McDONALD INSTITUTE MONOGRAPHS

Excavations at Kilise Tepe 1994–98

From Bronze Age to Byzantine in Western Cilicia

Volume 2: Appendices, References & Figures

Edited by Nicholas Postgate & David Thomas

BRITISH INSTITUTE AT ANKARA
BIAA Monograph No. 30

Published jointly by:

McDonald Institute for Archaeological Research
University of Cambridge
Downing Street
Cambridge, UK
CB2 3ER
(0)(1223) 339336
(0)(1223) 333538 (General Office)
(0)(1223) 333536 (FAX)
dak12@cam.ac.uk
www.mcdonald.cam.ac.uk

British Institute at Ankara
10 Carlton House Terrace
London, UK
SW1Y 5AH
(0)(20) 7969 5204
(0)(20) 7969 5401 (FAX)
biaa@britac.ac.uk
www.biaa.ac.uk

Distributed by Oxbow Books
 United Kingdom: Oxbow Books, 10 Hythe Bridge Street, Oxford, OX1 2EW, UK.
  Tel: (0)(1865) 241249; Fax: (0)(1865) 794449; www.oxbowbooks.com
 USA: The David Brown Book Company, P.O. Box 511, Oakville, CT 06779, USA.
  Tel: 860-945-9329; Fax: 860-945-9468

Undertaken with the assistance of the Institute for Aegean Prehistory.

ISBN: 978-1-902937-40-3 (2-vol. set)
ISBN: 978-1-902937-41-0 (vol. 1)
ISBN: 978-1-902937-42-7 (vol. 2)
ISSN: 1363-1349
(Volumes to be sold as a set)

© 2007 McDonald Institute for Archaeological Research

All rights reserved. No parts of this publication may be reproduced, stored in a retrieval system, or transmitted, in any form or by any means, electronic, mechanical, photocopying, recording or otherwise, without the prior permission of the McDonald Institute for Archaeological Research.

Edited for the Institute by Chris Scarre, Graeme Barker (*Series Editors*) and Dora A. Kemp (*Production Editor*).

Cover illustration: *Seal with hieroglyphic inscription naming 'Tarhunta-piya, charioteer' (No. 1470). (photograph: Bronwyn Douglas).*

Printed and bound by Short Run Press, Bittern Rd, Sowton Industrial Estate, Exeter, EX2 7LW, UK.

Contents

Figures   v

Appendices

Appendix 1   Archaeobotanical data   627

Appendix 2   List of Excavation Units   641

References   685

Figures
   Artefacts   705
   Maps, plans and sections   817
   Colour figures   861

Vol. 1 contents (printed as a separate volume)

Contributors   vii
Figures   ix
Tables   xvii
Preface   xix
Abbreviations and conventions   xxii
Note on numbers   xxiii

Part A   Introduction
Chapter 1   Introduction to the Project and the Publication   *by* Nicholas Postgate   3
Chapter 2   The Site of Kilise Tepe   *by* Nicholas Postgate   9
Chapter 3   The Kilise Tepe Area in Pre-Classical and Hellenistic Times   *by* Nicholas Postgate   15
Chapter 4   The Kilise Tepe Area in the Byzantine Era   *by* Mark Jackson   19
Chapter 5   The Excavations and their Results   *by* Nicholas Postgate   31

Part B   The Surface Collection
Chapter 6   The Surface Collection   *by* David Thomas   45

Part C   The Excavations
Chapter 7   Introduction to the Excavations   *by* Nicholas Postgate   67
Chapter 8   Fire Installations   *by* Nicholas Postgate   71
Chapter 9   Pits   *by* Nicholas Postgate   79
Chapter 10   Level V: the Early Bronze Age   *by* Lucy Seffen   87
Chapter 11   Level IV: the Middle Bronze Age   *by* Nicholas Postgate   103
Chapter 12   Level III: the Late Bronze Age   *by* Sarah Blakeney   111
Chapter 13   Level II: the End of the Bronze Age and the Iron Age   *by* Nicholas Postgate & David Thomas   121
Chapter 14   The East Slope   *by* Nicholas Postgate   165
Chapter 15   Trenches South of the Church   *by* Nicholas Postgate & Mark Jackson   171
Chapter 16   The Church   *by* Mark Jackson   185
Chapter 17   The Northwest Corner   *by* Mark Jackson   199
Chapter 18   The Northeast Corner Sub-surface Clearance   *by* Mark Jackson   211
Chapter 19   Architectural Fragments   *by* Mark Jackson & Dominique Collon   215

Part D   The Pottery
Chapter 20   Introduction to the Pottery   *by* Nicholas Postgate   237
Chapter 21   Pottery Fabrics and Technology   *by* Carl Knappett & Vassilis Kilikoglou   241
Chapter 22   Detailed Fabric Descriptions   *by* Carl Knappett   273

Contents

Chapter 23	The Early Bronze Age Pottery *by* Dorit Symington	295
Chapter 24	The Middle Bronze Age Pottery *by* Dorit Symington	319
Chapter 25	Pottery from Level III *by* Connie Hansen & Nicholas Postgate	329
Chapter 26	Pottery from Level II *by* Connie Hansen & Nicholas Postgate	343
Chapter 27	Geometric Pottery *by* Nicholas Postgate	371
Chapter 28	The Mycenaean Pottery *by* Elizabeth B. French	373
Chapter 29	Comparison of the NAA Data for Six Mycenaean-style Samples from Kilise Tepe with Chemical Reference Groups from Mainland Greece, Crete, Cyprus and the Levant *by* Jonathan E. Tomlinson	377
Chapter 30	Hellenistic Ceramics and Lamps *by* Lisa Nevett & Mark Jackson	379
Chapter 31	Pottery from Level One *by* Mark Jackson	387

Part E   *The Small Finds*

Chapter 32	The Small Finds: Introduction *by* Nicholas Postgate	437
Chapter 33	Seals with Hieroglyphic Inscriptions *by* Dorit Symington	441
Chapter 34	Other Glyptic *by* Dominique Collon	445
Chapter 35	Miscellaneous Clay Artefacts *by* Dominique Collon & Dorit Symington	449
Chapter 36	Loomweights *by* Dominique Collon & Dorit Symington	469
Chapter 37	Spindle Whorls *by* Dorit Symington & Dominique Collon	481
Chapter 38	Beads *by* Dominique Collon & Dorit Symington	499
Chapter 39	Glass *by* Dominique Collon	505
Chapter 40	Mosaic Tesserae *by* Dominique Collon	511
Chapter 41	Metalwork *by* Dominique Collon & Dorit Symington	515
Chapter 42	Bone, Horn and Ivory *by* Polydora Baker & Dominique Collon	531
Chapter 43	Fossils *by* Dominique Collon	541
Chapter 44	Lithics *by* Tim Reynolds	545
Chapter 45	Smaller Stone Artefacts *by* Dominique Collon & Dorit Symington	559
Chapter 46	Larger Stone Artefacts *by* Dominique Collon	567
Chapter 47	Coins *by* Koray Konuk	577

Part F   *Environmental Studies*

Chapter 48	Environmental Studies: Introduction *by* Nicholas Postgate	581
Chapter 49	The Archaeobotanical Assemblages *by* Joanna Bending & Sue Colledge	583
Chapter 50	Processing, Storing, Eating and Disposing: the Phytolith Evidence from Iron Age Kilise Tepe *by* Marco Madella	597
Chapter 51	Fish Remains from Bronze Age to Byzantine Levels *by* Wim Van Neer & Marc Waelkens	607
Chapter 52	Human Remains *by* Jessica Pearson	613
Chapter 53	Dating *by* Peter Ian Kuniholm, Maryanne W. Newton, Roy Switsur & Nicholas Postgate	619

Figures (vol. 2)

Artefact drawings

358.	Architectural fragments: *44, 61–2, 65, 72, 118, 127–8, 152c*.	705
359.	Architectural fragments: *60, 112, 131–2, 150, 190*.	706
360.	Architectural fragments: *70–71*; mouldings: *7, 49, 111, 113–17, 135, 137, 139a–b*.	707
361.	Architectural mouldings: *140, 142, 145–7, 152d, 158, 181*.	708
362.	LBA pottery recording sheet (a).	709
363.	LBA pottery recording sheet (b).	709
364.	LBA pottery recording sheet (c).	709
365.	Distribution of metamorphic rocks in Turkey (after Brinkmann 1976).	710
366.	Geological map of Kilise Tepe area (after Turkey, Geological Map of, 1950–65).	710
367.	Early Bronze Age ceramics *193–200*.	711
368.	Early Bronze Age ceramics *201–17*.	712
369.	Early Bronze Age ceramics *218–49*.	713
370.	Early Bronze Age ceramics *250–79*.	714
371.	Early Bronze Age ceramics *280–99*.	715
372.	Early Bronze Age ceramics *300–316*.	716
373.	Early Bronze Age ceramics *317–31*.	717
374.	Early Bronze Age ceramics *332–51*.	718
375.	Early Bronze Age ceramics *352–66*.	719
376.	Early Bronze Age ceramics *367–87*.	720
377.	Early Bronze Age ceramics *388–407*.	721
378.	Early Bronze Age ceramics *408–32*.	722
379.	Early Bronze Age ceramics *433–50*.	723
380.	Early Bronze Age ceramics *451–62*.	724
381.	Early Bronze Age ceramics *463–74*.	725
382.	Middle Bronze Age ceramics *475–99*.	726
383.	Middle Bronze Age ceramics *500–520*.	727
384.	Middle Bronze Age ceramics *521–31*.	728
385.	Middle Bronze Age ceramics *532–50*.	729
386.	Middle Bronze Age ceramics *551–67*.	730
387.	Late Bronze Age ceramics *568–603*.	731
388.	Late Bronze Age ceramics *604–29*.	732
389.	Late Bronze Age ceramics *630–57*.	733
390.	Late Bronze Age ceramics *658–77*.	734
391.	Late Bronze Age ceramics *678–92*.	735
392.	Level II ceramics *693–9*.	736
393.	Level II ceramics *700–705*.	737
394.	Level II ceramics *707–34*.	738
395.	Level II ceramics *735–50*.	739
396.	Level II ceramics *751–68*.	740
397.	Level II ceramics *769–83*.	741
398.	Level II ceramics *784–92*.	742
399.	Level II ceramics *793–803*.	743
400.	Level II ceramics *804–28*.	744
401.	Level II ceramics *829–50*.	745
402.	Level II ceramics *851–68*.	746
403.	Level II ceramics *869–89*.	747
404.	Level II ceramics *890–910*.	748
405.	Level II ceramics *911, 912–15, 916–19*.	749
406.	Level II ceramics *920–39*.	750
407.	Geometric ceramics *940–46*.	751
408.	Mycenaean ceramics *947–58*.	752

Figures

409.	*Mycenaean ceramics* **959–65**.	753
410.	*Hellenistic ceramics* **966–90**.	754
411.	*Hellenistic lamps* **991–5**, *Byzantine lamp* **996**.	755
412.	*Hellenistic ceramics* **997–1007**.	756
413.	*Late Roman/Byzantine ceramics* **1008–35**.	757
414.	*Late Roman/Byzantine ceramics* **1036–63**.	758
415.	*Late Roman/Byzantine ceramics* **1064–85**.	759
416.	*Late Roman/Byzantine ceramics* **1086–112**.	760
417.	*Late Roman/Byzantine ceramics* **1113–146**.	761
418.	*Late Roman/Byzantine ceramics* **1147–85**.	762
419.	*Late Roman/Byzantine ceramics* **1186–220**.	763
420.	*Late Roman/Byzantine ceramics* **1221–52**.	764
421.	*Late Roman/Byzantine ceramics* **1253–66**.	765
422.	*Late Roman/Byzantine ceramics* **1267–76**.	766
423.	*Late Roman/Byzantine ceramics* **1277–92**.	767
424.	*Late Roman/Byzantine ceramics* **1293–320**.	768
425.	*Late Roman/Byzantine ceramics* **1321–48**.	769
426.	*Late Roman/Byzantine ceramics* **1349–74**.	770
427.	*Late Roman/Byzantine ceramics* **1375–405**.	771
428.	*Late Roman/Byzantine ceramics* **1406–30**.	772
429.	*Late Roman/Byzantine ceramics* **1431–51**.	773
430.	*Late Roman/Byzantine ceramics* **1452–62**; *Byzantine tiles* **1463–9b**.	774
431.	*Seals* **1470–75**.	775
432.	*Seals and sealings* **1476–83**.	776
433.	*Sealings on pottery vessels* **1484–90**.	777
434.	*Clay stoppers (***1491**, **1498**, **1500**, **1502***) and figurines (***1505–6**, **1508***).*	778
435.	*Clay figurines (***1510–16***).*	779
436.	*Clay figurines (***1517–23***) and wheels (***1524–6***).*	780
437.	*Clay counters (***1527–9**, **1532**, **1535–6***), discs (***1539–40**, **1544**, **1546**, **1552**, **1567**, **1570**, **1575**, **1582**, **1586**, **1589**, **1593**, **1595***) and clay 'ball' (***1596***).*	781
438.	*Miscellaneous clay artefacts (***1597–8**, **1600**, **1610–11**, **1620**, **1622**, **1624***).*	782
439.	*Clay furniture (***1625**, **1627–8**, **1630–33***).*	783
440.	*Clay crescents (***1634**, **1636***) and clay ovoids (***1639–41***).*	784
441.	*Loomweights from Level V and IV (***1679**, **1681–3**, **1695**, **1700**, **1702–11***).*	785
442.	*Loomweights from Levels IV (***1712–13**, **1715**, **1725–6**, **1728–30***) and IIe (***1739**, **1740**, **1745***).*	786
443.	*Loomweights from Levels IIe (***1756–7**, **1760***), and IIf (***1761**, **1764–5**, **1775**, **1777–9**, **1783***).*	787
444.	*Loomweights from Level IIf (***1784**, **1788–9***), miscellaneous provenances (***1793**, **1807–8**, **1821–2**, **1824***), Q20 (***1812–16**, **1818**, **1820***), and possible stone weights (***1825–6**, **1835***).*	788
445.	*Spindle whorls from Level V (***1836–45**, **1848–54**, **1856–8***).*	789
446.	*Early Bronze Age spindle whorls (***1859–61**, unstratified, and ***1863–70**, **1872–80** from Level V).*	790
447.	*Spindle whorls from Levels V and IV (***1881–6**, **1888–90**, **1892–901***).*	791
448.	*Spindle whorls from Levels IV–III (***1902–8***) and later levels (***1909–13**, **1915–18**, **1920–28***).*	792
449.	*Spindle whorls from later levels (***1930–37**, **1939–43**, **1945–52**, **1954–8***).*	793
450.	*Spindle whorls from later levels (***1959–63**, **1966–8**, **1970–79***).*	794
451.	*Clay spindle whorls from later levels (***1980–92***), and in other materials (***1993–2000***).*	795
452.	*Beads (***2001–2**, **2007–8**, **2012**, **2020**, **2024–6**, **2033a–b**, **2038**, **2042–3**, **2052**, **2054**, **2057**, **2066–70a–b**, **2073–4**, **2079***) and glass vessels (***2080**, **2085–92***).*	796
453.	*Glass vessels (***2093–8**, **2100–14***), bangles (***2119**, **2121**, **2132**, **2139**, **2141**, **2155**, **2157***), and a ring (***2158***).*	797
454.	*Copper objects (***2213–20**, **2222–7**, **2231**, **2233–4**, **2237–8**, **2240**, **2243**, **2245***).*	798
455.	*Copper objects (***2246–53**, **2255**, **2257**, **2259–60**, **2265–6**, **2269**, **2271***).*	799
456.	*Copper objects (***2272–7**, **2279–85**, **2288–9***).*	800
457.	*Objects of copper, silver and iron (***2290**, **2293–5**, **2297**, **2306–7**, **2309–10***).*	801
458.	*Objects of iron (***2311–12**, **2315**, **2317**, **2319**, **2321–2**, **2384**, **2387**, **2392***).*	802

459. *Objects of iron (**2394, 2396, 2405, 2411, 2416**).* — 803
460. *Bone artefacts (**2421, 2423–4, 2445–6, 2455, 2460, 2463, 2465, 2469–72, 2474, 2478–9, 2483, 2486–7, 2489–92**).* — 804
461. *Lithics (**2533–52, 2554–64**).* — 805
462. *Lithics (**2565–6, 2568–73, 2575–85, 2587, 2591–5**).* — 806
463. *Smaller stone artefacts (**2597–603, 2605–7, 2609–10**).* — 807
464. *Smaller stone artefacts (**2611, 2613–18**).* — 808
465. *Smaller stone artefacts (**2619–21, 2623, 2630, 2632, 2634**).* — 809
466. *Smaller stone artefacts (**2636–7, 2639–43**).* — 810
467. *Smaller stone artefacts (**2644–7, 2649–52, 2654, 2656, 2658–9, 2665, 2667, 2670**).* — 811
468. *Larger stone artefacts (**2671, 2679, 2685, 2718–19, 2741, 2793, 2819**).* — 812
469. *Stele **2829** from Level IIc, Rm 3.* — 813

Maps, Plans and Sections

470. *General map of central and western Turkey.* — 817
471. *Map of Kilise Tepe area.* — 818
472. *Map of the Göksu valley.* — 819
473. *Kilise Tepe stratigraphic and chronological chart.* — 820
474. *H20: Phase Vl.* — 821
475. *H20: Phase Vk.* — 821
476. *H20: Phase Vj.* — 822
477. *H20: Phase Vi early.* — 822
478. *H20: Phase Vi late.* — 823
479. *H20: Phase Vh early.* — 823
480. *H20: Phase Vh late.* — 824
481. *H20: Phase Vg.* — 824
482. *H20: Phase Vf1–3.* — 825
483. *H20: Phase Vf4.* — 825
484. *H20: Phase Ve early.* — 826
485. *H20: Phase Ve middle.* — 826
486. *H20: Phase Ve late.* — 827
487. *H19/20: Phase IVa.* — 828
488. *H19/20: Phase IVb.* — 829
489. *NW Corner: Phases IIIa–b.* — 830
490. *NW Corner: Phase IIIc.* — 831
491. *NW Corner: Phases IIId and IIIe.* — 832
492. *Level IIc Stele Building and Eastern Building.* — 833
493. *Level IIb in J/K20.* — 834
494. *Level IIa/b Western Courtyard.* — 835
495. *Level IIc/d Western Courtyard (heavy stippling indicates dark ashy deposit).* — 836
496. *Level IId Stele Building.* — 837
497. *Level IIe in I19, J18/19, K18.* — 838
498. *Level IIe in K20, Rms e9–10.* — 839
499. *NW Corner: Level IIf.* — 840
500. *East slope, SE sector (Q19, Q–S18).* — 841
501. *East slope, NW sector - Q19/20.* — 842
502. *Q10a.* — 843
503. *N12a.* — 843
504. *I14: Level 3, Rms 91–4.* — 844
505. *I14 and J14a: Level 2 early, Rms 95–7.* — 844
506. *I–M14: Level 1a/b.* — 845
507. *Church, to show both phases.* — 846
508. *NW corner Level Ia–b.* — 847
509. *NW corner Level Ib–d (western part).* — 848

510.	NW corner Level Ib–d (eastern part).	849
511.	Section 1: H18b/d E section (Levels I & IId/e; see Figs. 497, 499, 508–9).	849
512.	Section 2: H20d/H19c E section (Level IIIa–c; see Figs. 479–91).	850
513.	Section 3: H19a/b S section (Level IIIa–c; see also Figs. 487–91).	851
514.	Section 4: I14a/b N section (Level 2; see Figs. 504–5).	852
515.	Section 5: I14a/b S section (Levels 1–3; see Figs. 504–5).	852
516.	Section 6: I19c/d S section (Levels I–IIf; see Figs. 494–5, 497, 499, 508–9).	853
517.	Section 7: I19b/d E section (Level IIa–f; see Figs. 151, 491, 494–5, 497, 499).	853
518.	Section 8: I20b/d E section (Levels IIb–e–IIId–e; see Fig. 491).	854
519.	Section 9: J18a/b S section (Levels I–IIf; see Figs. 492, 496–7, 499).	854
520.	Section 10: K14a S section (Levels 1–2 lower).	855
521.	Section 11: K14a W section (Level 2 middle–upper).	855
522.	Section 12: K18a/b S section (Levels I–IIf; see Figs. 492, 496–7, 499).	856
523.	Section 13: K19b/d E section (Levels I–IIc; see Figs. 492, 496–7, 508–9).	856
524.	Section 14: L19a/c E section (Levels I–IIc; see Figs. 492, 508–9).	857
525.	Section 15: L19c S section (Levels I–IIb; see Figs. 492, 508–9).	857
526.	Section 16: R18c W section (Levels E3a–E5a; see Fig. 500).	858
527.	Section 17: H20c E section (Level Ve/f–VI; see Figs. 474–91).	858

Colour Figures

528.	Thin sections of clay samples: S188–94, 196–7.	861
529.	Thin sections Level Vj–g, Groups A–E1.	861
530.	Thin sections Level Vj–g ctd, Groups F–N.	862
531.	Thin sections Level Vj–g ctd, Groups O–U.	862
532.	Thin sections Level Vf–e, Groups A–C.	863
533.	Thin sections Level IV, Groups A–D.	863
534.	Thin sections Level III, Groups A–C.	864
535.	Thin sections Level III ctd, Groups D–J.	864
536.	Thin sections Level IIa–d, Groups A–B.	865
537.	Thin sections Level IIa–d ctd, Groups C–G and IIe, Group A.	865
538.	Thin sections Level IIf, Groups A–B4.	866
539.	Thin sections Level IIf ctd, Groups B5–D.	866
540.	Mycenaean vessel **955**.	867
541.	Assorted Mycenaean sherds.	867
542.	**1001** (two pieces); waster from unit 2106.	867
543.	**1005, 1003, 1004**.	867
544.	**1011**, d533, **1016**.	868
545.	**1017**.	868
546.	**1027**.	868
547.	**1068, 1069, 1031; 1034, 1077, 1071**.	868
548.	d5446, **1062, 1053, 1056; 1309 1061, 1054, 1055**.	868
549.	**1073, 1288, 1060**.	868
550.	**1094**.	868
551.	**1112**.	868
552.	**1146, 1117, 1158; 1136, 1116**.	869
553.	**1145**.	869
554.	**99/4, 1144, 1167, 1155, 1142, 1143**.	869
555.	**1185, 1186**.	869
556.	**1189, 1182; 1178, 1181**.	869
557.	**1199**, unit 1260; **1187**, unit 194.	869
558.	**1177**.	869
559.	**1188, 1179**.	869
560.	**1257, 1255, 1256, 1258**.	870
561.	**1200**.	870

Figures

562.	*1172.*	870
563.	*1235, 1241, 1234; 1233, 1231, 1236.*	870
564.	*1220:* a) exterior; b) interior.	870
565.	*1266, 1265.*	870
566.	*1276, 1221, 1284; 1259, 1262, 1281.*	870
567.	*1267, 1268.*	871
568.	*1318, 1330, 1328, 1324.*	871
569.	*1335, 1336.*	871
570.	*1439, 1438, 1437, 1377, 1440, 1441.*	871
571.	*1440.*	871
572.	*1436.*	871
573.	*1135, 1134, 1118* local painted ware.	871
574.	*Glazed wares: unit 5000, d1378 (×2), unit 9600; unit 4801, unit 4800.*	871
575.	*Close-ups of cross-sections.*	872
576.	*Silica skeleton of cereal husk.*	873
577.	*Silica skeleton of a culm epidermis with typical smooth-sided long cells.*	873
578.	*A bulliform cell from the leaf mesophyll.*	874
579.	*A phytolith probably from a dicotyledon plant found in the coprolite and the residues from the pots.*	874
580.	*A phytolith (plate with perforations) from a dicotyledon plant found in the courtyard sediments.*	875
581.	*An idealized reconstruction of Kilise Tepe pits used for the storage of grains.*	875
582.	*Typical cereal (wheat/barley) husk silica skeleton.*	876
583.	*Silica skeleton from the husk of* Panicum/Setaria *(millets).*	876
584.	*Silica skeleton from a grass culm.*	877
585.	*Silica skeleton from grass culm with stepped cuts.*	877

Appendices

Appendix 1 **Archaeobotanical Data**   **627**
   1.1. *Percentages of cereal grains, legumes and wild cereals.*   627
   1.2. *Percentages of glume wheats, free-threshing and wild cereals.*   628
   1.3. *Percentages of grain species and wild seeds.*   629
   1.4. *Percentages of grain to chaff.*   630
   1.5. *Crop-processing groups.*   631
   1.6. *Categories of samples based on their composition.*   632
   1.7. *Total counts for each sample analysed.*   633

Appendix 2 **List of Excavation Units**   **641**

Appendix 1

Archaeobotanical Data

Appendix 1.1. *Percentages of cereal grains, legumes and wild cereals.*

Sample no.	Cereal grain	Legume	Wild	% Cereal grain	% Legume	% Wild
1	1	0	141	1%	0%	99%
2	24	9	6	62%	23%	15%
3	4	1	68	5%	1%	93%
4	4	1	80	5%	1%	94%
5	40	1	88	31%	1%	68%
6	0	0	10	0%	0%	100%
7	1	0	1	50%	0%	50%
8	351	0	209	63%	0%	37%
9	66	2	109	37%	1%	62%
10	2	2	2	33%	33%	33%
11	34	1	87	28%	1%	71%
12	11	0	25	31%	0%	69%
13	77	2	159	32%	1%	67%
14	27	210	176	7%	51%	43%
15	18	6	86	16%	5%	78%
16	4	256	20	1%	91%	7%
17	14	8	133	9%	5%	86%
18	9	4	177	5%	2%	93%
19	9	2	11	41%	9%	50%
20	10	6	116	8%	5%	88%
21	14	2	67	17%	2%	81%
22	34	7	305	10%	2%	88%
23	31	6	569	5%	1%	94%
24	3	2	48	6%	4%	91%
25	1564	1	55	97%	0%	3%
26	317	0	141	69%	0%	31%
27	169	2	92	64%	1%	35%
28	1	0	8	11%	0%	89%
29	330	1515	51	17%	80%	3%
30	112	16	137	42%	6%	52%
31	8	0	196	4%	0%	96%

Sample no.	Cereal grain	Legume	Wild	% Cereal grain	% Legume	% Wild
32	5	3	43	10%	6%	84%
33	499	0	122	80%	0%	20%
34	828	2	185	82%	0%	18%
35	18	4	94	16%	3%	81%
36	14	19	81	12%	17%	71%
37	4	1	13	22%	6%	72%
38	30	14	42	35%	16%	49%
39	18	4	14	50%	11%	39%
40	0	0	0	~	~	~
41	0	0	0	~	~	~
42	6	2	19	22%	7%	70%
43	98	9	21	77%	7%	16%
44	338	0	132	72%	0%	28%
45	88	22	423	17%	4%	79%
46	801	183	56	77%	18%	5%
47	193	0	25	89%	0%	11%
48	229	0	40	85%	0%	15%
49	617	0	11	98%	0%	2%
50	3	300	1	1%	99%	0%
51	128	3895	180	3%	93%	4%
52	1639	0	419	80%	0%	20%
53	555	1	146	79%	0%	21%
54	49	3	26	63%	4%	33%
55	50	0	0	100%	0%	0%
56	3	19	12	9%	56%	35%
57	1	0	7	13%	0%	88%
58	29	4	64	30%	4%	66%
59	8	5	98	7%	5%	88%
60	6	3	16	24%	12%	64%
61	51	2	20	70%	3%	27%

Appendix 1.2. *Percentages of glume wheats, free-threshing and wild seeds.*

Sample no.	% glume	%ft	%wild	Total	Sample no.	% glume	%ft	%wild	Total
1	0%	1%	99%	142	32	2%	2%	96%	45
2	22%	52%	26%	23	33	0%	80%	20%	615
3	0%	0%	100%	68	34	3%	78%	19%	962
4	0%	5%	95%	84	35	2%	11%	87%	108
5	7%	14%	79%	112	36	2%	8%	90%	90
6	0%	0%	100%	10	37	0%	7%	93%	14
7	0%	50%	50%	2	38	33%	3%	64%	66
8	29%	3%	68%	307	39	15%	31%	54%	26
9	15%	6%	79%	138	40	0%	0%	0%	0
10	0%	0%	100%	2	41	0%	0%	0%	0
11	11%	12%	78%	112	42	4%	20%	76%	25
12	0%	19%	81%	31	43	3%	79%	18%	117
13	5%	20%	76%	210	44	1%	71%	28%	468
14	3%	5%	92%	192	45	11%	4%	85%	497
15	1%	10%	89%	97	46	1%	56%	43%	1457
16	0%	9%	91%	22	47	84%	2%	15%	171
17	3%	3%	94%	141	48	85%	0%	15%	265
18	1%	2%	97%	182	49	98%	0%	2%	624
19	17%	22%	61%	18	50	50%	0%	50%	2
20	1%	7%	92%	126	51	14%	7%	79%	228
21	0%	3%	97%	69	52	0%	78%	22%	1940
22	1%	6%	93%	328	53	1%	78%	21%	682
23	1%	4%	95%	597	54	54%	0%	46%	57
24	0%	4%	96%	50	55	100%	0%	0%	50
25	83%	13%	4%	1554	56	0%	8%	92%	13
26	63%	5%	33%	431	57	0%	0%	100%	7
27	0%	62%	38%	244	58	0%	20%	80%	80
28	0%	11%	89%	9	59	0%	6%	94%	104
29	65%	16%	19%	273	60	0%	24%	76%	21
30	8%	35%	57%	241	61	18%	36%	45%	44
31	2%	0%	98%	200					

See Table 32 for key to amalgamated identification categories.

Appendix 1.3. *Percentages of grain species and wild seeds.*

Sample no.	Total	% einkorn	% emmer	% spelt	%ft wheat	% barley	% wild
1	142	0%	0%	0%	0%	1%	99%
2	23	22%	0%	0%	4%	48%	26%
3	68	0%	0%	0%	0%	0%	100%
4	84	0%	0%	0%	0%	5%	95%
5	112	7%	0%	0%	0%	14%	79%
6	10	0%	0%	0%	0%	0%	100%
7	2	0%	0%	0%	0%	50%	50%
8	307	22%	4%	4%	2%	1%	68%
9	138	11%	1%	3%	1%	4%	79%
10	2	0%	0%	0%	0%	0%	100%
11	112	11%	0%	0%	3%	9%	78%
12	31	0%	0%	0%	0%	19%	81%
13	210	5%	0%	0%	10%	9%	76%
14	192	3%	0%	1%	2%	4%	92%
15	97	1%	0%	0%	0%	10%	89%
16	22	0%	0%	0%	0%	9%	91%
17	141	1%	0%	1%	1%	2%	94%
18	182	1%	0%	0%	0%	2%	97%
19	18	17%	0%	0%	0%	22%	61%
20	126	1%	0%	0%	0%	7%	92%
21	69	0%	0%	0%	0%	3%	97%
22	328	0%	0%	0%	1%	5%	93%
23	597	0%	0%	0%	0%	4%	95%
24	50	0%	0%	0%	2%	2%	96%
25	1554	1%	0%	82%	7%	6%	4%
26	431	0%	0%	63%	0%	4%	33%
27	244	0%	0%	0%	0%	62%	38%
28	9	0%	0%	0%	0%	11%	89%
29	273	65%	0%	0%	0%	16%	19%
30	241	8%	0%	0%	1%	34%	57%
31	200	1%	1%	0%	0%	0%	98%
32	45	2%	0%	0%	0%	2%	96%
33	615	0%	0%	0%	0%	80%	20%
34	962	3%	0%	0%	0%	78%	19%
35	108	1%	1%	0%	0%	11%	87%
36	90	2%	0%	0%	0%	8%	90%
37	14	0%	0%	0%	0%	7%	93%
38	66	0%	3%	30%	0%	3%	64%
39	26	8%	0%	8%	0%	31%	54%
40	0	0%	0%	0%	0%	0%	0%
41	0	0%	0%	0%	0%	0%	0%
42	25	0%	4%	0%	0%	20%	76%
43	117	0%	2%	1%	0%	79%	18%
44	468	0%	1%	0%	0%	71%	28%
45	497	10%	0%	1%	1%	3%	85%
46	1457	1%	0%	0%	0%	56%	43%
47	171	84%	0%	0%	0%	2%	15%
48	265	84%	1%	0%	0%	0%	15%
49	624	98%	0%	0%	0%	0%	2%
50	2	0%	0%	50%	0%	0%	50%
51	228	0%	14%	0%	0%	7%	79%
52	1940	0%	0%	0%	0%	78%	22%
53	682	1%	0%	0%	0%	78%	21%
54	57	51%	4%	0%	0%	0%	46%
55	50	0%	2%	98%	0%	0%	0%
56	13	0%	0%	0%	0%	8%	92%
57	7	0%	0%	0%	0%	0%	100%
58	80	0%	0%	0%	0%	20%	80%
59	104	0%	0%	0%	0%	6%	94%
60	21	0%	0%	0%	0%	24%	76%
61	44	0%	0%	18%	32%	5%	45%

Appendix 1

Appendix 1.4. *Percentages of grain to chaff.*

Sample no.	% eingr	% eingl	% emgr	% emgl	% spel gr	% ftw gr	% ftw rach	% barley gr	% barley rachis	Sample no.	% eingr	% eingl	% emgr	% emgl	% spel gr	% ftw gr	% ftw rach	% barley gr	% barley rachis
1	0%	0%	0%	0%	0%	0%	0%	100%	0%	32	100%	0%	0%	0%	0%	0%	0%	100%	0%
2	100%	0%	0%	0%	0%	25%	75%	100%	0%	33	0%	0%	0%	0%	0%	0%	0%	100%	0%
3	0%	0%	0%	0%	0%	0%	0%	0%	0%	34	100%	0%	0%	0%	0%	0%	0%	100%	0%
4	0%	0%	0%	0%	0%	0%	0%	100%	0%	35	100%	0%	100%	0%	0%	0%	0%	100%	0%
5	100%	0%	0%	0%	0%	0%	0%	57%	43%	36	67%	33%	0%	0%	0%	0%	0%	100%	0%
6	0%	0%	0%	0%	0%	0%	0%	0%	0%	37	0%	0%	0%	0%	0%	0%	0%	100%	0%
7	0%	0%	0%	0%	0%	0%	0%	100%	0%	38	0%	0%	100%	0%	100%	0%	0%	100%	0%
8	100%	0%	100%	0%	100%	63%	38%	100%	0%	39	100%	0%	0%	0%	100%	0%	0%	100%	0%
9	100%	0%	67%	33%	100%	2%	98%	100%	0%	40	0%	0%	0%	0%	0%	0%	0%	0%	0%
10	0%	0%	0%	0%	0%	0%	0%	0%	0%	41	0%	0%	0%	0%	0%	0%	0%	0%	0%
11	100%	0%	0%	0%	0%	100%	0%	100%	0%	42	0%	0%	100%	0%	0%	0%	0%	100%	0%
12	0%	0%	0%	0%	0%	0%	100%	100%	0%	43	0%	100%	100%	0%	100%	0%	0%	100%	0%
13	80%	20%	0%	100%	0%	2%	98%	9%	91%	44	5%	95%	100%	0%	0%	0%	0%	100%	0%
14	100%	0%	0%	0%	100%	50%	50%	100%	0%	45	100%	0%	0%	0%	100%	100%	0%	100%	0%
15	50%	50%	0%	0%	0%	0%	0%	100%	0%	46	100%	0%	100%	0%	100%	2%	98%	99%	1%
16	0%	100%	0%	100%	0%	0%	0%	100%	0%	47	95%	5%	0%	0%	0%	0%	0%	100%	0%
17	80%	20%	0%	0%	100%	100%	0%	100%	0%	48	89%	11%	100%	0%	0%	0%	0%	0%	0%
18	67%	33%	0%	0%	0%	0%	0%	100%	0%	49	99%	1%	0%	0%	0%	0%	0%	0%	0%
19	86%	14%	0%	0%	0%	0%	0%	100%	0%	50	0%	0%	0%	0%	100%	0%	0%	0%	0%
20	100%	0%	0%	100%	0%	0%	0%	69%	31%	51	0%	0%	100%	0%	0%	0%	0%	100%	0%
21	0%	0%	0%	0%	0%	0%	0%	100%	0%	52	0%	0%	0%	0%	0%	0%	0%	100%	0%
22	67%	33%	100%	0%	100%	25%	75%	49%	51%	53	100%	0%	0%	0%	0%	0%	0%	100%	0%
23	100%	0%	100%	0%	100%	14%	86%	41%	59%	54	94%	6%	100%	0%	0%	0%	0%	0%	0%
24	0%	0%	0%	0%	0%	100%	0%	100%	0%	55	0%	0%	100%	0%	100%	0%	0%	0%	0%
25	100%	0%	0%	0%	100%	100%	0%	100%	0%	56	0%	0%	0%	0%	0%	0%	0%	100%	0%
26	0%	0%	0%	0%	100%	100%	0%	100%	0%	57	0%	0%	0%	0%	0%	0%	0%	0%	0%
27	0%	0%	0%	0%	0%	0%	0%	94%	6%	58	0%	100%	0%	0%	0%	0%	0%	100%	0%
28	0%	0%	0%	0%	0%	0%	0%	100%	0%	59	0%	0%	0%	0%	0%	0%	0%	75%	25%
29	99%	1%	0%	0%	0%	0%	0%	90%	10%	60	0%	0%	0%	0%	0%	0%	0%	100%	0%
30	14%	86%	0%	0%	0%	6%	94%	98%	2%	61	0%	100%	0%	0%	100%	100%	0%	100%	0%
31	100%	0%	100%	0%	0%	0%	0%	0%	0%										

See Table 32 for key to amalgamated identification categories.

Appendix 1.5. *Crop-processing groups.*

Sample no.	Crop processing ungrouped	Crop processing grouped
1	NA	NA
2	NA	NA
3	3	0
4	3	0
5	3	0
6	NA	NA
7	NA	NA
8	4	0
9	4	4
10	NA	NA
11	4	0
12	4	0
13	4	0
14	3	3
15	NA	NA
16	NA	NA
17	3	0
18	3	3
19	NA	NA
20	1	1
21	1	1
22	1	0
23	3	3
24	1	3
25	3	3
26	NA	NA
27	4	0
28	NA	NA
29	4	0
30	4	4
31	NA	NA

Sample no.	Crop processing ungrouped	Crop processing grouped
32	NA	NA
33	4	4
34	4	0
35	4	4
36	3	0
37	NA	NA
38	NA	NA
39	NA	NA
40	NA	NA
41	NA	NA
42	NA	NA
43	1	0
44	4	4
45	3	0
46	4	0
47	4	0
48	4	0
49	NA	NA
50	NA	NA
51	4	4
52	4	0
53	3	3
54	4	4
55	NA	NA
56	NA	NA
57	NA	NA
58	4	0
59	4	0
60	NA	NA
61	4	0

Appendix 1.6. *Categories of samples based on their composition.*

		Trench	Unit no.	Context type	Period	Phase
Clean product						
Einkorn	49	K19/99	1561	Occ. surf.	LBA/IA	IIc
Fig	40	J20/147	1388	Destr.	LBA	IIIe
	41	J120/153	1389	Destr.	LBA	IIIe
Lentil	50	K19/199	4507	Constr.	LBA/IA	IIc
	51	K19/204	4510	Destr.	LBA/IA	IIc
Spelt	55	K19/287	4822	Constr.	LBA/IA	?
Lathyrus sativus	29	J19/222	1686	Destr.	LBA/IA	IIc
Fine-sieve product						
Barley	33	J19/297	3927	Destr.	LBA/IA	IIc
	34	J19/308	3927	Destr.	LBA/IA	IIc
	44	K18/279	6141	Pit fill	LBA/IA	IIc
	53	K19/210	4510	Destr.	LBA/IA	IIc
Lathyrus sativus	16	I19/72	2818	Destr.	E/M IA	IId/e
Fine-sieve by-product						
	3	H18/116	2640	Constr.	LBA/IA	IId/e
Mixed crop (ft+gl)	18	I19/81	2825	Occ. seq.	LBA/IA	IId
ft	4	H18/116	2640	Constr.	LBA/IA	IId/e
	23	J19/4	1625	Pit fill	BYZ	I
Coarse-sieve product						
Barley	27	J19/204	1656	Pit fill	BYZ?	I?
	43	K18/256	6125	Pit fill	LBA/IA	IIc
	46	K19/96	1560	Destr.	LBA/IA	IIc
	52	K19/206	4510	Destr.	LBA/EIA	IIc
Einkorn (Hillman Stage 12)	47	K19/99	1561	Occ. surf.	LBA/IA	IIc
	48	K19/99	1561	Occ. surf.	LBA/IA	IIc
	54	K19/211	4511	Occ. dep.	LBA/IA	IIc
Lathyrus sativus	14	I19/70	2818	Destr.	LBA/IA	IId/e
Spelt	25	J19/110	1653	Pit fill	BYZ	I
	26	J19/129	1653	Pit fill	BYZ	I
Wild-seed dominated mixed/late crop-processing stages						
Mixed crop (gl+ft)	17	I19/80	2823	Pack. fill	LBA/IA	IId/e
	22	J19/4	1626	Pit fill	BYZ	I
	45	K19/72	1540	Occ. seq.	LBA/IA	IId
ft	20	J18/265	2370	Constr.	LIA	IIf
	21	J18/266	2391	Constr.	LIA	IIf
	24	J19/98	1644	Occ. seq.	BYZ	I
	35	J19/323	3927	Destr.	LBA/IA	IIc
	59	K20/171	1976	Occ. surf.	LBA/IA	IIb

		Trench	Unit no.	Context type	Period	Phase
Mixed crop + mixed/late crop-processing stages						
Mixrd crop (gl+ft)	5	H18/117	2636	Constr.	LIA	IIf
	8	I14/1	3459	Occ. seq.	LBA/IA	II
	9	I14/2	3458	Destr.	LBA/IA	II
	11	I19/44	1781	Pit fill	LIA	IIg
	13	I19/52	2802	Kiln	LIA	IIf
	30	J19/233	1690	Pit fill	LBA/IA	IIc/d
	36	J19/334	3943	Burnt surf.	LBA/IA	IIc/d
	61	K20/204	1994	Pit fill	LBA/IA	IId
ft	12	I19/50	2802	Constr.	LIA	IIf
	58	K20/166	1971	Occ. surf.	LBA/IA	IIb
Wild-seed dominated unanalysed						
Mixed crop (gl+ft)	15	I19/71	2817	Fire inst.	LIA	IIf
	32	J19/252	1696	Pit fill	LBA/IA	IIb
Single crop	1	H18/20	2607	Ash patch	BYZ	I
	31	J19/249	1688	Occ. seq.	LBA/IA	IIc
Unanalysed mixed crop and wild						
	38	J19/356	3963	Below floor	LBA/IA	IIb
	39	J19/396	6423	Occ. seq.	LBA/IA	IIb
Low counts						
	2	H18/98	2629	Pit fill	LIA	IIf
	6	H18/131	4263	Constr.	LBA/IA	IVa
	7	H19/224	4251	Destr.	MBA	IVb
	10	I19/26	1743	Fire inst.	BYZ/IA	I/IIh
	19	I20/1	4003	Pit fill	LBA/IA	IIb/e
	28	J19/204	1656	Pit fill	BYZ?	I?
	37	J19/341	3927	Destr.	LBA/IA	IIc
	42	K18/173	4344	Occ. seq.	IA	IIe
	56	K19/354	1566	Constr.	LBA/IA	IIc
	57	K20/154	1965	Occ. seq.	LBA/IA	IIb
	60	K20/183	1988	Constr.	LBA/IA	IId

See Table 32 for key to amalgamated identification categories.

Archaeobotanical Data

Appendix 1.7. *Total counts for each sample analysed.*

Sample no.	Trench	Unit/Context no.	Context type	Period	Phase	Charcoal density cm³/l	Fraction	T. monococcum 1 gr	T. monococcum 2 gr	cf. T. monococcum gr	T. monococcum/boeoticum gr	T. monococcum/dicoccum gr	T. dicoccum 2 gr	T. dicoccum cf. 2 gr	T. dicoccum 1 gr	cf. T. dicoccum gr	T. dicoccum/spelta gr	T. spelta gr	cf. T. spelta gr	Glume wheat indet.	T. aestivum/dicoccum gr	T. aestivum/durum/spelta gr	T. aestivum/durum gr	T. cf. aestivum/durum gr	T. aestivum var. compactum	Triticum indet.	cf. Triticum	TOTAL - Triticum gr
1	H18/20	2607	Ash patch	Byz	I	2.0	1	0	0	0	0	0	0	0	0	0	0	0	0	0	0	0	0	0	0	0	0	0
2	H18/98	2629	Pit fill	IA	IIf	5.3	1	4	1	0	0	0	0	0	0	0	0	0	0	0	0	0	0	1	0	0	4	0	10
3	H18/116	2640	Constr.	E/MIA	IId/e	5.2	1	0	0	0	0	0	0	0	0	0	0	0	0	0	0	0	0	0	0	0	0	0	0
4	H18/116	2640	Constr.	E/MIA	IId/e	7.7	1	0	0	0	0	0	0	0	0	0	0	0	0	0	0	0	0	0	0	0	0	0	0
5	H18/117	2636	Constr.	M/LIA	IIf	4.4	1	8	0	0	0	0	0	0	0	0	0	0	0	0	0	0	0	0	0	0	0	0	8
6	H18/131	4263	Constr.	LBA/IA	IVa	N/A	1	0	0	0	0	0	0	0	0	0	0	0	0	0	0	0	0	0	0	0	0	0	0
7	H19/224	4251	Destr.	MBA	IVb	N/A	1	0	0	0	0	0	0	0	0	0	0	0	0	0	0	0	0	0	0	0	0	0	0
8	I14/101	3459	Occ. surf.	LBA/IA	II	1.6	1/2	37	15	15	177	1	7	0	0	4	3	8	4	9	2	3	3	2	0	57	0	347
9	I14/98	3458	Destr.	LBA/IA	II	3.5	1/8	9	2	4	1	3	0	0	0	2	0	3	1	0	0	1	1	1	0	31	0	59
10	I19/26	1743	Fire inst.	BYZ/IA	I/IIh	4.0	1	0	0	0	0	0	0	0	0	0	0	0	0	0	0	0	0	0	0	2	0	2
11	I19/44	1781	Pit fill	MIA	IIg	5.2	1/2	10	0	2	0	0	0	0	0	0	0	0	0	0	0	1	2	0	0	6	0	21
12	I19/50	2802	Constr.	IA	IIf	18.2	1	0	0	0	0	0	0	0	0	0	0	0	0	0	0	0	0	0	0	3	2	5
13	I19/52	2802	Kiln	MIA	IIf	10.1	1/8	8	2	0	0	0	0	0	0	0	0	0	0	3	0	14	8	4	0	17	0	56
14	I19/70	2818	Destr.	LBA/IA	IId/e	4.6	1/2	3	0	2	0	2	0	0	0	0	0	1	0	0	0	1	2	0	0	7	0	18
15	I19/71	2817	Fire inst.	MIA	IIf	1.3	1	0	0	1	0	0	0	0	0	0	0	0	0	0	0	0	0	0	0	0	0	1
16	I19/72	2818	Destr.	LBA/IA	IId/e	N/A	1/4	0	0	0	0	0	0	0	0	0	0	0	0	0	0	2	0	0	0	0	0	2
17	I19/80	2823	Pack. fill	LBA/IA	IId/e	0.7	1/2	2	0	0	0	0	0	0	0	0	0	1	1	0	0	0	1	0	0	4	0	9
18	I19/81	2825	Occ. seq.	LBA/IA	IId	2.0	1/8	0	0	1	0	0	0	0	0	0	0	0	0	0	0	0	0	0	0	1	0	2
19	I20/47	4003	Pit fill	LBA/IA	IIb/e	1.4	1/8	1	1	1	0	0	0	0	0	0	0	0	0	0	0	0	0	0	0	1	0	4
20	J18/265	2370	Constr.	M/LIA	IIf	3.0	1	1	0	0	0	0	0	0	0	0	0	0	0	0	0	0	0	0	0	0	0	1
21	J18/266	2391	Constr.	IA	IIf	2.2	1	0	0	0	0	2	0	0	0	0	0	0	0	0	0	0	0	0	0	4	0	6
22	J19/74	1626	Pit fill	Hell/Byz	I	5.0	1/8	0	1	0	0	0	0	0	0	1	0	1	0	0	1	0	3	0	0	4	0	11
23	J19/74	1625	Pit fill	Hell/Byz	I	4.8	1/8	0	0	1	0	0	0	0	0	1	0	0	1	1	0	0	0	1	0	1	0	6
24	J19/98	1644	Occ. seq.	Byz	I	0.3	1/8	0	0	0	0	0	0	0	0	0	0	0	0	0	0	0	1	0	0	1	0	2
25	J19/110	1653	Pit fill	Byz	I	13.2	1/8	12	0	2	0	0	0	0	0	0	0	1057	220	0	0	17	111	0	0	48	0	1467
26	J19/129	1653	Pit fill	Byz	I	N/A	1/4	0	0	0	0	0	0	0	0	0	0	3	176	94	23	0	1	0	1	0	0	0	298
27	J19/204	1656	Pit fill	Byz?	I?	14.3	1	0	0	0	0	0	0	0	0	0	0	0	0	0	0	0	0	0	0	0	0	0
28	J19/204	1656	Pit fill	Byz?	I?	N/A	1/4	0	0	0	0	0	0	0	0	0	0	0	0	0	0	0	0	0	0	0	0	0
29	J19/222	1686	Destr.	LBA/IA	IIc	8.6	1/2	147	4	26	0	3	0	0	0	0	0	0	0	0	0	0	0	0	0	98	0	278
30	J19/233	1690	Pit fill	LBA/IA	IIc/d	6.1	1/2	7	4	8	0	0	0	0	0	0	0	0	0	0	0	2	1	0	0	0	0	22
31	J19/249	1688	Occ. seq.	LBA/IA	IIc	6.0	1	0	0	2	0	0	0	0	0	2	0	0	0	0	0	0	0	0	0	0	0	4
32	J19/252	1696	Pit fill	LBA/IA	IIb	0.9	1	0	0	1	0	2	0	0	0	0	0	0	0	0	0	0	0	0	0	1	0	4
33	J19/297	3927	Destr.	LBA/EIA	IIc	2.9	1/2	0	0	0	0	0	0	0	0	0	0	0	0	0	0	0	0	0	0	2	0	2
34	J19/308	3927	Destr.	LBA/EIA	IIc	6.9	1/8	28	0	0	0	12	0	0	0	0	0	0	0	0	0	0	0	0	0	0	0	40
35	J19/323	3927	Destr.	LBA/IA	IIc	1.2	1	0	0	1	0	0	0	1	0	0	0	0	0	0	2	0	0	0	0	1	0	5
36	J19/334	3943	Burnt surf.	LBA/IA	IIc/d	2.6	1	0	0	2	0	3	0	0	0	0	0	0	0	0	0	0	0	0	0	2	0	7
37	J19/341	3927	Destr.	LBA/EIA	IIc	0.8	1	0	0	0	0	0	0	0	0	0	0	0	0	0	0	0	0	0	0	0	0	0
38	J19/356	3963	Below floor	LBA/IA	IIb	4.5	1	0	0	0	0	0	2	0	0	0	6	20	0	0	0	0	0	0	0	0	0	28
39	J19/396	6423	Occ. seq.	LBA/IA	IIb	N/A	1/2	0	0	2	0	0	0	0	0	0	0	0	2	0	0	0	0	0	0	2	0	6
40	J20/147	1388	Destr.	LBA	IIIe	N/A	1	0	0	0	0	0	0	0	0	0	0	0	0	0	0	0	0	0	0	0	0	0
41	J120/153	1389	Destr.	LBA	IIIe	N/A	1	0	0	0	0	0	0	0	0	0	0	0	0	0	0	0	0	0	0	0	0	0
42	K18/173	4344	Occ. seq.	IA	IIe	9.8	1/8	0	0	0	0	0	1	0	0	0	0	0	0	0	0	0	0	0	0	0	0	1
43	K18/256	6125	Pit fill	LBA/IA	IIc	25.0	1	0	0	0	0	0	0	0	0	2	0	0	1	1	0	0	0	0	0	1	0	5
44	K18/279	6141	Pit fill	LBA/IA	IIc	N/A	1/8	1	0	0	0	0	1	1	0	1	0	0	0	0	0	0	0	0	0	1	0	5
45	K19/72	1540	Occ. seq.	LBA/IA	IId	1.3	1/2	43	0	8	0	0	0	0	0	0	0	4	0	0	1	0	4	0	0	11	0	71
46	K19/96	1560	Destr.	LBA/IA	IIc	4.5	1/4	11	1	0	0	0	6	0	0	0	1	0	5	0	1	0	0	1	0	0	73	0	288
47	K19/99	1561	Occ. surf.	LBA/EIA	IIc	N/A	1/64	109	0	34	0	0	0	0	0	0	0	0	0	0	0	0	0	0	0	45	0	188
48	K19/99	1561	Occ. surf.	LBA/EIA	IIc	N/A	1/16	210	3	9	0	0	0	3	0	0	0	0	0	0	0	0	0	0	0	0	0	225
49	K19/99	1561	Occ. surf.	LBA/EIA	IIc	60.0	1	412	4	197	0	0	0	0	0	0	1	0	0	0	0	0	0	0	0	3	0	617
50	K19/199	4507	Constr.	LBA/IA	IIc	11.1	1	0	0	0	0	0	0	0	0	0	0	0	0	1	2	0	0	0	0	0	0	3
51	K19/204	4510	Destr.	LBA/EIA	IIc	27.1	1/32	0	0	0	0	0	24	0	8	0	0	0	0	8	0	0	0	0	0	64	8	112
52	K19/206	4510	Destr.	LBA/EIA	IIc	285.0	1	0	0	0	0	0	0	0	0	0	0	0	0	0	0	0	0	0	0	0	0	0
53	K19/210	4510	Destr.	LBA/EIA	IIc	17.4	1/8	4	0	0	0	0	0	0	0	0	0	0	0	0	0	0	0	0	0	2	0	6
54	K19/211	4511	Occ. dep.	LBA/IA	IIc	3.5	1	19	0	10	0	0	0	0	0	0	0	2	0	0	0	0	0	0	0	10	0	41
55	K19/287	4822	Constr.	LBA/IA	?	N/A	1	0	0	0	0	0	1	0	0	0	0	49	0	0	0	0	0	0	0	0	0	50
56	K19/354	1566	Constr.	LBA/IA	IIc	0.9	1	0	0	0	0	0	0	0	0	0	0	0	0	0	0	0	0	0	0	0	0	0
57	K20/154	1965	Occ. seq.	LBA/EIA	IIb	3.0	1/8	0	0	0	0	0	0	0	0	0	0	0	0	0	0	0	0	0	0	1	0	1
58	K20/166	1971	Occ. surf.	LBA/EIA	IIb	2.0	1	0	0	0	0	0	0	0	0	0	0	0	0	0	0	0	0	0	0	0	0	0
59	K20/171	1976	Occ. surf.	LBA/EIA	IIb	9.8	1/8	0	0	0	0	0	0	0	0	0	0	0	0	0	0	0	0	0	0	0	0	0
60	K20/183	1988	Constr.	LBA/IA	IId	12.8	1/8	0	0	0	0	0	0	0	0	0	0	0	0	0	0	0	0	0	0	0	0	0
61	K20/204	1994	Pit fill	LBA/IA	IId	1.4	1/2	0	0	0	0	0	0	0	0	0	8	0	0	3	9	14	0	0	0	14	0	48
				Presence (number of samples)				22	11	21	2	9	6	3	1	9	4	10	11	6	7	6	13	9	1	32	2	46

The counts were multiplied as necessary to enable figures for the coarse and fine fractions to be added together to create a total for each sample.
This was based on the largest proportion of each fraction that had been sorted.

Appendix 1

Appendix 1.7. *(cont.)*

Sample no.	T. monococcum gl	cf. T. monococcum gl	T. monococcum/dicoccum gl	T. dicoccum gl	cf. T. dicoccum gl	TOTAL - Triticum gl.	T. aestivum rachis	T. durum rachis	T. aestivum/durum rachis	TOTAL - Triticum rachis	H. distichum/vulgare hulled indet.	H. distichum/vulgare cf. hulled	H. distichum/vulgare cf. naked	H. distichum/vulgare indet.	H. vulgare asymmetric	H. vulgare cf. asymmetric	H. distichum/vulgare symmetric	H. distichum/vulgare cf. symmetric	H. distichum/vulgare small hulled indet.	H. distichum/vulgare small indet.	H. distichum/vulgare cf. tail grains	H. distichum/vulgare/spontanaeum	Hordeum indet.	cf. Hordeum	TOTAL - Hordeum gr	H. distichum/vulgare rachis	Hordeum rachis cf. 2-row	Hordeum rachis indet.	TOTAL - Hordeum rachis	cf. Secale cereale gr	Triticum/Hordeum gr	Cereal gr indet.	TOTAL - Cereal gr	TOTAL - Cereal chaff
1	0	0	0	0	0	0	0	0	0	0	0	0	0	0	0	0	0	0	0	0	0	0	1	0	1	0	0	0	0	0	0	1	1	0
2	0	0	0	0	0	0	0	1	0	1	9	0	0	2	0	0	0	0	0	0	0	0	0	0	11	0	0	0	0	0	0	3	24	1
3	0	0	0	0	0	0	0	0	0	0	0	0	0	0	0	0	0	0	0	0	0	0	0	0	0	0	0	0	0	0	0	4	4	0
4	0	0	0	0	0	0	0	0	0	0	4	0	0	0	0	0	0	0	0	0	0	0	0	0	4	0	0	0	0	0	0	0	4	0
5	0	0	0	0	0	0	0	0	0	0	0	0	0	4	0	0	0	0	0	0	0	0	12	0	16	0	0	12	12	0	0	16	40	12
6	0	0	0	0	0	0	0	0	0	0	0	0	0	0	0	0	0	0	0	0	0	0	0	0	0	0	0	0	0	0	0	0	0	0
7	0	0	0	0	0	0	0	0	0	0	0	0	0	0	0	0	0	0	0	0	0	0	0	1	1	0	0	0	0	0	0	0	1	0
8	0	0	0	0	0	0	1	0	0	1	3	0	0	0	0	0	0	0	0	0	0	0	0	0	3	0	0	0	0	0	0	1	351	1
9	0	0	32	1	0	33	0	0	32	32	4	0	0	2	0	0	0	0	0	0	0	0	0	0	6	0	0	0	0	0	0	1	66	65
10	0	0	0	0	0	0	0	0	0	0	0	0	0	0	0	0	0	0	0	0	0	0	0	0	0	0	0	0	0	0	0	0	2	0
11	0	0	0	0	0	0	0	0	0	0	5	0	0	5	0	0	0	0	0	0	0	0	0	0	10	0	0	0	0	0	0	3	34	0
12	0	0	0	0	0	0	0	6	40	46	1	0	0	5	0	0	0	0	0	0	0	0	0	0	6	0	0	0	0	0	0	0	11	46
13	5	0	0	2	0	7	90	158	205	453	10	0	0	8	0	0	0	0	0	0	0	0	1	0	19	188	0	0	188	0	0	3	78	648
14	0	0	0	0	0	0	1	0	0	1	3	0	0	4	0	0	0	0	0	0	0	0	0	0	7	0	0	0	0	0	0	2	27	1
15	2	0	0	0	0	2	0	0	0	0	6	0	0	4	0	0	0	0	0	0	0	0	0	0	10	0	0	0	0	0	0	7	18	2
16	0	1	0	0	5	6	0	0	0	0	0	0	0	0	0	0	0	0	0	0	0	0	2	0	2	0	0	0	0	0	0	0	4	6
17	1	0	0	0	0	1	0	0	0	0	0	0	0	3	0	0	0	0	0	0	0	0	0	0	3	0	0	0	0	0	0	2	14	1
18	1	0	20	0	0	21	0	0	0	0	2	0	0	2	0	0	0	0	0	0	0	0	0	0	4	0	0	0	0	0	0	3	9	21
19	0	1	1	0	0	2	0	0	0	0	1	0	1	1	0	0	0	0	0	0	0	0	1	0	4	0	0	0	0	0	0	1	9	2
20	0	0	0	4	0	4	0	0	0	0	4	0	0	0	0	0	0	0	0	0	0	0	0	5	9	0	0	4	4	0	0	0	10	8
21	0	0	0	0	0	0	0	0	0	0	1	1	0	0	0	0	0	0	0	0	0	0	0	0	2	0	0	0	0	0	0	6	14	0
22	1	0	0	0	0	1	0	2	1	3	9	0	0	8	0	0	0	0	0	0	0	0	0	0	17	18	0	0	18	0	0	6	34	22
23	0	0	0	0	0	0	1	1	0	2	15	0	0	6	0	1	0	0	0	0	0	0	2	0	24	34	0	0	34	0	0	1	31	36
24	0	0	0	0	0	0	0	0	0	0	0	0	0	0	0	0	0	0	0	0	0	0	1	0	1	0	0	0	0	0	0	0	3	0
25	0	0	0	0	0	0	0	0	0	0	93	0	0	0	4	0	0	0	0	0	0	0	0	0	97	0	0	0	0	0	0	0	1564	0
26	0	0	0	0	0	0	0	0	0	0	19	0	0	0	0	0	0	0	0	0	0	0	1	0	19	0	0	0	0	0	0	0	317	0
27	0	0	0	0	0	0	0	0	0	0	121	0	0	29	2	0	0	0	0	0	0	0	0	0	152	9	0	0	9	0	0	17	169	9
28	0	0	0	0	0	0	0	0	0	0	0	0	0	1	0	0	0	0	0	0	0	0	0	0	1	0	0	0	0	0	0	0	1	0
29	2	0	8	0	0	10	0	0	0	0	44	0	0	1	0	0	0	0	0	0	0	0	0	0	45	5	0	0	5	0	7	0	330	15
30	229	0	1608	0	0	1837	1	0	16	17	11	0	0	71	0	0	0	0	0	0	0	0	0	0	82	2	0	0	2	0	0	8	112	1856
31	0	0	0	0	0	0	0	0	0	0	0	0	0	0	0	0	0	0	0	0	0	0	0	0	0	0	0	0	0	0	0	4	8	0
32	0	0	0	0	0	0	0	0	0	0	1	0	0	0	0	0	0	0	0	0	0	0	0	0	1	0	0	0	0	0	0	0	5	0
33	0	0	0	0	0	0	0	0	0	0	331	30	1	0	1	3	95	19	0	0	4	0	9	0	493	0	0	0	0	0	0	4	499	0
34	0	0	0	0	0	0	0	0	0	0	371	32	0	0	0	0	99	24	0	0	0	0	223	0	749	0	0	0	0	0	39	0	828	0
35	0	0	0	0	0	0	0	0	0	0	6	0	0	0	0	0	0	0	0	0	0	0	4	2	12	0	0	0	0	1	0	0	18	0
36	0	2	2	0	0	4	0	0	0	0	0	0	0	6	0	0	0	0	0	0	1	0	0	0	7	0	0	0	0	0	0	0	14	4
37	0	0	0	0	0	0	0	0	0	0	0	0	0	0	0	0	0	0	0	0	0	0	1	0	1	0	0	0	0	0	0	3	4	0
38	0	0	0	0	0	0	0	0	0	0	0	0	0	0	0	0	0	0	0	0	0	0	2	0	2	0	0	0	0	0	0	0	30	0
39	0	0	0	0	0	0	0	0	0	0	0	0	0	0	0	0	0	0	0	0	2	0	6	0	8	0	0	0	0	0	0	4	18	0
40	0	0	0	0	0	0	0	0	0	0	0	0	0	0	0	0	0	0	0	0	0	0	0	0	0	0	0	0	0	0	0	0	0	0
41	0	0	0	0	0	0	0	0	0	0	0	0	0	0	0	0	0	0	0	0	0	0	0	0	0	0	0	0	0	0	0	0	0	0
42	0	0	0	0	0	0	0	0	0	0	2	1	0	2	0	0	0	0	0	0	0	0	0	0	5	0	0	0	0	0	0	0	6	0
43	2	0	0	0	0	2	0	0	0	0	84	0	0	0	0	0	0	0	0	0	0	0	9	0	93	0	0	0	0	0	0	0	98	2
44	4	32	0	0	0	36	0	0	0	0	325	1	0	5	0	0	0	0	0	0	1	0	0	0	332	0	0	0	0	0	1	0	338	36
45	0	0	0	0	0	0	0	0	0	0	1	0	0	14	0	0	0	0	0	0	0	0	0	0	15	0	0	0	0	0	2	88	0
46	0	0	0	0	0	32	0	0	0	15	15	0	0	681	0	0	0	0	0	0	0	0	0	0	813	0	0	0	9	0	6	1107	56
47	14	0	65	0	0	79	0	0	0	0	0	1	0	0	0	0	0	0	0	0	2	0	0	0	3	0	0	0	0	0	0	2	193	79
48	56	0	90	0	0	146	0	0	0	0	0	0	0	0	0	0	0	0	0	0	0	0	0	0	0	0	0	0	0	0	4	0	229	146
49	0	16	28	0	0	44	0	0	0	0	0	0	0	0	0	0	0	0	0	0	0	0	0	0	0	0	0	0	0	0	0	0	617	44
50	0	0	0	0	0	0	0	0	0	0	0	0	0	0	0	0	0	0	0	0	0	0	0	0	0	0	0	0	0	0	0	0	3	0
51	0	0	0	0	0	0	0	0	0	0	8	0	0	0	0	0	0	0	0	0	0	0	0	8	16	0	0	0	0	0	0	0	128	0
52	0	0	0	0	0	0	0	0	0	0	477	170	8	768	0	8	8	3	3	76	0	0	0	0	1521	0	0	0	0	0	54	64	1639	0
53	0	0	0	0	0	0	0	0	0	0	92	20	0	0	0	0	0	0	8	44	0	0	368	0	532	0	0	0	0	0	0	17	555	0
54	0	4	0	0	0	4	0	0	0	0	0	0	0	0	0	0	0	0	0	0	0	0	0	0	0	0	0	0	0	0	0	8	49	4
55	0	0	0	0	0	0	0	0	0	0	0	0	0	0	0	0	0	0	0	0	0	0	0	0	0	0	0	0	0	0	0	0	50	0
56	0	0	0	0	0	0	0	0	0	0	0	0	0	0	0	0	0	0	0	0	1	0	0	0	1	0	0	0	0	0	0	2	3	0
57	0	0	0	0	0	0	0	0	0	0	0	0	0	0	0	0	0	0	0	0	0	0	0	0	0	0	0	0	0	0	0	0	1	0
58	2	0	0	0	0	2	0	0	0	0	0	0	0	0	4	0	0	0	0	0	0	0	12	0	16	0	0	0	0	0	13	0	29	2
59	0	0	0	0	0	0	0	0	0	0	2	0	0	0	0	0	0	2	0	0	0	0	2	0	6	0	2	0	2	0	0	2	8	2
60	0	0	0	0	0	0	0	0	0	0	0	0	0	3	0	0	0	0	0	0	1	0	0	0	5	0	0	0	0	0	0	1	6	0
61	1	0	0	0	0	1	0	0	0	0	0	0	0	2	0	0	0	0	0	0	0	0	0	0	2	0	0	0	0	0	0	1	51	1
	13	6	9	3	1	21	5	5	5	10	33	9	3	22	6	3	4	3	2	5	1	1	21	4	49	6	1	2	10	1	4	33	58	29

Appendix 1.7. *(cont.)*

Sample no.	Culm nodes	Silicified Culm nodes	Culm bases	TOTAL - Culm	Vicia faba	Vicia sativa	Vicia ervilia	cf. Vicia ervilia	V. ervilia/Lathyrus sativus	Lathyrus sativus	cf. Lathyrus sativus	small Lathyrus sativus	Pisum sativum	Pisum sp.	cf. Pisum	Lens sp.	cf. Lens sp.	Pisum/Lens	Astragalus-type (large legume type 2)	Large legume indet.	TOTAL - Legume	Panicum miliaceum	cf. Setaria viridis	Panicum sp.	cf. Panicum sp.	TOTAL - Millet	Linum sp.	cf. Linum sp.	Tuber
1	0	0	0	0	0	0	0	0	0	0	0	0	0	0	0	0	0	0	0	0	0	0	0	0	0	0	0	0	0
2	0	0	0	0	0	0	0	0	0	5	0	0	0	0	0	0	0	0	2	2	9	3	0	0	0	3	0	0	0
3	0	0	0	0	0	0	0	0	0	0	0	0	0	0	0	0	0	0	0	1	1	0	0	0	0	0	0	0	0
4	0	0	0	0	0	0	1	0	0	0	0	0	0	0	0	0	0	0	0	0	1	0	0	0	4	4	0	0	0
5	0	0	0	0	0	0	0	0	0	1	0	0	0	0	0	0	0	0	0	0	1	0	0	0	0	0	0	0	0
6	0	0	0	0	0	0	0	0	0	0	0	0	0	0	0	0	0	0	0	0	0	0	0	0	0	0	0	0	0
7	0	0	0	0	0	0	0	0	0	0	0	0	0	0	0	0	0	0	0	0	0	0	0	0	0	0	0	0	0
8	0	0	0	0	0	0	0	0	0	0	0	0	0	0	0	0	0	0	0	0	0	1	0	0	0	1	0	0	0
9	1	0	0	1	0	0	0	0	0	0	0	0	0	0	0	1	0	0	1	0	2	0	0	0	0	0	0	0	0
10	0	0	0	0	0	0	0	0	0	0	0	0	0	0	0	0	0	0	0	2	2	0	0	0	0	0	0	0	0
11	0	0	0	0	0	0	0	0	0	0	0	0	0	0	0	1	0	0	0	0	1	1	0	0	0	1	0	1	0
12	3	0	0	3	0	0	0	0	0	0	0	0	0	0	0	0	0	0	0	0	0	0	0	0	0	0	0	0	0
13	43	3	4	50	1	0	1	0	0	0	0	0	0	0	0	0	0	0	0	0	2	2	0	0	0	2	0	0	0
14	0	0	0	0	1	0	4	0	28	137	21	0	0	0	0	18	0	0	0	1	210	0	0	0	0	0	0	0	0
15	3	5	0	8	0	0	0	0	0	2	0	0	0	0	0	1	0	2	1	0	6	1	0	0	0	1	0	0	0
16	0	0	0	0	0	0	0	2	10	138	34	0	0	0	0	4	0	2	0	66	256	0	0	0	0	0	0	0	0
17	0	0	0	0	0	3	0	0	0	0	0	0	0	0	0	1	0	0	0	4	8	1	0	1	0	2	0	0	0
18	0	0	0	0	0	0	0	0	0	0	1	0	1	0	0	1	0	0	0	1	4	1	0	0	0	1	0	0	1
19	0	0	0	0	0	0	0	0	1	0	0	0	0	0	0	1	0	0	0	0	2	1	0	0	0	1	0	0	0
20	0	0	0	0	0	0	0	0	0	0	0	0	4	0	0	0	0	0	0	2	6	4	0	0	0	4	0	0	0
21	0	0	0	0	0	0	1	0	0	0	0	0	0	0	0	0	0	0	0	1	2	2	0	0	0	2	0	0	0
22	3	0	1	4	1	0	1	0	0	1	0	0	1	0	0	1	0	0	0	2	7	1	0	0	0	1	0	1	0
23	6	0	0	6	0	0	0	0	0	1	1	0	1	0	0	0	1	0	0	2	6	1	0	0	0	1	0	0	1
24	0	0	0	0	0	0	0	0	0	1	0	0	0	0	0	0	0	0	0	1	2	4	1	1	0	6	0	0	0
25	2	0	0	2	0	0	0	0	0	0	0	0	1	0	0	1	0	0	0	0	2	0	0	0	0	0	0	0	0
26	0	0	0	0	0	0	0	0	0	0	0	0	0	0	0	0	0	0	0	0	0	0	0	0	0	0	1	0	0
27	0	0	0	0	0	0	0	0	0	0	0	0	0	0	0	2	0	0	0	0	2	2	0	0	0	2	0	0	0
28	0	0	0	0	0	0	0	0	0	0	0	0	0	0	0	0	0	0	0	0	0	0	0	0	0	0	0	0	0
29	0	0	0	0	8	0	0	0	7	1384	56	42	0	0	0	1	0	0	0	17	1515	0	0	0	0	0	0	0	0
30	2	0	0	2	0	0	0	0	0	13	0	0	0	0	0	1	0	0	0	2	16	0	0	0	0	0	0	0	0
31	0	0	0	0	0	0	0	0	0	0	0	0	0	0	0	0	0	0	0	0	0	0	0	0	0	0	0	0	0
32	0	0	0	0	0	0	0	0	0	0	0	0	0	0	0	1	0	0	0	2	3	0	0	0	0	0	0	0	0
33	0	0	0	0	0	0	0	0	0	0	0	0	0	0	0	0	0	0	0	0	0	0	0	0	0	0	0	0	0
34	0	0	0	0	0	0	0	0	0	0	0	0	2	0	0	0	0	0	0	0	2	0	0	0	0	0	0	0	0
35	2	0	0	2	0	0	0	0	0	0	1	0	1	0	0	0	0	0	0	2	4	0	0	0	0	0	0	0	0
36	0	0	0	0	0	0	3	0	0	0	0	0	0	0	0	6	2	0	2	6	19	0	0	0	0	0	0	0	0
37	0	0	0	0	0	0	0	0	0	0	0	0	0	1	0	0	0	0	0	0	1	0	0	0	0	0	0	0	0
38	0	0	0	0	0	0	0	0	0	0	0	0	2	0	0	0	0	2	0	4	6	14	0	0	0	0	0	0	0	0
39	0	0	0	0	0	0	0	0	0	0	0	0	0	0	0	0	0	0	0	4	4	0	0	0	0	0	0	0	0
40	0	0	0	0	0	0	0	0	0	0	0	0	0	0	0	0	0	0	0	0	0	0	0	0	0	0	0	0	0
41	0	0	0	0	0	0	0	0	0	0	0	0	0	0	0	0	0	0	0	0	0	0	0	0	0	0	0	0	0
42	0	0	0	0	0	0	0	0	0	0	0	0	0	0	0	1	0	0	0	1	2	0	0	0	0	0	0	0	0
43	0	0	0	0	0	0	0	0	0	0	0	0	0	0	0	8	0	0	0	1	9	0	0	0	0	0	0	0	0
44	11	0	0	11	0	0	0	0	0	0	0	0	0	0	0	0	0	0	0	0	0	0	0	0	0	0	0	0	0
45	0	0	0	0	0	0	0	0	0	7	0	0	0.5	0	0	14	0	0	0	0.5	22	1	0	0	0	1	0	0	0
46	0	0	0	0	0	0	0	0	0	1	0	0	0	0	0	182	0	0	0	0	296	0	0	0	19	0	0	0	0
47	0	0	0	0	0	0	0	0	0	0	0	0	0	0	0	0	0	0	0	0	0	0	0	0	0	0	0	0	0
48	0	0	0	0	0	0	0	0	0	0	0	0	0	0	0	0	0	0	0	0	0	0	0	0	0	0	0	0	0
49	1	0	0	1	0	0	0	0	0	0	0	0	0	0	0	0	0	0	0	0	0	0	0	0	0	0	0	0	0
50	0	0	0	0	0	0	0	0	0	0	0	0	0	0	0	285	11	0	0	4	300	0	0	0	0	0	0	0	0
51	0	0	0	0	0	0	0	0	0	0	0	0	0	0	0	3267	268	0	0	360	3895	0	0	0	0	0	0	0	0
52	0	0	0	0	0	0	0	0	0	0	0	0	0	0	0	0	0	0	0	0	0	0	0	0	0	0	0	0	0
53	0	0	0	0	0	0	0	0	0	0	0	0	0	0	0	0	0	0	0	1	1	0	0	0	0	0	0	0	0
54	0	0	0	0	0	0	0	0	0	0	0	0	0	0	0	0	0	0	0	3	3	0	0	0	0	0	0	0	0
55	0	0	0	0	0	0	0	0	0	0	0	0	0	0	0	0	0	0	0	0	0	0	0	0	0	0	0	0	0
56	1	0	0	1	0	0	1	0	0	0	0	0	0	0	0	0	0	0	6	12	19	0	0	0	0	0	0	0	0
57	0	0	0	0	0	0	0	0	0	0	0	0	0	0	0	0	0	0	0	0	0	0	0	0	0	0	0	0	0
58	0	0	0	0	0	0	0	0	0	0	0	0	0	0	0	0	0	0	0	4	4	0	0	0	0	0	0	0	0
59	0	0	0	0	0	0	0	0	0	0	0	0	0	2	0	0	0	0	0	3	5	0	0	0	0	0	0	0	0
60	0	0	0	0	0	0	0	0	0	0	0	0	0	0	0	0	0	0	0	3	3	0	0	0	0	0	0	0	0
61	0	0	0	0	0	0	0	0	0	0	0	0	1	0	0	1	0	0	0	0	2	0	0	0	0	0	1	0	0
	12	2	2	12	4	1	7	1	4	12	6	1	9	1	2	22	5	2	8	28	43	15	1	2	1	17	2	2	2

Appendix 1

Appendix 1.7. *(cont.)*

Sample no.	Olea europaea (g)	Vitis sp.	Ficus sp. pip	cf. Ficus sp. pip	Ficus sp. fruit (g)	Pomegranate seed	cf. Pomegranate seed	Pomegranate skin (g)	Fruit flesh/skin indet. (g)	Fruit stone/Nut shell indet. (g)	Fruit type	Fruit type 1 (Pistachio-type)	Gypsophilia type	Silene sp.	Vaccaria cf. pyramidata	Vaccaria cf. segetalis	Vaccaria sp.	cf. Vaccaria sp.	Caryophyllaceae indet.	Atriplex sp.	Suaeda sp.	Chenopodium album	Chenopodium sp.	Chenopodiaceae indet.	Hypericum sp.	Filago type	Compositae indet.	Convovulus sp.	Convovulaceae indet.	Raphanus rugosum	Neslia paniculata	Neslia sp.	Crucifereae indet. - square types	Crucifereae indet.
1	0	14	1093	0	0	0	0	0	0	0	0	0	0	0	0	0	0	0	8	0	0	0	0	0	0	0	0	0	0	0	0	0	0	0
2	0	1	0	0	0	0	0	0	0	0	0	0	0	0	0	0	0	0	0	0	0	0	0	1	0	0	0	0	0	0	0	0	0	0
3	0.06	6	0	0	0	0	0	0	0	0	0	0	0	0	0	0	0	0	0	0	0	0	0	8	0	0	4	0	0	0	0	0	0	0
4	0	23	0	0	0	0	0	0	0	0	0	0	0	0	0	0	0	0	0	0	0	0	0	0	0	0	0	0	0	0	0	0	0	8
5	0	1	0	0	0	0	0	0	0	0	0	0	0	0	0	0	0	0	0	0	0	0	0	0	0	0	0	0	0	0	0	0	0	8
6	0	0	0	0	0	0	0	0	0	0	0	0	0	0	0	0	0	0	0	0	0	0	0	0	0	0	0	0	0	0	0	0	0	0
7	0	0	0	0	0	0	1	0	0	0	0	0	0	0	0	0	0	0	0	0	0	0	0	0	0	0	0	0	0	0	0	0	0	0
8	0	0	0	0	0	0	0	0	0	0	0	0	0	1	0	1	0	0	0	0	0	8	0	0	0	32	0	0	0	0	2	0	0	9
9	0	0	0	0	0	1	0	0	0	0	0	0	0	0	0	1	0	0	0	0	0	0	0	0	0	4	1	0	0	0	1	0	21	5
10	0	1	0	0	0	0	0	0	0	0	0	0	0	0	0	0	0	0	0	0	0	0	0	0	0	0	0	0	0	0	0	0	0	0
11	0	0	3	0	0	0	0	0	0	0	0	0	0	0	0	0	0	0	0	0	0	0	0	1	0	0	0	0	0	0	0	0	0	0
12	0	1	5	0	0	2	0	0	0.01	0.01	0	0	0	0	0	0	0	0	0	0	0	0	0	0	0	0	0	0	0	0	0	0	0	0
13	0.00375	3	4	2	0	4	0	0.29	0	0.00125	0	0	0	0	0	0	0	0	0	0	0	0	0	0	0	0	4	0	0	0	0	0	0	2
14	0.19	1	24	0	0	0	0	0	0	0.015	0	0	1	0	0	0	1	0	0	8	0	0	0	0	0	0	0	0	0	0	0	0	0	0
15	0.01	3	43	0	0	1	0	0	0	0	0	0	0	0	0	0	0	0	0	0	0	0	0	0	0	0	0	0	0	0	0	0	0	14
16	0	0	0	0	0	0	0	0	0	0.04	0	0	0	0	0	0	0	0	0	0	0	0	0	0	0	0	0	0	0	0	0	0	0	0
17	0.015	3	4	0	0	0	0	0	0	0.035	0	0	0	0	0	0	0	0	0	0	0	0	0	25	0	0	0	0	0	0	0	0	0	0
18	0.05	3	1	0	0	0	0	0	0	0	0	0	0	0	0	0	0	0	8	0	0	16	0	5	0	0	1	0	0	0	0	0	0	1
19	0	0	0	0	0	0	0	0	0	0	0	0	0	0	0	0	0	0	0	0	0	0	0	0	0	0	0	0	0	0	0	0	0	0
20	0.06	2	4	0	0	0	0	0	0	0	0	0	0	0	0	0	0	0	0	0	0	0	0	0	0	0	0	0	0	0	0	0	0	4
21	0.06	0	0	0	0	0	2	0	0	0	0	0	0	0	0	0	0	0	0	0	0	0	0	0	0	0	2	0	0	0	0	0	0	0
22	0.96125	1	0	0	0	0	0	0	0.00125	0.0025	0	1	0	0	1	0	1	0	1	0	0	1	1	8	8	0	0	0	0	42	0	0	0	0
23	0.48875	0	0	0	0	0	0	0	0	0	0	1	16	0	0	0	2	1	0	0	0	0	0	0	0	0	16	0	0	59	0	1	1	1
24	0	0	0	0	0	0	0	0	0	0	0	0	0	0	0	0	1	0	2	0	0	0	0	0	0	0	0	0	0	0	0	0	0	1
25	0.005	0	0	0	0	0	0	0	0	0	0	0	0	0	0	0	0	0	0	0	4	0	0	0	0	0	0	0	0	15	0	0	0	4
26	0	0	0	0	0	0	0	0	0	0	0	0	1	0	0	0	0	0	0	0	0	0	0	0	0	0	0	0	0	6	0	0	0	3
27	0.06	7	0	0	0	1	0	0	0.01	0	0	0	0	0	0	0	0	0	0	0	0	0	0	0	0	0	0	0	0	0	0	0	0	8
28	0	0	0	0	0	0	0	1	0	0	0	0	0	0	0	0	0	0	0	0	0	0	0	0	0	0	0	0	0	0	0	0	0	0
29	0	0	1	0	0	0	0	0	0	0	0	0	0	0	0	0	0	0	0	0	0	0	0	0	0	4	0	0	0	0	0	0	0	0
30	0.005	6	66	48	0	0	0	0	0	0.02	0	0	0	0	0	0	0	0	0	0	0	0	0	0	0	0	0	0	0	0	0	0	9	8
31	0	17	10	0	0	0	0	0	0	0	0	0	0	0	0	0	0	0	0	0	0	0	0	0	0	0	0	0	0	0	0	0	8	0
32	0.02	1	0	0	0	0	0	0	0	0	0	0	0	0	0	0	0	0	0	0	0	0	0	0	0	0	0	0	0	0	0	0	0	0
33	0	1	0	0	0	0	0	0	0	0	0	0	0	1	0	0	0	0	0	0	1	0	0	1	0	0	0	0	0	0	2	0	10	0
34	0	2	0	0	0	0	0	0	0	0	0	0	0	0	4	0	16	4	0	0	0	0	0	0	0	0	0	0	0	0	0	0	0	0
35	0.09	6	0	0	0	0	0	0	0	0	0	0	0	0	0	0	1	0	0	0	0	0	0	0	0	0	0	0	0	0	0	0	0	0
36	0	2	0	0	0	0	0	0	0	0.02	0	0	0	0	0	0	0	0	0	0	0	0	0	0	0	0	0	0	0	0	0	0	0	0
37	0.02	1	0	0	0	0	0	0	0	0	0	0	0	0	0	0	0	0	0	0	0	0	0	0	0	0	0	0	0	0	0	0	0	0
38	0.18	9	0	0	0	0	0	0	0	0	0	0	0	0	0	0	0	0	0	0	0	2	0	0	0	0	0	0	0	0	0	0	0	0
39	0	2	0	0	0	0	0	0	0	0	2	0	0	0	0	0	0	0	0	0	0	0	0	0	0	0	1	0	0	0	0	0	0	0
40	0	0	0	0	281.6	0	0	0	0	0	0	0	0	0	0	0	0	0	0	0	0	0	0	0	0	0	0	0	0	0	0	0	0	0
41	0	0	0	0	56	0	0	0	0	0	0	0	0	0	0	0	0	0	0	0	0	0	0	0	0	0	0	0	0	0	0	0	0	0
42	0.0025	1	0	0	0	0	0	0	0	0	0	0	0	0	0	0	0	0	0	0	0	0	0	0	0	0	0	0	0	0	0	0	0	0
43	0.06	3	5	0	0	0	0	0	0.01	0	0	0	0	0	0	0	0	0	0	0	0	0	0	0	0	0	0	0	0	0	0	0	5	0
44	0.07625	3	0	0	0	0	0	0	0	0	0	0	0	0	0	0	0	0	0	0	0	0	0	0	0	0	0	0	0	0	1	0	19	0
45	0	103	1130	360	0	0	0	0	0.005	0	0	0	0	0	0	0	0	0	0	0	0	0	0	0	0	0	0	0	0	0	0	0	32	0
46	0	0	0	0	0	0	0	0	0	0	0	0	0	0	0	0	0	0	2	0	0	0	0	0	0	0	0	0	0	0	0	0	0	0
47	0	0	0	0	0	0	0	0	0	0	0	0	0	0	0	0	1	0	0	0	0	0	0	0	0	0	0	0	0	0	0	0	0	0
48	0	0	0	0	0	0	0	0	0	0	0	0	0	0	0	0	0	0	2	0	0	0	0	0	0	0	0	0	0	0	0	0	0	0
49	0.01	0	0	0	0	0	0	0	0	0.01	0	0	0	0	0	0	0	0	0	0	0	0	0	0	0	0	0	0	0	0	0	0	0	0
50	0	0	0	0	0	0	0	0	0	0	0	0	0	0	0	0	0	0	0	0	0	0	0	0	0	0	0	0	0	0	0	0	0	0
51	0	0	0	0	0	0	0	0	0	0	0	0	0	0	0	0	3	0	0	0	0	0	0	0	0	0	0	0	0	0	0	8	0	0
52	0.01	1	0	0	0	0	0	0	0	0	0	0	0	0	0	0	8	0	0	0	0	0	0	0	0	0	0	0	0	0	0	0	8	0
53	0.00125	0	0	0	0	0	0	0	0.04	0	0	0	0	0	0	0	0	0	0	0	0	0	0	0	0	0	0	0	0	0	0	0	0	0
54	0	0	0	0	0	0	0	0	0	0	0	0	0	0	0	0	0	0	0	0	0	0	0	0	0	0	0	0	0	0	0	0	0	0
55	0	0	0	0	0	0	0	0	0	0	0	0	0	0	0	0	0	0	0	0	0	0	0	0	0	0	0	0	0	0	0	0	0	0
56	0.01	2	0	0	0	0	0	0	0	0	0	0	0	0	0	0	0	0	0	0	0	0	0	0	0	1	0	0	0	0	0	0	0	0
57	0.02125	3	0	0	0	0	0	0	0	0	0	0	0	0	0	0	0	0	0	0	0	0	0	0	0	0	0	0	0	0	0	0	0	0
58	0.36	6	0	0	0	0	0	0	0	0	0	0	0	0	4	0	0	0	0	0	0	0	0	0	0	0	0	0	0	0	0	0	0	0
59	0.23125	1	0	0	0	0	0	0	0	0	0	0	0	0	0	0	10	0	0	0	0	0	0	0	0	0	0	0	0	0	0	0	0	0
60	0.115	0	0	0	0	0	0	0	0	0	0	0	0	0	0	0	0	0	0	0	0	0	0	0	0	0	0	0	0	0	0	0	0	0
61	0	1	1	0	0	0	0	0	0.005	0	0	0	0	0	0	0	0	0	0	0	0	0	0	0	0	0	0	0	0	0	0	0	0	0
	28	35	15	3	2	5	3	1	5	8	1	2	3	1	4	0	13	3	5	1	2	3	1	10	1	3	5	0	0	4	5	1	9	14

Archaeobotanical Data

Appendix 1.7. *(cont.)*

Sample no.	Carex sp.	Scirpus spp.	Cyperaceae indet.	Fumaria densiflora	Erodium sp.	Aegilops sp.	cf. Aegilops sp.	Avena sp.	cf. Avena sp.	Avena/Bromus sp.	Bromus sterilis type	Bromus spp.	Bromus/Lolium sp.	Chloris sp.	Eragrostis spp.	Eremopyrum sp.	Hordeum cf. spontaneum	Hordeum spp. wild	Lolium temulentum	Lolium spp.	cf. Lolium	Lolium/Eremopyrum sp.	Lolium/Hordeum	Lophochloa sp.	Phalaris spp.	Setaria sp.	Triticum boeoticum	cf. Triticum boeoticum	Triticoid	Small grasses indet.	Gramineae indet.	Gramineae indet. >2 mm	Gramineae indet. <2 mm	Teucrium type	Labiateae indet.
1	0	0	0	0	3	0	0	0	0	0	0	0	0	0	0	0	0	0	0	0	0	0	0	0	0	0	0	0	0	0	0	0	0	0	0
2	0	0	0	0	0	0	0	0	0	0	0	0	0	0	0	0	0	0	0	0	0	0	0	0	0	0	0	0	0	0	0	4	0	0	0
3	0	0	0	0	0	0	0	0	0	0	0	0	0	0	0	0	0	0	0	4	0	0	0	0	0	0	0	0	0	28	0	0	0	0	0
4	0	0	0	0	0	0	0	0	0	0	0	0	0	0	0	0	0	0	0	0	0	0	0	0	0	0	0	0	0	28	8	0	0	0	0
5	0	0	0	0	0	0	0	0	0	0	0	0	0	0	0	0	0	0	0	4	0	0	0	0	0	0	0	0	0	32	0	0	0	0	0
6	0	0	0	0	0	0	0	0	0	0	0	0	0	0	0	0	0	0	1	1	0	0	0	0	0	0	0	0	0	5	0	1	0	0	0
7	0	0	0	0	0	0	0	0	0	0	0	0	0	0	0	0	0	0	0	0	0	0	0	0	0	0	0	0	0	1	0	0	0	0	0
8	0	0	0	0	0	1	0	7	0	0	0	4	0	0	0	0	0	0	42	92	0	0	0	0	0	0	1	8	1	0	0	0	0	0	0
9	1	0	0	0	0	0	0	0	0	0	0	0	0	0	0	0	9	0	29	7	0	0	0	0	0	0	0	0	0	4	0	0	0	0	0
10	0	0	0	0	0	0	0	0	0	0	0	0	0	0	0	0	0	0	0	0	0	0	0	0	0	0	0	0	0	0	0	0	0	0	0
11	1	1	0	0	0	0	0	0	0	0	0	2	0	0	8	0	1	0	2	2	0	0	0	0	0	0	0	0	0	16	0	0	0	0	0
12	0	0	0	0	0	0	0	0	0	0	0	2	0	0	0	0	0	0	1	3	0	0	0	0	1	0	0	0	0	0	0	7	3	0	0
13	0	1	0	1	0	0.5	0	3	0	0	1	19	1	0	0	1	1	11	9	25	0	2	0	0	0	1	0	0	0	48	0	0	0	0.5	0
14	0	18	1	0	0	0	0	0	0	0	0	1	0	0	2	0	0	0	2	3	0	0	0	0	0	0	0	0	0	16	0	0	0	1	0
15	0	0	0	1	0	0	0	0	0	0	0	0	0	0	0	0	0	0	0	0	0	0	0	0	1	0	0	0	0	8	5	0	0	0	0
16	0	0	0	0	0	0	0	0	0	0	0	0	0	0	0	0	0	0	2	0	0	0	0	0	0	0	0	0	0	15	0	0	0	0	0
17	0	1	0	0	0	0	0	0	0	0	0	1	0	0	0	0	0	0	2	2	0	0	0	0	0	0	1	0	0	0	72	0	2	0	0
18	1	22	0	0	0	0	0	2	0	1	0	0	0	0	0	0	0	0	1	1	0	0	0	0	0	4	0	0	1	0	1	6	0	0	0
19	0	0	0	0	0	0	0	0	0	0	0	0	0	0	0	0	0	0	0	1	0	0	0	0	0	0	0	0	0	0	0	0	0	0	0
20	0	0	0	0	0	0	0	0	0	0	0	0	0	0	0	0	0	0	4	0	0	0	0	0	0	0	0	0	0	44	0	0	0	0	0
21	0	0	0	0	0	0	0	0	0	0	0	0	0	0	0	0	0	0	0	0	0	0	0	0	0	0	0	0	0	40	0	8	0	0	0
22	0	0	0	0	0	0	0	10	0	0	1	22	0	0	0	0	0	1	5	3	0	0	0	0	1	0	0	0	0	0	0	1	0	0	0
23	1	0	0	0	0	0	0	3	0	2	0	1	0	0	0	0	16	0	0	0	0	0	9	0	0	0	0	1	0	0	0	3	0	0	0
24	1	0	5	0	0	0	0	0	0	0	0	0	0	0	0	0	0	1	0	0	0	0	0	0	0	0	0	0	0	10	0	1	0	0	0
25	0	1	0	0	0	0	0	6	0	0	0	0	0	0	0	0	0	0	4	0	0	0	0	0	0	0	1	0	0	0	0	0	0	0	0
26	0	0	0	0	1	0	0	0	0	0	0	0	0	0	0	0	0	0	1	0	0	0	0	0	0	0	0	0	0	102	0	0	1	0	0
27	0	0	0	0	0	0	0	1	0	0	0	0	0	0	0	0	0	19	0	3	0	0	0	0	0	0	0	0	0	8	0	0	0	0	0
28	0	0	0	0	0	0	0	0	0	0	0	0	0	0	0	0	0	0	0	0	0	0	0	0	0	0	0	0	0	4	0	0	0	0	0
29	0	0	0	0	0	0	0	0	0	0	0	0	0	0	4	0	0	0	7	19	0	0	0	0	0	0	0	0	0	0	0	0	0	0	0
30	0	3	0	0	0	0	0	1	0	0	0	0	0	0	0	0	3	0	13	8	0	3	0	0	8	0	0	0	0	40	1	0	0	0	0
31	0	0	0	0	0	0	0	0	0	0	0	0	0	0	0	0	0	0	2	0	0	0	0	0	0	0	0	0	0	152	0	20	0	0	0
32	0	0	0	0	0	0	0	0	0	0	0	0	0	0	0	0	0	0	0	0	0	0	0	0	4	0	0	0	0	32	0	2	0	0	0
33	0	0	0	0	0	0	0	5	0	0	0	0	0	0	0	0	4	0	15	2	0	0	0	0	0	0	0	0	0	8	0	1	4	0	0
34	0	0	0	0	0	0	0	20	0	0	0	0	0	0	0	0	0	0	32	76	0	0	0	0	0	0	0	0	0	0	25	0	0	0	0
35	0	0	0	0	0	0	1	1	0	0	0	0	4	0	0	4	0	5	13	0	0	0	4	0	0	0	0	0	12	0	0	2	0	0	0
36	0	0	0	0	0	0	0	0	0	0	0	0	0	0	0	0	0	0	2	0	0	0	0	4	0	0	0	0	0	4	0	5	0	0	0
37	0	0	0	0	0	0	0	0	1	0	0	0	0	0	0	0	0	0	2	0	0	0	10	0	0	0	0	0	0	0	0	0	0	0	0
38	0	0	0	0	0	0	0	0	0	0	0	0	0	0	0	0	0	0	4	0	0	0	0	0	0	0	0	0	0	2	0	0	1	0	0
39	0	0	0	0	0	0	0	0	0	0	0	0	0	0	0	0	0	0	2	2	0	0	0	0	0	0	0	0	0	0	0	4	0	0	0
40	0	0	0	0	0	0	0	0	0	0	0	0	0	0	0	0	0	0	0	0	0	0	0	0	0	0	0	0	0	0	0	0	0	0	0
41	0	0	0	0	0	0	0	0	0	0	0	0	0	0	0	0	0	0	0	0	0	0	0	0	0	0	0	0	0	0	0	0	0	0	0
42	0	0	0	0	0	0	0	0	0	0	0	0	0	0	0	0	0	0	0	0	0	0	0	0	0	0	0	0	0	2	0	0	0	0	0
43	0	0	0	0	0	0	0	1	0	0	0	0	0	0	0	0	0	0	3	0	0	0	0	0	0	0	0	0	0	0	1	0	0	0	0
44	0	0	0	0	0	0	0	2	0	0	0	0	0	0	0	0	9	0	4	0	0	0	0	0	0	0	0	0	0	0	4	32	0	0	0
45	0	1	0	0	0	0	0	0	0	0	0	0	0	0	4	0	15	20	0	9	0	0	16	0	0	0	280	0	0	0	0	0	0	0	0
46	0	0	0	0	0	0	0	0	0	0	0	0	0	0	5	5	0	35	0	0	0	0	0	0	0	0	0	0	0	0	0	0	0	0	0
47	0	0	0	0	0	0	0	1	0	0	0	0	0	0	0	0	0	0	17	0	0	0	0	0	0	2	0	0	2	0	0	0	0	0	0
48	0	0	0	0	0	0	0	6	0	0	0	0	0	0	0	0	0	0	31	0	0	0	0	0	0	0	0	0	0	0	0	0	0	0	0
49	0	0	0	0	0	0	0	0	0	0	0	0	0	0	0	0	0	0	1	0	0	0	0	0	0	0	0	0	0	0	0	2	4	0	0
50	0	0	0	0	0	0	0	0	0	0	0	0	0	0	0	0	0	0	0	0	0	0	0	0	0	0	0	0	0	0	0	0	0	0	0
51	0	0	0	0	0	0	0	0	0	0	0	0	0	0	0	0	0	0	40	0	0	0	0	4	0	0	0	0	0	12	0	0	0	0	0
52	0	0	0	0	0	0	0	8	0	0	0	0	0	0	0	0	0	0	24	163	144	0	0	0	0	0	0	0	0	16	0	8	16	0	0
53	0	0	0	0	0	0	0	0	0	0	0	0	0	0	0	0	0	0	10	24	4	0	0	0	0	0	0	0	0	0	0	0	6	0	0
54	0	0	0	0	0	0	0	2	0	0	0	0	0	0	0	0	0	0	1	4	0	0	0	0	0	0	0	0	0	4	0	0	3	0	0
55	0	0	0	0	0	0	0	0	0	0	0	0	0	0	0	0	0	0	0	0	0	0	0	0	0	0	0	0	0	0	0	0	0	0	0
56	0	0	0	0	0	0	0	0	0	0	0	0	0	0	0	0	0	0	0	0	0	0	0	0	0	0	0	0	0	4	0	1	0	0	0
57	0	0	0	0	0	0	0	0	0	1	0	0	0	0	0	0	0	0	0	1	0	0	0	0	0	0	0	0	0	0	0	0	0	0	1
58	0	4	0	0	0	0	0	0	0	0	0	0	0	0	0	0	0	0	8	4	0	0	0	0	0	0	0	0	0	24	0	0	0	0	0
59	0	0	0	0	0	0	0	0	0	0	0	0	0	0	0	0	0	0	2	18	0	0	0	4	0	0	0	0	0	28	0	0	4	0	0
60	0	0	0	0	0	0	0	0	0	0	0	0	0	0	0	0	0	0	0	2	0	0	0	1	0	0	0	0	0	0	1	0	0	0	0
61	0	0	0	0	0	0	0	10	0	0	0	1	0	0	0	0	0	0	1	2	0	1	0	0	0	0	0	0	0	0	0	0	0	0	0
	5	9	2	2	2	2	1	18	2	2	2	9	1	1	3	2	8	4	30	37	5	4	1	2	9	4	1	3	2	33	4	22	11	2	1

Appendix 1.7. *(cont.)*

Sample no.	Coronilla spp.	Lathyrus sp.	cf. Lathyrus	Medicago spp.	Scorpiurus sp.	Trifolium/Melilotis spp.	cf. Trifolium/Melilotis spp.	Trigonella astroides type	Trigonella/Astragalus spp.	Leguminoseae indet.	Bellevalia/Ornithogalum type	Liliaceae indet.	Malva sylvestris	Malvaceae indet.	Glaucium type	Papaver cf. dubidum	Papaver cf. hybridum	Papaver sp.	Polygonum sp.	Rumex conglomeratus	Rumex sp.	Polygonaceae indet.	Adonis m/d/f	Adonis sp.	Ranunculus sp.	Ranunculaceae indet.	Crataegus type
1	0	0	0	0	0	0	0	0	0	0	0	0	0	0	0	8	0	0	0	0	0	0	0	0	0	0	0
2	0	0	0	0	0	0	0	0	0	0	0	0	0	0	0	0	0	0	0	0	0	0	1	0	0	0	0
3	0	0	0	0	0	12	0	0	0	0	0	0	0	0	0	0	0	0	0	0	0	0	0	0	0	0	0
4	0	0	0	0	0	16	0	0	4	0	0	0	0	0	0	0	0	0	0	0	0	0	0	0	0	0	0
5	0	0	0	0	0	8	8	0	8	4	0	0	0	0	0	0	0	0	0	0	0	0	0	0	0	0	0
6	0	0	0	0	0	0	0	0	0	0	0	0	0	0	0	0	0	0	0	0	0	0	0	0	0	0	0
7	0	0	0	0	0	0	0	0	0	0	0	0	0	0	0	0	0	0	0	0	0	0	0	0	0	0	0
8	0	0	0	0	0	0	0	0	0	0	0	0	0	0	0	0	0	0	0	0	0	0	0	0	0	0	0
9	0	0	0	0	0	1	0	0	1	0	0	0	0	0	0	0	0	4	0	0	0	0	0	0	1	4	0
10	0	0	0	0	0	0	0	0	0	0	0	0	0	0	0	0	0	0	0	0	0	0	0	0	0	0	0
11	0	0	0	0	1	25	0	0	0	1	0	0	0	0	0	0	0	0	0	0	0	0	0	0	0	1	0
12	0	0	0	0	0	0	0	0	0	0	1	0	0	0	0	0	0	0	0	0	0	0	0	0	0	0	0
13	0	0	0	0	0	5	0	0	0	0	0	0	0	4	0	4	5	1	0	0	0	0	0	0	0	0	1
14	0	0	0	2	0	85	0	0	0	0	0	0	0	0	0	0	0	0	0	0	8	0	0	0	0	0	0
15	1	0	0	0	0	0	0	0	0	0	0	0	0	0	0	0	0	0	0	0	0	0	0	0	0	0	0
16	0	0	0	0	0	0	0	0	0	0	0	0	0	0	0	0	0	0	0	0	0	0	0	0	0	0	0
17	0	0	0	1	0	24	0	0	0	0	0	0	0	1	0	0	0	0	0	0	0	0	0	0	0	0	0
18	1	0	0	6	3	41	0	28	19	1	0	0	0	1	0	0	0	0	0	0	1	0	0	0	0	0	0
19	0	0	0	0	0	0	0	0	0	1	0	0	0	2	0	0	0	0	0	0	0	0	0	0	0	0	0
20	0	0	0	0	0	4	0	0	4	0	0	0	0	4	0	12	0	0	0	0	0	0	0	0	0	0	0
21	0	0	0	6	0	2	0	0	0	0	0	0	0	0	0	0	0	4	0	0	0	0	0	0	0	0	0
22	17	0	0	2	1	52	0	0	3	0	0	0	2	94	1	0	0	0	0	0	1	0	0	0	0	0	0
23	6	0	0	1	0	222	0	0	3	1	0	0	2	170	0	8	0	0	0	0	1	0	0	0	0	0	1
24	2	0	0	1	0	5	0	0	1	1	0	0	0	3	0	0	0	2	0	0	0	0	0	0	0	0	1
25	0	0	0	0	0	16	0	4	0	0	0	0	0	0	0	0	0	0	0	0	0	0	0	0	0	0	0
26	0	0	0	0	0	1	0	0	2	1	0	0	0	0	0	0	0	1	0	0	0	0	0	0	0	0	0
27	0	0	0	0	0	33	0	0	0	0	0	0	0	0	0	0	0	8	0	0	0	0	0	0	0	0	0
28	0	0	0	0	0	0	0	0	0	0	0	0	0	0	0	0	0	4	0	0	0	0	0	0	0	0	0
29	0	0	0	0	0	12	0	0	0	2	0	0	0	0	0	0	0	0	0	0	0	0	0	0	0	0	0
30	1	0	0	0	0	24	0	0	0	0	0	0	0	2	0	0	0	0	0	0	1	0	2	0	0	0	0
31	0	0	0	0	0	0	0	0	4	0	4	0	0	0	0	0	0	0	0	0	0	0	0	0	0	0	0
32	0	0	0	0	0	0	0	0	0	0	0	0	0	4	0	0	0	0	0	0	0	0	0	0	0	0	0
33	0	0	0	0	0	0	0	0	0	1	0	0	1	4	0	11	0	0	0	0	0	0	1	1	0	0	0
34	0	0	0	0	0	0	0	0	0	0	0	0	0	0	0	0	0	0	0	0	0	0	0	0	0	0	0
35	6	0	0	2	0	12	0	8	3	0	0	0	0	0	0	0	0	0	0	0	1	0	1	0	0	0	1
36	0	0	0	0	0	0	0	0	0	0	0	0	0	8	0	0	0	0	0	0	0	0	0	0	0	0	0
37	0	0	0	0	0	0	0	0	0	0	0	0	0	0	0	0	0	0	0	0	0	0	0	0	0	0	0
38	0	0	0	0	0	0	0	0	0	0	0	0	0	0	0	0	0	0	0	0	0	0	0	0	0	0	0
39	0	0	0	0	0	0	0	0	0	0	0	0	0	0	0	0	0	0	0	0	0	0	0	0	0	0	0
40	0	0	0	0	0	0	0	0	0	0	0	0	0	0	0	0	0	0	0	0	0	0	0	0	0	0	0
41	0	0	0	0	0	0	0	0	0	0	0	0	0	0	0	0	0	0	0	0	0	0	0	0	0	0	0
42	0	0	0	0	0	0	0	0	0	15	0	0	0	0	0	0	0	0	0	0	0	0	0	0	0	0	0
43	2	0	0	4	0	0	0	0	0	0	0	0	0	0	0	0	0	0	0	0	0	0	0	0	0	0	0
44	0	0	0	6	0	0	0	0	0	0	0	0	0	0	0	0	0	0	0	0	0	0	0	0	0	0	0
45	0	0	0	1	0	42	0	0	0	0	0	0	0	0	0	0	0	0	0	0	0	0	0	0	0	0	0
46	0	0	0	2	0	0	0	0	0	0	0	0	0	0	0	0	0	0	0	0	0	0	0	0	0	0	0
47	0	0	0	0	0	0	0	0	0	0	0	0	0	0	0	0	0	0	0	0	0	0	0	0	0	0	0
48	0	0	0	0	0	0	0	0	0	0	0	0	0	0	0	0	0	0	0	0	0	0	0	0	0	0	0
49	0	0	0	0	0	0	0	0	0	0	0	0	0	0	0	0	0	0	0	0	0	0	0	0	0	0	0
50	0	0	0	0	0	0	0	0	0	0	0	0	0	0	0	0	0	0	0	0	0	0	0	0	0	0	0
51	0	0	0	0	0	0	0	0	0	0	0	8	0	0	0	4	0	4	0	0	0	0	16	0	0	0	0
52	0	0	0	0	0	0	0	0	0	0	0	0	0	0	0	0	0	0	0	0	0	0	0	0	0	0	0
53	0	0	0	0	0	0	0	0	0	0	0	0	0	0	0	0	2	0	0	0	0	0	0	0	0	0	0
54	0	0	0	0	0	0	0	0	0	0	0	0	0	0	0	0	0	0	0	0	0	0	0	0	0	0	0
55	0	0	0	0	0	0	0	0	0	0	0	0	0	0	0	0	0	0	0	0	0	0	0	0	0	0	0
56	0	0	0	1	0	0	0	0	0	0	0	0	0	1	0	0	0	0	0	0	0	0	0	0	0	0	0
57	0	0	0	0	0	2	0	0	0	0	0	0	0	0	0	0	0	0	0	0	0	0	0	0	0	0	0
58	0	0	0	4	0	0	0	0	0	4	0	0	0	0	0	0	0	0	0	0	0	0	0	0	0	0	0
59	2	0	0	2	0	0	0	0	2	2	0	0	0	0	0	0	0	0	0	0	0	0	0	0	0	0	0
60	0	0	0	0	0	0	0	0	0	0	0	0	0	0	0	0	0	0	0	0	0	0	0	0	0	0	0
61	1	0	0	0	0	2	0	0	0	0	0	0	0	0	0	0	0	0	0	0	0	0	0	0	0	0	0
	10	0	0	15	3	23	1	3	12	12	2	1	3	12	1	6	1	8	1	1	6	0	5	1	1	2	4

Appendix 1.7. *(cont.)*

Sample no.	Galium spp.	Sharardia arvensis	Rubiaceae indet. (stunted type)	Bupleurum cf. lancifolium	Bupleurum sp.	cf. Bupleurum	Pimpinella type	Umbelliferae indet.	Wild type 2	Wild type 5	Pl quantifiable	Wild indet. quantifiable	TOTAL - wild spp.	Medicago sp. pod	Crucifereae/Leguminoseae pod	Stem	Thorn	Dung pellet
1	0	0	0	0	0	0	0	0	0	0	50	72	141	0	0	0	0	0
2	0	0	0	0	0	0	0	0	0	0	0	0	6	0	0	0	0	0
3	0	0	0	0	0	0	0	0	0	0	12	0	68	0	frags.	0	0	0
4	0	0	0	0	0	0	0	0	8	4	0	4	80	0	frags.	4	0	0
5	0	0	4	0	0	0	0	0	0	0	0	12	88	0	0	0	0	0
6	0	0	0	0	0	0	0	0	0	0	2	0	10	0	0	0	0	0
7	0	0	0	0	0	0	0	0	0	0	0	0	1	0	0	0	0	0
8	0	0	0	0	0	0	0	0	0	0	0	0	209	0	0	0	0	0
9	0	0	0	1	0	0	0	13	0	0	1	0	109	0	frags.	0	0	0
10	0	0	0	0	0	0	0	0	0	0	2	0	2	0	0	0	0	0
11	1	0	0	0	0	0	0	0	0	0	24	0	87	0	frags.	0	0	0
12	0	0	0	0	0	0	0	0	0	0	7	0	25	0	0	0	1	0
13	1	1	0	0	0	0	0	0	0	0	6	0	159	0	0	0	0	2
14	2	0	0	0	0	0	0	0	0	0	25	0	176	0	0	0	0	0
15	0	0	0	0	0	0	0	0	0	0	56	0	86	0	frags.	0	0	0
16	0	0	0	0	0	0	0	0	0	0	3	0	20	0	frags.	0	0	0
17	0	0	0	0	0	0	0	0	0	0	0	1	133	0	0	1	0	0
18	0	1	0	0	0	0	0	0	0	0	0	4	177	0	0	0	0	0
19	0	0	0	0	0	0	0	0	0	0	7	0	11	0	0	0	0	0
20	0	0	0	0	0	0	0	4	0	0	8	28	116	1	frags.	0	0	0
21	0	0	0	0	0	0	0	0	0	0	5	0	67	0	frags.	0	0	0
22	1	1	0	10	0	0	0	0	0	0	11	2	305	1	frags.	0	0	0
23	1	0	1	12	3	0	0	0	0	0	4	0	569	0	frags.	0	0	0
24	0	0	1	0	0	0	0	0	0	0	8	1	48	0	0	1	0	0
25	0	0	0	0	0	0	0	0	0	0	0	0	55	0	0	0	0	0
26	0	0	0	0	0	0	0	0	0	0	21	0	141	0	frags.	0	0	0
27	1	0	0	0	0	0	0	8	0	0	0	3	92	0	frags.	0	0	0
28	0	0	0	0	0	0	0	0	0	0	0	0	8	0	0	0	0	0
29	2	0	0	0	0	0	0	0	0	0	1	0	51	0	0	0	0	0
30	2	0	0	0	0	0	0	8	0	0	0	0	137	0	0	0	0	0
31	0	0	0	0	0	0	0	0	0	0	2	4	196	0	0	2	0	0
32	1	0	0	0	0	0	0	0	0	0	0	0	43	0	0	0	0	0
33	1	0	0	9	0	0	0	0	0	0	39	0	122	0	0	0	0	0
34	0	0	0	0	0	0	0	0	0	0	4	4	185	0	0	4	0	0
35	0	0	0	0	0	0	0	8	0	0	1	4	94	0	0	0	0	0
36	2	0	0	0	0	0	0	0	0	0	56	0	81	0	0	0	0	0
37	0	0	0	0	0	0	0	0	0	0	0	0	13	0	0	0	0	0
38	0	0	0	0	0	0	0	0	0	0	33	0	42	0	0	0	0	0
39	0	0	0	0	0	0	0	2	0	0	3	0	14	0	frags.	0	0	0
40	0	0	0	0	0	0	0	0	0	0	0	0	0	0	0	0	0	0
41	0	0	0	0	0	0	0	0	0	0	0	0	0	0	0	0	0	0
42	0	0	0	0	0	0	0	0	0	0	2	0	19	0	0	0	0	0
43	0	0	0	0	0	0	0	0	0	0	5	0	21	0	frags.	0	0	0
44	0	0	0	2	0	0	0	0	0	0	5	48	132	0	frags.	0	0	0
45	1	0	0	0	0	0	0	0	0	0	2	0	423	0	frags.	0	0	0
46	2	0	0	0	0	0	0	0	0	0	5	0	625	0	0	0	0	0
47	0	0	0	0	0	0	0	0	0	0	2	0	25	0	0	0	0	0
48	0	0	0	0	0	0	0	0	0	0	1	0	40	0	0	0	0	0
49	0	0	0	0	0	0	0	0	0	0	4	0	11	0	frags.	0	0	0
50	1	0	0	0	0	0	0	0	0	0	0	0	1	0	0	0	0	0
51	38	0	0	0	4	4	0	3	0	0	16	16	180	0	0	0	0	0
52	24	0	0	0	0	0	0	0	0	0	0	0	419	0	frags.	0	0	0
53	2	0	0	0	0	0	0	0	0	14	84	0	146	0	0	0	0	0
54	0	0	0	0	0	0	0	0	0	0	0	12	26	0	0	0	0	0
55	0	0	0	0	0	0	0	0	0	0	0	0	0	0	0	0	0	0
56	4	0	0	0	0	0	0	0	0	0	0	0	12	0	frags.	0	0	0
57	0	0	0	0	0	0	0	0	0	0	2	0	7	0	0	0	0	0
58	0	0	0	0	0	0	0	0	0	0	8	4	64	0	0	0	0	0
59	0	0	0	0	0	0	0	0	0	0	4	20	98	0	frags.	0	0	0
60	0	0	0	0	0	0	0	0	0	0	12	0	16	0	0	0	0	0
61	0	0	0	0	0	0	0	0	0	0	1	1	20	0	0	0	0	0
	18	3	3	5	2	1	0	7	1	2	41	18	58	2	0	5	1	1

Appendix 2

List of Excavation Units

Explanation of the headings

Unit: number assigned by excavator to each separately recorded archaeological operation. There was some divergence of practice, in that some area supervisors assigned one unit number to the outline of a feature (e.g. a pit), and another unit number to the contents. These are described in the unit list below as (e.g.) 'P95/33 cut' and 'P95/33 fill' respectively. Since the cuts marked only the interface between different deposits, they had no material existence and no contents. The symbol // introduces units which are stratigraphically equivalent.

Square: grid square (10 × 10 m: see Fig. 17) with quadrant (5 × 5 m) letter when appropriate (see p. 67).

Chapter
C1–17 denote the chapter or section of Part C in which the unit is referred to, as follows:
C8	Fire Installations
C9	Pits
C10	Level V
C11	Level IV
C12	Level III
C13.1	Level IIa–c
C13.2	Level IId
C13.3	Level IIe
C13.4	Level IIf
C14	The East Slope
C15.1	Square Q10
C15.2	Square N12
C15.3	Levels 2–3 in I14
C15.4	Level 2 in K14
C15.5	Level 1 in I–M14
C16	The Church
C17	The NW corner

Level: the following codes were used (see pp. 68–9 for the levels and their sub-divisions).
0 surface material including cuts from surface; also mixed units
1 Level 1 (away from NW corner)
2 Level 2 (away from NW corner)
3 Level 3 (away from NW corner)
I Level I (in NW corner)
II Level II (in NW corner)
III Level III (in NW corner)
IV Level IV (in NW corner)
V Level V (in NW corner)

E1–5 Strata on the East Slope (see p. 165).

Purity: the quality of stratigraphic control is indicated by a grade from a to d, as follows:
a believed pure
b slight, or slight risk of, contamination
c definitely and significantly contaminated
d no stratigraphic effort made

Context: a code from 1 to 9 assigning each unit to a deposit class. This was primarily intended for use in the Leverhulme project (see Matthews & Postgate 2001 from where the following definitions with some sub-divisions are taken).
1 Natural deposits — natural strata and deposits laid by natural agencies (e.g. wind, water, gravity)
2 Tip, midden, rubbish, dump — including single and repeated episodes
3 Structure — i.e. brick, stone, mortar, plaster etc. of walls and other constructed features
4 Construction materials — 'packing, fill'
   a. sand, clay, hard-core, bricky rubble, bricks
   b. refuse deposits with high organic content
   c. destruction debris, *in situ* and recycled [note the distinction between this (debris deposited in room as part of or after destruction) and 6b (materials belonging *in situ* and subjected to destruction)]
5 Occupation sequence
   a. laid floor material
   b. occupational accumulation on floor
   c. combinations of a and b
   d. combinations of a and b and (their) associated packing layers
6 *In situ* deposits — primary contexts where the deposits of artefacts and other material may be off the end of the quantitative spectrum
   a. grave contents
   b. room contents (incl. items involved in destruction)
   c. fire installation fill

Appendix 2

7. Pit fills
   a. residue from use of pit
   b. infill (striated accumulations)
   c. backfill (single episode, homogeneous)
8. Miscellaneous deposit type which cannot be put into 1–7
9. Mixed — units involving more than one of the above categories.

Description: this is a revised description of the unit in the light of subsequent interpretation, and therefore includes room numbers and other details not available at the time of excavation.

Unit	Square	Chapter	Level	Purity	Context	Description
99						Unprovenanced surface finds
100	K15		0	-	-	Surface
101	P15		0	-	-	Surface
102	L15		0	-	-	Surface
103	M15		0	-	-	Surface
104	N15		0	-	-	Surface
105	O15		0	-	-	Surface
106	K16		0	-	-	Surface
107	L16		0	-	-	Surface
108	M16		0	-	-	Surface
109	N16		0	-	-	Surface
110	O16		0	-	-	Surface
111	P16		0	-	-	Surface
112	Q16		0	-	-	Surface
113	Q15		0	-	-	Surface
114	Q17		0	-	-	Surface
115	P17		0	-	-	Surface
116	O17		0	-	-	Surface
117	N17		0	-	-	Surface
118	M17		0	-	-	Surface
119	L17		0	-	-	Surface
120	K17		0	-	-	Surface
121	K18		0	-	-	Surface
122	L18		0	-	-	Surface
123	M18		0	-	-	Surface
124	N18		0	-	-	Surface
125	O18		0	-	-	Surface
126	P18		0	-	-	Surface
127	Q18		0	-	-	Surface
128	R16		0	-	-	Surface
129	R17		0	-	-	Surface
130	R18		0	-	-	Surface
131	N21		0	-	-	Surface
132	M21		0	-	-	Surface
133	R15		0	-	-	Surface
134	L21		0	-	-	Surface
135	K20		0	-	-	Surface
136	J20		0	-	-	Surface
137	L20	C17	0	-	-	Surface
138	M20	C17	0	-	-	Surface
139	N20	C17	0	-	-	Surface
140	O20	C17	0	-	-	Surface
141	O21		0	-	-	Surface
142	P19		0	-	-	Surface
143	J15		0	-	-	Surface
144	J16		0	-	-	Surface
145	J17		0	-	-	Surface
146	J18		0	-	-	Surface
147	J19		0	-	-	Surface
148	I19		0	-	-	Surface
149	K19		0	-	-	Surface
150	I18		0	-	-	Surface
151	L19		0	-	-	Surface
152	M19		0	-	-	Surface
153	N19		0	-	-	Surface
154	O19		0	-	-	Surface
155	I15		0	-	-	Surface
156	I16		0	-	-	Surface
157	I17		0	-	-	Surface
158	H16		0	-	-	Surface
159	H15		0	-	-	Surface
160	H17		0	-	-	Surface
161	H18		0	-	-	Surface
162	H19		0	-	-	Surface
163	I20		0	-	-	Surface
164	Q19		0	-	-	Surface
165	S18		0	-	-	Surface
166	S17		0	-	-	Surface
167	S16		0	-	-	Surface
168	S15		0	-	-	Surface
169	T15		0	-	-	Surface
170	T16		0	-	-	Surface
171	T17		0	-	-	Surface
172	T18		0	-	-	Surface
173	Q19	C14	0	-	-	Sub-surface
174	S18		0	-	-	Sub-surface
175	P21		0	-	-	Surface
176	P20	C17	0	-	-	Surface
177	S18		-	-	-	Second sub-surface scrape
178	Q19	C14	-	-	-	Second sub-surface scrape
179	R18		0	-	-	Sub-surface
180	Q21		0	-	-	Surface
181	R18		-	-	-	Second sub-surface scrape
182	R19		0	-	-	Surface
183	Q20		0	-	-	Surface
184	Q20	C14	0	-	-	Sub-surface
185	O20	C17	0	-	-	Sub-surface

List of Excavation Units

Unit	Square	Chapter	Level	Purity	Context	Description
186	P14		0	-	-	Surface
187	Q14		0	-	-	Surface
188	O14		0	-	-	Surface
189	R14		0	-	-	Surface
190	N14		0	-	-	Surface
191	M14		0	-	-	Surface
192	L14		0	-	-	Surface
193	K14		0	-	-	Surface
194	L13		0	-	-	Surface
195	M13		0	-	-	Surface
196	N13		0	-	-	Surface
197	O13		0	-	-	Surface
198	P13		0	-	-	Surface
199	Q13		0	-	-	Surface
200	R13		0	-	-	Surface
201	K13		0	-	-	Surface
202	P12		0	-	-	Surface
203	O12		0	-	-	Surface
204	N12		0	-	-	Surface
205	M12		0	-	-	Surface
206	L12		0	-	-	Surface
207	K12		0	-	-	Surface
208	J14		0	-	-	Surface
209	I14		0	-	-	Surface
210	P20	C17	0	-	-	Sub-surface
211	J13		0	-	-	Surface
212	J12		0	-	-	Surface
213	J11		0	-	-	Surface
214	K11		0	-	-	Surface
215	L11		0	-	-	Surface
216	M11		0	-	-	Surface
217	N11		0	-	-	Surface
218	O11		0	-	-	Surface
219	P11		0	-	-	Surface
220	Q12		0	-	-	Surface
221	R12		0	-	-	Surface
222	R11		0	-	-	Surface
223	Q11		0	-	-	Surface
224	M10		0	-	-	Surface
225	L10		0	-	-	Surface
226	K10		0	-	-	Surface
227	N10		0	-	-	Surface
228	O10		0	-	-	Surface
229	P10		0	-	-	Surface
230	Q10	C15.1	0	-	-	Surface
231	M20	C17	0	-	-	Sub-surface
232	N20	C17	0	-	-	Sub-surface
233	R10		0	-	-	Surface
234	R9		0	-	-	Surface
235	Q9		0	-	-	Surface
236	P9		0	-	-	Surface
237	O9		0	-	-	Surface
238	N9		0	-	-	Surface
239	M9		0	-	-	Surface
240	L9		0	-	-	Surface
241	L20	C17	0	-	-	Sub-surface
242	N7		0	-	-	Surface
243	O8		0	-	-	Surface
244	O7		0	-	-	Surface
245	P8		0	-	-	Surface
246	P7		0	-	-	Surface
247	Q8		0	-	-	Surface
248	Q7		0	-	-	Surface
249	R8		0	-	-	Surface
250	R7		0	-	-	Surface
251	S8		0	-	-	Surface
252	S7		0	-	-	Surface
253	S6		0	-	-	Surface
254	T6		0	-	-	Surface
255	T7		0	-	-	Surface
256	T8		0	-	-	Surface
257	U6		0	-	-	Surface
258	U7		0	-	-	Surface
259	U8		0	-	-	Surface
260	V8		0	-	-	Surface
261	V7		0	-	-	Surface
262	W9		0	-	-	Surface
263	V9		0	-	-	Surface
264	U9		0	-	-	Surface
265	T9		0	-	-	Surface
266	S9		0	-	-	Surface
267	S10		0	-	-	Surface
268	T10		0	-	-	Surface
269	U10		0	-	-	Surface
270	V10		0	-	-	Surface
271	W10		0	-	-	Surface
272	W11		0	-	-	Surface
273	V11		0	-	-	Surface
274	U11		0	-	-	Surface
275	T11		0	-	-	Surface
276	S11		0	-	-	Surface
277	S12		0	-	-	Surface
278	T12		0	-	-	Surface
279	U12		0	-	-	Surface
280	S13		0	-	-	Surface
281	T13		0	-	-	Surface
282	U13		0	-	-	Surface
283	U14		0	-	-	Surface
284	T14		0	-	-	Surface
285	S14		0	-	-	Surface
286	U15		0	-	-	Surface
287	U16		0	-	-	Surface
288	V12		0	-	-	Surface
289	W12		0	-	-	Surface
290	V13		0	-	-	Surface
291	W13		0	-	-	Surface
292	V14		0	-	-	Surface
293	W14		0	-	-	Surface
294	V15		0	-	-	Surface

Appendix 2

Unit	Square	Chapter	Level	Purity	Context	Description
295	W15		0	-	-	Surface
296	V16		0	-	-	Surface
297	W16		0	-	-	Surface
298	W17		0	-	-	Surface
299	S19		0	-	-	Surface
300	T19		0	-	-	Surface
301	V19		0	-	-	Surface
302	I13		0	-	-	Surface
303	H13		0	-	-	Surface
304	G13		0	-	-	Surface
305	G12		0	-	-	Surface
306	I12		0	-	-	Surface
307	H12		0	-	-	Surface
308	H11		0	-	-	Surface
309	I11		0	-	-	Surface
310	I10		0	-	-	Surface
311	J10		0	-	-	Surface
312	I9		0	-	-	Surface
313	J9		0	-	-	Surface
314	K9		0	-	-	Surface
315	K8		0	-	-	Surface
316	J8		0	-	-	Surface
317	I8		0	-	-	Surface
318	L8		0	-	-	Surface
319	J7		0	-	-	Surface
320	K7		0	-	-	Surface
321	L7		0	-	-	Surface
322	M8		0	-	-	Surface
323	M7		0	-	-	Surface
324	L6		0	-	-	Surface
325	M6		0	-	-	Surface
326	N6		0	-	-	Surface
327	O6		0	-	-	Surface
328	P6		0	-	-	Surface
329	Q6		0	-	-	Surface
330	R6		0	-	-	Surface
331	N8		0	-	-	Surface
1000	Y9		9	d	9	Sanitary facility
1001			9	d	9	Sanitary facility
1002	J19		0	d	9	Modern robber pit
1003	J19		I	a	7	P94/29 cut
1004	J19		I	a	7	P94/29 upper fill
1005	J19		I	a	7	P94/29 central fill, below 1004
1006	J19		I	a	7	P94/29 lower fill, below 1005
1100	K20		0	d	9	Topsoil (//1901)
1101	K20		0	d	9	Topsoil, below 1100
1102	K20		I	b	3	W116 foundation
1103	K20a/b	C17	I/II	c	4	Clay packing N of W116 (//1914)
1104	K20c/d	C17	I/II	d	4	Occ. sequence S of W116
1105	K20a/c	C17	I	b	7	P94/13
1106	K20a	C13.1	IIc	b	6	Rm 15 FI94/7 fill against NW wall
1107	K20a	C17	I	a	7	P94/14
1108	K20a/b	C13.1, C13.2	IId?	d	6	Rm 12 FI94/8 fill
1109	K20b		I	b	7	P94/15
1110	K20d		I/II	c	7	P94/16
1111	K20b		I/II	c	7	Clay-lined depression
1112	K20b	C13.1, C13.2	IId?	b	6	Rm 12 FI94/8 fill
1113	K20c		I	d	2	Ash spread S of W116
1114	K20c	C17	I?	d	9	Fill of foundation trench for W116
1115	K20c		I	d	8	Ashy spread in SE corner
1116	K20c	C17	I/II	c	5	Floor beneath 1104
1117	K20c	C17	I/II	b	4	Packing beneath 1116
1118	K20c	C17	I	b	7	P94/17
1119	K20c		I	b	7	P94/18 = P96/42 (//1531)
1120	K20c		I/II	b	7	P94/19
1121	K20c	C13.3	IIe?	b	7	P94/20, upper fill
1122	K20c		I/II	b	7	P94/21
1123	K20c	C17	I	c	7	P94/22 (in base of P94/18)
1124	K20c		I/II	b	7	P94/23
1125	K20c	C13.3	IIe	b	5	Rm e10, occ. surface, below 1117 (//1924)
1126	K20c		I	d	4	Rubbly packing above 1117
1127	K20c	C13.3	I/II	b	7	P94/24
1128	K20c	C13.3	IIe	c	4	Rm e10, rubbly packing, below 1125 (//1136)
1129	K20c	C13.3	IIe	c	7	P94/20, lower fill
1130	K20c		IIc	a	3	W713 (//1932)
1131	K20	C13.1	IIc	a	4	Rm 15, ashy surface, below 1128 (//1141, 1142)
1132	K20c	C13.2	IId	b	4	Rm d2, burnt rubbly material S of W713, below 1128
1133	K20c	C13.2	IId	b	5	Rm d2, surface S of W713, below 1132
1134	K20c	C13.1	IIc	b	4	Fallen mud brick, Rm 2
1135	K20a/b	C13.1	IIc	b	5	Rm 15, occ. surface, below 1131 (//1146)
1136	K20c	C13.3	IIe	c	4	Rm e10, rubbly packing, below 1125 (//1128)
1137	K20c	C13.2	IId/e	c	6	FI94/9 and fill
1138	K20c	C13.1	IIc	b	7	P94/26, sealed by 1131
1139	K20c	C13.1	IIc	b	7	P94/27, cut by P94/26
1140	K20c	C13.1	IIc	c	7	P94/28, cut from 1135

List of Excavation Units

Unit	Square	Chapter	Level	Purity	Context	Description
1141	K20c	C13.1	IIc	b	4	Rm 15, ashy surface, below 1128 (//1131, 1142)
1142	K20c	C13.1	IIc	b	4	Rm 15, ashy surface, below 1128 (//1131, 1141, 1931)
1143	K20b		IIc	b	3	W716
1144	K20b	C13.1	IIc	b	6	Rm 15, FI94/10 and fill
1145	K20b	C13.1	IIc	b	6	Rm 15, FI94/11 and fill
1146	K20a/b	C13.1	IIc	b	5	Rm 15, occ. surface, below 1141–2 (//1135)
1147	K20c	C13.1	IIc	b	4	Rm 2, destr. debris, below 1133
1148	K20c	C13.1	IIc	a	5	Rm 2, clearing to plastered floor
1149	K20a	C13.1	IIb	c	5	Floor line in side of P94/13
1150	K20a	C13.1	IIb	b	5	Ash lying on 1149
1200	H20d		0	d	9	Topsoil
1201	H20d		0	d	9	Topsoil below 1200
1202	H20d	C12	IIId	b	8	Packing, below 1201
1203	H20d	C12	IIId	a	4	Rm 32, packing, below 1201
1204	H20d		0	d	9	Topsoil clearance
1205	H20d	C12	0	d	9	Topsoil, below 1201
1206	H20d	C12	IIId	c	7	Rm 36, post-hole in SW corner
1207	H20d	C12	0	c	4	Packing, below 1205
1208	H20d	C12	IIId	a	5	Rm 36, small patch of occ. surface
1209	H20d	C12	IIId	a	3	W100, W101 foundations
1210	H20d	C12	IIIc	a	3	W102 foundations
1211	H20d	C12	IIId	a	5	Rm 36, occ. surface
1212	H20d	C12	IIId	a	5	Rm 35, occ. surface
1213	H20d	C12	IIIa–d	c	4	Rm 35, below 1207
1214	H20d		IIIa–c	a	3	W103 foundation
1215	H20d	C12	IIIa–c	a	5	Rm 36, occ. surface, below 1211
1216	H20d	C12	IIIa–c	a	5	Rm 35, packing, below 1212
1217	H20d	C12	IIIa–c	c	5	Rm 36, packing, below 1215
1218	H20d	C11	IVb	a	4	Burnt occ. deposit, below 1223 (//1228)
1219	H20d	C11	IVb?	c	6	Burnt occ. deposit in NE (//1220)
1220	H20d	C11	IVb	a	5	Burnt occ. deposit, below 1217 (//1219)
1221	H20d	C12	IIIa/IVb	a	4	Fill, below 1208 (//1223)
1222	H20d		IIIa–c	a	3	W104 foundation
1223	H20d	C12	IIIa/IVb	a	4	Packing, below 1216 (//1221)
1224	H20d		-	d	9	S section straightening
1225	H20d		-	d	9	E section straightening
1226	H20d	C11	IVb	a	4	Packing, below 1220
1227	H20d	C11	IIIa/IVb	a	4	Packing, below 1223
1228	H20d	C11	IVb	c	6	Ashy deposits in SW (//1218)
1229	H20d	C11	IVb	c	6	FI94/2 ashy fill
1230	H20d	C11	IVb	c	6	FI94/3 ashy fill
1231	H20d	C11	IVb	a	6	Ashy deposits in NE (//1228)
1232	H20d	C11	IVa/b	b	4	Packing, below 1227
1233	H20d	C11	IVa/b	b	4	Packing, below 1232
1234	H20d		0	d	9	Topsoil
1235	H20d		0	d	9	Fill of animal burrow
1236	H20d	C11	IVa	a	4	Rm 42 E corner, destr. debris, below 1234
1237	H20d		IVa	a	3	W105 (NW wall Rm 41) //1298
1238	H20d		IVa	a	3	W106 (NE wall Rm 41) //1295
1239	H20d	C11	IVa	b	4	Rm 41, destr. debris in N angle
1240	H20d	C11	IVa	a	5	Rm 42 E corner, burnt occ. deposit
1241	H20d	C11	IVa	a	3	W107 (NE wall Rm 41)
1242	H20d	C11	IVa	c	5	Rm 43, burnt occ. deposit
1243	H20d	C11	IVa	a	5	Rm 42, occ. surface, below 1240
1244	H20d		IVa	a	5	Rm 42, occ. deposit, below 1243
1245	H20d	C11	IVa	a	5	Rm 42, occ. surface, below 1244
1246	H20d	C11	IVa	a	4	Rm 42, pebble packing, below 1245
1247	H20d	C11	IVa	a	5	Rm 42, occ. surface, below 1246
1248	H20d	C11	IVa	d	7	Post-hole in 1247
1249	H20d	C11	IVb?	d	5	Rm 43, mixed deposits, below 1227
1250	H20d		-	d	9	Section straightening
1251	H20d	C11	IVa	b	5	Rm 43, occ. surface, below 1249
1252	H20d	C10	IVa	b	7	P94/30
1253	H20d	C11	IVa	a	4	Rm 43, packing, below 1251
1254	H20d	C11	IVb	c	2	P95/85
1255	H20d	C11	IVb	b	7	Post-hole in 1253
1256	H20d	C11	IVb	a	7	P95/86
1257	H20d	C11	IVb	a	7	P95/37
1258	H20d	C11	IVa	a	4	Rm 43, destr. debris, below 1253
1259	H20d	C10	IVa	?	9	Brick feature round P95/37

Appendix 2

Unit	Square	Chapter	Level	Purity	Context	Description
1260	H20d		0	d	9	Back fill from robber tunnel
1261	H20d	C11	IVb	c	7	P95/38
1262	H20d	C11	IVb	c	7	P95/39
1263	H20d	C11	IVa	a	4	Packing, below W734
1264	H20d	C11	IVa	a	4	Packing against E face of W106
1265	H20d	C11	IVa	a	4	Rm 43, packing, below 1258
1266	H20d		IVa	a	3	W734
1267	H20d	C10	Ve	a	5	Packing, below W734
1268	H20d		-	d	9	Section straightening
1269	H20d	C10, C11	IVa	d	4	Rm 43, packing (//1265)
1270	H20d	C11	IVa	a	3	W734 removal
1271	H20d	C11	IVa?	b	8	Rm 43, post-holes along W106
1272	H20d	C10	IVa/Ve?	c	4/5	Packing/occ. surfaces
1273	H20d	C11	IVa	c	7	P97/2
1274	H20d	C10	Ve	a	3	FI97/1, below 1275
1275	H20d	C10, C11	IVa/Ve?	c	4	Mixed fill, below 1272, packing for IVa?
1276	H20d	C10	Ve	a	8	Fill of post-hole 1277
1277	H20d	C10	Ve	a	-	Cut for post-hole in NE
1278	H20d		Ve	a	3	W224
1279	H20d	C10	Ve	a	8	Fill of post-hole 1280
1280	H20d	C10	Ve	a	-	Cut for post-hole in SE
1281	H20d	C10	Ve	b	4	Fill S of W224
1282	H20d	C10	Ve	a	-	Foundation cut for W224
1283	H20d	C10	Ve	b	4	Fill N of W224
1284	H20d	C10	Ve	a	4	Clay packed rectangular feature in 1281
1285	H20d	C10	Ve	a	8	Fill of post-holes 1286
1286	H20d	C10	Ve	a	-	Cuts for post-holes into 1287
1287	H20d	C10	Ve	c	4	Fill, below 1281 and 1283
1288	H20d	C9	Ve	a	7	P97/7, below 1289
1289	H20d	C10	Ve	b	5	Fill, below 1287 (//1287)
1290	H20d	C10	Ve	a	7	P97/13, below 1289
1291	H20d		IVa	b	3	W228, foundation for W734
1292	H20d		Ve	a	3	W229
1293	H20d	C10	Ve	d	7	P97/14, below 1275
1294	H20d	C10	Ve	a	-	Foundation cut for W229
1295	H20d		IVa	b	3	W106 removal (//1238)
1296	H20d	C11	IVa	a	3	Rm 41, bench against S face of W105 removal
1297	H20d	C11	IVa	a	3	Rm 41, bench against W face of W106 removal
1298	H20d	C11	IVa	a	3	W105 removal (//1237)
1299	H20d	C10	Ve	c	7	P97/22, below 4278 (//5346)
1300	J20		0	d	9	Topsoil
1301	J20		0	d	9	Topsoil, below 1300
1302	J20d		I	b	3	W116 foundation (//1102)
1303	J20d		I	b	7	P94/6
1304	J20c	C17	I	b	7	P94/7, fill
1305	J20d		I	b	5	Burnt occ. layer N of W116
1306	J20c/d		I	b	5	Burnt occ. debris S of W116
1307	J20b	C13.1, C17	I	b	7	P94/10
1308	J20c		I	b	7	P94/7, clay lining
1309	J20d	C9	I	b	7	P94/7, ash, below 1308
1310	J20b		I/II	b	4	Packing, below 1301
1311	J20b	C17	I/II	c	7	P94/11
1312	J20b		IIb	a	4	Packing cut by P94/10
1313	J20b	C13.1	IIb	b	9	Mixed deposits, below 1310
1314	J20b		IIb	a	3	W118 foundation
1315	J20b		IIb	a	3	W119 foundation
1316	J20b	C13.1	IIb	b	5	Occ. deposits N of W118, below 1313
1317	J20b	C13.1	IIb	b	5	Occ. surface W of W119
1318	J20d		IId	b	3	W121 W end, below 1305
1319	J20d		I/II	c	7	P94/12
1320	J20d	C13.2	IId?	b	4	Packing, below W116
1321	J20d	C13.1	IIc	b	4	Rm 2, NW corner, destr. debris, below 1320
1322	J20d		IIc	b	3	W122, N end
1323	J20d	C13.1	IIc	b	4	Rm 2, NW corner, destr. debris, below 1322
1324	J20d	C13.2	IId	c	4	Packing W of W122
1325	J20d	C13.1	IIc	b	5	Rm 1, burnt occ. floor, below 1324
1326	J20b	C13.1	IIa/b	b	4	Packing, below 1316
1327	J20a	C12	IIIe	b	5	Ashy occ. deposit (//1418)
1328	J20b	C13.1	IIa/b	b	5	Packing W of W119, below 1317
1329	J20b	C13.1	IIa/b	b	5	Surface, below 1328
1330	J20a/b		IIa	a	3	W120, below 1317
1331	J20c	C13.1	IIb	c	5	W ctyd, ashy occ. deposit

List of Excavation Units

Unit	Square	Chapter	Level	Purity	Context	Description
1332	J20b	C13.1	IIa	b	4	Fill above ashy occ. surface, below 1326
1333	J20d	C13.1	IIc	b	4	Rm 1, bricks in destr. debris
1334	J20c	C13.1	IIb	b	6	W ctyd, FI94/5
1335	J20c	C13.1	IIb?	b	6	W ctyd, FI94/6
1336	J20c	C13.1	IIc/d	b	8	Rm 1, packing on W side
1337	J20c/d	C13.2	IId–f	b	7	P95/13 fill of N side
1338	J20c/d	C13.2	IId–f	a	7	P95/13 fill of N side, below 1337
1339	J20c/d	C13.2	IId–f	a	-	P95/13 cut
1340	J20c/d	C13.2	IId–f	b	7	P95/13 fill of S side (//1337)
1341	J20c/d	C13.2	IId–f	a	7	P95/13 fill of S side, below 1340
1342	J20c/d	C13.2	IId–f	a	7	P95/13 fill of S side, below 1341
1343	J20d		0	d	9	Topsoil, below 1300 (//1301)
1344	J20d	C13.2	IId–f	b	9	Mixed deposit cut by P95/13
1345	J20d		I/II	b	7	P95/51
1346	J20d		0	d	9	Topsoil W of 1343 (//1301)
1347	J20d		I/II	b	7	P95/50
1348	J20d	C13.1	IIc	b	4	Rms 2–3, destr. debris of W122, below 1346
1349	J20d		IId	b	3	W725, below 1343
1350	J20d	C13.1	IIc	b	4	Rms 2–3, destr. debris, below 1351
1351	J20d	C13.1	IIc	b	4	Rms 2–3, destr. debris at W end of W796
1352	J20d	C13.1	IIc/d	b	4	Packing, below W725
1353	J20d	C13.1	IIc	a	4	Rms 2–3, destr. debris, below 1350
1354	J20d	C13.1	IIc	a	5	Rms 2–3, burnt occ. deposit on floor
1355	J20d	C13.1	IIc	a	5	Rms 2–3, plastered floors
1356	J20d/J19b	C13.1	IIc	a	3	Rm 1, bench along E side
1357	J20c	C13.1	IIc	a	3	Rm 1, bench along W side
1358	J20c		IIc	a	3	W130, stone foundation
1359	J20c	C13.1	IIb/c	b	4	W ctyd, packing against W130
1360	J20c		-	d	9	Section cleaning
1361	J20d	C13.1	IIc	b	4	Rms 2–3, destr. debris
1362	J20c	C13.1	IIb–d	d	9	W ctyd, packing against W130
1363	J20c	C12, C13.1	IIb–d	b	7	P97/55, cut by P94/7
1364	J20c	C12, C13.1	IIb–d	a	7	P97/55, lower fill
1365	J20c	C13.1	IIb	c	4	W ctyd, packing N of P97/55
1366	J20c	C12, C13.1	IIb–d	a	7	P97/55, lowest fill
1367	J20c	C13.1	IIb	b	9	FI94/6 and contemporary packing
1368	J20c	C13.1	IIb	a	7	P97/71
1369	J20c	C13.1	IIb	b	4	W ctyd, packing, below 1367
1370	J20a	C12, C13.1	IIa/b	c	4	Packing of cut round NW corner of building
1371	J20a	C12	IIIe	c	4	E ctyd, packing
1372	J20a	C12	IIIe	c	4	E ctyd, burnt occ. deposits (//1388), below 1371
1373	J20a	C13.1	IIa–b	c	-	P95/73 cut
1374	J20a	C13.1	IIa–b	c	7	P95/73 fill (//1386)
1375	J20a	C12	IIId/e	b	4	E ctyd, packing, below 1372
1376	J20a	C12	IIId	b	4	E ctyd, destr. debris, below 1372
1377	J20a	C12	IIIe	b	3	FI95/9
1378	J20a	C12	IIIe	b	6	FI95/9 fill
1379	J20a	C12	IIIe	b	5	E ctyd, occ. surface
1380	J20a	C12	IIIe	b	3	Stone rimmed depression into 1379
1381	J20a	C12	IIIe	b	4	Burnt occ. deposit round FI95/9
1382	J20a	C12	IIId	b	5	E ctyd, occ. surface, below 1376
1383	J20a	C12	IIIe	c	5	Ash line over 1371
1384	J20a	C12	IIIe	c	4	Packing over 1383
1385	J20c	C13.1	IIb	b	4	W ctyd, packing, below 1367
1386	J20c	C13.1	IIa–b	c	4	Packing of cut round NW corner of building (P95/73)
1387	J20c	C12, C13.1	IIa/IIIe	b	4	Packing above IIIe floor deposits, below 1385 (//1399)
1388	J20c	C12	IIIe	a	5	E ctyd, burnt occ. deposits, below 1387 (//5700)
1389	J20c	C12	IIIe	b	4	E ctyd, packing, below 1388 (//5701)
1390	J20c	C12	IIIe	a	4	E ctyd, packing, below 1389
1391	J20c/d	C13.1	IIb	a	4	Rm 1, packing, below IIc floor
1392	J20c	C13.1	IIb	c	4	W ctyd, packing against W130 (//5702)
1393	J20c/d	C13.1	IIb	a	4	Rm 1, packing, below 1391
1394	J20c	C13.1	IIb	a	7	P97/90 into 1391

647

Appendix 2

Unit	Square	Chapter	Level	Purity	Context	Description
1395	J20c	C13.1	IIa/b	c	3	W ctyd, packing, below 1392
1396	J20d	C13.1	IIc	a	3	Rm 1, removal of bench against W122
1397	J20c/d	C13.1	IIc/d	c	9	Ashy debris along and within line of W122
1398	J20d	C13.1	IIc/d	c	8	Ashy debris in cut N of 1397
1399	J20c	C12, C13.1	IIa/IIIe	a	4	Packing above IIIe floor deposits, below 1395 (//1387)
1400	I20		0	d	9	Topsoil
1401	I20		0	d	9	Topsoil
1402	I20d		IIb?	a	3	W108
1403	I20d	C13.1	IIb–e	c	7	P94/1, N part (//4001)
1404	I20d	C12	I/II	c	4	Packing, below 1401
1405	I20b	C12	I/II	c	4	Packing, below 1401
1406	I20b/c		IIId/e	a	3	W109 foundation
1407	I20b	C12	IIId/e	c	4	Loose packing N of W109
1408	I20b	C12	IIId/e	b	8	E ctyd, ash line
1409	I20b	C12, C13.1	IIb	c	7	P94/2, below 1417
1410	I20b	C12	IIId	b	4	E ctyd, destr. debris
1411	I20b	C12	IIId	c	4	Packing NE of W109 and W110
1412	I20b	C12	IIId	c	4	Destr. debris NW of W109 and W110
1413	I20b		IIId/e	a	3	W110 foundation
1414	I20b	C12	IIId	c	7	P94/3, below 1405
1415	I20b	C12	IIId	c	7	P94/4, below 1405
1416	I20b	C12	IIId	b	5	Occ. surface, N of W109
1417	I20d	C12, C13.1	IIb	c	4	E ctyd, packing, below 1404
1418	I20d	C12	IIIe	b	5	E ctyd, burnt occ. deposits (//1327, 1372, 4016)
1419	I20c		I/II	c	4	Packing, below 1401
1420	I20d	C12, C13.1	IIb	b	5	E ctyd, occ. deposit, below 1417
1421	I20d	C12, C13.1	IIb	c	7	P94/5 (//4004)
1422	I20c		II/III	c	4	Packing, below 1419
1423	I20d		IIId/e	a	3	W111
1424	I20c		IIId/e	a	3	W112
1425	I20d	C12	IIId/e	a	4	Packing S of W109
1426	I20d	C12	IIIe	c	4	E ctyd, loose packing, below 1418 (//4017)
1427	I20d	C12	IIId/e	b	5	E ctyd, surface, below 1426
1428	I20d	C12	IIId	a	4	E ctyd, destr. debris, below 1427
1429	I20d	C12	IIId	a	5	E ctyd, burnt occ. deposit, below 1428
1430	I20d		IIIe	a	3	W113 foundation
1431	I20c	C12	IIId	c	4	Packing W of W112, below 1422
1432	I20c/d	C12	IIId/e	a	3	?Packing E of W112
1433	I20c	C12	IIId	b	5	Packing W of W112, below 1431
1434	I20d		II/III	a	4	E ctyd, packing
1435	I20d	C12	IIId	b	5	E ctyd, occ. surface, below 1429
1436	I20d	C12	II/IIIe	c	5	E ctyd, packing, below 1420 (//4014)
1437	I20c	C12	IIId/e	b	5	Occ. surface E of W112
1500	K19	C17	0	d	9	Topsoil
1501	K19	C17	I	d	9	Sub-surface clearance
1502	K19	C17	I	c	8	Surface, below plough soil
1503	K19a/b		I	b	3	W700 foundation
1504	K19a		I	b	3	W701 foundation
1505	K19a		I	a	3	Wall foundation or collapse (W702)
1506	K19a		I	b	8	Door socket in W701
1507	K19b		I	a	3	W703 foundation
1508	K19c		I	a	3	W704 foundation
1509	K19d		I	a	3	W705 foundation
1510	K19d	C17	I	b	5	Occ. surface, below 1501
1511	K19d		I	b	3	W706 foundation
1512	K19	C17	-	c	9	Cleaning prior to renewed excavation
1513	K19	C17	-	d	9	Cleaning masonry of wall foundations
1514	K19	C17	I	b	9	Material between Level I walls
1515	K19b/d		I	b	5	S of W700, below 1514
1516	K19a+b		I/II	b	5	N of W700, below 1514
1517	K19d	C17	I	b	7	P96/32
1518	K19a/b		I	b	3	W701 removal
1519	K19c		I	c	3	W704 removal
1520	K19a/b	C17	I	b	7	P96/23
1521	K19a/b	C17	I	b	7	P96/24
1522	K19a/b		I	b	7	P96/25
1523	K19a/b		I	b	7	P96/26
1524	K19c		I	-	3	W706 removal
1525	K19a/b		I	a	3	W700 removal
1526	K19b		I	c	8	Jar base sunk through 1514 and 1516, N of W700
1527	K19a/b	C17	IIe	b	4	N of W700, below 1516 (//1528)
1528	K19b	C17	IIe	c	4	S of W700, below 1515 (//1527)
1529	K19a		I	b	7	Lens within 1527
1530	K19b	C17	I	c	7	P96/40, sealed by W700
1531	K19a		I	b	7	P96/42 = P94/18 (//1119)

648

List of Excavation Units

Unit	Square	Chapter	Level	Purity	Context	Description
1532	K19a		I	b	7	Lens within 1527
1533	K19b	C13.3	IIe	b	5	Rm e9 S end, occ. surface, below 1527
1534	K19a/b	C13.3	IId/e	b	4	Packing material, below 1527
1535	K19b	C13.2	IId	a	5	Occ. surface E of W770, below 1527
1536	K19a/b	C13.3	IIe	b	7	P96/52, sealed by 1527
1537	K19a	C17	I/II	b	7	P96/53
1538	K19a		I/II	b	7	P96/54
1539	K19a		I/II	b	7	P96/55
1540	K19b	C13.2	IId	a	4	Occ. layer E of W770, below 1535
1541	K19a/b	C13.2	IId	b	4	Rm d3, destr. debris W of W770, below 1534
1542	K19a/b	C13.2	IId	a	5	Rm d3, occ. surface W of W770, below 1541 (//1983)
1543	K19a/b	C13.2	IId	a	5	Occ. surface S of W771, below 1541
1544	K19a	C13.2	IId	b	7	P96/92, below 1541
1545	K19b	C13.2	IId	a	5	Surface E of W770, below 1540
1546	K20d	C13.2	IId	a	7	P96/97
1547	K19b	C13.2	IId	a	7	P96/99, E of W770
1548	K19b	C13.2	IId/e	b	7	P96/100, E of W770
1549	K19a/b	C13.1	IIc/d?	b	5	Occ. surface S of W771, below 1543
1550	K19b	C13.1	IIc/d	c	7	P96/101, NE corner of Rm d5, sealed by 1543
1551	K19a/b	C13.1	IIc/d	a	4	Packing material N of W771, below 1542 (//1991)
1552	K19a/b	C13.1	IIc/d	b	4	Packing material S of W771, below 1542 (//1551)
1553	K19a/b		IId	b	3	W771 removal
1554	K19a	C13.1	IIc	b	4	Rm 3, destr. debris, below 1552 (//1560)
1555	K19b	C13.1	IIc	b	4	Rm 4, destr. debris, below 1551/2
1556	K19a	C13.1	IIc/d	b	7	Rm 3, P96/122
1557	K19a	C13.1	IIc	a	5	Rm 3, plastered floor, below 1554
1558	K19a	C13.1	IIc	a	8	Rm 3, E door, socket for jamb
1559	K19a	C13.1	IIc	a	3	Rm 3, diagonal brick feature
1560	K19a	C13.1	IIc	a	4	Rm 3, destr. debris in SE corner (//1554)
1561	K19b	C13.1	IIc	b	5	Rm 4, occ. surface, below 1555 (//1995)
1562	K19b	C13.2	IIc/d	b	7	Rm 4, P96/127 (//1565)
1563	K19		-	d	9	Cleaning prior to renewed excavation
1564	K19c	C17	I	d	9	Surface, below plough soil
1565	K19a/b	C13.2	IIc/d	a	7	Rm 4, P96/127, continued (//1562)
1566	K19a/b	C13.1	IIc	a	4	Rm 4, destr. debris, below 1551/2 (//1572)
1567	K19d	C17	I/II	b	9	Surface, below plough soil
1568	K19a/b	C13.1	IIc	a	4	Rm 4, S end, destr. debris, below 1566 (//1572)
1569	K19a/b	C13.1, C13.2	IIc/d	a	7	Rm 4, P97/3, below 1551 or 1555
1570	K19a/b	C13.1	IIc	a	4	Rm 4, N end, destr. debris, below 1551 or 1555
1571	K19c	C17	I/II	a	9	Material between Level I walls, below 1564
1572	K19a	C13.1	IIc	c	4	Rm 4, destr. debris along E wall (//1566 and 1568)
1573	K19d	C17	I	c	7	P97/8
1574	K19c		I/II	b	9	Material S of W610 and W611, below 1564
1575	K19d	C17	I/II	c	7	P97/9
1576	K19d		-	d	9	Cleaning quadrant
1577	K19d	C17	I	d	9	Material cut by W612, below 1567
1578	K19c	C17	I	a	9	Material N of W610 and W611, below 1564
1579	K19c		I	a	3	W611 removal
1580	K19c		I	a	3	W610 removal
1581	K19c		II	a	7	P97/15, cut by W611
1582	K19c	C17	I/II	a	7	P97/16, cut by W610 and W611
1583	K19d	C17	I/II	b	9	Material cut by W612, below 1577
1584	K19c		I/II	a	7	P97/17
1585	K19c		I/II	a	7	P97/18
1586	K19d		I/II	a	8	Bricky material N side of 1577
1587	K19d	C13.2	IIc/d	c	7	P97/20, S side sealed by 1586 (//4561)
1588	K19a	C13.1, C13.2	IIc/d	a	7	Rm 4, P97/21
1589	K19a	C13.1	IIc	a	5	Rm 4, destr. debris in doorway
1590	K19a/b	C13.1	IIc	a	8	Rm 4, basket impression
1591	K19c		I/II	d	9	Material beneath W610 and W611, below 1574 and 1578
1592	K19a	C13.1	IIc/d	a	7	P97/23
1593	K19c		I/II	d	8	Ashy occ. layer in SE, below 1574

Appendix 2

Unit	Square	Chapter	Level	Purity	Context	Description
1594	K19a	C13.1	IIc	a	4	Rm 4, N end, destr. debris
1595	K19c		I/II	a	7	P97/26
1596	K19c		I/II	c	7	P97/28
1597	K19c		I/II	b	3	FI97/4 removal
1598	K19c		I/II	c	7	P97/48, below 1593 (//4319)
1599	K19c		I/II	c	7	P97/35
1600	J19		0	d	9	Topsoil
1601	J19b/d		0	d	9	Topsoil, below 1600
1602	J19b/d	C17	I	b	5	Striated ash layers, below 1601 (//2306)
1603	J19b	C17	I	b	-	P95/14 cut
1604	J19b	C17	I	a	7	P95/14 fill
1605	J19d	C17	I	a	5	Occ. surface, below 1602 (//1627)
1606	J19d	C17	I	c	3	W717
1607	J19d		I	c	3	W718
1608	J19b/d	C17	I	a	-	P95/15 cut
1609	J19b/d	C17	I	b	7	P95/15 upper fill
1610	J19b/d	C17	I	b	7	P95/15 lower fill
1611	J19b	C17	IIe/f	a	-	P95/16 cut
1612	J19b	C13.3, C17	IIe/f	b	7	P95/16 fill
1613	J19b	C13.2, C17	IIe/f	b	-	P95/17 cut
1614	J19b	C13.2, C17	IIe/f	b	7	P95/17 upper fill
1615	J19d		IId/e	a	5	Packing?, below 1605, W720
1616	J19b	C13.2	IIe/f	b	7	P95/17 clayey fill, below 1614
1617	J19b	C13.2	IIe/f	c	7	P95/17 fill, below 1614 and 1616
1618	J19b	C13.1	IIc	a	5	Rm 3, destr. debris, below P95/17
1619	J19d	C17	I	a	-	P95/21 cut
1620	J19d	C17	I	a	7	P95/21 fill
1621	J19d/J20d	C17	I	c	-	P95/31 cut
1622	J19b/J20d	C17	I	c	7	P95/31 fill of S half
1623	J19b	C17	I	a	-	P95/32 cut
1624	J19b	C17	I	b	7	P95/32 fill, below 1605
1625	J19d	C17	I	c	-	P95/33 cut
1626	J19d	C17	I	c	7	P95/33 fill
1627	J19b	C17	I	a	5	Occ. surface, below 1602 (//1605)
1628	J19b	C8, C13.2	IId	a	3	FI95/5
1629	J19d		IId/e?	a	3	W719
1630	J19d		IId/e	a	3	W720 stone foundation
1631	J19b		IId/e	a	3	W721 stone foundation
1632	J19b	C13.3	IId/e	b	5	Occ. surface, below 1602
1633	J19b	C13.2	IId	a	3	Clay platform for FI95/5 (1628)
1634	J19b	C13.2	IId	a	3	Mud bricks in platform 1633
1635	J19b	C13.2	IId	b	5	Burnt occ. surface, below 1631
1636	J19d		IId/e	c	3	W724, below 1605
1637	J19b	C13.2	IId	a	4	Rm d4, packing, below 1635
1638	J19b/d		IId/e	b	3	W722, below 1627
1639	J19b/d		IId/e	a	3	W723, below 1627
1640	J19b	C13.1	IIc	a	4	Rm 3, destr. debris, below 1635
1641	J19a/c		0	c	9	Topsoil
1642	J19b/d	C13.1	IIc	a	4	Rm 3, destr. debris, below 1640
1643	J19c	C17	I	b	5	Occ. surface, below 1644
1644	J19c	C17	I	b	5	Ashy striation, below 1645
1645	J19c	C17	I	c	5	Clayey striation, below 1646
1646	J19c	C17	I	c	5	Ashy striation, below 1647
1647	J19c	C17	I	c	5	Clayey striation, below 1648
1648	J19c	C17	I	c	5	Ashy striation, below 1649 (//1730)
1649	J19c	C17	I	c	5	Clayey striation, below 1641 (//1729)
1650	J19a/c	C17	I	b	5	Ashy striation, below 1643
1651	J19a/c	C17	II?	a	5	Occ. surface, below 1650
1652	J19a/c	C17	I	c	7	P96/16
1653	J19a	C17	I	b	7	P96/11
1654	J19a	C17	I	c	7	P96/17
1655	J19c		-	d	9	Cleaning W section
1656	J19b	C17	I?	b	7	P96/19
1657	J19b/d	C13.2	IId?	c	7	P96/20, below 1640
1658	J19c	C17	II?	b	7	P96/21
1659	J19c		II?	a	4	Packing, below 1651
1660	J19	C17	I	c	7	P96/35
1661	J19c	C17	I?	c	7	P96/36
1662	J19c		II?	a	4	Packing, below 1659
1663	J19c		II?	c	7	P96/44, below 1659
1664	J19c		II?	a	4	Packing, below 1662
1665	J19a/c		II?	c	7	P96/47
1666	J19a		II?	a	9	Packing, below 1651
1667	J19a		II?	a	4	Packing, below 1666
1668	J19a		IIe/f	c	7	P96/56, below 1651
1669	J19a		IIe/f	c	7	P96/56 lower fill
1670	J19a		I	d	9	P96/11, removal of clay lining

650

List of Excavation Units

Unit	Square	Chapter	Level	Purity	Context	Description
1671	J19a		II?	c	7	P96/64, upper fill, below 1667
1672	J19a		II?	c	7	P96/64, fill, below 1671
1673	J19a/c		-	d	9	Cleaning W section
1674	J19a		II?	a	5?	Packing, below 1667
1675	J19a		II?	c	7	P96/71, below 1667
1676	J19a/b		II?	c	7	P96/72, below 1667
1677	J19a		II?	c	7	P96/76, stony fill
1678	J19a		II?	c	4	Packing, below 1674
1679	J19a		II?	c	7	P96/79, below 1667
1680	J19a		II?	c	7	P96/83, below 1674
1681	J19a	C13.2	IId?	b	4	Rm d6, packing, below 1678
1682	J19a		0	d	9	Animal burrow
1683	J19a	C17	I/II	b	7	P96/90
1684	J19a		II?	c	7	P96/89, below 1678
1685	J19a	C13.1	IIc	a	4	Rm 1, destr. debris, below P96/90
1686	J19b	C13.1	IIc	a	4	Rm 3, destr. debris, below 1642
1687	J19a		I/II	a	1	Water-laid deposit in pit base?
1688	J19b	C13.1	IIc	a	5	Rm 3, burnt occ. deposit, below 1686
1689	J19b	C13.1	IIc	a	5	Rm 3, occ. surface, below 1688
1690	J19b/d	C13.1	IId	b	7	P96/102, below W718
1691	J19c	C13.2	IId	a	4	Rm d7, packing, below 1664 (//3901)
1692	J19d	C13.2	IId	c	4	Rm d9, packing, below 1691
1693	J19c	C13.2	IId	a	4	Rm d7, destr. debris, below 1691 (//3901)
1694	J19b	C13.1	IIc	a	3	Rm 3, steps in SW corner
1695	J19b	C13.1	IIc	a	3	FI96/18, partition wall on W side
1696	J19b	C13.1	IIb	a	7	FI96/18 central hearth
1697	J19d		IIe?	c	7	P96/116, below W764.
1698	J19d	C13.2	IIe?	c	7	P96/117, cut by P96/116
1699	J19b	C13.1	IIc	c	4	Rm 3, S side, destr. debris, below 1686
1700	I19		0	d	9	Topsoil
1701	I19d	C17	I	d	3	Area of stone paving
1702	I19d	C17	I	c	5	Clay surface assoc. with 1701
1703	I19d	C17	I	a	3	W727
1704	I19b	C13.3	IIe/f?	c	4	W ctyd, Rm e4, packing
1705	I19c		I	-	3	W728
1706	I19c/d		I	-	3	W729
1707	I19b		I/IIh	c	-	P95/1 cut
1708	I19b	C9, C13.4	IIf–h	b	7	P95/1 fill, N part
1709	I19b		-	c	9	Baulk around P95/1
1710	I19b		IIg–h	c	-	P95/2 cut
1711	I19b		IIg–h	c	7	P95/2 fill
1712	I19b	C13.2	IIc/d	c	4	W ctyd, packing, below W730
1713	I19b	C13.4	IIf–h	c	-	P95/3 cut
1714	I19b	C9, C13.4	IIf–h	c	7	P95/3 fill
1715	I19b	C13.4	IIf–h	c	-	P95/4 cut
1716	I19b	C13.4	IIf–h	c	7	P95/4 fill
1717	I19b	C13.4	IIf–h	c	-	P95/10 cut
1718	I19b	C13.4	IIf–h	c	7	P95/10 fill
1719	I19b	C8	IId	c	3	FI95/1 cut by P95/2
1720	I19b		IIg–h	c	-	P95/11 cut
1721	I19b		IIg–h	c	7	P95/11 fill
1722	I19b		IId?	a	3	W730 stone foundation (//2860)
1723	I19b		IId?	a	3	W731
1724	I19b	C13.2	IId?	c	4	Loose bricky packing N of W730
1725	I19b	C13.1	IIc	a	3	W732
1726	I19b	C13.1	IIc	a	3	W733
1727	I19b	C8, C13.1	IIc	c	6	FI95/6
1728	I19b	C13.1	IIc	c	5	Rm 18, occ. surface, below 1712
1729	I19d	C17	I	c	4	Packing E of W727 (//1649)
1730	I19d	C17	I	c	5	Ash line E of W727, below 1729 (//1648)
1731	I19d	C17	I	c	4	Packing E of W727, below 1730
1732	I19d	C17	I	c	9	Rubble filling Byzantine cut (//2703)
1733	I19d	C17	I	c	4	Packing with sherds, below 1701 (//1740)
1734	I19d		I	c	7	P96/2
1735	I19d		I	c	7	P96/3
1736	I19d		I	c	7	P96/4
1737	I19d	C17	I	c	5	Ash line E of W727, below 1731
1738	I19d	C17	I	c	5	Packing E of W727, below 1737
1739	I19d	C17	I	c	4	Ash line E of W727, below 1738
1740	I19d	C17	I	c	5	Packing, below W727 and 1739 (//1733)
1741	I19d	C17	I	c	4	Packing, below 1733, 1740
1742	I19d/c	C17	I/IIh?	c	5	Packing, below 1741
1743	I19d		I/IIh?	c	6	FI96/1 ashy contents
1744	I19c/d	C17	I/IIh?	c	4	Packing, below 1742
1745	I19c/d		I	c	3	W750 foundation
1746	I19d		I/IIh?	c	4	Packing W of W751
1747	I19d		I/IIh?	c	4	Packing E of W751
1748	I19d		I/IIh	c	5	Deposit E of W751, below 1747

651

Appendix 2

Unit	Square	Chapter	Level	Purity	Context	Description
1749	I19c/d		I	c	3	W750 removal (//1745)
1750	I19c/d		I/IIh	c	4	Packing beneath W750
1751	I19d		I/IIh	c	4	Packing S of W752
1752	I19c		I/IIh	b	3	W753 removal
1753	I19c/d		I	c	4	P96/22
1754	I19d		IIh	c	5	Occ. deposit, below 1751
1755	I19d		IIh	c	5	Occ. surface, below 1754
1756	I19d		I/IIh	b	4	Fill SE of W778
1757	I19d		I	c	3	W752 removal
1758	I19d	C8	IIg?	c	3	FI96/26, hearth?
1759	I19d	C8	IIg?	c	3	FI96/27, hearth?
1760	I19d		IIg?	c	3	FI96/5 tannour
1761	I19d		IIg?	b	3	Feature against W side of FI96/5
1762	I19c		IIh	b	3	W728 removal
1763	I19d		IIg?	b	6	Upper fill of FI96/5
1764	I19d		IIg?	a	6	Lower fill of FI96/5
1765	I19d		IIg?	a	6	Clay base of FI96/5
1766	I19c/d		IIh	b	4	Packing N of W778
1767	I19c/d		II	b	4	Fill above 1778
1768	I19d		IIg/h	b	6	FI96/7, ashy fill
1769	I19d		IIg/h	b	6	FI96/8, ashy fill
1770	I19c/d		IIg/h	b	3	W778 removal
1771	I19d		IIg/h	b	3	W751 removal
1772	I19d		IIg	b	4	Burnt occ. deposit W of FI96/15, below 1755
1773	I19d	C8	IIg	c	5	Occ. surface, below 1772
1774	I19c/d		IIg/h	b	3	Wall trench for W751 and W778
1775	I19c/d		IIg/h	b	4	Fill of 1774
1776	I19c/d		IIg/h	b	4	Packing, below 1766 (or W778?)
1777	I19d	C13.4	IIf/g	b	4	Destr. debris inside FI96/15
1778	I19c/d		IIg	b	5	Cobbled surface E of W757
1779	I19c		IIg	b	4	Packing S of W757
1780	I19d		IIg?	b	4	Fill of cut 1794
1781	I19d		IIg	b	7	P96/48
1782	I19d		IIg	b	7	P96/49
1783	I19c	C13.4	IIf	b	4	Destr. debris from FI96/14
1784	I19c		IIg	a	4	Packing, below 1779
1785	I19d		IIg	c	7	P96/50, fill of N side
1786	I19d	C13.4	IIf	a	4	Packing W of FI96/15, below 1789
1787	I19c/d		IIg	b	7	P96/51
1788	I19d		IIf/g	b	4	Packing N of FI96/15
1789	I19d		IIf/g	a	4	Packing W of FI96/15, below 1772
1790	I19c	C13.4	IIf	a	4	Packing, below 1784, cut by FI96/11
1791	I19c		IIg	b	6	FI96/11 ashy fill
1792	I19c/d		IIg	b	7	P96/60
1793	I19d		IIg	b	7	P96/61, below 1794
1794	I19d		IIg?	b	-	Shallow cut running NE–SW
1795	I19d	C13.3	IIe	b	7	P96/63, cut by P96/61
1796	I19c		IIg?	b	3	W757 removal
1797	I19c/d		IIg?	b	4	Packing, below W757 and 1778
1798	I19c/d	C13.4	IIf	b	5	Surface, below 1799
1799	I19c/d	C13.4	IIf	a	4	Burnt occ. debris, below 1790
1800	H20c		0	d	9	Loose soil clearance
1801	H20c		-	d	9	Cleaning E section
1802	H20c		0	c	9	Modern backfill
1803	H20c		Vf	a	4	Packing above W249
1804	H20c		0	c	9	Modern backfill
1805	H20c		0	c	9	Modern backfill
1806	H20c	C11	IVa	a	5	Rm 42, E corner, floor and benches
1807	H20c	C11	IVa/Ve	a	4	Rm 42, packing, below 1806
1808	H20c	C11	IVa/Ve	a	4	Rm 42, packing N of 1807
1809	H20c	C10	Ve	a	4	E strip, clay band N of W105, below 1807, 1808
1810	H20c	C10	Ve/f	a	4	E strip, packing, below 1807
1811	H20c	C10	Ve	a	5	E strip, ashy lens, below 1809
1812	H20c	C10	Vf	b	6	Rm 55, fill, below 1810
1813	H20c	C10	Vf?	a	4/5	Mixed deposits N of W735 (//1820)
1814	H20c	C10	Vf	a	4	E strip, pebble packing within 1813
1815	H20c	C10	Ve?	a	4	NE corner, clay packing, below 1809
1816	H20c	C10	Vf	a	4	E strip, fallen stones, below 1813
1817	H20c	C10	Vf4	a	3	W735 removal
1818	H20c	C10	Vf4	a	3	W736 removal
1819	H20c	C10	Vf4	a	4	E strip, packing in foundation trench for W735–6
1820	H20c	C10	Vf	a	4	E strip, fill (//1813)
1821	H20c	C10	Ve/f	a	-	P95/65 cut, sealed by 1811
1822	H20c	C10	Ve	a	7	P95/65 fill
1823	H20c	C10	Vf3/4	a	4	E strip, packing, below 1819
1824	H20c	C10	Vf	a	8	Ash lens within 1823
1825	H20c	C10	Vf/g	a	5	E strip, packing, below 1823

List of Excavation Units

Unit	Square	Chapter	Level	Purity	Context	Description
1826	H20c	C10	Vf/g	a	4	E strip, packing, below 1823
1827	H20c		-	d	9	Cleaning loose soil
1828	H20d		-	d	9	Cleaning loose soil
1829	H20c	C10	Vf/g	a	4	E strip, fill, below 1826
1830	H20c		-	d	9	Baulk straightening
1831	H20c	C10	Vg	a	4	Rm 61, destr. debris
1832	H20c	C10	Vf/g	a	7	P96/13
1833	H20c	C10	Vg	a	4	Rm 62, destr. debris
1834	H20c	C10	Vf1	a	3	W785 removal
1835	H20c	C10	Vg	a	4	Rm 62, pocket of fill under 1833
1836	H20c	C10	Vg/h	a	4	Rm 62, fill, below occ. surface, below 1831, 1835
1837	H20c		Vg	a	3	W784 removal
1838	H20c	C10	Vg/h	a	4	Packing, below phase Vg floors
1839	H20c	C10	Vg	d	9	Baulk straightening in SW corner
1840	H20c		-	d	9	Modern back fill
1841	H20c	C10	Vg	a	4	Rm 60, destr. debris
1842	H20c	C11	IVb/Ve	b	9	Mixed deposits in NE corner
1843	H20c	C10	Vf	b	9	Mixed deposits in NE corner, below 1842
1844	H20c	C10	Vg	a	9	Rm 61, destr. debris in NE corner, below 1843
1845	H20c		Vg/h	a	4	Rm 60, fill, below plastered floor, below 1841
1846	H20c	C10	Vh	a	5	Rm 70, occ. surface, below 1845
1847	H20c	C10	Vg/h	a	4	Packing NW of W786, below 1838
1848	H20c		Vh2	a	3	W786, N alignment
1849	H20c	C10	Vh1	a	3	W786, S alignment upper courses
1850	H20c	C10	Vh	a	5	Rm 70, clay floors
1851	H20c	C10	Vh/i	a	4	E half, packing, below W786
1852	H20c	C10	Vi	a	4	E half, packing, below 1851
1853	H20c	C8, C10	Vi	a	4	E half, packing assoc. with W792, below 1852
1854	H20c		Vi	a	3	W790 removal
1855	H20c	C10	Vi	a	7	P96/96
1856	H20c		-	d	9	Straightening H20c/d section
1857	H20c	C10	Vh/i	a	7	P96/103
1858	H20c	C10	Vj	a	4	Rm 83, destr. debris
1859	H20c	C10	Vj	a	4	Rm 83, destr. debris, below 1858
1860	H20c		-	d	9	Trench cleaning
1861	H20c	C10	Vj	a	5	Rm 83, burnt occ. surface
1862	H20c		Vj	b	3	W226 (//1875)
1863	H20c	C10	Vi/j	c	5	E half, packing over W225
1864	H20c	C10	Vj	a	4	Rm 84, destr. debris
1865	H20c	C10	Vi/j	a	7	Rm 84, fill of 1866, below 1864
1866	H20c	C10	Vj	a	-	Rm 84, post-hole into 1870
1867	H20c	C10	Vj	a	8	Rm 84, fill of 1868, below 1864
1868	H20c	C10	Vj	a	-	Rm 84, post-hole into 1870
1869	H20c	C10	Vj	a	3	Rm 84, plastered circular feature
1870	H20c	C10	Vj	a	5	Rm 84, occ. surface, below 1864 (//5425)
1871	H20c	C10	Vj	a	4	Rm 83, destr. debris
1872	H20c	C10	Vf-i	a	7	P97/5
1873	H20c	C10	Vj	a	3	Rm 83, plastered rectangular feature
1874	H20c	C10	Vj	a	3	W225 removal
1875	H20c	C10	Vj	a	3	W226 removal (//1862)
1876	H20c		Vj	a	3	W227 removal
1877	H20c		Vj/k	a	8	Fill of 1878, below W225
1878	H20c		Vj/k	a	-	E half, post-hole into 1879
1879	H20c	C10	Vj/k	d	4	E half, packing, below W225, W226 (//5427)
1880	H20c	C10	Vj/k	a	7	Fill of 1881, below 1879
1881	H20c	C10	Vj/k	a	-	E half, post-hole into 1882
1882	H20c	C10	Vj/k	a	5	E half, occ. surface, below 1879
1883	H20c	C10	Vj/k	a	4	E half, packing, below 1882 (//5428)
1884	H20c	C10	Vk	a	4	Packing NE of W230, W231, below 1883
1885	H20c	C10	Vk	a	4	Packing W of W230, W231, below 1883
1886	H20c	C10	Vk	a	4	Packing SE of W231, below 1883
1887	H20c		Vk	a	3	W230 removal
1888	H20c		Vk	a	3	W231 removal
1889	H20c	C10	Vk	a	8	Fill of 1890, below 1885
1890	H20c	C10	Vk	a	-	E half, post-hole into 1891
1891	H20c	C10	Vk	a	5	E half, construction surface, below 1884–8 (//5429)
1892	H20c	C10	Vk	a	4	E half, packing, below 1891

Appendix 2

Unit	Square	Chapter	Level	Purity	Context	Description
1893	H20c		Vi	a	1	E half, natural conglomerate (//5431)
1894	H20c		Vi	a	7	P97/30, below 1892
1895	H20c		Vi	a	3	W233
1896	H20c		Vi	a	3	W234
1897	H20c		Vi	a	3	W235
1898	H20c	C10	Vi	a	4	W half, packing, below W233–5
1899	H20c	C10	Vi/j	a	4	W half, packing, below 1898
1901	K20d		0	d	9	Topsoil (//1100)
1902	K20d	C16, C17	I	b	7	P95/6
1903	K20d	C17	I	a	3	W707 foundation
1904	K20d		I	a	3	W708 foundation
1905	K20d		I/II	b	4	Occ. surface W of W708
1906	K20d	C17	I	a	-	P95/6 cut
1907	K20d		I/II	c	-	P95/9 cut
1908	K20d		I/II	c	7	P95/9 fill
1909	K20d	C17	I/II	a	3	FI95/2
1910	K20b	C13.3	IIe	a	3	Rm e9, FI95/3
1911	K20d	C13.3	IIe	b	5	Rm e9, occ. surface
1912	K20d		IIe	a	3	W712
1913	K20b	C13.3	IIe	a	8	Rm e9, loose bricks, below 1905
1914	K20c		I/II	c	4	Clay packing N of W710 (//1103)
1915	K20d	C17	I/II	b	5	Surface W of W708, below 1905
1916	K20c/d	C13.3	IIe	a	5	Rm e9, occ. layer, below 1915 (//1911)
1917	K20b		IIe ?	a	3	W710 foundation
1918	K20b	C13.3	IIe	a	4	Rm e9, rubbly packing S of W710, below 1905
1919	K20d		I		7	P95/40 cut
1920	K20d		I	b	7	P95/40 fill
1921	K20d	C13.3	IIe	b	6	Rm e10, occ. layer
1922	K20b/d	C13.3	IId/e	a	-	P95/42 cut
1923	K20b/d	C13.3	IIe	a	7	Rm e9, P95/42 feature in floor 1911
1924	K20b/d	C13.3	IIe	a	5	Rm e9, occ. surface, below 1911 (//1125)
1925	K20b	C13.3	IIe	b	5	Rm e9, occ. surface N of W710, below 1914
1926	K20b	C13.3	IIe	b	8	Ashy feature in 1925 surface
1927	K20d		I/IIf	b	-	P95/48 cut, post 1911
1928	K20d		I/IIf	b	7	P95/48 fill, post 1911
1929	K20d	C13.3	IIe	b	-	Rm e9, P95/49 cut
1930	K20d	C13.3	IIe	b	7	Rm e9, P95/49 fill
1931	K20a/c	C13.1	IIc	a	5	Rm 15, ashy surface (//1142, 1948)
1932	K20d		IIc	a	3	W713 (//1130)
1933	K20a/b		IIc	a	3	W714
1934	K20d	C13.3	IId/e	b		Rm e10, packing, below 1921
1935	K20a/c	C13.1	IIb	b	5	Rm 15, occ. levels, below 1931
1936	K20c	C13.1	IIc/d	b	6	Rm 2, below 1133?
1937	K20c		-	d	9	P95/55
1938	K20b/d	C13.3	IId/e	b	4	Rm e9, rubbly packing sealing W713, below 1924
1939	K20d	C13.1	IIc/d	a	4	Rm 2, destr. debris, below 1938 (//1943)
1940	K20c		I?	b	-	P95/59 cut
1941	K20c		I?	b	7	P95/59 fill
1942	K20b/d	C13.1	IIc/d	a	4	Rubbly destruction material N of W713, below 1938
1943	K20d	C13.1	IIc/d	a	4	Rm 2, destr. debris, below 1938 (//1939)
1944	K20b/d	C13.1	IIc	b	4	Rm 15, destr. debris on floor, below 1942
1945	K20a/b	C13.1	IIc	a	4	Rm 11, destr. debris on floor, below 1942
1946	K20d		IIc	a	3	W715
1947	K20b/d		IIc	a	3	W716
1948	K20b/d	C13.1	IIc	a	5	Rm 15, floor surface, below 1944 (//1931)
1949	K20d	C13.1	IIc	a	5	Rm 11, floor surface, below 1945
1950	K20a/b	C13.3	IId/e	b	-	P95/69 cut
1951	K20b/d	C13.3	IId/e	b	7	P95/69 fill
1952	K20d	C13.1	IIc	b	3	Rm 15, FI95/7, below 1944
1953	K20d	C13.1	IIc	a	3	Rm 11, FI95/8, below 1945
1954	K20a/b	C13.3	IId/e		-	P95/74 cut
1955	K20a/b	C13.3	IId/e	a	7	P95/74 fill
1956	K20b/d	C13.3	IId/e		-	P95/82 cut
1957	K20b/d	C13.3	IId/e	a	7	P95/82 fill
1958	K20c	C13.1	IIb	a	5	Rm 15, occ. surface, below 1935
1959	K20b/d	C13.3	IId/e		-	P95/82 cut
1960	K20b/d	C13.3	IId/e	a	7	P95/82 fill
1961	K20a	C13.1	IIb/c	b	6	Rm 13, FI96/3
1962	K20a/c	C13.1	IIb/c	b	4	Rm 13, packing material
1963	K20a		II	b	7	Rm 15, P96/1
1964	K20a		II	b	7	Rm 15, P96/10
1965	K20a	C13.1	IIb	a	5	Rm 15, occ. surface, below 1958
1966	K20a/c	C13.1	IIb?	a	6	Rm 15, FI96/4
1967	K20a/c	C13.1	IIb	a	5	Rm 15, occ. surfaces (//1935, 1958)
1968	K20a/c	C13.1	IIb/c	b	4	Rm 13, packing material (//1962)
1969	K20a	C13.1	IIb/c	b	4	Rm 13, packing material, below 1968
1970	K20a/c		II	b	7	P96/46

List of Excavation Units

Unit	Square	Chapter	Level	Purity	Context	Description
1971	K20a/c	C13.1	IIb	a	5	Rm 15, occ. surface, below 1965
1972	K20a/c	C13.1	IIb	a	5	Rm 15, occ. surface, below 1971
1973	K20a/c	C13.1	IIb?	b	6	Rm 15, FI96/10
1974	K20a/c		IIc?	b	4	W714, decayed brickwork
1975	K20a/c	C13.1	IIb	a	5	Rm 15, occ. surface, below 1972
1976	K20a/c	C13.1	IIb	a	5	Rm 15, occ. surface, below 1975
1977	K20a/c	C13.1	IIb	a	5	Rm 15 (S), packing material, below 1976
1978	K20a/c	C13.1	IIb	a	6	Rm 15 (N), occ. layer, below 1976
1979	K20a/c		IIb?	a	3	W794 foundation
1980	K20a/c	C13.2	IId	b	5	Rm d2, occ. surface
1981	K20a/c	C13.1	IIb?	a	2	Rm 15 (N), spread of stones along W794, below 1972
1982	K20a/c	C13.1	IIb/c	a	5	Rm 13, packing material, below 1969
1983	K20c/d	C13.2	IId	a	6	Rm d3, fill? on floor (//1542, 1987)
1984	K20c	C13.1	IIc	b	5	Rm 2, cleaning to plastered floor (//1148)
1985	K20c/d		II	b	7	P96/82
1986	K20a/c	C13.1	IIa?	a	5	Rm 15, packing material
1987	K20d	C13.2	IId	b	6	Rm d3, fill? on floor (//1542, 1983)
1988	K20c	C13.2	IId	b	4	Rm d2, packing below 1980
1989	K20c	C13.1	IIc	a	4	Rm 2, destr. debris on floor, below 1988
1990	K20c		II	a	7	P96/107
1991	K20c/d	C13.1	IIc/d	b	4	Rm 2, packing material, below 1988 (//1551)
1992	K20c/d	C13.2	IId	a	3	W795 removal
1993	-		-	-	-	-
1994	K20d	C13.2	IId	b	7	Rm 4, P96/121 upper fill
1995	K20d	C13.1	IIc	a	5	Rm 4, occ. surface (//1561, 2908)
1996	K20c	C13.1, C13.2	IIc/d?	b	7	Rm 2, P96/119
1997	K20c	C13.2	IIc/d?	b	7	Rm 2, P96/120
1998	-		-	-	-	-
1999	K20d	C13.1, C13.2	IIc/d	b	7	Rm 4, P96/121 lower fill (//2906)
2000	R18a	C14	0	d	9	Topsoil removal
2001	R18a	C14	0	d	7	P94/47 upper fill in SW corner
2002	R18a	C14	E5b	d	4	Packing, below 2001 in SW corner
2003	R18a	C14	E5b	d	4	Ashy layer, below 2002
2004	R18a	C14	E5a/b	d	9	Mixed material at W side
2005	R18a	C14	E5a/b	d	9	Mixed material, below 2004
2006	R18a	C14	E5b	d	9	Stratified fill, below 2001
2007	R18a	C14	E5b	d	9	Loose packing at N side, below 2002
2008	R18a	C14	-	d	9	Cleaning unit
2009	R18a	C14	0	d	9	Animal burrow
2010	R18a	C14	9	d	9	Mixed material, below 2007
2011	R18a	C14	9	d	9	Mixed material W of 2010
2012	R18a	C14	0	c	7	P94/48 fill, below 2009
2013	R18a	C14	0	d	9	Animal burrow
2014	R18a	C14	E5b	c	4	Stratified material, below 2010
2015	R18a	C14	0	c	9	Mixed deposits in NW corner
2016	R18a	C14	E5b	c	7	P94/49 fill, below 2014
2017	R18a	C14	E5b	c	7	P94/49 lower fill, below 2016
2018	R18a	C14	E5b	c	4	Loose packing, below 2014
2019	R18a	C14	E5b	a	4	Hard yellow packing, below 2018
2020	R18a	C14	E5b	c	7	P94/50 fill, sealed by 2018
2021	R18a	C14	-	d	9	Section straightening
2022	R18a	C14	E5a	c	7	P94/51 fill, below 2015
2023	R18a	C14	0	d	9	Topsoil, below 181 in SW corner
2024	R18a	C14	E5a	c	7	P94/52 fill, below FI94/13 (//2422)
2025	R18a	C14	E5a	c	7	P94/53 upper fill, cut by 2024
2026	R18a	C14	E5a	c	7	P94/53, fill, below 2025
2027	R18a	C14	E5a	c	7	P94/53, fill, below 2026
2028	R18a	C14	-	d	9	Section straightening
2029	R18a	C14	E5b	c	4	Packing layer in SW corner
2030	R18a	C14	E5a	c	7	P94/52 fill, below FI94/13
2031	R18a	C14	E5a	c	7	P94/53, fill, below 2027
2032	R18a	C14	E5b	a	4	Stratified material E of P94/53
2033	R18a	C14	E5a	c	7	P94/53, fill, below 2031

Appendix 2

Unit	Square	Chapter	Level	Purity	Context	Description
2034	R18a	C14	E5a	c	7	Basal fill of P94/51 in NW corner
2035	R18a	C14	E5b	b	4	Stratified material, below 2015
2036	R18a	C14	E5a	c	7	P94/54 fill
2037	R18a	C14	E5a	c	7	P94/55 fill, cut by 2036 (//2050)
2038	R18a	C14	E5a	c	7	P94/53 fill, cut by 2030
2039	R18a	C14	E5a	c	7	P94/53 fill, below 2038 (//2414)
2040	R18a	C14	E5a	c	7	P94/53 fill, below 2039
2041	R18a	C14	0	d	9	Topsoil, below 181, overlying FI94/13
2042	R18a	C14	E5a	c	7	P94/53 fill, below 2040
2043	R18a	C14	E5a	c	7	P94/53 fill, below 2042
2044	R18a	C14	E5b	c	4	Fill E of P94/53, below 2032
2045	R18a	C14	-	d	9	Section straightening, below FI94/13
2046	R18a	C14	E5a	c	7	P94/53 fill, below 2043
2047	R18a	C14	E5a	c	7	P94/53 fill, below 2046
2048	R18a	C14	E5a	c	7	P94/56 fill, below 2034
2049	R18a	C14	E5a	c	7	P94/53 fill, below 2047
2050	R18a	C14	E5a	c	7	P94/55 fill, cut by 2048 (//2037)
2051	R18a	C14	-	d	9	Section straightening, below FI94/13
2052	R18a	C14	-	c	9	Unstratified sherds, below 2006 & 2018
2053	R18a	C14	E5b	c	8	Post-hole in 2006
2100	Q19c/d	C14	E2b	d	4	Mixed fill W of W301
2101	Q19d	C14	E2b	d	4	Fill E of W301, overlying W300 & W303
2102	Q19b	C14	E2b	d	4	Fill overlying W300
2103	Q20a	C14	E2a	c	7	Pottery in cuts from surface
2104	Q20a	C14	E2a	c	7	P94/46 upper fill
2105	Q19c/d	C14	E2b	c	4	Mixed fill W of W301, below 2100
2106	Q19c	C14	E2a	c	7	P94/41, upper fill
2107	Q19c/d	C14	E2a	c	7	P94/41, lower fill
2108	Q19c/d	C14	E2b/c	c	4	Fill E of P94/41 beneath W301 floor
2109	Q19c/d	C14	E2b	b	7	Fill of P94/42
2110	Q19c	C14	E3b/4b	a	5	Occupation material, below 2108
2111	Q19		E2b	a	3	W301 and W302
2112	Q19d	C14	E2c	c	4	Fill between drain and W302
2113	Q19d	C14	E3b	c	4	Fill between drain and W303, below 2112
2114	Q19d		E2c	a	3	W303
2115	Q19d	C14	E3b	c	9	Fill between W300 & W305, below 2113
2116	Q19d	C14	E3b	c	4	Fill of stone-lined drain
2117	Q19d	C14	E4b	c	4	Fill of room to E of and above drain
2118	Q19d	C14	E4a	c	7	P94/44 upper fill, below ~99.70
2119	Q19c/d	C14	E4b	d	9	Fill, below P94/41, W of drain
2120	Q19d	C14	E3b	a	3	Stone-lined drain
2121	Q19	C14	E2b	b	5	Fill to W of W301
2122	Q19d	C14	E2b	c	4	Fill beneath 2121
2123	Q19d	C14	E4a	c	7	P94/44 lower fill, below +99.18
2124	Q19d	C14	E2c	c	4	Fill of cut for W303
2125	Q19c/d	C14	E2/3	d	9	Mixed pit (P94/43) & room fill, W of drain
2126	Q19c/d	C14	E3b	d	4	Fill of cut for stone-lined drain
2127	Q19c/d	C14	E4b	c	5	Fill of room, below 2119
2128	Q19d	C14	E4b	d	4	Post-hole sealed by 2127
2129	Q19c/d	C14	E2/3	d	7	P94/43 fill, below 2125
2130	Q19c/d	C14	E4b	b	5	Occupation material over burnt floor, below 2127
2131	Q19d		E4b	a	8	W304, highest brickwork
2132	Q19d		E4b	a	3	W304, S part, below 2131 (//2137)
2133	R19a/c	C14	E4a	d	7	P94/57, upper fill
2134	Q19d	C14	E4b	a	8	Fill N of W306, E of drain
2135	Q19d	C14	E4c	a	8	Packing, below W304
2136	R19a/c		E4a	d	9	Definition of rim of P94/57
2137	Q19d		E4b	a	3	W304, N part, below 2131 (//2132)
2138	R19a/c	C14	E4a	d	7	P94/57, fill , below 2133
2139	Q19d	C14	E4c	a	8	Packing NW of W306, below 2134
2140	Q19d	C14	E4c	a	8	Fill, below and W of W304, below 2135 & 2139
2141	Q20	C14	E2a	b	8	Ash around sherds in P94/45
2142	Q20	C14	E2a	d	7	P94/46 lower fill
2150	Q20a/b		0	d	9	Topsoil clearance
2151	Q20		0	d	9	Rubbly fill over stones of W300

List of Excavation Units

Unit	Square	Chapter	Level	Purity	Context	Description
2201	Q18b	C14	0	d	9	Topsoil clearance
2202	Q18b	C14	E2b	a	3	W303
2203	Q18 b	C14	E2b	d	9	Fill above masonry of W300
2300	J18a		0	d	9	Topsoil
2301	J18a		0	c	9	Topsoil, below 2300
2302	J18a	C17	I	b	5	SW corner, occ. surface, below 2301
2303	J18a		I	c	4	NW corner, stone tumble, below 2301
2304	J18a		0	c	9	NE corner, lower topsoil, below 2301
2305	J18a	C17	I	a	7	P97/1
2306	J18a	C17	I	b	5	Striated ash layers, below 2301–4 (//1602)
2307	J18a		-	d	9	Baulk with J19 removal
2308	J18a	C17	I	b	5	Striated ash layers, below 2306
2309	J18a		I	b	4	Packing in SE corner, below 2308
2310	J18a		I	b	4	Packing in SW corner, below 2308
2311	J18a	C17	I	b	4	Packing, below 2308
2312	J18a		IIg/h?	b	5	Packing W of W422, below 2311
2313	J18a		IIg/h?	b	4	Packing E of W422, below 2311
2314	J18a		IIg/h?	b	5	Fill W of W422, below 2312
2315	J18a		IIg/h?	b	4	N half, packing E of W422, below 2313
2316	J18a		IIf?	b	4	Packing E of W424, below 2311, 2315
2317	J18a		IIg/h?	c	3	W422 and W423 removal
2318	J18a		IIg/h?	c	4	SW corner, packing above W424, below 2311
2319	J18a		IIg/h?	b	7	P97/29
2320	J18b		0	d	9	Topsoil
2321	J18b		IIf	b	4	Packing W of W424, below 2312, 2314
2322	J18a	C13.4	IIf	b	8	Cut for vessel, below 2316
2323	J18a	C13.4	IIf	b	4	Fill/packing E of W424, below 2316
2324	J18a	C13.4	IIf	a	7	P97/31
2325	J18a	C13.4	IIf	b	5	Packing at S side, below 2323
2326	J18a	C13.4	IIf	a	7	P97/32
2327	J18a	C13.4	IIf	a	8	Jar base in P97/32
2328	J18a	C13.4	IIf	b	7	P97/33
2329	J18b	C17	I	c	8	Ashy deposits, below 2320
2330	J18b	C17	I	b	4	Striated ash layers, below 2329
2331	J18a	C13.4	IIf?	c	7	P97/36, disturbed by animal burrow
2332	J18a	C13.4	IIf	b	8	Jar installation, below 2316
2333	J18a	C13.4	IIf	b	8	Post-hole, below 2316
2334	J18b		I	b	4	E side, packing material above W421
2335	J18a	C13.4	IIf	a	3	W424
2336	J18b		I	b	4	Packing with stones, below 2329
2337	J18b	C17	I	b	5	W side, striated ash layers, below 2330
2338	J18b	C13.4, C17	I	a	7	P97/37, below 2336
2339	J18b	C17	I	b	4	E side, packing material, below 2334, 2336
2340	J18a	C13.4	IIf	a	5	Packing material in Rm f3, below 2323
2341	J18a	C13.4	IIf	a	5	Occ. sequence, below 2340
2342	J18a	C13.4	IIf	a	5	Occ. sequence, below 2341
2343	J18b	C17	I	b	4	E of W425 packing, below 2337 (//2350)
2344	J18b	C17	I/IIf	a	5	Packing W of W425, below 2337
2345	J18b		I	c	4	Mixed material over W425, S end, below 2337
2346	J18b		I	c	9	Displaced stones of W425, below 2337
2347	J18b	C13.4	I/II?	b	7	P97/43, below 2337
2348	-	-	-	-	-	-
2349	J18b	C13.4	IIf	b	4	Mudbrick packing W of W425, below 2344
2350	J18b	C17	I	b	4	Packing E of W425 (//2343)
2351	J18b	C13.4	IIf	b	4	Mudbrick packing W of W425, below 2349
2352	J18b	C17	I	b	7	P97/44, cuts W425
2353	J18b	C13.4, C17	I	b	4	Packing E of W425, below 2343
2354	J18b	C13.4, C17	I	a	4	Packing E of W425, below 2353
2355	J18b	C13.4, C17	I	a	3	W425
2356	J18b	C13.4	IIf	b	5	Packing beneath W425, below 2353
2357	J18b		-	d	9	Baulk with J19d removal
2358	J18b	C13.4	IIf	b	4	W half, packing, below 2356
2359	J18a/b	C13.4	IIf	b	3	Mudbrick benches, below 2323, 2358

Appendix 2

Unit	Square	Chapter	Level	Purity	Context	Description
2360	J18a	C13.4	IIf	a	4	Packing material S of mudbrick bench/wall
2361	J18a	C13.4	IIf	a	5	Packing material SW corner of room, below 2323
2362	J18a	C13.4	IIf	a	3	Mudbrick benches, below 2323
2363	J18a	C13.4	IIf	b	3	Mudbrick benches along N face of mudbrick bench/wall
2364	J18a	C13.4	IIf	a	3	Mudbrick bench/wall, below 2316
2365	J18a	C13.4	IIf?	c	4	Disturbed area in SW corner of room, below 2331
2366	J18a	C13.4	IIf	a	3	Mudbrick bench along E face W424, below 2323
2367	J18a	C13.4	IIf	a	7	P97/53, below 2364
2368	J18a	C13.4	IIf	a	5	Occ. surface in S half, below 2361, 2363
2369	J18b	C13.4	IIf	a	3	Mudbrick benches and walls removal
2370	J18a	C13.4	IIf	b	4	Packing under mudbrick features, below 2368–9 (//2374)
2371	J18b	C13.4	IIf	b	8?	Small plaster-lined depression, below 2358
2372	J18a	C13.4	IIf	a	3	Mudbrick bench, SE corner (//2382)
2373	J18b		I	c	-	Packing round base of W421, below 2356
2374	J18a	C13.4	IIf	c	4	SE corner, packing (//2370)
2375	J18a	C13.4	IIf	a	7	P97/60, plaster-lined pit, below 2364
2376	J18a	C13.4	IIf	c	7	P97/61, animal hole
2377	J18a	C13.4	IIf?	b	4	Patch of earth on E side, below 2370
2378	J18b	C13.4	IIf	b	4	Packing layer, below 2369 (//2381, 2384)
2379	J18b	C13.4	-	d	9	Removal of baulk with J19c
2380	J18a	C13.4	IIf	c	4	Packing, below bench 2366
2381	J18b	C13.4	IIf1	a	5	Occ. sequence, below 2378 (//2378, 2384)
2382	J18b	C13.4	IIf	a	3	Mudbrick bench in SW corner (//2372)
2383	J18a	C13.4	IIf1	a	3	Earlier mudbrick bench along W424, below 2380 (2395)
2384	J18b	C13.4	IIf1	d	4	Deposits against W face of bench 2383 (//2378, 2381)
2385	J18a/b	C13.4	IIf1	a	3	Earlier mudbrick bench, below 2382
2386	J18a/b	C13.4	IIf1	a	4	Packing under bench 2385 (//2370)
2387	J18a	C13.4	IIf	a	4	Packing within mudbrick feature, below 2366
2388	J18a	C13.4	IIf1	a	8	Post-hole, below 2370
2389	J18a	C13.4	IIf1	a	3	W427, N wall of mudbrick feature
2390	J18a	C13.4	IIf1	b	5	Occ. surface, below 2370
2391	J18a	C13.4	IIf1	a	4	S half, packing, below 2390
2392	J18a	C13.4	IIf1	b	4	N half, packing, below 2390
2393	J18a	C13.3	IIe	b	5	N half, Rm e5 occ. surfaces (E of W424), below 2392
2394	J18a	C13.3	IIe	b	5	S half, Rm e5 occ. surfaces, below 2391
2395	J18a	C13.4	IIf1	b	4	Bench against S face of W764 (//2383)
2396	J18a	C13.4	IIf1	b	4	N half, packing, below 2390 along E face of W424
2397	J18a	C13.4	IIf1	a	4	Fill of mudbrick feature against W424, below 2391, 2396
2398	J19c		IIf	a	3	W764, removal of N end (//3918)
2399	J18a	C13.4	IId/e	c	7	P97/85 upper fill, below 2393
2400	R18a	C14	0	d	9	Surface clearance
2401	R18a	C14	0	d	8	Mixed material round pits
2402	R18a	C9, C14	E5a	a	7	P95/5 fill
2403	R18a	C14	E5b	b	4	Bricky debris E of P95/5 (//2453)
2404	R18a	C14	E5a	a	-	P95/5 cut
2405	R18c	C14	0	d	9	Topsoil removal E of W300
2406	R18a	C14	E5a	a	7	P95/70, cut by P95/5
2407	R18c	C14	0	c	9	Mixed fill, below 2405
2408	R18a	C14	E5b	a	4	Bricky debris, below 2403
2409	R18c		E3a	a	3	W930 (= W300)
2410	R18c	C14	0	c	7	P95/45 fill
2411	R18c	C14	E5a	a	7	P95/24 fill
2412	R18c	C14	E5a	a	7	P95/35 fill
2413	R18c	C14	E5a	a	-	P95/24 cut, below W300
2414	R18c	C14	E5a	a	7	Fill of P94/53 (//2039)
2415	R18c	C14	E5a	a	-	P95/35 cut, below W300
2416	R18c	C14	E5a	a	7	P95/36, upper fill
2417	R18c	C14	E5a	a	-	P95/36 cut, below W300

List of Excavation Units

Unit	Square	Chapter	Level	Purity	Context	Description
2418	R18c	C14	E5a	a	7	P95/36, lower fill
2419	R18c	C14	0	a	7	P95/43 fill
2420	R18c	C14	E5a	a	7	Base of P94/53, below 2414
2421	R18c	C14	0	b	-	P95/43 cut
2422	R18c	C14	E5a	a	7	P95/44 fill (//2024)
2423	R18c	C14	E5a	a	-	P95/44 cut, below W300
2424	R18c	C14	E5a/b	c	9	Mixed stratified and fill of P95/46
2425	R18c	C14	0	c	-	P95/45 cut
2426	R18c	C14	E5a	a	7	P95/46, upper fill
2427	R18c	C14	E5a	a	-	P95/46 cut, cut by P95/35 & P95/36
2428	R18c	C14	E5a	a	7	Fill of P94/53, below 2414
2429	R18c	C14	E5a/b	c	9	Stratified fill mixed with fill of P95/46
2430	R18c	C14	E5a	a	7	Basal fill of P95/46
2431	R18c	C14	E5a/b	a	4 or 7	Stratified or pit fill, below 2428
2432	R18d	C14	0	d	9	Topsoil removal
2433	R18c	C14	E5b	a	4	Stratified fill in NW, below 2431, 2428
2434	R18c	C14	E5a	a	7	P95/53 fill
2435	R18c	C14	E5a/b	a	4 or 7	Stratified or pit fill, below 2430
2436	R18c	C14	E5b	a	4	Stratified material, below 2433
2437	R18c	C14	E5b	b	4	Bricky debris in NW, below 2428
2438	R18c	C14	E5a	a	-	P95/53 cut, below 2418
2439	R18d	C14	0	d	9	Topsoil removal, W half, below 2432
2440	R18c	C14	E5a	a	7	P95/52 fill
2441	R18c	C14	E5a	a	-	P95/52 cut, below 2435
2442	R18c	C14	E5b	a	4	Stratified material, below 2436 (//2446)
2443	R18c	C14	E5a	b	7	P95/58 fill
2444	R18c	C14	E5b	a	7	P95/54 fill
2445	R18c	C14	E5b	a	-	P95/54 cut, below 2442
2446	R18c	C14	E5b	b	4	Stratified material in SW (//2442)
2447	R18c	C14	0	c	7	P95/57 fill
2448	R18c	C14	0	c	-	P95/57 cut, below topsoil
2449	R18c	C14	E5a	b	-	P95/58 cut, below 2425 and 2438
2450	R18c	C14	E5b	b	4	Stratified material, below 2442 and 2446
2451	R18c	C14	E5b	a	7	P95/60 fill
2452	R18c	C14	E5b	a	-	P95/60 cut, below 2450
2453	R18c	C14	E5b	b	4	Stratified material, below 2450 (//2403)
2454	R18c	C14	E5b	a	7	P95/66 fill
2455	R18c	C14	E5b	a	-	P95/66 cut, below 2450
2456	R18c	C14	0	d	9	Topsoil removal, E half, below 2405
2457	R18d	C14	0	d	9	Topsoil removal in SE corner, above W935
2458	R18c	C14	E5b	a	7	P95/68 fill
2459	R18c	C14	E5b	a	-	P95/68 cut, below 2453
2460	R18a/c	C14	E5c	a	5	Occ. layer at N side of R18c (//2463)
2461	R18a	C14	E5a	b	7	P95/70 fill, below 2406
2462	R18c	C14	E5c	b	4 or 5	Fill above occ. surface N of W947
2463	R18c	C14	E5c	a	5	Occ. deposit, below 2462 (//2460)
2464	R18a	C14	E5b	a	4	Packing, below 2401
2465	R18c	C14	9	a	9	Mixed deposits in NW corner
2466	R18a	C14	E5a	b	-	P95/70 cut, below 2406
2467	R18c		E5c	a	3	W931
2468	R18c		E5c	a	3	W932
2469	R18c		E5c	a	3	W947
2470	R18c	C14	E5b	a	4	Fill overlying and S of W947
2471	R18c	C14	E5b	b	7	P95/71 fill
2472	R18a	C14	0	b	7	P95/72 fill
2473	R18c	C14	E5b	b	-	P95/71 cut, below 2453
2474	R18a	C14	0	b	-	P95/72 cut
2475	R18c	C14	E5d	a	5	Occ. layer, below 2463 and W931–2
2476	R18c	C14	E5d	a	5	Occ. layer, below 2475
2500	S18a	C14	0	d	9	Topsoil
2501	T15b/d	C14	0	d	9	Topsoil round conglomerate rocks
2502	S18c		E1	a	3	W933
2503	S18a/c		E1	c	3	W934
2504	S18c	C14	E1	c	4	Fill above W933, below 2504
2505	S18c	C14	E1	b	4	Fill N of W933
2506	S18c	C14	E1	b	4	Upper fill S of W933, below 2504
2507	S18c	C14	E1	a	4	Lower fill S of W933, below 2506
2508	S18c	C14	E1	a	4	Lower fill N of W933, below 2505
2509	S18/R18d		E1	a	3	W935
2600	H18		0	d	9	Topsoil

Appendix 2

Unit	Square	Chapter	Level	Purity	Context	Description
2601	H18d		I	a	3	W side of W775
2602	H18b/d		I	c	4	Fill, W of W775
2603	H18b/d		0	c	9	Topsoil, W of W774
2604	H18b/d		I	a	4	Fill against W face W775, below 2602
2605	H18b/d		0	c	9	Topsoil and fill, below 2603
2606	H18b/d		I	a	4	Packing against W face W775, below 2603
2607	H18d		I	a	6	Patch of ashy debris, below 2606
2608	H18b/d		I	a	3	W774 removal
2609	H18b/d		I	a	4	Packing E of W774
2610	H18b/d		0	c	9	Topsoil and fill W of W774
2611	H18b/d		I	a	3	W775
2612	H18b/d		I	a	4	Packing against W face W774
2613	H18b/d		I	a	4	Packing W of W775, below W774
2614	H18d		I	a	7	P96/14
2615	H18b/d		I	a	4	Packing, below 2613
2616	H18d		I	a	7	P96/15, below 2613
2617	H18b/d		I	a	4	Packing, below 2615
2618	H18d		I/II	a	4	Loose fill in SE corner, below 2615
2619	H18b/d	C13.4	IIf	a	3	W777
2620	H18d		I	c	9	Loose fill at S, below 2615
2621	H18b/d		I	b	4	Packing against E face W777
2622	H18d		I/II	a	4	Fill, below 2618
2623	H18b/d		I/II	a	4	Fill, below 2622
2624	H18b/d	C9, C13.4	IIf	b	5	Ashy layer, below 2623
2625	H18b/d	C13.4	I/II	c	9	Sounding in centre of square
2626	H18b	C13.4	IIf	a	4	Packing assoc. with W779
2627	H18b	C13.4	IIf	c	9	Fill in E part of sounding
2628	H18b	C13.4	IIf	a	4	Fill in NE, below 2624
2629	H18b	C13.4	IIf	b	7	P96/78, below 2628
2630	H18d	C13.3	IIe/f	b	4	Rm e2, debris overlying FI96/13
2631	H18b/d	C13.4	IIf	c	7	P96/86, upper fill, below 2624
2632	H18b	C13.3	IIe/f	b	4	Rm e3, debris overlying FI96/17
2633	H18b	C13.3	IIe/f	a	4	Rm e3, packing, below 2628
2634	H18b	C13.3	IId/e	a	6	FI96/17 loose fill
2635	H18b	C13.3	IId/e	a	4	Rm e3, destr. debris assoc. with FI96/17
2636	H18b/d	C9, C13.4	IIf	a	7	P96/86 lower fill, below 2631
2637	H18b	C13.3	IIe/f	a	4	Rm e3, fill, below 2633
2638	H18b	C13.3	IId/e	c	4	Rm e3, packing N of W779
2639	H18b	C13.3	IIe/f	a	4	Rm e3, packing E of W780
2640	H18b	C13.3	IId/e	a	4	Rm e3, packing and burned debris (//2653, 2655)
2641	H18b	C13.3	IId/e	b	4	Rm e3, destr. debris, below 2639 (//2653, 2655)
2642	H18b		IIe/f	a	3	W780 removal
2643	H18b	C13.3	IId/e	a	4	Rm e3, destr. debris over FI96/19
2644	H18b	C13.3	IIe/f	a	4	Rm e3, packing against W face W775, below 2637
2645	H18b/d	C13.3	IId/e	a	5	Rm e2/3, occ. surface, below 2640, 2641
2646	H18b	C13.3	IId/e	a	4	Rm e3, destr. debris below 2644
2647	H18b	C13.3	IId/e	c	9	Rm e3, packing, below 2644
2648	H18b	C13.3	IId/e	a	7	P96/104
2649	H18b	C13.3	IIe/f	a	7	P96/105
2650	H18b/d	C13.3	IId/e	b	4	Rm e1, packing
2651	H18b	C13.3	IIe/f	c	7	P96/110, cut by P96/86
2652	H18d	C13.3	IIe/f	a	4	Rm e2, packing S of FI96/13, below 2624
2653	H18d	C13.3	IId/e	a	4	Rm e2, destr. debris (//2640–41)
2654	H18d	C13.3	IId/e	b	3	FI96/13 removal
2655	H18d	C13.3	IId/e	a	4	Rm e2, destr. debris E of 2653 (//2640–41)
2656	H18b/d	C13.3	IId/e	a	4	Rm e1, destr. debris, below 2650
2657	H18b	C13.3	IIe/f	a	7	P96/118 fill including much charcoal
2658	H18b/d	C13.3	IId/e	b	4	Rm e1, destr. debris, below 2656
2659	H18b/d	C13.3	IId/e	b	5	Rm e1, burnt deposit W of 2658
2660	H18d		IIe/f	a	7	P96/126, below 2658
2661	H18b/d		IId/e	a	3	W779 removal
2662	H18d		IId/e	a	3	W782 removal
2663	H18c		IId/e	a	3	W783 removal
2664	H18b		IIe/f	a	3	W781 removal
2665	H18b	C13.3	IIc/d	-	5	Burnt fill, below 2645 (unexc.)
2666	H18b		IId/e	-	6	FI96/25 fill (unexc.)
2667	H18b/d	C13.3	IId/e	-	5	Rm e1, occ. surface, below 2658 (unexc.)
2700	I18a		0	d	9	Topsoil
2701	I18a	C17	0	d	9	Topsoil and loose fill, below 2700
2702	I18a	C17	I	a	7	P96/88 into W775

List of Excavation Units

Unit	Square	Chapter	Level	Purity	Context	Description
2703	I18a	C17	I	c	7	Stone filling of cut E of W775 (//1732)
2704	I18a		0	c	9	Topsoil in NW corner, below 2701
2705	I18a		I	a	7	P96/68
2706	I18a		I	a	4	Packing, N of W775
2707	I18a	C17	I	b	4	Stony backfill, NE of W775
2708	I18a		I	a	4	Packing N of W775, below 2706
2709	I18a		I	a	4	Pebbly packing, below 2708
2710	I18a		I	b	3	Mudbrick superstructure of W814
2711	I18a	C17	I/II	b	4	Loose fill, cut by W814–15
2800	I19d	C13.4	IIf	c	7	P96/37, below FI96/26–7
2801	I19d	C13.3	IIe/f	b	7	P96/69, below FI96/15
2802	I19d	C13.4	IIf	b	4	FI96/15, light ashy fill, below 1777
2803	I19d	C13.4	IIf	b	3	FI96/15, structure
2804	I19d	C13.3	IIe/f	b	7	P96/70, below FI96/15
2805	I19c	C13.3	IIe	b	7	P96/73, below 1798
2806	I19c/d	C13.3	IIe–h	b	7	P96/74, below W760
2807	I19c/d	C13.3	IIe–h	b	7	P96/75
2808	I19c	C13.4	IIf	b	4	Packing, below 1798 (//2816)
2809	I19d	C13.4	IIf/g	b	7	P96/80, below 1794
2810	I19d	C13.4	IIf/g	b	7	P96/81, below 1794
2811	I19d/c		-	d	9	Baulk straightening
2812	I19c	C13.3	IIe	b	7	P96/84, below 2808
2813	I19d	C13.4	IIf/g	b	7	P96/85, below 1788
2814	I19c/d	C13.4	IIf	a	5	W ctyd, clayey occ. surface, below 2815
2815	I19c/d	C13.4	IIf	b	5	W ctyd, ashy occ. deposit, below 2808
2816	I19d	C13.4	IIf	b	4	W ctyd, packing on E side (//2808)
2817	I19c	C13.4	IIf	a	6	FI96/14, ashy fill at base
2818	I19c/d	C13.3	IId/e	a	4	W ctyd, destr. debris, below 2814
2819	I19d	C13.4	IIf	b	7	P96/93, cut by FI96/15
2820	I19c/d	C13.3	IId/e	a	5	W ctyd, occ. surface, below 2818
2821	I19c	C13.4	IIf	b	3	FI96/11 removal
2822	I19c	C13.4	IIe/f	a	7	P96/109, cut by W759
2823	I19c	C13.2, C13.3	IId/e	a	4	W ctyd, Rm e4, packing, below 2820 (//2827)
2824	I19c	C13.3	IIe	a	7	P96/108, below 2814
2825	I19c/d	C13.2	IId	a	5	W ctyd, ashy occ. deposit, below 2823
2826	I19c	C13.4	IIf	a	3	FI96/14, flooring clay and small stones
2827	I19c	C13.3	IId/e	b	4	W ctyd, Rm e4, packing, below 2820 (//2823)
2828	I19c/d	C13.4	IIf	c	3	W760 removal
2829	I19c/d	C13.2	IId	a	5	W ctyd, ashy occ. layer, below 2825
2830	I19c/d		I/II	b	7	P96/111
2831	I19c	C13.2	IId	a	4	W ctyd, Rm e4, packing, below 2814
2832	I19c	C13.3	IIe	a	4	W ctyd, Rm e4, packing W of W759
2833	I19c	C13.3	IIe–h	b	7	P96/113
2834	I19c	C13.1	IIc?	a	4	Bricky feature at base of P96/84, prob. part of FI97/2
2835	I19d	C13.4	IIf/g	a	7	P96/114, cut by P96/85
2836	I19c		IIf	b	3	W816 removal
2837	I19c	C13.3	IIe	c	4	W ctyd, Rm e4, fill, below W816
2838	I19c		IId/e/f	c	3	W762 removal
2839	I19c		IIf	b	3	W759 removal
2840	I19c/d	C13.1	IIc	b	4	W ctyd, destr. debris
2841	I19c/d	C13.1	IIc/d	b	4	W ctyd, packing, below 2829
2842	I19c	C13.2	IId	b	4	Packing W of W759, below 2832
2843	I19c	C13.1	IIc	b	4	W ctyd, destr. debris
2844	I19c	C13.4	IIf	b	3	FI96/14 stone lining on W side
2845	I19c/d	C13.1	IIc	b	5	W ctyd, occ. surface, below 2841
2846	I19d	C13.1	IIc-f	d	9	Mixed deposits N of FI96/15
2847	I19c	C13.4	IIf	b	3	FI96/14 removal of N side
2848	I19d	C13.1	IIc	a	7	P97/6 lower fill, below 2858
2849	I19c	C13.1	IIc	c	4	W ctyd, loose destr. debris, below 2843
2850	I19c	C13.1	IIc	b	5	W ctyd, occ. surface, below 2849
2851	I19c	C13.1	IIc	b	4	Destr. debris W of W818
2852	I19c	C13.1	IIc	a	5	Occ. surface W of W818, below 2851
2853	I19c	C13.2	IId–h	b	7	P97/4
2854	I19a/c	C13.1	IIc	b	4	FI97/2, debris in fill
2855	I19c		IIb	b	3	Stone feature at S end W818
2856	I19a	C13.1	IIc–e	c	7	P97/10
2857	I19c	C13.4	IIf–h	c	7	P97/11
2858	I19d	C13.1	IIc	a	7	P97/6, destr. debris in upper fill
2859	I19a	C13.3	IIe/f	c	7	P97/12

Appendix 2

Unit	Square	Chapter	Level	Purity	Context	Description
2860	I19b		IIf–h?	b	3	W730 removal (//1722)
2861	I19b	C13.1	IIc/d	d	9	Mixed deposits W of Rm 17
2862	I19b	C13.1	IIc	b	5	Occ. surface W of Rm 17, below 2861
2863	I19b	C13.1	IIc–e	b	7	P97/19
2864	I19d	C13.1	IIb/c	a	4	W ctyd, packing, below 2845
2865	I19a/c	C13.1	IIb/c	b	7	P97/25, below FI97/2
2866	I19b	C13.1	IIb-c	b	4	Packing, below 2862 and W732–3
2867	I19b	C13.1	IIb	a	5	W ctyd, occ. surface, below 2866
2868	I19b		IIc	a	3	W733 removal
2869	I19d	C13.1	IIb	b	5	W ctyd, packing, below 2864
2870	I19c		IIc	b	3	W818 removal
2871	I19b	C13.1	IIb	a	4	W ctyd, packing, below 2867
2872	I19b	C13.1	IIb	a	5	W ctyd, occ. surface, below 2871, 2873
2873	I19b	C13.1	IIb	b	4	W ctyd, packing, below 2867
2874	I19b		IIb/c	b	3	W732 removal
2875	I19b	C13.1	IIb	a	4	W ctyd, packing, below 2867
2876	I19b		IIb/c?	a	3	W819 removal
2877	I19b	C13.1	IIb	b	5	Packing, below 2872, W of W823
2878	I19b	C13.1	IIb	b	4	Packing, below 2872, E of W823
2879	I19b	C13.1	IIb	a	5	Occ. surface, below 2878
2880	I19b	C13.1	IIa/b	b	4	Packing, below 2879
2881	I19b	C13.1	IIa/b	b	5	Occ. surface W of W823, below 2877
2882	I19b	C13.1	IIb	a	4	Packing within Rm 17, below 2879
2883	I19b	C13.1	IIb	a	7	P97/41, below 2873
2884	I19b	C13.1	IIa/b	a	5	Occ. surface W of W823, below 2880
2885	I19b	C13.1	IIb/c	c	9	Mixed deposits N of W827
2886	I19b/I20	C9, C13.1	IIb	c	7	P95/34, fill of SW quarter (//4008)
2887	I19d		-	d	9	Section straightening
2888	I19a	C13.1	IIb/c	b	4	W ctyd, fill, below 2850
2889	I19a	C13.1	IIb	b	4	W ctyd, packing, below 2888
2890	I19b	C13.1	IIb	a	5	Rm 17 occ. surface, below 2882
2891	I19a	C13.1	IIa/b	c	4	Packing S of W825
2892	I19a	C13.1	IIb	c	9	Mixed deposits N of W825
2893	I19b	C13.1	IIa/b	a	4	Rm 17, packing against foundations, below 2890
2894	I19b	C13.1	IIb	c	9	Packing layers N of W827, below 2885 (//5502)
2895	I19b	C13.1	IIa/b	a	3	FI97/6 removal
2896	I19b		IIb	a	3	W823 removal (//5503)
2897	I19b	C13.1	IIa	a	5	W ctyd, occ. surface N of W826
2898	I19b	C13.1	IIa	a	3	Pebble feature assoc. with 2897
2899	I19b	C13.1	IIa	a	3	Plastered feature against N face W826
2900	K20c	C13.1	IIc	a	6	Rectangular feature at NW end of W796
2901	K20c	C13.2	IId	c	7	P96/82 at E end of Rm 2
2902	K20c	C13.1	IIc	b	3	Cleaning N face of W796
2903	K20c	C13.2	IIc/d	c		P96/119 fill
2904	K20d	C13.1	IIb	d	9	Rm 4, NE corner, sounding, below IIc floor
2905	K20d	C13.1	IIb	d	9	Rm 4, sounding, below 2904
2906	K20c/d	C13.1	IIc/d	a	7	P96/121, further fill (//1999)
2907	K20c	C13.1	IIb/III	a	9	Rm 4, NW corner, sounding, below IIc floor
2908	K20c	C13.1	IIc	a	6	Rm 4, NW corner, occ. surface (//1995)
3000	K14a		0	d	9	Topsoil
3001	K14a		1	a	3	W400–402
3002	K14a	C15.5	1	b	6	FI94/14, ashy fill
3003	K14a	C15.5	1	b	5	Ashy layer on W side
3004	K14a	C15.5	1	b	5	Ashy layer on E side
3005	K14a	C15.5	1	d	5	Ashy fill around FI94/15
3006	K14a	C15.5	1	a	9	SE corner deposits overlying W403, below 3002
3007	K14a	C15.5	1/2	d	9	Mixed deposits
3008	K14a	C15.5	1	b	6	FI94/15 lower fill
3009	K14a		1	a	4	Fill S of W404
3010	K14a		1	a	4	Fill W of W401
3011	K14a	C15.5	1	c	6	FI94/15, below 3008
3012	K14b	C9, C15.5	0	d	9	Topsoil
3013	K14b	C15.5	1	b	9	Mixed deposits, below 3012
3014	K14b	C15.5	1	b	4	Fill S of W413, below 3012
3015	K14b	C15.5	1	c	7	P95/7 fill
3016	K14b	C15.5	1	b	4	Fill N of W413, below 3013
3017	K14b		1	d	3	W413 removal
3018	K14a		1	a	3	W403 removal

662

List of Excavation Units

Unit	Square	Chapter	Level	Purity	Context	Description
3019	K14b		-	-	-	-
3020	K14b	C15.5	1	b	-	P95/7 cut
3021	K14b		1a	a	3	W917 foundation (//3040)
3022	K14b	C15.5	1	b	7	P95/7 fill
3023	K14b	C15.5	1	a	-	P95/8 cut
3024	K14b	C15.5	1	c	7	P95/8 fill
3025	K14a		1	a	3	W401 removal
3026	K14a	C15.4, C15.5	2 upper	a	4	SE corner, packing sealed by W403
3027	K14a	C15.4, C15.5	2 upper	a	4	SE corner, packing, below 3026
3028	K14a		-	d	9	Straightening E section
3029	K14b	C15.5	1	b	4	Packing S of W404, below 3016
3030	K14b	C15.5	1	a	-	P95/22 cut, sealed by W401
3031	K14b	C9, C15.5	1	a	7	P95/22, E half fill
3032	K14a		1a	a	3	W915
3033	K14b	C15.4, C15.5	1/2	b	4	Fill E of W915, below 3029
3034	K14b	C15.4, C15.5	1/2	b	4	Fill W of W915, below 3029
3035	K14b	C15.4, C15.5	2 upper	a	4	S side, fill, below 3014
3036	K14b	C15.4, C15.5	2 upper	c	4	Fill E of W915, beow 3033
3037	K14a	C15.4	2 upper	b	9	S side, fill, below 3027
3038	K14a	C15.4	2 upper	b	4	S side, fill, below 3037
3039	K14b		1a	a	3	W916
3040	K14b		1a	a	3	W917 (//3021)
3041	K14b		1a	a	3	W918
3042	K14b		1a	a	3	W919
3043	K14a	C15.4	2 upper	d	4	N side, packing, below 3009?
3044	K14a	C15.4	2 upper	c	5	N side, patch of occ. debris, below 3043
3045	K14a		-	d	9	Animal burrow
3046	K14a	C15.4	2 upper	d	4	Packing, below 3038, 3044
3047	K14a	C9	1	a	7	P95/22 lower fill
3048	K14a	C15.4	2 upper	c	-	P95/67 cut
3049	K14a	C15.4	2 upper	c	7	P95/67 and intersecting pits
3050	K14a	C15.4	2 middle	d	9	W side, mixed fill, below 3046
3051	K14a	C15.4	2 middle	d	9	N side, mixed fill, below 3050
3052	K14a	C15.4	2 middle	d	4	N side, packing E of P95/67
3053	K14a	C15.4	2 middle	b	5	N side, loose fill, below 3052
3054	K14a	C15.4	2 middle	b	5	N side, soft fill E of P95/67, below 3052
3055	K14a	C15.4	2 middle	b	4	N side, fill E of P95/67, below 3054
3056	K14a	C15.4	2 middle	b	4	N side, pebbly fill, below 3051
3057	K14a	C15.4	2 lower	a	7	Fill of post-hole, cut into 3058
3058	K14a	C15.4	2 lower	a	4	N side, orange sandy fill W of 3055
3059	K14a	C15.4	2 lower	b	4	Orange sandy fill, below 3058
3060	K14a		1	a	3	W400
3061	K14a		1a	a	3	W921
3062	K14a		-	d	9	Section straightening
3063	K14a	C15.4	2 middle	c	4	S half, fill, below 3046
3064	K14a	C15.4	2 upper	a	7	P96/5
3065	K14a	C15.4	2 middle	c	9	S half, fill, below 3063
3066	K14a	C15.4	2 upper	a	7	P96/6
3067	K14a	C15.4	2 upper	c	7	P96/7, cut by P96/6
3068	K14a	C15.4	2 middle	a	4	S half, fill E of P96/7, below 3065
3069	K14a	C15.4	2 middle	b	4	S half, yellow packing S of 3068, below 3065
3070	K14a	C15.4	2 middle	b	4	S half, yellow packing W of P96/7, below 3065
3071	K14a	C15.4	2 lower	b	4	S half, fill assoc. with W812 (upper), below 3069
3072	K14a	C15.4	2 lower	a	5	Plastered surface NW of P96/7, below 3070
3073	K14a	C15.4	2 lower	b	4	Packing SW of P96/7, below 3070
3074	K14a	C15.4	2 middle	b	7	P96/34, W side, below 3073
3075	K14a	C15.4	2 lower	a	4	Packing, below 3073
3076	K14a	C15.4	2 middle	b	7	P96/34, E side, below 3071
3077	K14a	C15.4	2 middle	a	7	P96/34, W side, soft orange, below 3074
3078	K14a	C9, C15.4	2 middle	a	7	P96/33, cut by P96/7
3079	K14a	C15.4	2 lower	a	7	Fill of shallow cut in SE corner
3080	K14a	C15.4	2 middle	b	7	P96/34, layers, below 3076, 3077
3081	K14a	C15.4	2 middle	b	7	P96/38 sealed by P96/34
3082	K14a	C15.4	2 lower	a	4	Ash-filled pit assoc. with FI95/10

663

Appendix 2

Unit	Square	Chapter	Level	Purity	Context	Description
3083	K14a	C15.4	2 middle	b	7	P96/45
3084	K14a	C15.4	2 lower	a	5	Ashy occ. deposit assoc. with FI96/16
3085	K14a	C15.4	2 lower	b	5	Packing in SE corner, below 3071
3086	K14a	C15.4	2 middle	b	7	P96/62, upper fill
3087	K14a	C15.4	2 lower	a	5	Ashy occ. deposits in SW corner, below 3085
3088	K14a		-	d	9	Cutting access steps
3089	K14a	C15.4	2 middle	b	7	P96/62, fill, below 3086
3090	K14a	C15.4	2 lower	a	5	Ashy occ. debris along S side, below 3085
3091	K14a	C15.4	2 lower	a	5	Occ. surface assoc. with W813, below 3087
3092	K14a	C15.4	2 lower	a	5	Burned surfaces in cut, below 3090
3093	K14a	C15.4	2 lower	b	5	Occ. debris in cut, below 3092
3094	K14a	C15.4	2 lower	a	4	Occ. debris, below 3091
3095	K14a	C15.4	2 lower	a	4	N side, occ. debris, below 3057
3096	K14a	C15.4	2 middle	a	7	P96/98 into 3803, below 3093
3097	K14a	C15.4	2 lower	a	5	Packing in NE corner, below 3095
3098	K14a	C15.4	2 lower	a	5	Occ. surface assoc. with W811–12
3099	K14a	C15.4	2 lower	a	3	FI96/16
3100	Q10a	C15.1	0	d	9	Sub-surface scrape
3101	Q10a	C15.1	1	d	9	Sub-surface fill, below 3100
3102	Q10a	C15.1	1	d	9	Sub-surface fill, below 3101
3103	Q10a	C15.1	1	d	9	Fill between W600 and W601
3104	Q10a	C15.1	1	c	9	Fill E of W602
3105	Q10a	C15.1	1	c	4	Fill inside building W of W602
3106	Q10a	C15.1	1	c	4	Fill E of W602, below 3104
3107	Q10a	C15.1	1	c	4	Fill, below 3105 and 3103
3108	Q10a	C15.1	1	c	4	Mixed deposits, below 3106
3109	Q10a	C15.1	1	c	7	S half of P94/36
3110	Q10a	C15.1	1	c	7	N half of P94/36
3111	Q10a	C15.1	1	c	4	Fill E of W604
3112	Q10a		1	c	4	Fill NW corner, below 3105
3113	Q10a	C15.1	1	c	4	Fill in E half, below 3111
3114	Q10a	C15.1	1	c	4	Fill E of W604, below 3113
3115	Q10a		1	c	4	Fill W of W604, below 3113
3116	Q10a		1	c	7	Fill E of W604, below 3114
3117	Q10a	C15.1	1	d	4	Sounding to SW of P94/36, S of 3115
3118	Q10a	C15.1	1	d	8	Contents of Q10/36
3200	N12a	C15.2	0	d	9	Topsoil
3201	N12a	C15.2	1	d	4	Grey sub-topsoil fill, N of W500
3202	N12a	C15.2	1	d	4	Mixed ashy material, below 3201
3203	N12a	C15.2	1	b	6	FI94/17 in 3202
3204	N12a	C15.2	1	d	4	Fill S of W500, S of 3205 (//3205)
3205	N12a	C15.2	1	d	4	Fill S of W500, N of 3204 (//3204)
3206	N12a	C15.2	1	b	6	FI94/18
3207	N12a	C15.2	1	d	4	Fill between walls W502 and W500
3208	N12a	C15.2	1	d	5	Fill S of W502
3209	N12a	C15.2	1	d	4	Fill between walls W502 and W500
3210	N12a	C15.2	1	c	5	Fill, below 3208
3211	N12a	C15.2	1	c	5	Fill, below 3210
3212	N12a	C15.2	1	c	5	Fill, below 3211
3213	N12a	C15.2	1	d	4	Fill, below 3209
3214	N12a	C15.2	1	d	4	Fill N of W500, below 3202
3215	N12a	C15.2	1	d	4	Fill, below 3214
3216	N12a	C15.2	1	d	7	P94/40
3300	J14b	C15.5	0	d	9	Topsoil (//3309)
3301	J14b	C15.5	1	a	4	Fill, below 3300
3302	J14b	C15.5	1	a	4	Packing S of W400, below 3301
3303	J14b	C15.5	1	d	4	Packing N of W407
3304	J14b	C15.5	1	d	4	Packing S of W403, below 3302
3305	J14b	C15.5	1	d	4	Packing N of W403, below 3302
3306	J14b	C15.5	1	d	4	Packing, below 3305
3307	J14b	C15.5	1	d	4	Packing, below 3306
3308	J14b	C15.5	1	d	4	Packing S of W403
3309	J14a		0	d	9	Topsoil (//3300)
3310	J14a	C15.5	1	d	4	Fill, below 3309
3311	J14b	C15.5	1	d	4	Packing, below 3303
3312	J14a	C15.5	1	b	7	P95/18
3313	J14a	C15.5	1	b	7	P95/19
3314	J14a	C15.5	1	b	4	Packing, below 3310
3315	J14b	C15.5	1	d	4	Packing, below 3311
3316	J14a	C15.5	1	d	4	Packing, below 3314
3317	J14b	C15.5	1	d	4	Packing, below W407–8
3318	J14a	C15.5	1	d	5	Surface, below 3316

List of Excavation Units

Unit	Square	Chapter	Level	Purity	Context	Description
3319	J14b		1	a	3	W407–8 removal
3320	J14b		1	a	3	W406 removal
3321	J14b	C15.5	1	d	5	Occ. debris, below W403
3322	J14b	C15.5	1	a	7	P95/20
3323	J14b		1	a	6	Group of potsherds on 3328
3324	J14b		1	a	5?	Patch of ashy material, below 3316
3325	J14a/b		1	a	3	W411 / W909
3326	J14a/b		1	a	3	W406 removal (W part)
3327	J14b	C15.5	1	a	6	Group of potsherds, below 3317
3328	J14a		1	a	7	Pit or cut containing 3323
3329	J14a		1	a	6	Storage vessel partly in I14
3330	J14b		1	a	3	W409 removal
3331	J14a/b	C15.5	1	d	4	Packing, below W409
3332	J14a		1	a	3	W414/W910
3333	J14a/b		1	a	3	W911 (W part)
3334	J14a		1	a	8	Lower fill of 3329
3335	J14b		1	a	-	P95/20 cut for jar
3336	J14b		1	a	-	P95/29 cut
3337	J14b	C15.5	1	a	7	P95/29 fill
3338	J14b		1	a	-	P95/30 cut
3339	J14b	C15.5	1	a	7	P95/30 fill, below 3317
3340	J14a		1/2	d	4	Fill, below 3318
3341	J14b		1/2	c	8	Fragmentary feature of unbaked clay
3342	J14b		1/2	b	7	P95/41 upper fill
3343	J14b		1/2	b	7	P95/41 upper fill NE of 3342 (//3345)
3344	J14b		1/2	b	-	P95/41 cut
3345	J14b		1/2	b	7	P95/41 lower fill
3346	J14a/b		1/2		5	Surface S of 3341, below 3354–5
3347	J14b		1/2	d	4	Fill, below 3346
3348	J14b	C15.5	1/2	d	4	Fill, below 3317
3349	J14b		1/2	d	4	Packing, below 3347
3350	J14b		-	a	9	Animal burrow in SE
3351	J14b		1/2	b	3	Possible hearth base N of 3341
3352	J14a/b		1/2	b	4	Fill assoc. with 3341, 3351
3353	J14a		1/2	d	8	Fill, below 3340
3354	J14a/b		1/2	d	8	Fill, below 3340 (//3355)
3355	J14a		1/2	d	8	Fill, below 3348–9 (//3354)
3356	J14b		1/2	d	8	Sounding in NW corner
3357	J14a		1/2	a	7	P95/56 fill
3358	J14a		1/2	a	-	P95/56 cut
3359	J14b		1/2	a	5	Occ. debris in N, below 3354
3360	J14b		1/2	d	4	Packing in SE, below 3354
3361	J14b		1/2	a	7	Fill of cut or pit in NE, below 3354
3362	J14b		1/2	d	4	Packing in SE, below 3360
3363	J14b		1/2	d	7	Packing in SW, below 3354
3364	J14a/b		1/2	a	7	P95/64 fill, below 3354
3365	J14a/b		1/2	a	-	P95/64 cut
3366	J14b		1/2	d	4	Packing in NW, below 3359
3367	J14a		2k	c	7	Mixed fill of ditch
3368	J14a	C15.3	2k	a	7	Fill of ditch 3433 (//3424, 3465)
3369	J14a		1/2	b	9	Fill E of ditch
3370	J14a	C15.3	2k	a	-	E side of ditch cut
3371	J14a		2k	b	3	W810
3400	I14a/b	C15.5	0	b	9	Topsoil
3401	I14a/b	C15.5	1	b	4	Fill, below 3400
3402	I14a	C15.5	1	a	6	Fill on S side, below 3401
3403	I14a/b	C15.5	1	b	4	Wall collapse, below 3401–2
3404	I14a		1	b	6	Wall rubble, below 3403
3405	I14a		1/2k	b	4	Fill, below 3404
3406	I14a	C15.3	1/2k	a	4	Packing, below 3405
3407	I14a	C15.3	1/2k	a	5	Ashy areas, below 3406
3408	I14a		1	a	3	W901
3409	I14a	C15.3	1/2k	b	5	Ashy area, below 3407 (FI95/4)
3410	I14a	C15.3	1	a	6	FI95/4
3411	I14a	C15.3	1	b	7	P95/25 fill
3412	I14a	C15.3	1	a	7	P95/26 fill, below 3406
3413	I14a	C15.3	1	a	8	Cut for depression in 3432
3414	I14a	C15.3	1	a	7	P95/27 fill, below 3406
3415	I14a		-	c	9	Fill of animal burrow
3416	I14a	C15.3	1	a	7	Post-hole into 3432, below 3406
3417	I14a	C15.3	1	a	7	Fill of post-hole 3428, below 3406
3418	I14a	C15.3	1	a	7	Fill of post-hole 3429, below 3406
3419	I14b	C15.5	1	a	5	Burnt occ. layer, below 3401
3420	I14b		1	a	3	W902
3421	I14b	C15.5	1	a	5	Occ. surface W of W902
3422	I14b	C15.5	1/2	a	5	Occ. surface E of W902

665

Appendix 2

Unit	Square	Chapter	Level	Purity	Context	Description
3423	I14b	C15.5	1/2	a	5	Burnt deposit overlying 3422
3424	I14b	C15.3	2k	a	7	Fill of ditch 3433 (//3368, 3465)
3425	I14a	C15.3	1	b	-	P95/25 cut
3426	I14a	C15.3	1	a	-	P95/26 cut
3427	I14a	C15.3	1	b	-	P95/27 cut
3428	I14a	C15.3	1	a	-	Post-hole into 3432 (fill = 3417)
3429	I14a	C15.3	1	a	-	Post-hole into 3432 (fill = 3418)
3430	I14b	C15.3	1/2k	b	4	Packing W of 3424, below 3404
3431	I14b	C15.3	1/2k	b	4	Packing, below 3430
3432	I14a/b	C15.3	2	a	5	Occ. surface W of ditch (S half) (//3466)
3433	I14b	C15.3	2k	a	-	W side of ditch cut (//3467)
3434	I14a/b	C15.3	2	a	7	P95/61 fill
3435	I14a/b	C15.3	2	a	-	P95/61 cut, into 3432
3436	I14a/b	C15.3	2	a	7	P95/62 fill
3437	I14a/b	C15.3	2	a	-	P95/62 cut, into 3432
3438	I14b	C15.3	2	a	7	P95/76 fill
3439	I14b	C15.3	2	a	-	P95/76 cut, into 3432
3440	I14a	C15.3	2	a	8	Fill of post-hole 3441
3441	I14a	C15.3	2	a	-	Post-hole into 3432
3442	I14b		2	a	3	W802 upper courses (//3464)
3443	I14a	C15.3	2	a	7	P95/77 fill, below 3432
3444	I14a	C15.3	2	a	7	P95/77 cut, into 3445
3445	I14a/b	C15.3	2	b	4	Packing, below 3432
3446	I14a	C15.3	2	b	7	P95/78 fill, below 3445
3447	I14a	C15.3	2	b	-	P95/78 cut, into 3448
3448	I14a/b	C15.3	2	b	4	Packing, below 3445
3449	I14b	C15.3	2	a	7	P95/79 fill, below 3448
3450	I14b	C15.3	2	a	7	P95/80 fill, below 3448, cut by 3433 (//3471)
3451	I14a/b	C15.3	2	a	4	Packing, below 3448 (//3472)
3452	I14b	C15.3	2	a	-	P95/79 cut, into 3451
3453	I14b	C15.3	2	a	-	P95/80 cut, into 3451
3454	I14a		2	a	3	W904 (//3490)
3455	I14a	C15.3	2	b	7	P95/81 fill, below 3448
3456	I14a	C15.3	2	a	-	P95/81 cut, into W904
3457	I14a/b	C15.3	2	b	4	Rm 97, packing, below 3451
3458	I14a/b	C15.3	2	a	4	Rm 97, destr. debris, below 3457 (//3474)
3459	I14a/b	C15.3	2	a	5	Rm 97, burnt occ. deposit, below 3458 (//3474)
3460	I14a/b	C15.3	2	a	5	Rm 97 occ. surface, below 3459 (//3475)
3461	I14a/b	C15.3	2	b	-	P95/87 cut
3462	I14a/b	C15.3	2	a	7	P95/84 fill, below 3459
3463	I14a/b	C15.3	2	a	-	P95/84 cut, into 3460
3464	I14b		2	a	-	W802 upper courses (//3442)
3465	I14b	C15.3	2k	b	7	Fill of ditch 3433 (//3368, 3424)
3466	I14a/b	C15.3	2	b	5	N half, occ. surface W of ditch (//3432)
3467	I14b	C15.3	2k	a	-	W side of ditch cut (//3433)
3468	I14a	C15.3	2	b	7	P96/8, below 3466
3469	I14b	C15.3	2	a	7	P96/9, below 3466
3470	I14a	C15.3	2	b	7	P96/12, below 3466
3471	I14b	C15.3	2	b	7	P95/80 fill (//3450)
3472	I14a/b	C15.3	2	b	4	Rm 97, packing, below 3466 (//3451)
3473	I14a	C15.3	2	b	4	Rm 95, packing, below 3466 (//3445)
3474	I14a/b	C15.3	2	b	5	Rm 97, burnt deposit, below 3472 (//3458–9)
3475	I14a/b	C15.3	2	b	5	Rm 97, occ. surface, below 3474 (//3460)
3476	I14a/b	C15.3	2	b	7	P96/27, below 3474
3477	I14a	C15.3	2	c	7	P96/28, below 3474
3478	I14a	C15.3	2	b	7	P96/29, below 3475
3479	I14a	C15.3	2	a	7	P96/30, below 3474
3480	I14a	C15.3	2	b	7	P96/31, below 3474
3481	I14a		1	b	3	W901
3482	I14a	C15.3	2	a	6	FI96/6, internal ashy fill.
3483	I14a		1	a	-	W901 foundation cut
3484	I14a		2	b	3	W800
3485	I14b		2	b	3	W802 lowest course
3486	I14a	C15.3	2	a	5	Rm 96, occ. surface, below 3446
3487	I14a	C15.3	2	a	5	Rm 95, occ. surface NW of FI96/6
3488	I14b	C15.3	2	b	7	P96/41, below 3474
3489	I14a/b	C15.3	2/3	a	4	Packing, below 3475
3490	I14a		2	a	3	W904 (//3454)
3491	I14a/b	C15.3	2	b	7	P96/58, below 3475
3492	I14a		2	b	3	W801
3493	I14a	C15.3	2	a	7	P96/59, cut by P96/41
3494	I14a	C15.3	3	a	5	Rm 92, occ. deposit, below 3705
3495	I14a	C15.3	2/3	b	7	P96/65, below 3489
3496	I14b	C15.3	2	a	7	P96/66, below 3459
3497	I14a	C15.3	2	a	8	Post-hole into 3475, below 3459
3498	I14a/b	C15.3	2	a	8	Post-hole into 3489, below 3475
3499	I14	C15.3	2	a	7	P96/77, below 3473
3500	M14a	C15.5	0	d	9	Topsoil

List of Excavation Units

Unit	Square	Chapter	Level	Purity	Context	Description
3501	M14a	C15.5	1	b	4	Fill starting at top of walls
3502	M14a		1	a	3	W922
3503	M14a		1	a	3	W923
3504	M14b	C15.5	0	d	9	Topsoil
3505	M14a	C15.5	1	b/c	4	Fill between W922 and W923
3506	M14a	C15.5	1	b/c	4	External fill, outside W922 and W923
3507	M14b	C15.5	0	d	9	Sub-topsoil fill
3508	M14b		1	a	3	W924
3509	M14b		1	a	3	W925
3510	M14a		1	a	3	W926
3511	M14a		1	a	3	W927
3512	-	-	-	-	-	-
3513	M14b		1	a	3	W928
3514	M14b		1	a	3	W929
3600	L14a	C15.5	0	d	9	Topsoil
3601	L14b	C15.5	0	c	9	Topsoil
3602	L14a	C15.5	1	b	8	Fill, entire quadrant
3603	L14a	C15.5	1	b	4	Fill
3604	L14b	C15.5	1	b	9	Fill
3605	L14a		1	b	3	W943
3606	L14a	C15.5	1	b	4	Fill, entire quadrant
3607	L14b		1	a	3	W944
3608	L14b	C15.5	1	a	4	Fill
3700	I14a	C15.3	2	a	7	Post-hole into 3475, below 3459
3701	I14a/b	C15.3	2	a	7	Post-hole into 3489, below 3475
3702	I14b	C15.3	3	a	4	Rm 91, packing, below 3489
3703	I14a	C15.3	2/3	a	7	P96/94, below 3489
3704	I14a/b	C15.3	2/3	a	7	P96/95, below 3489
3705	I14a	C15.3	3	a	4	Rm 92, packing, below 3489
3706	I14b		3	a	3	W803
3707	I14b		3	a	3	W804
3708	I14	C15.3	3	a	5	Rm 91, occ. surface, below 3702
3709	I14a	C15.3	3	a	5	Rm 92, occ. surface, below 3494
3710	I14b	C15.3	2	a	7	P96/112, cut by P96/59
3711	I14a/b	C15.3	3	a	4	Rm 93, packing, below 3489
3712	I14a/b	C15.3	3	a	4	Rm 94, packing, below 3489
3713	I14a/b	C15.3	3	a	5	Rm 93, occ. surface, below 3711
3714	I14a/b	C15.3	3	a	5	Rm 94, occ. surface, below 3712
3715	I14a/b		-	d	9	Section straightening
3716	I14a/b	C15.3	3	b	5	Rm 94, surface, below 3714
3717	I14b	C15.3	3	d	9	Sounding, below base of ditch
3800	K14a	C15.4	2 lower	a	5	Fill, below occ. surface 3098
3801	K14a		2 lower	a	3	W811
3802	K14a	C15.4	2 lower	a	3	W812
3803	K14a	C15.4	2 lower	a	5	Occ. surface assoc. with W811 and W812
3804	K14a		2 lower	a	3	W813
3900	J19c		IIc	a	3	W766 removal
3901	J19c	C13.2	IId	b	5	Rm d7, packing and destr. debris, below W766 (//1691, 1693)
3902	J19c		II?	c	7	P96/64 lower fill, below 1672
3903	J19c	C13.2	IId	a	6	Rm d7, unbaked clay vessel J19/282
3904	J19c	C13.2	IId	a	5	Rm d7, occ. surface, below 1693
3905	J19c	C13.2	IId	a	3	Rm d7, bench against N and E walls
3906	J19d	C13.1	IIc		4	Rm 3, destr. debris over steps
3907	J19a/c		IId?	c	7	P96/123
3908	J19a		I/II		7	P96/124
3909	J19b/d	C13.1	IIc		3	Rm 3, rectangular feature in W624
3910	J19a		-		9	Removal of baulk with I19b
3911	J19a	C13.2	IId/e	d	9	Mixed deposits above IIc
3912	J19c		I	b	5	Baulk with I19d, ash lines, below topsoil
3913	J19c		I/II	a	4	Baulk with I19d, below 3912
3914	J19c	C13.4	IIf	a	3	W765, E side of FI96/15, below 3913
3915	I19d	C13.4	IIf	a	3	FI96/15, W and N walls removal
3916	J19d	C13.2	IId	b	4	Rm d9, destr. debris
3917	J19d	C13.1	IIc	b	8	Rm 10, burnt surfaces above P97/73, below W763
3918	J19c	C13.2, C13.4	IIf	d	3	W764 removal (//2398)
3919	J19c	C13.4	IIf	d	9	Mixed deposits E of FI96/15
3920	J19c	C13.2	IId	a	4	Rm d10, burnt occ. deposit, below W764
3921	J19c	C13.2	IId	a	4	Rm d10, ceramics within 3920
3922	J19c	C13.1	IId	b	4	Rm d10, destr. debris, below W764
3923	J19d		0	c	7	Modern robber pit (//1002)
3924	J19c		IId	b	4	Removal of W724 and assoc. walls
3925	J19d	C13.2	IIe/f	d	7	P96/16 and P96/17 fill
3926	J19c	C13.2	IId	b	9	Rm d7, fill to base of walls

667

Appendix 2

Unit	Square	Chapter	Level	Purity	Context	Description
3927	J19c	C13.1	IIc	a	4	Rms 7 and 8, destr. debris
3928	J19d	C13.1	IIc/d	a	4	Rm 7, packing above destr. debris
3929	J19d	C13.1	IIc	a	4	Rm 7, burnt occ. deposit
3930	J19d	C13.2	IId/f	a	7	P97/42
3931	J19d	C13.1	IIc/d	a	4	Rm 7, packing, below W764
3932	J19c	C13.1	IIc	b	4	Rms 7–8, destr. debris
3933	J19c	C13.2	IId	b	4	Rm d8, occ. deposit against W768
3934	J19d	C13.1	IIc	a	4	Rm 7, destr. debris, below 3929
3935	J19c/d	C13.1	IIc/d	a	7	Rm 7, P97/49 in NW corner
3936	J19	C13.4	IIf	c	3	FI96/15, removal of upper walls
3937	J19d	C13.1	IIc/d	a	4	SW corner of Rm 7, packing and destr. debris
3938	J19	C13.1	IIc	a	5	Rm 7, occ. surface
3939	-	-	-	-	-	-
3940	J19a	C13.2	IId	d	9	Rm d6, packing material S of W617
3941	J19a	C13.2	IId	b	4	Rm d6, packing S of W617
3942	J19a	C13.2	IId	a	5	Rm d6, occ. deposit, below 3941
3943	J19d	C9, C13.1	IIc/d	a	8	Rm 10, burnt surfaces above P97/73
3944	J19d		II	c	7	P95/33
3945	J19a	C13.2	IId	c	4	Packing above W617
3946	J19a	C13.2	IId	b	4	Rm d1, occ. surface N of W617
3947	J19a	C13.1	IIc	b	4	Rm 9, destr. debris
3948	J19d		IIc	a	3	W615
3949	J19		IIc	a	3	W616
3950	J19a	C13.1	IIc	b	4	Rm 9, destr. debris, below 3947
3951	J19a	C13.1	IIc?	b	7	Rm 9, P97/66, below 3947
3952	J19a	C13.1	IIb/c	b	4	Rm 9, packing, below 3942
3953	J19a		II	b	7	P97/67, cut by P97/68
3954	J19a		II	c	7	P97/68
3955	J19a	C13.1	IIc?	b	7	P97/66, below 3951
3956	J19a		IId	b	3	W617 removal
3957	J19d	C13.1	IIc/d	a	8	Rm 10, burnt surfaces, below 3943
3958	J19a		II	c	7	P97/75, below 3959
3959	J19a		II	c	7	P97/75, upper fill
3960	J19b	C13.1	IIb/c	b	4	Mud brick and packing in W122
3961	J19b/d		II	b	7	P97/76
3962	J19a	C13.1	IIc/d	b	4	Packing, below 3946 and W617
3963	J19d	C13.1	IIb	b	8	Rm 7, sounding, below IIc floor
3964	J19d/c	C13.1	IIc/d	a	7	Rm 7, cleaning edges of P97/49
3965	J19d	C13.1	IIb	a	5	Rm 7, sounding, below 3963
3966	J19c	C13.4	IIf	c	3	FI96/15, removal of lower walls
3967	J19d	C13.1	IIc	c	7	P97/73, below 3957
3968	J19d	C13.1	IIc	a	7	P97/73, below 3967
3969	J19d	C13.1	IIc	b	7	P97/73, below 3968
3970	J19a	C13.1	IIc	c	4	Courtyard packing W of W130
3971	J19a		II	a	7	P98/25, base only
3972	J19a		II	a	7	P98/26, base only
3973	J19a	C13.1	IIb/c	a	4	Courtyard packing, W of W130 below IIc floor
3974	J19a	C13.1	II	b	7	P98/54 base only, fill
3975	J19a	C13.1	IIb	a	7	P98/55 fill
3976	J19a	C13.1	IIb	b	4	Courtyard packing, W of W130
3977	J19a	C13.1	IIb	b	4	Courtyard packing, S of W633
3978	J19a	C13.1	IIb/c	b	7	P98/90 E half
3979	J19a	C13.1	IIb	a	4	Courtyard packing, below 3976, 3977
3980	J19a	C13.1	IIb	b	4	Courtyard packing N of W633, below 3976
3981	J19a	C13.1	IIb	a	4	Courtyard packing N of W633, below 3980
3982	J19a	C13.1	IIb	b	4	Courtyard packing S of W633, below 3979
3983	J19a	C13.1	IIb?	b	7	P98/91, E part
3984	J19a		II	b	4	Courtyard packing E of 3980, 3981
4001	I20d	C13.1	IIb-e	c	7	P94/1 S part (//1403), cut by P94/5
4002	I19b/I20d	C13.1	IIb-e	c	-	P95/12 cut
4003	I19b/I20d	C13.1	IIb-e	c	7	P95/12 fill
4004	I20d	C13.1	IIb	b	7	P94/5, cut by P95/28 and P95/34 (//1421)
4005	I20d	C13.1	IIb-e	c	-	P95/28 cut
4006	I20d	C13.1	IIb-e	c	7	P95/28 fill, cut by P95/34
4007	I20d	C13.1	IIb	c	-	P95/34 cut
4008	I20d	C13.1	IIb	c	7	P95/34 fill (//2886)
4009	I20d	C13.1	IIb	c	9	W ctyd, strata above P95/34
4010	I20d	C13.1	IIb	c	4	Packing S of W108
4011	I20c/d	C12, C13.1	IIa/b	c	4	Orange layer S of W108, below 4010
4012	I20c/d	C12, C13.1	IIa/b	c	5	Packing, below 4011
4013	I20c/d	C12, C13.1	IIa/IIIe	b	4	Reddish layer, below 4012

List of Excavation Units

Unit	Square	Chapter	Level	Purity	Context	Description
4014	I20d	C12	IIIe	c	4	E ctyd, packing, below 4011 (//1436)
4015	I20d	C12	IIIe	b	4	E ctyd, packing, below 4014
4016	I20	C12	IIIe	b	5	E ctyd, burnt occ. deposits (//1327, 1372, 1418)
4017	I20b/d	C12	IIIe	b	4	E ctyd, packing, below 4016 (//1426)
4018	I20b/d	C12	IIIe	b	5	E ctyd, occ. surface, below 4017
4019	I20c/d	C13.1	IIb	c	4	Packing E of W108
4020	I20c/d	C13.1	IIb	c	4	Packing, below 4019, above 4011
4021	I20b/d	C12	IIIe	b	5	E ctyd, clay surface, below 4018
4022	I20d	C12	IIId/e	b	4	E ctyd, packing, below 4021
4023	I20b/d	C12	IIId	b	5	E ctyd, occ. surface, below 4022
4024	I20c/d	C12	IIIe	b	4	Packing, below 4013
4025	I20c/d		IIId/e	a	3	W742
4026	I20c/d	C12	IIId/e	b	4	Packing S of W742
4027	I20c	C12	IIId/e	b	4	Packing W of W112, below 4024 (Rm 32)
4028	I20c/d	C12	IIId/e	b	5	Rm 30, occ. surface, below 4026 (//5521)
4029	I20c	C12	IIId/e	b	5	Rm 30, occ. deposit on 4028
4030	I20c	C12	IIId	b	4	Ashy occ. deposit W of W112, below 4027 (Rm 32)
4200	H19b		0	d	9	Topsoil
4201	H19b	C12, C13.1	IIb	a	8	Packing, below topsoil
4202	H19b		IIId	a	3	W737
4203	H19b		IIId	a	3	W738
4204	H19b	C12	II/III	a	7	P95/47 fill
4205	H19b	C12	IIId	a	4	Packing assoc. with W737–8
4206	H19b	C12	IIId	a	3	W739
4207	H19b	C12	IIIc	b	4	Rm 35, packing assoc. with W739
4208	H19b	C12	IIId	a	4	Rm 33, packing
4209	H19b		IIIc/d	a	5	Rm 32, occ. surface, below 4205
4210	H19b	C12	IIId	-	-	Foundation trench for W738
4211	H19b	C12	IIIc/d	a	4	Mixed fill, Rms 32, 34, below 4209 (4225)
4212	H19b	C9, C12	IIIc/d	a	7	P95/63 fill sealed by 4205
4213	H19b	C12	IIIc/d	-	-	P95/63 cut sealed by 4205
4214	H19b	C12	IIId	c	9	Mixed deposits from baulk in NE, below 4200 (//4219)
4215	H19b	C12	IIId	c	9	Mixed deposits, below 4214 (//4205, 4209, 4211)
4216	H19b		IIIc	a	3	W740 (//4241)
4217	H19b	C12	IIIc	a	4	Packing assoc. with W740, below 4211
4218	H19b	C12	IIIc	a	4	Packing W of W741
4219	H19b		-	c	9	Mixed deposits from baulk in NW (//4214)
4220	H19b		IIIc	a	3	W741 (//4244)
4221	H19b		0	-	-	P95/83 cut
4222	H19b	C12	0	a	7	P95/83 fill
4223	H19b	C12	IIIc	a	4	Packing N of W740, below W739
4224	H19a/b	C12	IIIc	b	9	Packing assoc. with W703 and W744
4225	H19b	C12	IIIc/d	a	4	Mixed fill in SE corner (//4211)
4226	H19b		-	d	9	Trench cleaning
4227	H19b	C12	IIIc	a	4	Material, below 4225, to W (//4228)
4228	H19b	C12	IIIc	a	4	Material, below 4225, to E (//4227)
4229	H19b	C12	IIIc	a	5	Occ. layers in SE corner, below 4227–8
4230	H19b	C12	IIIc	a	4	Packing layer, below 4229
4231	H19b	C12	IIIc	a	4	Packing, below 4230
4232	H19b	C12	IIIc/d	a	4	Packing above W741
4233	H19b		-	d	9	Baulk straightening
4234	H19b	C12	IIIc	a	4	Packing assoc. with W740, 741
4235	H19b	C12	IIIa/IVb	b	8	Ashy lens
4236	H19b	C12	IIIa–b	a	4	Packing assoc. with W745
4237	H19b	C12	IIIa–b	a	4	Packing N of W740
4238	H19b	C12	IIIc/d	a	4	Packing W of W741
4239	H19a	C12	IIIb or c?	a	4	Surface W of W744
4240	H19a	C12	IIIb	a	7?	Fill, below 4239
4241	H19b	C12	IIIc	a	3	W740 removal (//4216)
4242	H19a/b	C12	IIIb	a	3	Mud-brick floor surface, below 4240
4243	H19a	C12	IIIa	a	4	Packing, below W703 and W744
4244	H19b	C12	IIIc	a	3	W741, removal of upper courses (//4220)
4245	H19b	C12	IIIb	a	3	W745, removal
4246	H19b	C12	IIIb	a	5	Packing E of W745
4247	H19b	C12	IIIa	a	3	W703, W744, W746 removal
4248	H19a/b	C11	IIIa/IVb	b	4	Packing, below W703, W744, W746
4249	H19a/b	C11	IVb	b	6	Burnt debris on IVb surface, below 4248
4250	H19a		0	d	9	Topsoil at W side

Appendix 2

Unit	Square	Chapter	Level	Purity	Context	Description
4251	H19a/b	C11	IVb	a	4	Burnt occ. deposits on IVb surface, below 4249
4252	H19a/b		IIIa	a	3	W747 removal, below 4238
4253	H19b	C11	IVb	a	7	P96/67, pot emplacement
4254	H19a/b	C11	IVb	a	5	NW sector, IVb floor and underlying material
4255	H19a/b	C11	IVa/b	a	4	Packing, below 4254 (//4272)
4256	H19b		-	d	9	Straightening H19/20 section
4257	H19a/b	C11	IVa/b	a	4	Rm 41, packing, below 4255 (//4261)
4258	H19a	C11	IVa	a	4	Rm 42, collapsed masonry etc.
4259	H19a	C11	IVb	a	7	P96/87, below 4243
4260	H19a	C11	IVb	a	4	Packing, below 4249
4261	H19a/b	C11	IVa/b	a	4	Rm 41, packing, below 4255, above 4264 (//4257)
4262	H19a/b	C11	IVb	c	4	Packing above W748
4263	H19a/b	C11	IVa	a	4	Rm 41, NW, collapsed masonry, below 4257 (//4273)
4264	H19a/b	C11	IVa	a	4	Rm 41, N, destr. debris, below 4261, 4263 (//4273)
4265	H19a		0	c	9	Topsoil in W
4266	H19a		0	b	9	Packing, below 4265
4267	H19a	C11	IVa	a	4	Rm 40, packing, below 4265
4268	H19b	C11	IVb	b	4	Rm 43, SE sector, packing, below 4248 (//4275)
4269	H19a	C11	IVa	b	4	Rm 44, burnt occ. deposit, below 4266
4270	H19b	C11	IVb	a	7	P96/106, within 4268
4271	H19a	C11	IVb	a	7	P96/87, lower fill
4272	H19a/b	C11	IVb	a	4	Rm 41 SE, packing, below 4249 (//4255)
4273	H19a/b	C11	IVa	a	4	Rm 41 SE, collapsed masonry etc. (//4263-4)
4274	H19a	C11	IVa	a	4	Rm 41, tumbled masonry of W748
4275	H19b	C11	IVb	a	4	Packing overlying W106 S end (//4268)
4276	H19b	C11	IVa	a	4	Rm 43, destr. debris, below 4268, 4275
4277	H19b	C11	IVa	a	4	Rm 45, destr. debris, below 4272
4278	H19a/b	C11	IVa	a	6	Rm 41, burnt occ. surface
4300	K18a		0	d	9	Topsoil
4301	K18a		0	d	9	Topsoil, below 4300
4302	K18a		I	c	9	Mixed deposits, below 4301
4303	K18a	C17	I	b	4	Fill S of W421, below 4302
4304	K18a	C17	I	b	4	Fill W of W420, below 4302
4305	K18a		-	d	9	Baulk on N side removal (//4300–302)
4306	K18a	C17	I	b	4	NE corner, beneath white surface, below 4301
4307	K18a	C17	I	c	4	S half, fill E of W420, below 4302
4308	K18a	C17	I	b	4	S half, fill E of W420, below 4307
4309	K18a	C17	I	c	4	N half, fill S of W421, below 4303
4310	K18a	C17	I/II	b	4	W side, fill beneath W420 and 4304
4311	K18a		I	b	7	P97/24
4312	K18a	C17	I	b	4	N half, fill S of W421, below 4309–10
4313	K18a	C17	-	c	9	N half, cleaning spit S of W421, below 4312
4314	K18a	C17	I	c	4?	Fill above white surface, below 4313, 4316
4315	K18a		I/II	c	7	P97/50
4316	K18a	C17	I	b	4?	Packing above white surface, SE part, below 4308
4317	K18a	C17	I	b	4?	Packing above white surface, SW part, below 4308
4318	K18a		I/II	c	7	P97/51
4319	K18a		I/II	b	7	P97/48 (//1598)
4320	K18a	C17	I	b	4	Packing, below 4316–17; cobbles set into it in SE (//4398, 6104-5)
4321	K18a		II	b	9	Packing, below 4320
4322	K18a		IIf	b	4	SE corner, packing, below 4321
4323	K18a		IIf	b	8	*In situ* vessel sealed by 4320
4324	K18a		IIf	c	4	Packing, below 4321
4325	K18a		IIf	c	4	E side, packing, below 4322, 4324
4326	K18a		IIf	c	4	E side, packing, below 4325
4327	K18a		IIf	c	9	E side, cleaning, below 4326
4328	K18a		IIe/f	c	4	E side, packing, below 4327
4329	K18a		IIf?	c	7	Mixed pit fills SW of P97/50
4330	K18a		II	c	9	E side, cleaning, below 4328

List of Excavation Units

Unit	Square	Chapter	Level	Purity	Context	Description
4331	K18a		IIe/f	c	4	E side, packing material, below 4330
4332	K18a	C13.2	0	c	9	Cleaning animal burrow on E side
4333	K18a		I	a	3	W420, foundations (//4389)
4334	K18a	C13.2	IId?	a	3	W421, foundations removal (//5830)
4335	K18a	C13.3	IIe/f?	a	4	Rm e6, packing beneath W421 and above W426
4336	K18a	C13.3	IIe/f?	d	4	Rm e6, W side packing S of 4335
4337	K18a	C13.3	IIe/f?	d	4	Rm e6, W side, packing beneath 4335–6
4338	K18a	C13.2, C13.3	IIe	c	5	Rm e6, W side, occ. surface S of W426, below 4337
4339	K18a	C13.3	IIe	c	4	Rm e6, W side, packing material beneath 4338
4340	K18a	C13.3	IIe	c	7	Rm e6, pit like feature cut from 4338
4341	K18a	C13.3	IIe	d	4	Rm e6, W side, packing material S of W426, below 4338
4342	K18a	C13.3	IIe	c	5?	Rm e6, orange patch at base of 4338
4343	K18a	C13.3	IIe	b	4	Rm e6, E side, packing, below 4331
4344	K18a	C13.3	IIe	a	5	Rm e6, E side, burnt occ. deposit, below 4343
4345	K18a	C13.3	IIe	b	9	Rm e6, SE corner, material above occ. surface, below 4331 (//4343–4)
4346	K18a	C13.3	IIe	c	9	Rm e6, W side, material above 4356, below 4341, 4339
4347	K18a		IIe	a	3	W426 (//4381)
4348	K18a	C13.3	IIe	b	4	Rm e6, SW corner, material above 4352, below 4339
4349	K18a		-	d	9	Baulk on N side removal
4350	K18a	C13.3	-	c	9	Baulk on N side removal, lower part, fill N of Rm e6
4351	K18a	C13.3	IId/e	a	4	Packing N of Rm e6
4352	K18a	C13.3	IIe	b	5	S half, Rm e6 occ. surface, below 4343, 4348 (//4356)
4353	K18a	C13.3	IIe/f	a	7	Rm e6, P97/79
4354	K18a	C13.3	IIe/f	b	7	Rm e6, P97/78
4355	K18a	C13.3	IIe	a	5	Rm e6, packing material against S face W426
4356	K18a	C13.3	IIe	b	5	N half, Rm e6, occ. surface, below 4343, 4346 (//4352)
4357	K18a	C13.3	IIe/f	a	7	Rm e6, P97/80
4358	K18a	C13.3	IIe/f	a	7	Rm e6, P97/81, cut by P97/79 and P97/80
4359	K18a	C13.3	IIe	a	5	Rm e6, occ. surface against S face W426
4360	K18a	C13.3	IIe	a	5	Rm e6, burnt occ. surface/deposit S of 4359, below 4356
4361	K18a	C13.3	IIe	b	4	N half, Rm e6, packing above 4363, below 4356 (//4362)
4362	K18a		IIe	b	4	S half, packing above burnt occ. deposit, below 4352 (//4361)
4363	K18a	C13.3	IIe	a	5	N half, Rm e6 burnt occ. surface/deposit, below 4361
4364	K18a	C13.3	IIe	a	4	Rm e6, packing above 4370, below 4362
4365	K18a	C13.3	IIe	b	8	Fill of jar K18/134
4366	K18a	C13.3	IIe	a	3	Rm e6, bench along E face of W434
4367	K18a	C13.2	IId	a	5	Rm d9, packing N of W426
4368	K18a		-	d	9	Baulk straightening
4369	K18a	C13.3	IIe	a	4	Rm e6, burnt occ. deposit over SE bench, below 4364
4370	K18a	C13.3	IIe	a	4	Rm e6, burnt occ. surface/deposit, below 4364
4371	K18a	C13.3	IIe	a	5	N half, Rm e6 occ. deposit, below 4363
4372	K18a	C13.3	IIe	a	5	W half, Rm e6 occ. surface, below 4363 (//4374)
4373	K18a	C13.3	IIe	a	3	Rm e6, FI97/9
4374	K18a	C13.3	IIe	a	5	E half, Rm e6 occ. surface, below 4363–4 (//4372)
4375	K18a	C13.3	IIe	a	3	Rm e6, bench along W face of W446
4376	K18a	C13.3	IIe	a	5	Rm e6, occ. surface, below 4372 and 4374
4377	K18a	C13.3	IIe	a	3	Rm e6, lower bench along E face of W447
4378	K18a	C13.3	IIe	a	3	Rm e6, bench along W face of W446
4379	K18a	C13.3	IIe	a	3	Rm e6, bench along S face of W426
4380	K18a		IId	a	3	W614 mud brick removal
4381	K18a		IIe	a	3	W426 removal (//4347)

671

Appendix 2

Unit	Square	Chapter	Level	Purity	Context	Description
4382	K18a	C13.2	IId	b	5	Rm d9, burnt occ. deposit, below W426
4383	K18a	C13.2	IId	a	5	Rm d9, occ. surface, below 4382
4384	K18a	C13.1	IIc	c	9	Rm 6, destr. debris etc., under W426, below 4380, 4383
4385	K18a	C13.3	IId/e	a	4	Rm e6, packing, below W446
4386	K18a	C13.2	IId?	b	5	Occ. deposit E of W446
4387	K18a	C13.1	IIc	c	9	Rm 6, destr. debris etc., below 4376
4388	K18a	C13.3	IIe	a	8	Rm e6, post-holes in 4376
4389	K18a		I	a	3	W420 (//4333)
4390	K18b		0	d	9	Topsoil
4391	K18b		0	d	9	Topsoil E of W430, below 4390
4392	K18b	C17	0	d	9	Topsoil W of W430, below 4390
4393	K18b		I	b	4	Packing E of W430, below 4391
4394	K18b		I	a	3	W430 (//6102)
4395	K18b	C17	I	a	4	Packing E of W430, below 4393
4396	K18b		I	a	3	W431
4397	K18b	C17	I	b	4	Packing W of W430, below 4392
4398	K18b	C16, C17	I	b	4	Packing above cobble paving W of W430 (//4320, 6104-5)
4399	K18b		I	a	3	W432
4400	I15a/b	C16	0	d	9	Topsoil
4401	I15b		0	d	9	Topsoil
4402	I15a	C16	0	d	9	Topsoil
4403	I15a/b		1		3	Wall 503 (not removed)
4500	K19d	C17	I	c	9	P97/39
4501	K19d	C17	I	c	7	P97/40
4502	K19c	C17	I/II	b	9	Material beneath 1591
4503	K19c	C13.2	IId/e	d	9	Material beneath 4502
4504	K19c	C13.2	IId	d	4	Occ. surface, below 4503
4505	K19c	C13.2	IId/e	c	5	Ashy occ. layer assoc. with FI97/4
4506	K19c	C13.1	IIc/d	d	4	Packing material above Rms 5 and 6, below 4504/5
4507	K19c	C13.1	IIc	d	4	Rms 5 and 6, destr. debris, below 4506
4508	K19c		I/II	c	7	P97/52
4509	K19c	C13.1	IIc	a	4	Rm 6, destr. debris, below 4507
4510	K19c	C13.1	IIc	a	4	Rm 5, destr. debris, below 4507
4511	K19c	C13.1	IIc	a	6	Rm 6, carbonized matter in occ. deposit
4512	K19c	C13.2	IId/e	a	7	P97/57 = P97/59 upper fill
4513	K19c	C13.1	IIc	a	5	Rm 5, occ. surface, below 4510
4514	K19c	C13.2	IId/e	a	7	P97/59 lower fill, below 4512
4515	K19c	C13.1	IIc	a	4	Rm 6, destr. debris
4516	K19c	C13.1	IIc/d?	a	4	Rm 6, material below P97/59
4517	K19d	C13.2	IId	d	4	Packing material in W half of quadrant, below 4500
4518	K19c	C13.1	IIc	b	5	Burned occ. deposit between Rms 6 and 7
4519	K19d	C13.2	IId/e	b	7	P97/65
4520	K19d	C13.2	IId	c	5	Packing material in W half of quadrant, below 4517 (//4595)
4521	K19a	C13.1	IIb/c	a	5	Rm 4, floor round storage jar in SW corner
4522	K19d	C13.1	IIc/d	c	4	Packing material in W half of quadrant, below 4520
4523	K19d	C13.2	IIc/d	d	4	Packing material against E face of W770
4524	K19d	C13.2	IId/e	a	3	Rm 20, orange and white layers above destruction
4525	K19d	C13.1	IIc	c	4	Rm 20, destr. debris W half of quadrant
4526	K19c	C13.2	IId/e	d	9	Clearance to IId surface in SW corner of quadrant
4527	K19c	C13.2	IId	a	9	Surface above W615 in SW corner of quadrant
4528	K19d	C13.1	IIc	b	4	Rm 20, destr. debris, W half of quadrant
4529	K19c	C13.2	IId/e	b	9	Material above W773
4530	K19c	C13.2	IId/e	b	8	Material above W773, below 4529
4531	K19d	C13.1	IIc	a	4	Rm 20, mudbrick destr. debris, below 4528
4532	K19c	C13.2	IId	a	5	Packing material above W773
4533	K19d	C13.2	IId/e	b	7	P97/86
4534	K19a	C13.1	IIb/c	d	9	Rm 4, sounding, below IIc floor in SW corner
4535	K19a	C13.1	IIb/c	d	9	Rm 3, sounding, below IIc floor in NE corner
4536	K19d		I	d	7	P97/77, upper part
4537	K19c	C13.1	IIc	d	5	Rm 6, occ. deposit

List of Excavation Units

Unit	Square	Chapter	Level	Purity	Context	Description
4538	K19d		I	a	7	P97/77, N half
4539	K19d	C13.4	I	d	7	P97/77, S half
4540	K19a	C13.1	IIb	d	9	Rm 2, sounding, below IIc floor
4541	K19b		IId	a	3	W 770 removal
4542	K19b	C13.1	IIc/d	a	4	Packing material, below W770
4543	K19b		-	d	4	Cleaning E of W770, below 1545
4544	K19d	C13.3	IId/e	d	9	Stone scatter, below 4524
4545	-	-	-	-	-	-
4546	K19d	C13.1	IIc/d	d	9	Investigation of W613
4547	K19d	C13.3	IId/e	d	3	Removal of stones in 4544
4548	K19d	C13.1	IIc	d	4	Rm 20, destr. debris, below 4544
4549	K19d	C13.2	IId/e	a	7	P97/87
4550	K19d	C13.2	IId	a	4	Packing over SW corner Rm 20
4551	K19a	C13.1	IIb	d	9	Rm 3, additional sounding to SW of 4535
4552	K19d	C13.1	IIc	d	4	Rm 20, SW corner, destr. debris, below 4550
4553	K19d	C13.1	IIc	d	4	Rm 20, SW corner, destr. debris, below 4552
4554	K19c	C13.2	IId	a	4	Exposure of top of W773, below 1432
4555	K19d	C13.1	IIc?	a	4	Rm 20, destr. debris E of W770
4556	K19d		IIc	a	8	Rm 20, SW corner, burnt occ. deposit
4557	K19d	C13.1	IIc	b	6	Rm 20, SW corner, ashy deposit above floor
4558	K19d	C13.1	IIc	a	4	Rm 6, destr. debris, below W614
4559	K19d		IId	a	3	W614 removal
4560	K19d	C13.2	IId	a	5	Occ. surface S of W614
4561	K19b/d	C13.1	IIc/d	a	7	P97/20 N side (//1587)
4562	K19d	C13.1, C13.3	IIc	d?	4	Rm 20, destr. debris
4563	K19b	C13.1	IIc	d	9	Rm 4, cleaning
4564	K19c	C13.1	IIc	a	6	Rm 20, SW corner destr. debris
4565	K19d		-	d	9	Cleaning, Rm 20
4566	K19d		IId	b	3	W770 S end, removal
4567	K19a	C13.1	IIc	a	6	Plastered face of diagonal feature
4568	K19d	C13.3	IIe	d	9	Removal of access steps
4569	K19d	C9, C13.3	IIe	c	7	P98/35 and P97/20 mixed fill
4570	K19d	C9, C13.3	IIe	b	7	P98/35
4571	K19b		-	d	9	Cleaning NE part of quadrant
4572	K19a	C13.1	IIc	d	9	Rm 3, E door, socket for jamb (//1558)
4573	K19b	C13.3	IIe	b	7	P97/20
4574	K19b	C13.3	IIe	c	7	P98/15 and P98/16 mixed fills
4575	K19b	C13.3	IIe	a	7	P98/15 upper fill
4576	K19b	C13.3	IIe	a	7	P98/16
4577	K19d		I/II	d	9	Material N of W612, below 4568 (//4579)
4578	K19d	C13.1	IIc	a	6	Rm 20 destr. debris
4579	K19d	C13.3	IIe	d	8	Material S of W612 (//4577)
4580	K19d	C13.3	IIe?	b	7	P98/27 (E half)
4581	K19d	C13.3	IIe?	a	7	P98/28 (E half)
4582	K19d	C13.3	IIe	a	9	Material cut by W612, below 4577/9
4583	K19d	C13.3	IIe	b	7	P98/30, cut by P98/29
4584	K19d	C13.2	IId	a	4	Packing material, below 4582
4585	K19d	C13.2	IId	a	4	Packing material, below 4584
4586	K19d	C13.2	IId	a	5	Burnt occ. layer, below 4585
4587	K19b	C13.2	IId	b	4	Packing material, below 1545
4588	K19d	C13.2	IId	a	7	P98/42, sealed by 4586
4589	K19b	C13.1	IIc	a	3	W626
4590	K19b	C13.1	IIc	a	3	W627
4591			-	-	-	-
4592	K19d	C13.3	IIe	d	9	Material S of W612
4593	K19d	C13.3	IIe	a	7	P98/49 upper fill
4594	K19d	C13.3	IIe	a	7	P98/49 lower fill
4595	K19d	C13.2	IId	a	5	Packing material in E half of quadrant (//4520)
4596	K19d	C13.1	IIc	a	4	Rm 22, destr. debris
4597	K19b	C13.1	IIc	a	6	Rm 20, N end, destr. debris
4598	K19d	C13.1	IIc	a	5	Rm 20, N end, burnt occ. layer, below 4597
4599	K19b	C13.3	IIe	a	7	P98/15 lower fill
4600	I16	C16	0	c	9	Topsoil
4601	I16	C16	0	d	9	Topsoil
4602	I16b/d		1	a	3	Wall W503
4603	I16b		1	b	5	Ash lens
4604	I16a/b		1	a	3	Wall W508
4700	J16	C16	0	c	9	Topsoil
4701	J16		1	d	3	W510 (not removed)
4702	J16		1	d	3	W517 (not removed)
4703	J16		1	d	3	W509 (not removed)
4704	J16		1	d	3	W940 foundation

Appendix 2

Unit	Square	Chapter	Level	Purity	Context	Description
4705	J16	C16	1		9	W510 (not removed)
4706	J16	C16	1		9	W517 (not removed)
4720	J16c	C16	1	b	4	Fill of W side of sondage
4721	J16c	C16	1	a	3	Mortar floor on E side of sondage
4722	J16c	C16	1	a	4	Mortar layer immediately, below 4721
4723	J16c	C16	1	a	4	Fill beneath 4721
4724	J16c	C16	1	a	7	P98/82
4725	J16c	C16	1	a	4	Fill beneath 4723
4726	J16d	C16	1	a	9	Fill from sondage, below floor 4721
4727	J16c	C16	1	b	9	Arbitrary spit, below 4725, to base of W510
4800	K16	C16	0	c	9	Topsoil
4801	K16		1	d	3	W941
4802	K16	C16	1	b	4	Rubble fill
4803	K16	C16	0	d	9	Topsoil inside later church
4804	K16	C16	0	d	9	Fill, below topsoil
4805	K16b/d	C16	0	d	9	Topsoil
4806	K16b/d		1	c	9	Rubble fill
4807	K16b	C16	1	c	9	Fill inside W516 and W515
4808	K16b	C16	1	c	4	Fill outside W516, above W512
4809	K16b/d	C16	1	c	9	Fill outside W516, above W512
4810	K16d	C16	0	d	9	Topsoil
4811	K16d	C16	1	c	9	Sub-topsoil fill
4812	K16d	C16	1	c	9	Robber trench
4813	K16d	C16	1	b	7	P97/89
4814	K16d		1	b	3	W516
4815	K16d		1	b	3	W512
4900	J17	C16	0	c	9	Topsoil
4901	I17d	C16	0	d	9	Topsoil
4902	I17c	C16	0	d	9	Topsoil
4903	I17c	C16	0	c	9	Topsoil
5000	J17	C16	0	c	9	Topsoil
5001	J17		1	d	3	W506
5002	J17		1	d	3	W943 foundation
5003	J17		1	d	3	W944 foundation
5101	L17c	C16	0	b	9	Topsoil
5102	L17c	C16	0	a	4	Sub-topsoil clearance
5103	L17c	C16	1	a	4	Soil, below 5102, E side of trench
5104	L17c	C16	1	a	4	Rubble, below 5102, W side of trench
5105	L17c	C16	1	a	4	Same as 5103
5106	L17c	C16	1	a	4	Same as 5104
5107	L17c	C16	1	a	5	Ashy deposit on floor 5110
5108	L17c	C16	1	a	4	Soft fill, below 5105
5109	L17c	C16	1	a	9	Robber trench fill
5110	L17c	C16	1	a	6	Mortar floor (//9610)
5111	L17a	C16	0	b	9	Topsoil, N of W521
5112	L17a	C16	0	a	4	Sub-topsoil, N of wall W521, above W520
5113	L17a	C16	1	a	4	Material below 5112, N of wall W520
5114	L17c	C16	1	a	4	Hard deposit beneath 5118
5300	H20d	C10	Ve	b	5	Occ. deposits in SW, below 1289
5301	H20d	C10	Ve	b	4	Ashy deposit, below 5300
5302	H20d	C10	Ve	c	9	Mixed fill, below 1289
5303	H20d	C10	Ve	b	7	P97/27, below 5302
5304	H20d	C10	Ve	c	4	NE sounding, fill, below 5302 (//5313)
5305	H20d	C10	Ve	c	7	P97/34
5306	H20d	C10	Ve	c	4	NE sounding, fill, below 5304 (//5313, 5318)
5307	H20d	C10	Ve/f	d	4	NE sounding, fill, below 5306 (//5319)
5308	H20d		Vf4	a	3	W232
5309	H20d	C10	IVa/Ve	d	7	P97/38
5310	H20d	C10	Vf4	a	5	Rm 52, fill, below 5307
5311	H20d	C10	Ve	a	6	FI97/7, secondary fill
5312	H20d	C10	Ve	a	3	FI97/7
5313	H20d	C10	Ve	a	4	Fill, below 5302 (//5304, 5306)
5314	H20d	C10	Vf4	a	5	Rm 52, plastered floor, below 5310
5315	H20d	C10	IVa/Ve	a	7	P97/45
5316	H20d	C10	IVa/Ve	a	7	P97/46
5317	H20d	C10	IVa/Ve	b	7	P97/47
5318	H20c	C10	Ve	d	4	Fill, below 5313 (//5306)
5319	H20d	C10	Ve/f	d	4	Fill, below 5318 (//5307)
5320	H20d	C10	Vf4	a	3	W240, below 5313
5321	H20d	C10	Ve	a	7	P97/54
5322	H20d		IVa/Ve	b	7	P97/58
5323	H20d	C10	Vf	a	4	Rm 53, fill, below 5319
5324	H20d	C10	Vf	b	7	P97/63
5325	H20d	C10	Ve	b	7	P97/64
5326	H20d	C10	Vf4	a	3	W238, below 5319
5327	H20d	C10	Vf4	b	4	Rm 53, fill, below 5319
5328	H20d	C10	Vf4	a	8	Rm 53, filling of cut for W238
5329	H20d	C10	Ve	a	-	Cut for FI97/7
5330	H20d	C10	Vf4	a	-	Cut for W238
5331	H20d	C10	Vf4	b	4	Fill, below 5327
5332	H20d	C10	Vf4	b	4	Fill, below 5331
5333	H20d	C10	Ve	a	7	P97/82, below FI97/7

List of Excavation Units

Unit	Square	Chapter	Level	Purity	Context	Description
5334	H20d	C10	Vf4	d	4	Rm 53, fill, below 5332
5335	H20d	C10	Vf4	a	5	Rm 51, occ. layers, below 5331
5336	H20d	C10	Vf4	a	5	Rm 51, plastered floor, below 5335
5337	H20d	C10	Vf3	a	3	Stone lining of P98/17, W side (//5349)
5338	H20d	C10	Vf	d	4	Rm 53, fill, below 5334
5339	H20d	C10	Vf	a	3	Rm 54, brick along W face W238
5340	H20d	C10	Vf4	a	7	P97/88, below 5338
5341	H20d	C10	Vf4	-	-	Cut for W238
5342	H20d	C10	Vf?	b	4	Rm 50, fill, below 5331
5343	H20d		-	d	9	Section straightening
5344	H20d	C10	Vf?	d	9	Mixed deposits, below 5338, 5342, etc.
5345	H20d		0	d	9	P97/82 modern backfill
5346	H20d	C10	Ve	c	7	Removal of H20/838 from P97/22 (//1299)
5347	H20d	C10	Vf4	a	3	W239 removal
5348	H20d		Vf4	a	3	W240 removal
5349	H20d	C10	Vf3	b	3	P98/17, removal of stone lining on W (//5337)
5350	H20d	C10	Vf3	c	4	Rm 52, packing, below 5314
5351	H20d	C10	Vf	d	7	P97/88, removal of stone lining
5352	H20d	C10	Vf	c	4	Rm 53, packing in SE, below 5344
5353	H20d	C10	Vf	c	4	Rm 54, packing, below 5344
5354	H20d	C10	Vf3	c	4	Rm 50, packing, below 5344
5355	H20d		Vf3	a	3	W243 removal
5356	H20d	C10	Vf3	a	3	W244 removal
5357	H20d	C10	Vf3	d	8	Rm 50, deposit on floor
5358	H20d		Vf4	a	3	W232
5359	H20d	C10	Vf3/4	a	4	Packing in NE corner, below 5347, 5357 and W232
5360	H20d	C10	Vf3	b	4	Packing, below 5359
5361	H20d	C10	Vf3?	c	9	Mixed deposits in SE corner, below 5352
5362	H20d	C10	Vf3?	a	7	P98/17 lower fill, below 5361
5363	H20d	C10	Vf2/3	b	5	Packing in SW corner, below 5354
5364	H20d	C10	Vf	c	7	P98/21
5365	H20d	C10	Vf	c	4	Clay packing over stones of P98/17 N lining
5366	H20d	C10	Vf3?	a	4	Packing in NE corner, below 5360
5367	H20d	C10	Vf	b	4	Clay packing over stones of P98/17 W lining
5368	H20d	C10	Vf	b	4	Packing in NW corner, below 5357 and W232
5369	H20d	C10	Vf1	b	4	Packing E of W246, below 5363
5370	H20d	C10	Vf2?	b	4	Packing in NE, below 5366
5371	H20d	C10	Vf?	d	9	Mixed deposits between P98/17 and P97/88
5372	H20d	C10	Vf	a	4	Packing in SW corner, below 5363
5373	H20d	C10	Vf2	a	3	Mud-brick feature in Rm 52
5374	H20d	C10	Vg	a	4	Rm 62, SE corner, destr. debris
5375	H20d	C10	Vf?	d	7	P98/24, cut by P97/82, P97/88
5376	H20d	C10	Vf1	c	4	Robbed cut for W247 within W246/249
5377	H20d	C10	Vf?	d	7	P98/34, cut by P97/82, P98/24
5378	H20d	C10	Vf1	c	4	Robbed cut for W247, E of W246/249
5379	H20d	C10	Vg	b	8	Rubble filled cut in E face of W246
5380	H20d	C10	Vg	a	4	Rm 63, destr. debris
5381	H20d	C10	Vf	d	9	Section straightening in SE corner
5382	H20d	C10	Vg	a	4	Rm 63, SE corner, destr. debris
5383	H20d	C10	Vg	b	4	Rm 63, N end, packing, below 5368
5384	H20d	C10	Vg	a	4	Rm 64 rubble fill, below 5370 (//6304)
5385	H20d	C10	Vg?	c	4	Rm 66, mixed fill, below 5368
5386	H20d	C10	Vf2	a	7	Plastered post-hole E of W245
5387	H20d	C10	Vg	b	4	Rm 62, destr. debris
5388	H20d	C10	Vg	a	4	Rm 63, destr. debris, below 5380
5389	H20d	C10	Vg	a	5	Rm 64, plastered floor surface, below 5384
5390	H20d	C10	Vf?	b	4	Packing under P98/24
5391	H20d	C10	Vg	a	5	Rm 62, plastered floor surface
5392	H20d	C10	Vf1-2	c	7	P98/58 sealed by W242
5393	H20d	C10	Vg	a	5	Rm 63, W side, plastered floor, below 5388

675

Appendix 2

Unit	Square	Chapter	Level	Purity	Context	Description
5394	H20d	C10	Vf	b	7	P98/61
5395	H20d		Vf1	a	3	W247 removal
5396	H20d		Vf1	a	3	W248 removal
5397	H20d	C10	Vf/g	c	4	Rm 64, mixed packing
5398	H20d	C10	Vg	a	3	Rm 66, bricky debris from W249
5399	H20d	C10	Vh1–2	a	5	Rm 73, occ. deposit, below 5384
5400	H20c	C10	Vi	a	8	Fill of 5401
5401	H20c	C10	Vi	a	-	W half, post hole cutting 1899
5402	H20c	C10	Vi	a	4	W half, packing, below 1899
5403	H20c	C10	Vi	a	4	W half, occ. surface, below 5402
5404	H20c	C10	Vi	a	3	FI97/5
5405	H20c	C10	Vh/i	a	4	Cleaning down to W233-5
5406	H20c	C10	Vj	a	4	W half, destr. debris
5407	H20c	C10	Vj	a	8	Grave overlying W225, below 5406
5408	H20c		Vj	a	7	Fill of grave 5407
5409	H20c		Vj	a	3	W236
5410	H20c		Vj	a	3	W237
5411	H20c	C10	Vj	a	5	Rm 82, plastered floor, below 5406
5412	H20c	C10	Vj	a	4	W half, destr. debris N of W225 (//5417)
5413	H20c		Vj	a	3	W half, W225
5414	H20c		Vj	a	-	Post-hole into W225
5415	H20c		Vj	a	8	Fill of 5414, below 5408
5416	H20c	C10	Vj	a	4	W half, Rm 84, destr. debris
5417	H20c	C10	Vj	a	4	W half, destr. debris N of W225 (//5412)
5418	H20c		Vj	a	8	Fill of 5419, below 5408
5419	H20c		Vj	a	-	Post-hole into W225
5420	H20c		Vj	a	8	Fill of 5421, below 5417
5421	H20c		Vj	a	-	Post-hole into W225
5422	H20c	C10	Vj	a	8	Fill of 5423, below W236?
5423	H20c	C10	Vj	a	-	Post-hole into 5427
5424	H20c	C10	Vj	a	5	Rms 81-2, burnt occ. surface, below 5412, 5417
5425	H20c		Vj	a	5	Rm 84 (W half), burnt occ. surface, below 5427 (//1870)
5426	H20c		Vj	a	-	Cut for W236
5427	H20c	C10	Vj/k	a	4	W half, packing, below 5424-5 & W225 (//1879)
5428	H20c	C10	Vk	a	4	W half, packing, below 5427 (//1883)
5429	H20c	C10	Vk	a	4	W half, construction surface, below 5428 (//1891)
5430	H20c		Vk	a	3	W241
5431	H20c	C10	Vl	a	1	W half, natural conglomerate (//1893)
5500	I19b	C13.1	IIa	a	5	W ctyd, occ. surface E of W823, below 2897
5501	I19b	C9, C13.1	IIa	b	7	P97/69, fill of NW part
5502	I19b	C13.1	IIa	b	4	W ctyd, packing, below 2884, 2897 (//2894, 5517)
5503	I19b		IIb	a	3	W823 removal (//2896)
5504	I19b	C13.1	IIa/b	a	5	Occ. deposit, below 5502 (//5526)
5505	I19b	C12	IIIe	a	5	Rm 30, packing, below 5504
5506	I19b	C12	IIIe	a	4	E ctyd, packing
5507	I19b	C12	IIIe	a	5	Rm 31, packing, below 5504
5508	I19a	C13.1	IIa/b	b	4	Packing assoc. with W828-9
5509	I19b	C12	IIIe	a	4	Rm 30, packing layer, below 5505
5510	I19b	C12	IIIe	a	4	Rm 31, packing layer, below 5507
5511	I19a	C13.1	IIa/b	c	5	Surface assoc. with W828–9, below 5508 (//5530?)
5512	I19a		IIa–b	a	3	W828 removal
5513	I19a		IIa/b	b	3	W829 removal
5514	I19a	C13.1	IIa	b	4	Mixed deposits, below W828 and 5511 (//5531)
5515	I19a	C13.1	IIa	b	5	Occ. deposit, below 5514
5516	I19a	C12, C13.1	IIa	c	7	P97/70, fill of N side (//5523, 5538)
5517	I19a	C13.1	IIa	a	4	W ctyd, packing, below 5515 (//5502)
5518	I19a	C13.1	IIa/IIIe	a	5	Packing layer, below 5517
5519	I19b/a	C12	IIIe	a	4	Rm 30, packing, below 5509
5520	I19b/a	C12	IIIe	a	4	Rm 30, packing, below 5519
5521	I19b/a	C12	IIIe	a	5	Rm 30, occ. surface, below 5520 (//4028)
5522	I19b/I20d		IIIe	c	3	W113b removal of mud brick
5523	I19a	C13.1	IIa/b	b	7	P97/70 fill (//5516, 5538)
5524	I19b		IIIe	b	3	W113b, removal of stone foundation
5525	I19b		IIIe	b		Rm 30, mixed deposits in SE corner

676

List of Excavation Units

Unit	Square	Chapter	Level	Purity	Context	Description
5526	I19a		II/III	a?	5	Occ. deposit round P97/70 (//5504)
5527	I19a/b	C12	IIIe	a	5	Rm 30, occ. surface, below 5521
5528	I19a/b	C12	IIId	a	4	Rm 30, packing, below 5527
5529	I19a	C13.1	IIa/b	c	9	Mixed deposits in SW of quadrant
5530	I19a	C13.1	IIa/b	b	5	Occ. surface N of W829 (//5511?)
5531	I19a	C13.1	IIa/b	a	4	Packing N of W829 foundation (//5514, 5535)
5532	I19a	C13.1	IIa/b	a	4	Packing S of W829
5533	I19a	C13.1	IIa	a	4	Packing layer, below 5531, 5535
5534	I19a		IIa	a	3	W829 removal
5535	I19a	C13.1	IIa	a	4	Packing S of W829 foundation (//5531)
5536	I19a	C12	IIId/e	a	4	Rm 32, packing, below 5533
5537	I19a	C12, C13.1	IIb	b	7	P98/18, N side
5538	I19a	C12, C13.1	IIa	b	7	P97/70 fill on W side (//5516, 5523)
5539	I19a	C12	IIId/e	a	4	Rm 32, packing, below 5536
5540	I19a	C12	IIId/e	a	4	Rm 32, packing on S side of quadrant
5541	I19a	C12	IIId/e	a	5	Rm 32, occ. surface, below 5540
5542	I19c	C13.4	IIf?	c	6	FI98/4 loose fill
5600	L16a	C16	0	d	9	Topsoil
5601	L16a	C16	1	c	4	Rubble fill, below 5600
5602	L16a	C16	1	c	9	W512 cleaning
5603	L16a	C16	0	d	9	Topsoil
5604	L16a	C16	1	c	4	Rubble fill, below 5603
5620	L16a	C16	0	c	9	Topsoil
5621	L16a	C16	0	a	4	Sub-topsoil
5622	L16a	C16	1	a	4	Material below 5621
5623	L16a	C16	1	a	4	Rubble fill in robber trench over wall W522 (//5625)
5624	L16a	C16	1	a	4	Material between 5622 and 5623
5625	L16a	C16	1	a	4	Rubble fill in robber trench (//5623)
5626	L16a	C16	1	a	6	Grave fill in P98/38
5627	L16a	C16	0	a	9	Topsoil
5628	L16a	C16	1	b	4	Rubble fill of robber trench over W522
5629	L16a	C16	1	a	4	Deposit below 5623, 5624
5630	L16a	C16	1	a	4	Reddish fill incl. many ceramics
5631	L16a	C16	1	a	4	Fill below 5629, above 5632
5632	L16a	C16	1	a	4	Surface E of W522
5633	L16a	C16	1	a	5	Plaster surface lying partly over and between walls W512 and W522
5634	L16a	C16	1	a	4	Fill between walls W512 and W522, below plaster
5635	L16a	C16	1	a	4	Fill beneath 5632, cut by 5636
5636	L16a	C16	1	b	4	Fill cutting 5635
5637	L16a	C16	1	a	4	Fill beneath 5630
5638	L16a	C16	1	a	4	Fill beneath 5634
5639	L16a	C16	1	a	4	Fill beneath 5638, more stones
5700	J20c	C12	IIIe	a	5	E ctyd, burnt occ. deposits, below 1399 (//1388)
5701	J20c	C12	IIIe	a	4	E ctyd, packing, below 5700 (//1389)
5702	J20c	C12, C13.1	IIa/IIIe	b	4	W ctyd, packing N of 5701 (//1392)
5703	J20	C12	IIId	a	4	Burnt debris overlying FI97/10
5704	J20	C12	IIId	b	8	Loose stones overlying FI97/10
5705	J20	C12	IIId	a	6	FI97/10
5800	J18a	C13.4	IIf1	a	3	Wall of mudbrick feature against W424
5801	J18a	C13.4	IIf	a	7	P97/84, lower part of P97/61
5802	J18a	C13.2	IId	a	4	Rm d10, destr. debris against E face W429
5803	J18a	C13.4	IIf	a	7	P97/84
5804	J19c	C13.2	IId/e?	d	9	Rm d8, removal of baulk under W764
5805	J18a	C13.2	IId	a	5	Rm d10, occ. surface, below 5802
5806	J18a		IId	a	3	W429
5807	J19c	C13.2	IId	a	4	Rm d8, destr. fill, below 5804
5808	J18a	C13.2	IId/e	a	7	P97/85
5809	J18a	C13.1	IIc/d	a	4	Rm 7, packing under floor, below 5805
5810	J18a	C13.2	IId/e	c	7	P97/85 fill, below 2399?
5811	J18a	C13.1	IIc/d	c	9	Packing W of W424, below 2393
5812	J18a	C13.1	IId/e	a	7	P97/85, fill, below 5810 (N part)
5813	J18a	C13.1	IId/e	b	7	P97/85, fill, below 5810 (S part)
5814	J18a	C13.1	IIc/d	c	7	Mixed pit fills in NE corner, below 5809, 5811
5815	J18a	C13.1	IIc	b	4	Rm 7, destr. debris, below 5809

677

Appendix 2

Unit	Square	Chapter	Level	Purity	Context	Description
5816	J18a	C13.1	IIc	a	4	Rm 7, destr. debris, below 5815
5817	J19c	C13.1	IIc	b	4	Rm 8, destr. debris
5818	J18a	C13.1	IId/e	b	7	P97/85, fill S of 5813
5819	J18a	C13.1	IIc/d	c	4	Packing deposit, below 5818
5820	J18a	C13.1	IId/e	c	7	P97/85 lower fill, below 5812, 5813
5821	J18a	C13.4	IIf	a	8	Post-hole cut into 2386, below 2385
5822	J18a/b	C13.4	-	d	9	Cleaning at start of season
5823	J18b	C13.4	IIf	b	4	Packing S of W421, below 2339
5824	J18b	C13.4	IIf	b	5	Stony surface S of W421, below 5823
5825	J18b	C13.4	IIf	b	4	Packing, below 5824
5826	J18b	C13.4	IIf	b	4	Packing to W of 5825
5827	J18b	C13.3	IIe?	b	7	P98/1
5828	J18b	C13.3	IIe?	b	7	P98/2
5829	J18b	C13.4	II1/2	b	4	Packing, below 5826
5830	J18b		I	a	3	W421 removal (//4334)
5831	J18b	C13.3	IIe?	c	7	P98/3
5832	J18b	C13.4	-	c	9	Baulk with J19d removal
5833	J18b	C13.4	IIf1/2	c	4	Packing under W421, below 2373
5834	J18b	C13.4	IIf1	b	7	P98/5, below 2373
5835	J18b	C13.4	IIf1	b	7	P98/4, below 5833
5836	J18b	C13.4	IIf1	c	7	P95/6, below 5829
5837	J18b		IIf1?	b	4	S side packing, below 5829
5838	J18b	C13.4	IIf1	a	4	Packing N of 5837, below 5833
5839	J18b		IIf1	c	4/7	SE corner, packing, below 5837 (possibly top 5843)
5840	J18b	C13.4	IIf1	b	4	S side, stony packing, below 5829
5841	J18b	C13.4	IIf1	b	4	NE corner packing, below 5833
5842	J18b	C13.4	IIf1	b	4	N side packing, below 5833
5843	J18b	C13.3	IIe/f1	b	7	P98/8, below 5839
5844	J18b	C13.4	IIe/f1	b	7	P98/9, below 5838, 5841
5845	J18b	C13.4	IIe/f1	b	7	P98/10, below 5838, 5841–2
5846	J18b	C13.4	IIf1	b	7	P98/11, below 5839
5847	J18b	C13.3	IIe/f1	b	7	P98/12, below 5837
5848	J18b	C13.4	IIf	c	9	SW side, mixed deposit
5849	J18b	C13.4	IIe	b	4	NW corner packing, below 1997
5850	J18b	C13.3	IIe?	b	7	P98/19, cut by P98/5 and P98/12
5851	J18b	C13.3	IIe?	a	7	P98/20, below 5848
5852	J18b	C13.3	IIe?	b	7	P98/22, below 5848
5853	J18b	C13.4	IIe	b	4	NE corner, packing, below 5841–2
5854	J18b	C13.3	IIe	b	4	SE corner, Rm e5 packing layer, below 5837–8
5855	J18b	C13.3	IIe	b	4	Rm e5, burnt debris, below 5848
5856	J18b	-	-	-	-	Unassigned
5857	J18b	C13.2, C13.3	IIe?	b	4	S side, Rm e5 burnt debris, below 5839, 5840
5858	J18b	C13.3	IIe	b	4	Rm e5, packing E of W434
5859	J18b	C13.4	IIe?	c	4	S side, packing, below 5857
5860	J18b	C13.3	IIe?	c	7	P98/29, below 5859
5861	J18b	C13.3	IIe	b	4	E side, Rm e5 packing
5862	J18b	C13.2	IId	b	5	Rm d10, destr. debris, below 5849
5863	J18b	C13.3	IIe?	b	7	P98/32, below 5861
5864	J18b	C13.2	IId	a	5	Rm d10, occ. surface, below 5862
5865	J18b	C13.3	IIe	a	7	P98/33, below 5862
5866	J18b	C13.2	IId/e	c	5	Debris N of W433, below 5849
5867	J18b	C13.4	IIe?	b	3	S side, steps
5868	J18b	C13.2	IId/e	a	5	W side, occ. deposit, below 5857
5869	J18b	C13.3	IIe	b	5	SW corner, Rm e5 surface, below 5867
5870	J18a	C13.1	IIc	a	8	Rm 7, cache, below floor plaster
5871	J18b	C13.2	IId	b	8	Rm d10, post-hole, below 5868
5872	J18b	C13.3	IIe?	b	7	P98/40, below 5858
5873	J18b	C13.2	IId	a	5	Rm d10, occ. surface, below 5864, 5868
5874	J18b	C13.2	IId?	a	7	P98/41, below 5868
5875	J18b	C13.3	IIe	b	3	Rm e6, bench against E face of W434
5876	J18b	C13.2	IId	a	8	Rm d10, post-hole, below 5862
5877	J18b	C13.2	IId	b	5	Rm d10, occ. deposits, below 5861
5878	J18b	C13.3	IIe	a	3	W434 removal
5879	J18b	C13.2	IId	b	4	Rm d10, packing, below 5862 (//5881)
5880	J18b	C13.2	IId	c	9	Rm d9, mixed deposit N of W433
5881	J18b	C13.2	IId	b	4	Rm d10, E half, packing, below 5877 (//5879)
5882	J18b	C13.2	IId	a	3	W433 removal
5883	J18b	C13.3	IId/e?	c	9	Rm e5, packing W of W434, below 5861

678

List of Excavation Units

Unit	Square	Chapter	Level	Purity	Context	Description
5884	J18b	C13.3	IIe?	c	9	Rm e6, SE corner, cut into W435
5885	J18b		IIe	b	3	W435
5886	J18b	C13.1	IIc?	c	9	Mixed deposits E of W436, below W434
5887	J18b	C13.1	IIc	b	4	Rm 7, destr. debris, below 5879
5888	J18a/b	C13.2	IId	c	7	P98/46, below 5879
5889	J18b	C13.1	IIc/d	b	4	Rm 7, packing, below 5881
5890	J18b	C13.2	IId/e	b	4	Rm 6, packing E of W436
5891	J18b	C13.1	IIc	c	4	Rm 7, E side, destr. fill, below 5889
5892	J18b	C13.1	IIc	b	4	Rm 6, destr. fill, below 5890
5893	J18b/K18a	C13.1	IIc	b	7	P98/52, below 4387, 5890
5894	J18b	C13.1	IIc/d	c	4	Packing above IIc walls, below 5879
5895	J18b/J19d	C13.1	IIc	a	5	Rm 7, plastered floor, below 5891
5896	J18b	C13.1	IIc	a	5	Rm 7, SE sounding, earlier plastered floor, below 5895
5897	J18b	C13.1	IIc	a	4	Rm 7, SE sounding, packing, below 5896
5898	J18b	C13.1	IIb/c	b	4	Rm 7, SE sounding, packing, below 5897
5899	J18b	C13.1	IIb/c	b	5	Occ. surface S of W437, below 5894
5900	L19c		0	d	9	Topsoil
5901	L19a		0	d	9	Topsoil along S side of quadrant
5902	L19c		0	d	9	Topsoil, below 5900
5903	L19c		I	b	9	Fill N of W950, below 5902
5904	L19c		I	d	9	Fill N of W950, W of W951
5905	L19c		I	a	4	Fill S of W950
5906	L19a	C17	0	d	9	Topsoil N of 5901
5907	L19c		I	a	3	W950 removal
5908	L19a/c		I	a	3	W951 removal
5909	L19c		I	a	3	W952
5910	L19a/c		I	a	3	W953
5911	L19a	C17	0	b	9	Topsoil, below 5906
5912	L19a		0	c	9	Topsoil on NE side, below 5906 (//5913)
5913	L19a		0	c	9	Topsoil on SE side, below 5906 (//5912)
5914	L19a		I/II	c	4	Fill NE of W953, W954
5915	L19a	C17	I	a	6	FI98/1 fill
5916	L19a		I	a	3	FI98/1 removal
5917	L19a		0	c	9	W954 robber cut at E end
5918	L19a		I/II	c	4	Fill NE of W953 and W954, below 5914
5919	L19a		I/II	b	4	Loose rubble area within 5918, below W955
5920	L19c		0	c	9	Topsoil above W952 and W953
5921	L19a/c	C17	I/II	c	4	Packing between W952–4
5922	L19a/c		I/II	c	4	Packing W of W953
5923	L19c		I	c	4	Packing S of W952
5924	L19a/c		II?	a	5	Packing above occ. surface, below 5921 (//5927)
5925	L19c		I	d	9	Fill above W956 (//5920)
5926	L19a/c		II?	c	5	Occ. surface W of W953, below 5922
5927	L19a/c		II?	a	5	Packing above occ. surface, below 5921 (//5924)
5928	L19c		I/II	c	4	Packing S of W952, below 5923
5929	L19a/c	C17	I	c	4	Fill of trenches for W952–4
5930	L19c		I/II	c	4	Packing S of W952, below 5928
5931	L19c		I	a	3	W956 removal
5932	L19c		I/II	c	4	Fill S of W952, below 5930 (//5939)
5933	L19a/c	C8, C17	I	b	3	FI98/2 removal
5934	L19a		I/II	b	7	P98/31
5935	L19c		II?	a	5	Occ. surface S of W952, below 5932
5936	L19c		I	a	3	W957 removal
5937	L19c		I	c	4	Packing W of W957
5938	L19c		I	b	5	Occ. surface, below 5937
5939	L19c		I/II	a	4	Packing, below 5938 (//5932)
5940	L19c		I	c	4	Wall trench for S side of W952
5941	L19a/c		II	c	4	Fill N of W952, below 5924
5942	L19c		II	b	4	Packing S of W952, below 5935, 5939
5943	L19a		I/II	c	7	P98/43
5944	L19a/c		I	a	3	W952-954 removal
5945	L19a/c		I	d	9	Mixed deposits W of W953, below 5926
5946	L19a/c	C13.4	IIf	a	7	P98/44
5947	L19a/c	C13.4	IIf	b	7	P98/44, upper fill on W
5948	L19a		I/II	d	9	Mixed deposits N of W954
5949	L19c	C13.4	IIf	b	7	P98/47, below 5942
5950	L19c	C13.4	IIf	a	7	P98/48, below 5942
5951	L19c	C13.4	IIf	b	4	Packing, below 5940

679

Appendix 2

Unit	Square	Chapter	Level	Purity	Context	Description
5952	L19a/c	C13.3	IIe/f	d	9	Mixed deposits W of P98/44
5953	L19a	C13.3	IIe/f	a	7	P98/50, cut by P98/44
5954	L19a/c	C13.3	IIe/f	b	7	P98/51, cut by P98/44
5955	L19c	C13.4	IIf	b	9	Mixed deposits in SW
5956	L19a/c	C9	II	b	7	P98/35
5957	L19a/c		I/II	d	9	Mixed deposits, below W952
5958	L19a/c	C13.2	IId	a	5	Burnt occ. surface, below 5959
5959	L19a/c	C13.2	IId/e	a	4	Packing above 5958
5960	L19c	C13.4	IIf	a	7	P98/53
5961	L19c	C13.4	IIf	a	7	P98/56, cut by P98/44
5962	L19a/c	C13.4	IIf	a	7	P98/57, cut by P98/51
5963	L19a/c	C13.4	IIf	a	7	P98/59, cut by P98/51
5964	L19c	C13.4	IIf	b	7	P98/60, cut by P98/57
5965	L19a/c	C13.3	IIe/f	b	7	P98/62, below 5952
5966	L19c	C13.2	IId/e	a	4	Packing above 5958 in SW
5967	L19c		I/II	a	7	P98/49, fill of E part
5968	L19a/c	C13.2	IId	a	4	Packing, below 5958
5969	L19a/c	C13.2	IId	a	5	Ashy surface, below 5968
5970	L19c	C9, C13.3	IIe/f	a	7	P98/66
5971	L19c	C13.2	IId/e	a	7	P98/67
5972	L19a	C13.3	IIe/f	d	9	Mixed deposits above 5969 in N
5973	L19a/c	C13.1	IIc/d	a	4	Packing, below 5969
5974	L19a/c	C13.3	IIe/f	a	7	P98/71, cut by P98/44
5975	L19c	C13.1	IIc	a	4	Rm 22, destr. debris
5976	L19a/c	C13.1	IIc	b	4	Rm 21, destr. debris
5977	L19a	C13.1	IIb/c	a	4	Packing N of Rm 21
5978	L19c	C13.1	IIc	a	7	P98/85, below 5975
5979	L19c	C13.1	IIc	a	5	Rm 22, occ. surface
5980	L19a/c	C13.1	IIc	a	5	Rm 21, occ. surface
5981	L19c	C13.1	IIc	a	8	Rm 22, storage vessel in NE corner within 5975
5982	L19c	C13.1	IIc	c	4	Rms 21–2, brick debris against W958
6000	K18d		0	c	9	Topsoil
6001	K18d		0	c	9	2nd spit of topsoil
6002	K18d		0	b	9	Fill beneath topsoil (//9614)
6003	K18d		I	a	4	Fill beneath topsoil (//9615)
6004	K18d		I	a	4	Hard deposit, below 6003, above 6007 (//9615)
6005	K18d		I	a	7	Ashy deposit in depression in 6007
6006	K18d		I	a	7	P98/7, fill
6007	K18d		I	b	4	Hard deposit, below 6004 (//6009, 6015)
6008	K18d		I	a	4	Soft powdery deposit, below 6007, above 6011
6009	K18d		I	a	4	2nd spit of 6007 (//6015)
6010	K18d		I	a	7	P98/23, fill
6011	K18d	C16	I	a	5	Mortar surface
6012	K18d		I	a	-	P98/23, cut
6013	K18d		I	a	-	P98/7, cut
6014	K18d		I	a	4	Cobbles, rubble and loose soil, south of Wall W430
6015	K18d		I	a	4	Deposit below 6014, abutting wall W430 (//6007/9)
6100	K18b		I	a	3	W706
6101	K18b	C17	I	b	5	Surface and packing material E of W430, below 4395
6102	K18b		I	b	3	W430 (//4394)
6103	K18b		I?	b	7	P98/49
6104	K18b		I	b	4	Packing material under W706 (//4320, 4398)
6105	K18b		I	b	4	Packing material under W430 (//4320, 4398)
6106	K18b		IIf?	c	9	NW corner, mixed deposits, below 4398
6107	K18b		IIf?	c	9	SW corner, mixed deposits, below 4398
6108	K18b	C13.4	IIf?	c	7	P98/64, cut by P98/65
6109	K18b	C13.4	IIf?	b	7	P98/65
6110	K18b	C13.4	IIf	b	4	Wall trench for W438 foundation
6111	K18b	C13.4	IIf	b	4	Packing material on W, below 6106
6112	K18b	C13.4	IIf	b	4	Packing material N of P98/65
6113	K18b	C13.4	IIf	b	5	NW corner, ashy occ. deposit, below 6106
6114	K18b	C13.4	IIf?	c	7	Mixed pit fills
6115	K18b	C13.4	IIf?	c	9	S half, mixed deposits, below 6107
6116	K18b	C13.4	IIf	b	4	Surface and packing material in NW, below 6113
6117	K18b	C13.4	IIf?	c	4	Packing material N of W438
6118	K18b	C13.4	IIf?	b	7	P96/68
6119	K18b	C13.4	IIe/f	c	7	P98/69, cut by P98/70
6120	K18b	C13.4	IIf?	c	9	S of W438, mixed deposits
6121	K18b	C13.4	IIf?	b	7	P98/70, sealed by W438
6122	K18a	C9, C13.1	IIc	b	7	P98/72, upper fill
6123	K18b	C13.4	IIf	b	3	W438 removal
6124	K18b	C13.4	IIf	b	7	P98/75
6125	K18a	C13.1	IIc	b	7	P98/72 fill, below 6122

List of Excavation Units

Unit	Square	Chapter	Level	Purity	Context	Description
6126	K18a	C13.1	IIc	a	7	P98/72, sieved portion of 6125
6127	K18b	C13.3	IIe	c	4	Mixed packing material N of Rm e7, below 6111 and 6116 (//6128)
6128	K18b	C13.3	IIe	b	4	Packing material along N face W439 (//6127)
6129	K18b	C13.3	IIe	c	4	Packing material, below 6127
6130	K18b		IIe	a	3	W440 removal
6131	K18b	C13.2	IId	c	9	Rm d11, mixed deposit, below 6129–30
6132	K18b	C13.2	IId	a	5	Rm d11, burnt occ. deposit, below 6131
6133	K18b	C13.2	IId	b	4	Rm d11, packing, below 6131
6134	K18b		IIe	b	3	W441 removal
6135	K18b	C13.2	IId	a	5	Rm d11, occ. surface N of W639
6136	K18b	C13.4	IIf	c	4	SE corner packing layers, below 6107
6137	K18b	C13.4	IIf	b	4	Packing along S side, below 6107
6138	K18b	C13.4	IIe/f?	c	4	Mixed packing S of W439
6139	K18a	C13.1	IIc	a	7	P98/72 lower fill, below 6125
6140	K18b	C13.4	IIe?	c	9	Mixed deposit S of W439, below 6138
6141	K18a	C13.1	IIc	a	7	P98/72, carbonized seed sample in 6139
6142	K18b	C13.2	IId/e?	b	7	P98/86, below 6140
6143	K18b	C13.1	IIc	c	4	Rm 24, destr. debris, below 6132, 6135
6144	K18b		IIe	a	3	W439 removal
6145	K18a	C13.1	IIc	a	7	P98/72, fill against W side
6146	K18b	C13.1	IIc	b	4	Rm 24, destr. debris below 6135 (//6153, 6156)
6147	K18b	C13.2	IId	b	9	Mixed deposits S of 6146
6148	K18b	C13.2	IId/e?	b	7	P98/88
6149	K18b		IId/e?	c	9	Loose fill in cut into W442
6150	K18b	C13.2	IId	b	5	Rm d11, occ. surface E of W442, below 6147
6151	K18b	C13.2	IId	a	8	Post-holes or pits in 6150 surface, below 6147
6152	K18b		IId	a	3	W442 removal
6153	K18b	C13.1	IIc	b	4	Rm 24, destr. debris below P98/86 (//6146, 6156)
6154	K18b	C13.2	IId	a	8	Post-hole in 6156, below 6150
6155	K18b	C13.2	IId	b	8	Shallow cut in 6156, below 6150
6156	K18b	C13.1, C13.2	IIc/d	b	4	Rm 24, destr. debris S of 6146 (//6146, 6153)
6157	K18b		IId	b	3	W443 removal
6158	K18b	C13.1	IIc?	b	7	P98/89, below 6156
6159	K18b	C13.1	IIc	b	4	Rm 24, destr. debris, below 6156
6160	K18b	C13.1	IIc	b	4	Rm 24, destr. debris, below 6153, 6159
6161	K18b	C13.1	IIc	b	3	W444 collapsed masonry
6162	K18b	C13.1	IIc	b	7	P98/94, sealed by 6160
6163	K18a	C13.1	IIc	a	8	Rm 6, post-hole in floor surface, below 4387
6164	K18a	C13.1	IIc	a	8	Rm 6, shallow cut into floor surface, below 4387
6200	K19b	C13.1	IIc/d	a	4	Rm 23, packing, below 4587
6201	K19b	C13.1	IIc/d	b	5	Rm 23, occ. layer, below 6200
6202	K19b	C13.1	IIc/d	a	7	P98/76, sealed by W770
6203	K19b	C13.1	IIb/c	a	4	Rm 23, packing, below 6201 (//6205, 6207)
6204	K19b		I/II	d	9	Rm 23, removal of access steps
6205	K19b	C13.1	IIb/c	a	4	Rm 23, packing, below 6203 (//6203, 6207)
6206	K19b	C13.1	IIb/c	b	7	P98/92, feature within 6205
6207	K19b	C13.1	IIb/c	a	4	Rm 23, packing, below 6205 (6203, 6205)
6208	K19b		IIb/c	a	3	W627
6209	K19a/b	C13.1	IIc	a	3	Rm 3, diagonal brick feature
6210	K19d	C13.1	IIc	a	3	W628, vitrified masonry
6211	K19a		IIc	a	8	Rm 4, carbonized log within brickwork of W797
6212	K19a		IIc	a	8	Rm 2, carbonized timber within W796
6300	H20d	C10	Vf3	c	7	P98/81, below 5361
6301	H20d		Vf/g	b	-	Cut or pit in W side P97/82
6302	H20d		V?	b	7	Fill of 6301
6303	H20d	C10	Vg	b	6	Rm 63, FI98/5
6304	H20d	C10	Vg	a	6	Rm 64, destr. debris under 5397 (//5384)
6305	H20d	C10	Vg	a	3	W246 removal
6306	H20d	C10	Vg/h	b	4	Rm 66, rubble fill under W247
6307	H20d	C10	Vh1–2	a	5	Rm 73, occ. surface, below 5399

Appendix 2

Unit	Square	Chapter	Level	Purity	Context	Description
6308	H20d	C10	Vh	b	4	Rm 72, fill, below 5393
6309	H20d	C10	Vh1	a	5	Rm 72, pebble layer, below 6308
6310	H20d	C10	Vh	a	4	Packing above W253
6311	H20d		Vg	c	4	Foundation cut and packing for W250
6312	H20d	C10	Vh	a	4	Mixed deposit at base of P98/17
6313	H20d	C10	Vh1	a	5	Rm 72, plaster floor
6314	H20d	C10	Vg/h	b	4	Rm 64, packing, below 5389
6315	H20d	C10	Vg	a	3	W249 removal
6316	H20d	C10	Vg	a	3	W250 removal
6317	H20d	C10	Vh?	a	4	Packing, below W249
6318	H20d	C10	Vh1–2	b	3	Rm 73, mudbrick block on 6307
6319	H20d	C10	Vh3	a	5	Rm 71, surface, below 6306
6320	H20d	C10	Vh/i	b	4	Rm 73, packing, below 6307
6321	H20d	C10	Vh/i	a	4	Rm 73, burnt material, below 6320
6322	H20d	C10	Vg?	c	4	Foundation cut through Rm 71 and W254
6323	H20d	C10	Vh2	a	4	Rm 71, packing, below 6319
6324	H20d	C10	Vh/i	c	6	Rm 73, cut in 6321
6325	H20d	C10	Vh1–2	b	4	Rm 74, packing S of W251
6326	H20d	C10	Vh2	a	5	Rm 71, yellow clay floor, below 6323
6327	H20d	C10	Vg	a	3	Rm 62, removal of threshold
6328	H20d		Vh2	a	3	W253 removal
6329	H20d	C10	Vh1	a	4	Rm 72 (N), fill over floor, below 6326
6330	H20d	C10	Vh1–2	a	3	W251 removal
6331	H20d		Vh2	a	3	W254 removal
6332	H20d		Vh2	a	3	W255 removal
6333	H20d	C10	Vh/i	a	4	Rm 73, along W252, burnt filling material, below 6321
6334	H20c		Vi?	c	8	Sherd displaced from H20c/d section
6335	H20c	C10	Vg	a	8	Hole with carbonized post, SW corner W249
6336	H20d		Vf2	b	3	W245 removal
6337	H20d		Vh1–2	a	3	W252 removal
6400	J19b	C13.1	IIc	c	5	Rm 3, surface round FI96/18
6401	J19b	C13.1	IIc	b	5	Rm 3, occ. surface N of FI96/18
6402	J19b	C13.1	IIc	b	5	Rm 3, surround of FI96/18
6403	J19b	C13.1	IIc	b	5	Rm 3, occ. surface N of FI96/18, below 6401
6404	J19b	C13.1	IIc	a	3	Partition wall W630, W side of FI96/18
6405	J19b	C13.1	IIb/c	a	5	Rm 3, surface below FI96/18
6406	J19b	C13.1	IIb/c	a	4	Packing, below W630
6407	J19b	C13.1	IIc	a	7	P98/73, below 6401
6408	J19b	C13.1	IIc	a	7	P98/74, below 6401
6409	J19b	C13.1	IIb	a	5	Rm 3, occ. deposit N of FI96/18, below 6405
6410	J19b		IId		7	P96/102 lower fill
6411	J19b	C13.1	IIb/c	c	5	Rm 3, sub-floor packing round FI96/18
6412	J19b	C13.1	IIc	b	5	Rm 3, occ. surface W of W630
6413	J19b	C13.1	IIb	b	6	Rm 3, FI96/18 earlier phase
6414	J19b	C13.1	IIb	b	5	Rm 3, occ. deposits, below 6406
6415	J19b	C13.1	IIb	a	5	Rm 3, NW corner, occ. surface, below 6411
6416	J19b	C13.1	IIb	b	7	Rm 3, P98/83, below 6411
6417	J19b	C13.1	IIb	a	7	P98/84, cut by P98/83
6418	J19b	C13.1	IIb	a	4	Rm 3, S side, packing, below 6415
6419	J19b	C13.1	IIb	a	5	Rm 3, ashy occ. deposit assoc. with 6413
6420	J19b	C13.1	IIb	a	4	Rm3, S side, packing, below 6415 (//6418)
6421	J19b	C13.1	IIb	a	7	Rm 3, P98/87
6422	J19b	C13.1	IIb	a	4	Rm 3, W side, packing, below 6415
6423	J19b	C13.1	IIb	a	5	Rm 3, occ. deposits, below 6420, 6422
6424	J19b	C13.1	IIb	a	5	Rm 3, occ. deposits round FI96/18
6500	J18b		IIc	a	3	SE sounding, W437 removal
6501	J18b	C13.1	IIb	a	4	SE sounding, packing, below W437, and 5899
6502	J18b	C13.1	IIb?	b	4	SE sounding, packing, below 5898, 6501
6503	J18b	C13.1	IIb?	c	4	SE sounding, packing, below 6502
6504	J18b		IIc	a	3	W436
9600	K17		0	d	9	Topsoil
9601	K17c	C16	0	d	9	Topsoil
9602	K17c	C16	0	c	9	Topsoil
9603	K17c	C16	0	c	9	Sub-topsoil
9604	K17c		1	b	3	W508
9605	K17d		0	b	9	Topsoil
9606	K17d	C16	0	d	9	Topsoil

List of Excavation Units

Unit	Square	Chapter	Level	Purity	Context	Description
9607	K17d		1	c	9	Rubble fill
9608	K17d	C16	-	d	9	Baulk removal
9609	K17d	C16	1	c	9	Brown fill beneath rubble
9610	K17d	C16	1	b	5	Mortar surface (//5110)
9611	K17b		0	c	9	Topsoil
9612	K17b		0	c	9	Topsoil
9613	K17b		0	b	9	Topsoil
9614	K17b	C16	1	a	4	Fill, below topsoil abutting W521 (//6002)
9615	K17b	C16	1	a	4	Hard, below 9614 (//6003–4)
9616	K17b		1	a	7	P98/14, fill
9617	K17b	C16	1	a	4	Fill below 9615 (//6003–4)
9618	K17b	C16	1	a	4	Fill below 9617 (//9668, 9686)
9619	K17b		1	a	4	Fill below 9618 (//9620, 9668, 9686)
9620	K17b	C16	1	a	4	Fill below 9618, above W520 (//9619, 9668, 9686)
9621	K17d	C16	0	c	9	Topsoil
9622	K17d	C16	0	c	9	Sub-topsoil
9623	K17d	C16	0	b	9	Sub-topsoil
9624	K17d	C16	1	a	4	Rubble fill (//9626, 9628, 9630, 9632)
9625	K17d	C16	1	a	4	Sub-topsoil
9626	K17d	C16	1	a	4	Fill of robber trench above W520 (//9624)
9627	K17d	C16	1	?	5	Light ashy layer, below 9626 (//9637)
9628	K17d	C16	1	a	4	Rubble fill (//9624, 9626, 9630, 9632, 9639)
9629	K17d	C16	1	a	5	Dark ashy layer, below 9627 (//9638)
9630	K17d	C16	1	a	4	Rubble fill (//9624, 9626, 9628, 9632)
9631	K17d	C16	1	a	5	Light grey ash deposit on mortar floor 9610 (//9641)
9632	K17d	C16	1	a	4	Rubble fill similar to 9624, 9626, 9628 and 9630
9633	K17d	C16	1	a	4	Fill W of 9628, above 9634
9634	K17d	C16	1	a	4	Compact deposit above 9662
9635	K17d	C16	0	c	9	Topsoil
9636	K17d	C16	1	a	4	Rubble fill, below 9635 S of wall W521
9637	K17d	C16	1	a	5	Light ash, below 9636 (//9627)
9638	K17d	C16	1	a	5	Dark ash (//9629)
9639	K17d	C16	0	c	9	Topsoil
9640	K17b		1	a	-	P98/14, cut
9641	K17d	C16	1	a	5	Light ash, below 9638 (//9631)
9642	K17d		1	a	4	Fill beneath 9639
9643	K17d	C16	1	a	4	Rubble on mortar floor, below 9642
9644	K17d		1	a	4	Rubble fill in robber trench above W511
9645	K17d	C16	1	a	4	Rubble fill E of 9644
9646	K17c	C16	0	c	9	Topsoil
9647	K17c	C16	1?	a	4	Soft deposit containing large stones, below 9646
9648	K17c	C16	1	a	4	Deposit E of 9647, below 9646
9649	K17c	C16	1	a	4	Relatively hard, ceramic-rich, below 9648
9650	K17c	C16	1	a	4	Deposit E of P98/36 (//9652)
9651	K17c	C16	1	a	7	Fill of P98/36
9652	K17c	C16	1	a	4	Deposit S of P98/36 (//9650)
9653	K17c	C16	1	a	4	5 cm spit continuing 9650 and 9652
9654	K17b	C16	1	a	4	Softer deposit, below 9620
9655	K17b		1	a	4	Harder deposit, below 9620
9656	K17b	C16	1	a	4	Fill below 9654–5
9657	K17b	C16	1	a	4	Fill below 9656
9658	K17b	C16	1	a	4	Stony layer, below 9657
9659	K17b	C16	1	a	4	Cobbles and stone layer, below 9658
9660	K17b		1	a	4	Fill below 9615
9661	K17b		1	a	4	Fill E of W524
9662	K17d	C16	1	a	4	Compact deposit with stones & pottery, beneath 9634
9663	K17c		1	-	-	P98/36, cut
9664	K17d	C16	1	a	7	P98/37, fill
9665	K17d		1	-	-	P98/37, cut
9666	K17d	C16	1	a	7	P98/37, middle fill
9667	K17d	C16	1	a	7	P98/37, lower fill
9668	K17b		1	a	4	Material beneath 9660 (//9618–20)
9669	K17b		1	c	4	Fill below 9668 (//9656–7)
9670	K17b		1	c	4	Fill below 9669 (//9658–9)
9671	K17b		1	a	4	Soft fill, below 9670 and 9659
9672	K17b		1	a	4	Soft deposit, below 9615, above 9677
9673	K17b		1	a	4	Hard deposit, below 9615, above 9677

Appendix 2

Unit	Square	Chapter	Level	Purity	Context	Description
9674	K17b		1	a	3	Capstones of cist burial (unexcavated)
9675	K17d		1	b	9	Animal hole at bottom of fill of pit P98/39
9676	K17d		1	-	-	P98/39, cut of animal hole
9677	K17b	C16	1	a	5	Mortar surface (//6011)
9678	K17b		1	a	7	Fill from top of grave visible beneath 9674 (unexcavated)
9679	K17b		1	a	4	Fill E of W524, below 9661
9680	K17b		1	a	4	Harder deposit below 9661, N of 9679
9681	K17d		1	a	4	Very hard deposit clinging to W face of W520
9682	K17d		1	a	5	Occ. deposit in N aisle
9683	K17b		1	a	4	Sounding beneath floor 9677
9684	K17b	C16	0	b	9	Topsoil
9685	K17b	C16	0	a	4	Sub-topsoil beneath 9684
9686	K17b	C16	1	a	4	Fill above wall W520, beneath 9685 (//9618–20)

References

Abbreviations used

AA	*Archäologischer Anzeiger*
AAA	*Annals of Archaeology and Anthropology* (Liverpool)
AJA	*American Journal of Archaeology*
An. St.	*Anatolian Studies*
AST	*Araştırmaları Sonuçları Toplantısı*
BAR	*British Archaeological Reports*
BASOR	*Bulletin of the American Schools of Oriental Research*
BIAA	British Institute of Archaeology at Ankara
BSA	*(Annual of the) British School at Athens*
BSAI	British School of Archaeology in Iraq
CNRS	Centre National de la Recherche Scientifique
ÉRC	*Éditions Recherche sur les Civilisations*
JAS	*Journal of Archaeological Science*
KST	*Kazı Sonuçları Toplantısı*
PACT	*Journal of the European Study Group on Physical, Chemical and Mathematical Techniques Applied to Archaeology*
SIMA	*Studies in Mediterranean Archaeology*
TÜBA-AR	*Türkiye Bilimler Akademisi Arkeoloji Dergisi*
ZA	*Zeitschrift für Assyriologie und Vorderasiatische Archäologie*

Acsádi, G.T.F. & J. Nemeskéri, 1970. *History of Human Lifespan and Mortality.* Budapest: Akadémiai Kiadó.

Adams, R.M., 1981. *Heartland of Cities.* Chicago (IL): University of Chicago Press.

Adan-Beyitz, D., M. Artzy & F. Asaro (eds.), forthcoming. *Nuclear Chemistry and its Influence on Modern Science.*

Ahrweiler, H., 1962. L'Asie Mineure et les invasions arabes (VIIe–IXe siècles). *Revue Historique* CCXXVII, 1–32.

Aitchinson, J., 1990. Relative variation diagrams for describing patterns of compositional variability. *Mathematical Geology* 22, 487–511.

Aitken, M.J., 1985. *Thermoluminescence Dating.* London: Academic Press.

Albert, R.M. & S. Weiner, 2001. Study of phytoliths in prehistoric ash layers from Kebara and Tabun caves using a quantitative approach, in Meunier & Colin (eds.), 251–66.

Alföldi Rosenbaum, E., 1980. *Necropolis of Adrassus (Balabolu) in Rough Cilicia (Isauria).* Vienna: Österreichische Akademie der Wissenschaften.

Allan, J.W., 1982. *Nishapur: Metalwork of the Early Islamic Period.* New York (NY): Metropolitan Museum of Art.

Alp, S., 1968. *Zylinder- und Stempelsiegel aus Karahöyük bei Konya.* Ankara: Türk Tarih Kurumu.

Amiet, P., 1980. *La Glyptique Mésopotamienne Archaïque.* Paris: CNRS.

Anderson, P.C., 1998. The history of harvesting and threshing techniques for cereals in the prehistoric Near East, in *The Origins of Agriculture and Crop Domestication*, eds. A.B. Damania, J. Valkoun, G. Willcox & C.O. Qualset. Aleppo: ICARDA, 141–55.

Anderson, P.C., 1999. *Prehistory of Agriculture: New Experimental and Ethnographic Approaches.* Los Angeles (CA): Institute of Archaeology, University of California.

Anderson, P.C. & M.-L. Inizan, 1994. Utilisation du tribulum au début du IIIe millénaire: des lames «cananéennes» lustrées à Kutan (Ninive V) dans la région de Mossoul, Iraq. *Paléorient* 20/ii, 85–103.

Anderson-Gerfaud, P.C., 1992. Experimental cultivation, harvest and threshing of wild cereals and their relevance for interpreting the use of Epipalaeolithic and Neolithic artifacts, in *Préhistoire de l'Agriculture: Nouvelles Approches Expérimentales et Ethnographiques*, ed. P.C. Anderson-Gerfaud. Paris: CRA, 159–209.

Arndt, A., W. Van Neer, B. Hellemans, J. Robben, F. Volckaert & M. Waelkens, 2003. Roman trade relationships at Sagalassos (Turkey) elucidated from mtDNA of ancient fish remains. *JAS* 30, 1095–105.

Arvites, J.A., 1983. The defense of Byzantine Anatolia during the reign of Irene (780–802), in *Armies and Frontiers in Roman and Byzantine Anatolia: Proceedings of a colloquium held at University College Swansea in April 1981*, ed. S. Mitchell. (British Archaeological Reports International Series 156.) Oxford: BAR, 219–38.

Bahar, H. & Ö. Koçak, 2003. Konya-Hatunsaray yerleşmesinde Erken Demir Çağı çanak çömleği, in Fischer *et al.* (eds.), 193–8.

Bahar, H. & Ö. Koçak, 2004. *Eskiçağ Konya Araştırmaları* 2. Konya: Kömen Yayınları.

Bahar, H., G. Karauğuz & Ö. Koçak, 1996. *Eskiçağ Konya Araştırmaları* 1. Istanbul.

Bailey, D., 1988. *A Catalogue of Lamps in the British Museum III: the Roman Provincial Lamps.* London: British Museum.

Bailiff, I.K., 1982. Beta-TLD apparatus for small samples. *PACT* 6, 72–6.

Baird, D., 1996. Konya Plains Survey: aims and methods, in Hodder (ed.), 41–6.

Baird, D., 2003. The Konya Plains Survey, Central Anatolia. (http://www.liv.ac.uk/sacos/research/projects/konya.html accessed 10/05/2004).

Baird, D., 2004. Settlement expansion on the Konya Plain, Anatolia: 5th–7th centuries AD, in *Recent Research on the Late Antique Countryside*, eds. W. Bowden, L. Levan & C. Machado. Leiden: Brill, 219–46.

Baker, H.D., D. Collon, J.D. Hawkins, T. Pollard, J.N. Postgate, D. Symington & D. Thomas, 1995. Kilise Tepe 1994. *An. St.* 45, 139–91.

Baker, P., 2001. Analysis of zooarchaeological data: Kilise Tepe 1995–1997, in Matthews & Postgate (eds.), 2001.

Baker, P., 2005. The Vertebrate Remains from Kilise Tepe, Southcentral Turkey: the 1994–1998 Excavations. Unpublished archive report.

Baker, P., C. Forcey, S. Jundi & R. Witcher (eds.), 1999. *TRAC 98 Proceedings of the Eighth Annual Theoretical Roman Archaeology Conference Leicester 1998*. Oxford: Oxbow.

Bakla, E., 1993. *Tophane Lüleciliği [The Pipe-Making Industry of Tophane]*. Istanbul: Dışbank.

Ball, J.W., 1993. Pottery, potters, palaces and polities: some socio-economic and political implications of Late Classic Maya ceramic industries, in *Lowland Maya Civilization in the Eighth Century AD: a Symposium at Dumbarton Oaks, 7th and 8th October 1989*, eds. J.A. Sabloff & J.S. Henderson. Washington (DC): Dumbarton Oaks, 243–72.

Ball, T.B., J.S. Gardner & N. Anderson, 2001. An approach to identifying inflorescence phytoliths from selected species of wheat and barley, in Meunier & Colin (eds.), 289–301.

Balty, J.-C., 1981. *Guide d'Apamée*. Brussels: Centre belge de recherches archéologiques à Apamée de Syrie.

Banning, E.B., 2002. *Archaeological Survey*. New York (NY): Kluwer Academic/Plenum Publishing.

Barag, D., 1985. *Catalogue of Western Asiatic Glass in the British Museum I*. London: British Museum.

Barber, E.J.W., 1991. *Prehistoric Textiles*. Princeton (NJ): Princeton University Press.

Barnett, R.D., 1939–40. The Greek pottery. *AAA* 26, 98–130.

Barnett, R.D., 1957. *A Catalogue of the Nimrud Ivories*. London: BSAI.

Bass, G.F., 1967. *Cape Gelidonya: a Bronze Age Shipwreck*. (Transactions of the American Philosophical Society 57, Part 8.) Philadelphia (PA): American Philosophical Society.

Bass, G.F., 1984. The nature of the Serçe Limani glass. *Journal of Glass Studies* 26, 64–9.

Bass, G.F. & F.H. van Doornick Jr, 1982. *Yassı Ada*, vol. I: *A Seventh-century Byzantine Shipwreck*. College Station (TX): Texas A&M University Press.

Bass, W., 1995. *Human Osteology: a Laboratory and Field Manual*. Columbia (MO): Missouri Archaeological Society.

Bayliss, R., 1999. Usurping the urban image: the experience of ritual topography in late Antique cities of the Near East, in Baker *et al.* (eds.), 59–71.

Bayliss, R., 2001. Provincial Cilicia and the Archaeology of Temple Conversion. Unpublished PhD thesis, Newcastle University.

Baysal, A. & K.I. Wright, 2002. Analysis of ground stone artefacts from Çatalhöyük, excavations of 1995–1999. Catalhoyuk Website Archive Reports 2002 (http://catal.arch.cam.ac.uk//catal/Archive_rep02/a10.html).

Bazin, M., 1991. Le pays de Taşeli (Cilicie Trachée): les apports de la géographie actuelle à la compréhension de l'occupation antique. *De Anatolia Antiqua* 1, 243–52.

Beal, R.H., 1992a. *The Organisation of the Hittite Military*. Heidelberg: C. Winter.

Beal, R.H., 1992b. The location of Cilician Ura. *An. St.* 42, 65–73.

Bean, G.E. & T.B. Mitford, 1970. *Journeys in Rough Cilicia 1964–1968*. (Denkschriften der Österreichische Akademie der Wissenschaften, phil.-hist. Kl., 102.) Vienna: Bohlau.

Bending, J.M., 1999. Hittite to Byzantine: Archaeobotanical Assemblages from Kilise Tepe, Southern Turkey. Unpublished MSc dissertation, University of Sheffield.

Berlin, A., 1997. The plain wares, in *Tel Anafa II.i: the Hellenistic and Roman Pottery*, ed. S.C. Herbert. (*Journal of Roman Archaeology* Supplement 10, Part II.i.). Ann Arbor (MI): Kelsey Museum of the University of Michigan, 1–244.

Bernabò-Brea, L., 1964. *Poliochni: città preistorica nell'isola di Lemnos*, vol. 1/i. Rome: Bretschneider.

Beyer, D., 1982. Le sceau-cylindre de Shahurunuwa, roi de Karkémish, in *La Syrie au Bronze Récent*. Paris: Editions Recherche sur les civilisations, 67–78.

Bilgi, Ö., 1982. *M.Ö. binyılında Anadolu'da bulunmuş olan matara biçimli kaplar*. Istanbul: Edebiyat Fakültesi Basımevi.

Binford, L.R., 1972. *An Archaeological Perspective*. New York (NY): Seminar Press.

Bittel, K., 1983. Die archäologische Situation in Kleinasien um 1200 v. Chr. und während der nachfolgenden vier Jahrhunderte, in *Griechenland, die Ägäis und die Levante während der 'Dark Ages' vom 12. bis zum 9. Jh. v. Chr.*, ed. S. Deger-Jalkotzy. (Sitzungsberichte der Österreichische Akad. der Wissenschaften, phil.-hist. Kl., 418.) Vienna: Österreichische Akademie der Wissenschaften, 25–65.

Bittel, K., G. Neumann, P. Neve, W. Orthmann & H. Otten, 1984. *Funde aus den Grabungen bis 1979 (Boğazköy-Hattuša VI)*. Berlin: Gebr. Mann.

Blanton, R.E., 2000. *Hellenistic, Roman and Byzantine Settlement Patterns of the Coast Lands of Western Rough Cilicia*. (BAR International Series 879.) Oxford: Archaeopress.

Blaylock, S.R., 1999. Iron Age pottery from Tille Höyük, south-eastern Turkey, in *Iron Age Pottery in Northern Mesopotamia, Northern Syria and South-eastern Anatolia: Papers presented at the meetings of the international 'table ronde' at Heidelberg (1995) and Nieborów (1997)*, eds. A. Hausleiter & A. Reiche. (Altertumskunde des Vorderen Orients Band 10.) Münster: Ugarit-Verlag. 263–86.

Blegen, C.W., J.L. Caskey, M. Rawson & J. Sperling, 1950. *Troy I. General Introduction. The First and Second Settlements*. Princeton (NJ): Princeton University Press.

Blegen, C.W., J.L. Caskey & M. Rawson, 1951. *Troy II. The Third, Fourth, and Fifth Settlements*. Princeton (NJ): Princeton University Press.

Blinnikov, M., A. Busacca & K. Whitlock, 2001. A new 100,000-year phytolith record from the Columbia Basin, Washington, USA, in Meunier & Colin (eds.), 27–55.

Boardman, J., 1965. Tarsus, Al-Mina and Greek chronology. *Journal of Hellenic Studies* 85, 5–15.

Boardman, J., 1999. The excavated history of Al-Mina, in

References

Ancient Greeks West and East, ed. G.R. Tstetskhladze. (*Mnemosyne* Suppl. 196). Leiden: Brill.

Boehmer, R.M., 1972. *Die Kleinfunde von Boğazköy aus den Grabungskampagnen 1931–1939 und 1952–1969 (Boğazköy-Hattuša VII)*. Berlin: Gebr. Mann.

Boehmer, R.M., 1979. *Die Kleinfunde aus der Unterstadt von Boğazköy, Grabungskampagnen 1970–1978 (Boğazköy-Hattuša X)*. Berlin: Gebr. Mann.

Boehmer, R.M., 1983. *Die Reliefkeramik von Boğazköy (Boğazköy-Hattuša XIII)*. Berlin: Gebr. Mann.

Boehmer, R.M. & H.G. Güterbock, 1987. *Die Glyptik aus dem Stadtgebiet von Boğazköy.* (Die Glyptik von Boğazköy II). Berlin: Gebr. Mann.

Boehmer, R.M. & H. Hauptmann (eds.), 1983. *Beiträge zur Altertumskunde Kleinasiens: Festschrift für Kurt Bittel.* Mainz: von Zabern.

Boessneck, J., 1969. Osteological differences between sheep (*Ovis aries* Linné) and Goat (*Capra hircus* Linné), in Brothwell & Higgs (eds.), 331–58.

Bogutskaya, N.G., 1997. Contribution to the knowledge of leuciscine fishes of Asia Minor, part 2: An annotated check-list of leuciscine fishes (Leuciscinae, Cyprinidae) of Turkey with descriptions of a new species and two new subspecies. *Mitteilungen aus dem Hamburgischen Zoologischen Museum und Institut* 94, 161–86.

Bol, P.C., 1989. *Argivische Schilde* (Olympische Forschungen XVII). Berlin: de Gruyter.

Borger, R., 1956. *Die Inschriften Asarhaddons Königs von Assyrien.* (Archiv für Orientforschung, Beiheft 9.) Graz.

Börker-Klähn, J., 1982. *Altvorderasiatische Bildstelen und vergleichbare Felsreliefs.* (Baghdader Forschungen 4.) Mainz: von Zabern.

Bottema, S., 1999. Landscape archaeology and reconstruction of the Mediterranean environment based on palynology, in *Environmental Reconstruction in Mediterranean Landscape Archaeology*, eds. P. Leveau, F. Trement, K. Walsh & G. Barker. Oxford: Oxbow, 9–17.

Bowdery, D., 2001. Phytolith and starch data from an obsidian tool excavated at Bitokora, New Britain Province, Papua New Guinea: a 3400-year-old hafting technique, in Meunier & Colin (eds.), 225–38.

Branstetter, S., 1989. Carcharhinidae, in *Fishes of the Northeastern Atlantic and the Mediterranean*, eds. P.J.P. Whitehead, M.-L. Bauchot, J.-C. Hureau, J. Nielsen & E. Tortonese. Paris: UNESCO, 102–14.

Brinkmann, R., 1976. *Geology of Turkey*. Amsterdam: Elsevier.

Brixhe, Cl., 1991. Les inscriptions paléo-phrygiennes de Tyane: leur intérêt linguistique et historique, in *La Cappadoce méridionale jusqu'à la fin de l'époque romaine: état des recherches: actes du Colloque d'Istanbul (Institut Français d'études anatoliennes) 13–14 avril 1987*, eds. B. Le Guen-Pollet, & O. Pelon. Paris: ÉRC, 37–46.

Broneer, O., 1930. *Corinth,* vol. IV, part II: *Terracotta Lamps.* Cambridge (MA): Harvard University Press.

Bronk Ramsey, C., 1995. Radiocarbon calibration and analysis of stratigraphy: the OxCal program. *Radiocarbon* 37(2), 425–30.

Bronk Ramsey, C., 2001. Development of the radiocarbon program OxCal. *Radiocarbon* 43 (2A), 355–63.

Bronk Ramsey, C., P.B. Pettitt, R.E.M. Hedges, G.W.L. Hodgins & D.C. Owen, 2000. Radiocarbon dates from the Oxford AMS system: Archaeometry Datelist 30. *Archaeometry* 42 (2).

Brooks, E.W., 1898. The Arabs in Asia Minor (641–750), from Arabic sources. *The Journal of Hellenic Studies* 18, 182–208.

Brooks, E.W., 1901. Arabic lists of the Byzantine themes. *Journal of Hellenic Studies* 21, 67–77.

Brothwell, D.R., 1981. *Digging up Bones.* Oxford: Oxford University Press/British Museum.

Brothwell D. & E. Higgs (eds.), 1969. *Science in Archaeology.* London: Thames & Hudson.

Broudy, E., 1979. *The Book of Looms: a History of the Handloom from Ancient Times to the Present*. New York (NY): van Nostrand Reinhold.

Brown, G.H., 1967. Prehistoric pottery from the Antitaurus. *An. St.* 17, 123–64.

Brown, P., 1971. The rise and function of the Holy Man in late antiquity. *Journal of Roman Studies* 61, 80–101.

Brundage, J., 1962. *The Crusades: a Documentary History.* Milwaukee (WI): Marquette University Press.

Bruneau, P., 1965. *Les Lampes*. (Exploration Archéologique de Délos faite par l'Ecole Française d'Athènes; fasc. XXVII.) Paris: de Boccard.

Bryan, N.D., E.B. French, S.M.A. Hoffmann & V.J. Robinson, 1997. Pottery sources in Bronze Age Cyprus: a provenance study by neutron activation. *Report of the Department of Antiquities, Cyprus 1997*, 31–64.

Buchanan, B. & P.R.S. Moorey, 1984. *Catalogue of Ancient Near Eastern seals in the Ashmolean Museum,* vol. II: *The Prehistoric Stamp Seals*. Oxford: Oxford University Press.

Buchholz, H.-G. & V. Karageorghis, 1973. *Prehistoric Greece and Cyprus: an Archaeological Handbook*. London: Phaidon.

Buchwald, A., 1981. Church of St John the Theologian in Alaşehir (Philadelphia). *Jahrbuch der Österreichischen Byzantinistik* 30, 301–18.

Burke, R.B., 1998. *From Minos to Midas: the Organization of Textile Production in the Aegean and Anatolia.* UCLA PhD dissertation. Ann Arbor (MI): UMI Dissertation Services.

Buxeda i Garrigós, J., 1999. Alteration and contamination of archaeological ceramics: the perturbation problem. *JAS* 26, 295–313.

Buxeda i Garrigós, J. & V. Kilikoglou, 2003. Total variation as a measure of variability in chemical data-sets, in *Patterns and Process, a Festschrift in honor of Edward V. Sayre,* ed. L. van Zelst. Washington (DC): Smithsonian Center for Materials Research and Education. 185–98.

Cadogan, G. (ed.), 1986. *The End of the Early Bronze Age in the Aegean.* Leiden: E.J. Brill.

Calder, W.M. & G.E. Bean, 1958. *A Classical Map of Asia Minor.* London: BIAA.

Campbell, A.S. (ed.), 1971. *Geology and History of Turkey*. Tripoli: Petroleum Exploration Society of Libya.

Caneva, I. & V. Sevin, 2004. *Mersin-Yumuktepe, a Reappraisal.* Lecce: Congedo Editore.

Carnelli, A.L., M. Madella & J.-P. Theurillat, 2001. Biogenic silica production in selected Alpine plant species and plant communities. *Annals of Botany*, 87, 425–34.

Cartland, B.M., 1918. Balls of thread wound on pieces of pottery. *Journal of Egyptian Archaeology* 5, 139.

Caskey, J.L., 1986. Did the Early Bronze Age end?, in Cadogan (ed.), 9–30.

Castro Curel, Z., 1985. Pondera. Examen cualitativo, cuantitativo, espacial y su relación con el telar con pesas. *Empúries: Revista de Prehistòria, Arqueologia i Etnologia (Barcelona)* 47, 230–53.

Catling, H.W., 1964. *Cypriot Bronzework in the Mycenaean world*. Oxford: Clarendon Press.

Catling, H.W., 1972. An early Byzantine pottery factory at Dhiorios in Cyprus. *Levant* 4, 1–82.

Catling, H.W. & A.I. Dikigoropoulos, 1970. The Kornos Cave: an early Byzantine site in Cyprus. *Levant* 2, 37–63.

Cato, M., 1933. *On Farming*, trans. E. Brehaut. New York (NY): Columbia University Press.

Cecchini, S.M., 2000. The textile industry in northern Syria during the Iron Age according to the evidence of the Tell Afis excavations, in *Essays on Syria in the Iron Age*, ed. G. Bunnens. (Ancient Near Eastern Studies, Supplement 7.) Louvain: Peeters, 211–33.

Cheetham, L., 1982. Threshing and winnowing — an ethnographic study. *Antiquity* 56, 127–30.

Choyke, A.M., 2000. Bronze Age bone and antler manufacturing at Arslantepe (Anatolia), in *Archaeozoology of the Near East IVA*, eds. M. Mashkour, A.M. Choyke, H. Buitenhuis & F. Poplin. Groningen: Centre for Archaeological Research and Consultancy, 171–84.

Civil, M., 1994. *The Farmer's Instructions: a Sumerian Agricultural Manual*. Barcelona: Editorial AUSA.

Clarke, D.L., 1973. Archaeology: the loss of innocence. *Antiquity* 47, 6–18.

Coldstream, J.N., 1968. *Greek Geometric Pottery: a Survey of Ten Local Styles and their Chronology*. London: Methuen.

Coldstream, J.N., 1984. Cypriaca and Cretocypriaca from the North Cemetery of Knossos. *Report of the Department of Antiquities, Cyprus 1984*, 122–37.

Coldstream, J.N. & H.W. Catling, 1996. *Knossos North Cemetery: Early Greek Tombs*. Athens: BSA.

Colledge, S., 2001. Final Report on the Archaeobotanical Analysis, in Matthews & Postgate (eds.), 2001.

Collon, D., 1975. *The Seal Impressions from Tell Atchana/Alalakh*. (Alter Orient und Altes Testament 27.) Neukirchen-Vluyn: Neukirchener Verlag.

Collon, D., 1995. Pottery from the surface collection, in Baker et al. (eds.), 157–72.

Columella, 1941. *De Re Rustica*. Cambridge (MA): Harvard University Press.

Courtois, J.-C. & L. Courtois, 1978. Corpus céramique de Ras Shamra-Ugarit, niveaux historiques d'Ugarit Bronze Moyen et Bronze Récent, in *Ugaritica* VII (Mission de Ras Shamra XVIII). Paris/Leiden: Brill, 191–370.

Courtois, J.-C., J. Lagarce & E. Lagarce, 1986. *Enkomi et le Bronze Récent à Chypre*. Nicosia: Zavallis.

Courtois, L., 1971. Déscription Physico-Chimique de la Céramique Ancienne: La Céramique de Chypre au Bronze Récent. Unpublished thesis, Université de Clermont.

Crespin, A.-S., 1999. Between Phrygia and Cilicia: the Porsuk area at the beginning of the Iron Age. *An. St.* 49, 61–71.

Crewe, L., 1998. *Spindle Whorls: a Study of Form, Function and Decoration in Prehistoric Bronze Age Cyprus*. Jonsered: Paul Åströms Förlag.

Cribb, R., 1991. *Nomads in Archaeology*. Cambridge: Cambridge University Press.

Curtis, J., 1984. *Nush-i Jan. 3: the Small Finds*. London: British Institute of Persian Studies.

Curtis, J. & A. Green, 1997. *Excavations at Khirbet Khatuniyeh*. London: British Museum.

Dagron, G., 1978. *Vie et Miracles de Sainte Thècle, Texte grec, traduction, et commentaire*. (Subsidia Hagiographica, 62.) Brussels: Société des Bollandistes.

Darga, M.A., 1986. Karatepe — Azatiwattaya Kalesinin Çanak Çömlek Buluntuları. *Anadolu Araştırmaları*, 371–99.

Dark, K., 2001. *Byzantine Pottery*. Stroud: Tempus.

Davesne, A., 1991. La campagne 1989 à Meydancıkkale. *KST* 12/ii, 349–54.

Davesne, A. & F. Laroche-Traunecker (eds.), 1998. *Gülnar I. Le Site de Meydancıkkale. Recherches Entreprises sous la Direction d'Emmanuel Laroche (1971–1982)*. Paris: ÉRC.

Davesne, A., A. Lemaire & H. Lozachmeur, 1987. Le site archéologique de Meydancıkkale (Turquie): du royaume de Pirindu à la garnison ptolémaïque. *Comptes rendus de l'Académie des inscriptions et belles-lettres*, 359–82.

Davis, E.J., 1879. *Life in Asiatic Turkey: a Journey of Travel in Cilicia (Pedias and Trachaea), Isauria, and Parts of Lycaonia and Cappadocia*. London: Stanford.

Davis, P.H. (ed.), 1965–88. *Flora of Turkey and the East Aegean Islands*. Edinburgh: Edinburgh University Press.

Davis, S.J.M., 1994. Even more bones from Khirokitia: the 1988-1991 excavations, in *Fouilles récentes a Khirokitia (Chypre 1988–1991)*, ed. A. Lebrun. Paris: ÉRC, 305–33.

Day, P.M., 1995. Pottery production and consumption in the Sitia Bay area during the New Palace Period, in *Achladia: Scavi e ricerche della Missione Greco-Italiana in Creta Orientale (1991–1993)*, eds. M. Tsipopoulou & L. Vagnetti. Roma: Gruppo editoriale internazionale. 149–75.

Day, P.M. & H.W. Haskell, 1995. Transport stirrup jars from Thebes as evidence of trade in Late Bronze Age Greece, in *Trade and Production in Premonetary Greece: Aspects of Trade: Proceedings of the Third International Workshop, Athens 1993*, eds. C. Gillis, C. Risberg & B.L. Sjöberg. Jonsered: Paul Åstroms Förlag, 87–109.

de Contenson, H., 1993. Meule dormante, in *Syrie, Mémoire et Civilisation, Exposition realisée par l'Institut du Monde Arabe, Le Ministère de la Culture de la République Arabe Syrienne*, ed. S. Muhesen. Paris: Institut du Monde Arabe.

de Grossi Mazzorin, J., 2000. État de nos connaissances concernant le traitement et la consommation du poisson dans l'antiquité à la lumière de l'archéologie. *Mélanges de l'École Française de Rome, Antiquité* 112, 155–67.

de Paepe, P. & B. Gratien, 1995. Petrological and chemical

analysis of pottery from Tell el-Herr (Egypt): Nile mud wares and marl wares, in Meyza & Mlynarczyk (eds.), 61–83.

De Vries, K., P.I. Kuniholm, G.K. Sams & M.M. Voigt, 2003. New dates for Iron Age Gordion, *Antiquity* 77, no. 296 June 2003 (http://antiquity.ac.uk/ProjGall/devries/devries.html).

Delougaz, P. & R.A. Haines, 1960. *The Byzantine Church at Khirbat al-Karak.* (Oriental Institute Publications 85.) Chicago (IL): University of Chicago Press.

Demirtaşlı, E., N. Turhan, A.Z. Bilgin & M.A. Selim, 1984. Geology of the Bolkar Mountains, in Tekeli & Göncüoğlu (eds.), 125–41.

Dennell, R.W., 1976. The economic importance of plant resources represented on archaeological sites. *JAS* 3, 229–47.

Dennis, G.T., 1985. *Three Byzantine Military Treatises.* (Corpus Fontium Historiae Byzantinae XXV.) Washington (DC): Dumbarton Oaks.

Deshayes, J., 1960. *Les Outils de bronze, de l'Indus au Danube.* Paris: Geuthner.

Desideri, P., 1991. Strabo's Cilicians. *De Anatolia Antiqua* 1, 299–304.

Desideri, P. & A.M. Jasink, 1990. *Cilicia dall'età di Kizzuwatna alla conquista macedone.* Torino: Casa Editrice Le Lettere.

Diamant, S. & J. Rutter, 1969. Horned objects in Anatolia and the Near East and possible connections with the Minoan 'Horns of Consecration'. *An. St.* 19, 147–77.

Diederichs, C., 1980. *Salamine de Chypre IX: Céramiques Hellénistiques, Romaines et Byzantines.* Paris: de Boccard.

Dikaios, P. & J.R. Stewart, 1962. *The Stone Age and Early Bronze Age in Cyprus.* (The Swedish Cyprus Expedition IV, pt IA.) Lund: Swedish Cyprus Expedition.

Dinçol, A., 1983. Hethitische Hieroglyphensiegel in den Museen zu Adana, Hatay und Istanbul. *Anadolu Araştırmaları* 9, 213–49.

Dinçol, A.M., 1998. Die Entdeckung des Felsmonuments in Hatıp und ihre Auswirkungen über die historischen und geographischen Fragen. *TÜBA-AR* 1, 27–34.

Dinçol, A. & B. Dinçol, 1985. Neue Hieroglyphensiegel in den Museen zu Ankara und Mersin. *Akkadica* 45, 33–40.

Dinçol, A.M., B. Dinçol & E. Jean, 1998. Unpublished Hittite seals in the collections at Adana. *Anatolia Antiqua* 6, 183–93.

Dinçol, A.M., J. Yakar, B. Dinçol & A. Taffet, 2000. The borders of the appanage kingdom of Tarhuntassa — a geographical and archaeological assessment. *Anatolica* 26, 1–29.

Dinçol, A.M., J. Yakar, B. Dinçol & A. Taffet, 2001. Die Grenzen von Tarhunbtašša im Lichte geographischer Beobachtungen, in Jean *et al.* (eds.), 79–86.

Dothan, T. & A. Zuckerman, 2004. A preliminary study of the Mycenaean IIIC:1 pottery assemblages from Tel Miqne-Ekron and Ashdod. *BASOR* 333, 1–54.

Drews, R., 1993. *The End of the Bronze Age. Changes in Warfare and the Catastrophe c. 1200 BC.* Princeton (NJ): Princeton University Press.

du Plat Taylor, J., 1959. The Cypriot and Syrian pottery from Al Mina, Syria. *Iraq* 21, 62–92.

Dupré, S., 1983. *La Céramique de L'âge du Bronze et de L'âge du Fer.* Paris: Institut Français d'Études Anatoliennes.

Duru, R., 1983. Excavations at Kuruçay Höyük, 1981. *Anadolu Araştırmaları* 9, 41–50.

Easton, D.F., 2002. *Schliemann's Excavation at Troia 1870–1873.* (Studia Troica Monograph 2.) Mainz: von Zabern.

Easton, D.F., J.D. Hawkins, A.G. Sherratt & E.S. Sherratt, 2002. Troy in recent perspective. *An. St.* 52, 75–109.

Edgar, C.C., 1925. *Zenon Papyri I (Catalogue Général des Antiquités Égyptiennes du Musée de Caire).* Cairo: Service des Antiquités de l'Égypte.

Edwards, G.R., 1975. *Corinth, vol. VII part III: Corinthian Hellenistic Pottery.* Princeton (NJ): American School of Classical Studies at Athens.

Edwards, R.W., 1982. Ecclesiastical architecture in the fortifications of Armenian Cilicia. *Dumbarton Oaks Papers* 36, 155–77.

Edwards, R.W., 1987. *The Fortifications of Cilician Armenia.* Washington (DC): Dumbarton Oaks.

Edwards, R.W., 1999. Isauria, in *Late Antiquity: a Guide to the Postclassical World*, eds. G.W. Bowersock, P. Brown & O. Grabar. London: Harvard, 515–16.

Efe, T., 1988. *Demircihüyük III.2: Die frühbronzezeitliche Keramik der jüngeren Phasen (ab Phase H).* Mainz: von Zabern.

Egloff, E., 1977. *Kellia. La poterie copte III,1.* Geneva: Georg.

Eichner, I., 2000. Frühbyzantinische Wohnhäuser in Kilikien: Bericht über die Kampagne 1999. *AST* 18/i, 221–30.

Elliott, C., 1991. The ground stone industry, in *Arts et industries de la pierre*, ed. M. Yon. (Ras Shamra-Ougarit 6.) Paris: ÉRC, 9–99.

Elton, H., 1996. *Frontiers of the Roman Empire.* London: Batsford.

Elton, H., 2000a. Illus and the Imperial aristocracy under Zeno. *Byzantion* 70, 393–407.

Elton, H., 2000b. The nature of the 6th century Isaurians, in *Ethnicity and Culture in Late Antiquity*, eds. S. Mitchell, & G. Greatrex. London: Duckworth, 293–307.

Elton, H., 2002a. Alahan and Zeno. *An. St.* 52, 153–7.

Elton, H., 2002b. Göksu Archaeological Project. *Anatolian Archaeology* 8, 24.

Elton, H., 2004. Romanization and some Cilician cults, in *Roman Rule and Civic Life: Local and Regional Perspectives*, eds. L. de Ligt, E.A. Hemelrijk & H.W. Singor. Amsterdam: J.C. Gieben, 231–41.

Emre, K., 1971. *Anatolian Lead Figurines and their Stone Moulds.* (Türk Tarih Kurumu Yayınları VI/14.) Ankara: Türk Tarih Kurumu.

Emre, K., M. Mellink, B. Hrouda & N. Özgüç (eds.), 1989. *Anatolia and the Ancient Near East, Studies in Honor of Tahsin Özgüç.* Ankara: Türk Tarih Kurumu.

Equini Schneider, E., 1970. *Malatya II. Rapporto preliminare delle campagne 1963–1968. Il livello romano bizantino e le testimonianze islamiche.* Rome: Centro per le Antichità e la Storia dell'Arte del Vicino Oriente.

Equini Schneider, E., 1999. *Elaiussa Sebaste I — Campagne di scavo 1995–1997.* Rome: Bretschneider.

Equini Schneider, E., 2003. *Elaiussa Sebaste II — Un porto tra Oriente e Occidente.* Rome: Bretschneider.

Eriksson, K.O., 1991. Red Lustrous Wheelmade Ware: a

product of Late Bronze Age Cyprus, in *Cypriot Ceramics: Reading the Prehistoric Record*, eds. J.A. Barlow, D.L. Bolger & B. Kling. Philadelphia (PA): University Museum of Archaeology and Anthropology, 81–96.

Eriksson, K.O., 1993. *Red Lustrous Wheel-made Ware.* (SIMA 103.) Jonsered: Paul Åströms Förlag.

Erinç, S. & N. Tunçdilek, 1952. The agricultural regions of Turkey. *Geographical Review* 42, 179–203.

Eyice, S., 1981. Einige Byzantinische Kleinstädte im Rauhen Kilikien, in *150 Jahre Deutsches Archäologisches Institut (Festschrift)*. Mainz: von Zabern, 204–9.

Eyice, S., 1988. Ricerche e scoperte nella regione di Silifke nella Turchia Meridionale. *Milion* 1, 15–33.

Feldtkeller, A., 2003. Nierenförmige Webgewichte — wie funktionieren sie? *Archaeological Textiles Newsletter* 37 (Autumn), 16–19.

Finkbeiner, U., 1991. *Uruk Kampagne 35–37, 1982–1984. Die archäologische Oberflächenuntersuchung.* Mainz: von Zabern.

Finnegan, M., 1978. Non-metric variations of the infracranial skeleton. *Journal of Anatomy* 125, 23–37.

Fischer, B., H. Genz, É. Jean & K. Köroğlu (eds.), 2003. *Identifying Changes: the Transition from Bronze to Iron Ages in Anatolia and its Neighbouring Regions (Proceedings of the International Workshop, Istanbul, November 8–9, 2002)*. Istanbul: Türk Eskiçağ Bilimleri Enstitüsü.

Fischer, F., 1963. *Die hethitische Keramik von Boğazköy (Boğazköy/Hattuša IV)*. Berlin: Gebr. Mann.

Fitzgerald, G.M., 1939–40. Pottery of Levels V, VI and VII, *AAA* 26, 131–5.

Foley, R., 1981. *Off Site Archaeology and Human Adaptation in Eastern Africa: an Analysis of Regional Artefact Density in the Amboseli, Southern Kenya.* (BAR International Series 97.) Oxford: BAR.

Forsberg, S., 1995. *Near Eastern Destruction Datings as Sources for Greek and Near Eastern Iron Age Chronology: Archaeological and Historical Studies: the Cases of Samaria (722 BC) and Tarsus (696 BC)*. Uppsala: Uppsala Universitet.

Forsyth, G.H., 1957. Architectural notes on a trip through Cilicia. *Dumbarton Oaks Papers* 11, 223–36.

Forsyth, G.H., 1961. An Early Byzantine church at Kanlidivane in Cilicia, in *De artibus Opuscula XL: Essays in Honour of Erwin Panofsky*, ed. M. Meiss. New York (NY): New York University Press, 127–37.

Forsyth, G.H., 1968. The Monastery of St Catherine at Mount Sinai: the church and fortress of Justinian. *Dumbarton Oaks Papers* 22, 3–19.

Foss, C., 1975. The Persians in Asia Minor and the end of Antiquity. *English Historical Review* 90, 721–43.

Foss, C., 1995. The Near Eastern countryside in late antiquity: a review article, in *The Roman and Byzantine Near East*, ed. J.H. Humphrey. Ann Arbor (MI): *Journal of Roman Archaeology*, Suppl. 14. 213–23.

Freed, R.E., 1982. *Egypt's Golden Age: the Art of Living in the New Kingdom, 1558–1085 BC*. Boston (MA): Museum of Fine Arts.

French, D.H., 1965. Prehistoric sites in the Göksu Valley. *An. St.* 15, 177–201.

French, D.H., 1969. Prehistoric sites in northwest Anatolia II (c): the Balıkesir and Akhisar/Manisa Areas. *An. St.* 19, 41–98.

French, D.H., 1970. Notes on site distribution in the Çumra Area. *An. St.* 20, 139–48.

French, D.H., 1984. The site of Dalisandus. *Epigraphica Anatolica* 4, 85–98.

French, D.H., 1992. Roads in Pisidia, in *Forschungen in Pisidia*, ed. E. Schwertheim. (Asia Minor Studien 6.) Bonn: Habelt, 167–73.

French, D.H. & Çilingiroğlu, A. (eds.), 1994. *Anatolian Iron Ages 3*. London: BIAA.

French, E., 1965. Late Helladic IIIA2 pottery from Mycenae. *BSA* 60, 159–202.

French, E., 1975. A reassessment of the Mycenaean pottery at Tarsus. *An. St.* 25, 53–75.

French, E., 1993. Turkey and the East Aegean, in Zerner *et al.* (eds.), 155–8.

French, E., 1999. The postpalatial levels at Mycenae, an up-date. Mycenaean Seminar 17/3/99. *Bulletin of the Institute for Classical Studies* 43, 222–3.

French, E., forthcoming a. Postpalatial Mycenae: the stratified material. (Well Built Mycenae, Fascicule 16.)

French, E., forthcoming b. Minoans and Mycenaeans in Anatolia. *The Archaeology of Anatolia: an Encyclopedia*.

French, E., forthcoming c. Cilicia, in *Proceedings of the International Workshop The Philistines and other 'Sea Peoples'* (Haifa and Beer Sheba, May 2001).

French, E., forthcoming d. The origin and date of Aegean type pottery in the Levant, in *Proceedings of the International Workshop: The Philistines and other 'Sea Peoples'* (Haifa & Beer Sheba, May 2001).

French, E., forthcoming e. The impact on correlations to the Levant of the recent stratigraphic evidence from the Argolid, in *The Proceedings of the 2nd EuroConference SCIEM 2000, Vienna 2003*.

French, E.B. & J.E. Tomlinson, 1999. The mainland 'conical cup', in *MELETEMATA. Studies in Aegean Archaeology Presented to Malcolm H. Wiener as he enters his 65th Year*, eds. P.P. Betancourt, V. Karageorghis, R. Laffineur & W.-D. Niemeier. Liège: Université de Liège, 259–65.

Frend, W.H.C., 1972. *The Rise of the Monophysite Movement*. Cambridge: Cambridge University Press.

Freu, J., 2001. Le traité Sunassura et la fin du Kizzuwatna autonome, in Jean *et al.* (eds.), 25–39.

Friend, G., 1998. *The Loom Weights* (Tell Taannek 1963–1968 III, The Artifacts, 2.) Birzeit: Palestinian Institute of Archaeology, Excavations and Surveys.

Fulford, M.G. & D.P.S. Peacock, 1984. *Excavations at Carthage, The British Mission*, vol. I, 2: *The Avenue du President Bourgiba, Salammbo: the Pottery and other Ceramic Objects from the Site*. Sheffield: University of Sheffield Department of Prehistory and Archaeology.

Gallet de Santerre, H. & J. Tréheux, 1947–48. Dépôt égéen et géométrique de l'Artémision à Délos. *Bulletin de Correspondance Héllenique*, 71–2.

Garstang, J., 1939. Explorations in Cilicia. The Neilson expedition: fifth interim report. Excavations at Mersin: 1938–39. *AAA* 26, 89–158.

Garstang, J., 1953. *Prehistoric Mersin: Yümük Tepe in Southern Turkey; the Neilson Expedition in Cilicia*. Oxford: Clarendon Press.

Gates, M.-H., 2001. Potmarks at Kinet Höyük and the Hittite

References

ceramic industry, in Jean *et al.* (eds.), 137–57.

Geldiay, R. & S. Balık, 1996. *Türkiye tatlısu balıkları*. Izmir: Ege Üniversitesi.

Genz, H., 2000. Die Eisenzeit in Zentralanatolien im Lichte der keramischen Funde vom Büyükkaya in Boğazköy/Hattuša. *TÜBA-AR* 3, 35–54.

Genz, H., 2003. Früheisenzeitliche Keramik von Büyükkale in Boğazköy/Hattuša. *Istanbuler Mitteilungen* 53, 113–129.

Genz, H., 2004. *Büyükkaya I. Die Keramik der Eisenzeit. Funde aus den Grabungskampagnen 1993 bis 1998 (Boğazköy/Hattuša XXI)*. Berlin: Gebr. Mann.

Ghirshman, R., 1939. *Fouilles de Sialk près de Kashan, 1933, 1934, 1937*, vol. II. Département des Antiquites Orientales, sér. archéologique V). Paris: Geuthner.

Gilchrist, R. & C.H. Mytum, 1986. Experimental archaeology and burnt animal bones from archaeological sites. *Circaea* 4(1), 29–38.

Gilmour, G., 1997. The nature and function of astragalus bones from archaeological contexts in the Levant and Eastern Mediterranean. *Oxford Journal of Archaeology* 16, 167–75.

Gjerstad, E., 1948. *The Cypro-Geometric, Cypro-Archaic and Cypro-Classical Periods*. (The Swedish Cyprus Expedition IV/2.) Stockholm: The Swedish Cyprus Expedition.

Gjerstad, E., 1977a. Pottery from various parts of Cyprus, in Gjerstad (ed.), 23–59.

Gjerstad, E. (ed.), 1977b. *Greek Geometric and Archaic Pottery found in Cyprus* (Acta Instituti Atheniensis Regni Sueciae 4°, 26.) Stockholm: Svenska Institutet i Athen.

Gjerstad, E., 1980. *Ages and Days in Cyprus*. Göteborg: Paul Åströms Förlag.

Gjerstad, E., E.J. Lindros, E. Sjøqvist & A. Westholm, 1935. *Finds and Results of the Excavations in Cyprus 1927–1931*. (The Swedish Cyprus Expedition II.) Stockholm: The Swedish Cyprus Expedition.

Goldman, H., 1935. Preliminary expedition to Cilicia, 1934, and excavations at Gözlü Kule, Tarsus, 1935. *AJA* 39, 526–49.

Goldman, H., 1937. Excavations at Gözlü Kule, Tarsus, 1936. *AJA* 41, 262–86.

Goldman, H. (ed.), 1950. *Excavations at Gözlü Kule, Tarsus, I. The Hellenistic and Roman Periods*. Princeton (NJ): Princeton University Press.

Goldman, H. (ed.), 1956. *Excavations at Gözlü Kule, Tarsus, II. From the Neolithic through the Bronze Age*. Princeton (NJ): Princeton University Press.

Goldman, H. (ed.), 1963. *Excavations at Gözlü Kule Tarsus, III. The Iron Age*. Princeton (NJ): Princeton University Press.

Goldman, H. & F.F. Jones, 1950. The lamps, in Goldman (ed.), 84-133.

Gorelick, L. & A.J. Gwinnett, 1989. 'Collars' in the holes of Near Eastern cylinder seals. *Archeomaterials* 3, 39–46.

Gorny, R.L., 1993. The biconvex seals of Alişar Höyük. *An. St.* 43, 163–91.

Gough, M., 1955. Early churches in Cilicia. *Byzantinoslavica* 16/ii, 210–11.

Gough, M., 1957. A Church of the iconoclast (?) period in Byzantine Isauria. *An. St.* 7, 153–63.

Gough, M., 1958. Report on archaeological work carried out at Alahan in 1957. *Türk Arkeoloji Dergisi* 8/ii, 6.

Gough, M., 1959a. Dağ Pazarı. *An. St.* 9, 8.

Gough, M., 1959b. Karlık and Dağ Pazarı, 1958. *Türk Arkeoloji Dergisi* 9/ii, 5–6.

Gough, M., 1960. Dağ Pazarı 1959. *Türk Arkeoloji Dergisi* 10/ii, 23–4.

Gough, M., 1962. The Church of the Evangelists at Alahan: a preliminary report. *An. St.* 12, 173–84.

Gough, M., 1963. Excavations at Alahan monastery: second preliminary report. *An. St.* 13, 105–16.

Gough, M., 1964. Excavations at Alahan monastery: third preliminary report. *An. St.* 14, 185–90.

Gough, M., 1968. Excavations at Alahan monastery: fifth preliminary report. *An. St.* 18, 159–67.

Gough, M., 1972. The Emperor Zeno and some Cilician churches. *An. St.* 22, 199–212.

Gough, M.R.E., 1974. Notes on a visit to Mahras monastery in Isauria. *Byzantine Studies* 1, 65–72.

Gough, M. (ed.), 1985. *An Early Christian Monastery in Southern Turkey. Based on the Work of Michael Gough*. Toronto: Pontifical Institute of Mediaeval Studies.

Grayson, A.K., 1975. *Assyrian and Babylonian Chronicles*. (Texts from Cuneiform Sources 5.) Locust Valley (NY): J.J. Augustin.

Grayson, A.K., 1996. *Assyrian Rulers of the Early First Millennium BC*, vol. II *(858–745 BC)*. (The Royal Inscriptions of Mesopotamia. Assyrian periods 3.) Toronto: University of Toronto Press.

Green, A. (ed.), 1993. *The 6G Ash-tip and its Contents: Cultic and Administrative Discard from the Temple?* (Abu Salabikh Excavations 4.) London: BSAI.

Greenwood, P.H. & G. Howes, 1973. Fish remains, in *Salamis V. Excavations in the Necropolis of Salamis III*, ed. V. Karageorghis. Nicosia: Zevallis Press, 259–68.

Gurney, O.R., 1997. The Annals of Hattusilis III. *An. St.* 47, 127–39.

Güterbock, H.G., 1942. *Siegel aus Boğazköy II*. (Archiv für Orientforschung, Beiheft 7.)

Guyer, S., 1909/10. Ala Kilise — ein kleinasiatischer Bau des V. Jahrhunderts. *Zeitschrift für Geschichte der Architectur* 3, 192–9.

Haldon, J., 1999. *Warfare, State and Society in the Byzantine World, 565–1204*. London: University College London.

Haldon, J. & H. Kennedy, 1980. The Arab–Byzantine frontier in the eighth and ninth centuries: military organization and society in the borderlands. *Zbornik Radova Biz. Inst.* 19, 79–116.

Hanfmann, G.M.A., 1963. The Iron Age pottery of Tarsus, in Goldman (ed.), 18–332.

Hansen, C.K. & J.N. Postgate, 1999. The Bronze to Iron Age transition at Kilise Tepe. *An. St.* 49, 111–21.

Hardy-Smith, T. & P.C. Edwards, 2004. The garbage crisis in prehistory: artefact discard patterns at the Early Natufian site of Wadi Hammeh 27 and the origins of household refuse disposal strategies. *Journal of Anthropological Archaeology* 23, 253–89.

Harrison, R.M., 1980. The monastery on Mahras Dağ in Isauria. *Yayla: Third Report of the Northern Society for*

Anatolian Archaeology (Newcastle upon Tyne), 22–4.

Harrison, R.M., 1985. The inscriptions and chronology of Alahan, in Gough (ed.), 21–35.

Hawkins, J.D., 1972–75. Hilakku. *Reallexikon der Assyriologie* Band IV, 402–3.

Hawkins, J.D., 1992. The inscriptions of the Kızıldağ and the Karadağ in the light of the Yalburt inscription, in *Hittite and Other Anatolian and Near Eastern Studies in honour of Sedat Alp*, eds. H. Otten, E. Akurgal, H. Ertem & A. Süel. Ankara: Türk Tarih Kurumu, 259–75.

Hawkins, J.D., 1995. *The Hieroglyphic Inscription of the Sacred Pool Complex at Hattusa (SÜDBURG).* (Studien zu den Bogazköy-Texten Beiheft 3.) Wiesbaden: Harrassowitz.

Hawkins, J.D., 2000. *Corpus of Hieroglyphic Luwian Inscriptions*, vol. I: *Inscriptions of the Iron Age*. Berlin: de Gruyter.

Hawkins, J.D., 2002. Anatolia: the end of the Hittite Empire and after, in *Die nahöstlichen Kulturen und Griechenland an der Wende vom 2. zum 1. Jahrtausend v. Chr.: Kontinuität und Wandel von Strukturen und Mechanismen kultureller Interaktion*, eds. E.A. Braun-Holzinger & H. Matthäus. Möhnesee: Bibliopolis, 143–51.

Hayes, J.W., 1972. *Late Roman Pottery*. London: British School at Rome.

Hayes, J.W., 1980. Problèmes de la céramique des VIIème–IXème Siècles à Salamine et à Chypre, in *Salamine de Chypre Histoire et Archéologie État des recherches 13–17 mars 1978.* (Actes du Colloque International 578.) Paris: CNRS, 375–93.

Hayes, J.W., 1991. *Paphos III: the Hellenistic and Roman Pottery*. Nicosia: Department of Antiquities of Cyprus.

Hayes, J.W., 1997. Ceramics of the Byzantine period, in Meyers (ed.), 471–5.

Hayes, W.C., 1959. *The Scepter of Egypt*, part II: *The Hyksos Period and the New Kingdom (1675–1080 BC)*. New York (NY): The Metropolitan Museum of Art.

Headlam, A.C., 1892. *Ecclesiatical Sites in Isauria (Cilicia Tracheia).* (The Society for the Promotion of Hellenic Studies. Supplementary papers 2.) London: The Society for the Promotion of Hellenic Studies.

Heberdey, R. & A. Wilhelm, 1896. *Reisen in Kilikien ausgeführt 1891 und 1892 im Aufträge der Kaiserlichen Akademie der Wissenschaften.* (Denkschriften der Kaiserliche Akademie der Wissenschaften in Wien, phil.-hist. Klasse, Band XLIV/6.) Vienna: Öster. Akad. der Wissenschaften.

Hein, A. & H. Mommsen, 1999. Element concentration distributions and most discriminating elements for provenancing by NAA of ceramics from Bronze Age sites in Greece. *JAS* 25, 1053–8.

Hein, A., T. Beier & H. Mommsen, 2002. A complete chemical grouping of the Perlman/Asaro neutron activation analysis databank of Mycenaean and Minoan pottery, in Kilikoglou *et al.* (eds.), 143–50.

Hellenkemper, H., 1994. Early church architecture in southern Asia Minor, in *'Churches built in Ancient Times': Recent Studies in Early Christian Archaeology*, ed. K. Painter. London: Society of Antiquaries of London, 213–38.

Hendy, M., 1985. *Studies in the Byzantine Monetary Economy c. 300–1450.* Cambridge: Cambridge University Press.

Henrickson, R.C., 1994. Continuity and discontinuity in the ceramic tradition of Gordion during the Iron Age, in French & Çilingiroğlu (eds.), 92–129.

Henrickson, R.C., 2002. Hittite pottery and potters: the view from Late Bronze Age Gordion, in *Across the Anatolian Plateau: Readings in the Archaeology of Ancient Turkey*, ed. D.C. Hopkins. Boston (MA): Annual of the American Schools of Oriental Research 57, 123–32.

Herbordt, S., 1998. Seals and sealings of Hittite officials from the Nisantepe Archive, Boğazköy, in *Acts of the IIIrd International Congress of Hittitology, Ankara*, eds. S. Alp & A. Süel. Ankara: Grafik, Teknik Hazırlık Uyum Ajans, 309–18.

Herbordt, S., 2005. *Die Prinzen- und Beamtensiegel der hethitischen Grossreichszeit auf Tonbullen aus dem Nişantepe-Archiv in Hattuša (Boğazköy/Hattuša XIX).* Mainz: von Zabern.

Herzfeld, E. & S. Guyer, 1930. *Meriamlik und Korykos. Zwei christliche Ruinenstatten des Rauhen Kilikiens* (Monumenta Asiae Minoris Antiqua 2.) Manchester: Manchester University Press.

Hild, F. & H. Hellenkemper, 1990. *Tabula Imperii Byzantini 5. Kilikien und Isaurien.* (Öster. Akad. der Wissenschaften, phil.-hist. Kl., 215.) Vienna: Öster. Akad. der Wissenschaften.

Hild, F., H. Hellenkemper & G. Hellenkemper Salies, 1984. Kommagene–Kilikien–Isaurien. *Reallexikon zur Byzantinischen Kunst* 4, 182–356.

Hill, S., 1979. Dağ Pazarı and its monuments: a preliminary report. *Yayla* 2, 8–12.

Hill, S., 1996. *The Early Byzantine Churches of Cilicia and Isauria.* Aldershot: Variorum.

Hill, S., 1998. Alahan and Dağ Pazarı, in Matthews (ed.), 315–39.

Hillman, G., 1981. Reconstructing crop husbandry practices from charred remains of crops, in *Farming Practice in British Prehistory*, ed. R. Mercer. Edinburgh: Edinburgh University Press, 123–64.

Hillman, G., 1984. Interpretation of archaeological plant remains: the application of ethnographic models from Turkey, in Van Zeist & Caspare (eds.), 1–41.

Hodder, I. (ed.), 1996. *On the Surface: Çatalhöyük 1993–95.* (McDonald Institute Monographs/BIAA Monograph 22.) Cambridge: McDonald Institute for Archaeological Research/London: BIAA.

Hodson, M.J. & A.G. Sangster, 1988. Silica deposition in the inflorescence bracts of wheat (*Triticum aestivum* L.), I. Scanning electron microscopy and light microscopy. *Canadian Journal of Botany* 66, 829–38.

Hoffmann, S.M.A. & V.J. Robinson, 1993. Neutron activation groupings of imported material from Tell Abu Hawam, appendix to E.B. French, Wace and Blegen: Some introductory thoughts and a case study, in Zerner *et al.* (eds.), 7–10.

Hoffmann, S.M.A., V.J. Robinson & E.B. French, 1992. Report on the Perlman/Asaro analysis of selected Nichoria sherds, in *Excavations at Nichoria in Southwest Greece*, vol. 2: *The Bronze Age Occupation*, eds. W.A. McDonald

& N.C. Wilkie. Minneapolis (MN): University of Minnesota Press, 779–82.
Hoffmann, S.M.A., V.J. Robinson, E.B. French & R.E. Jones, forthcoming. The problems of the North East Peloponnese and progress to its solution: effects of measurement errors and element-element correlations in defining ceramic reference groups, in *Nuclear Chemistry and its Influence on Modern Science*, eds. D. Adan-Beyitz, M. Artzy & F. Asaro.
Hölbl, G., 2001. *A History of the Ptolemaic Empire*. London: Routledge.
Hopwood, K., 1991. The links between the coastal cities of western Rough Cilicia and the interior during the Roman period. *De Anatolia Antiqua (=Eski Anadolu)* 1, 305–10.
Houwink ten Cate, P.H.J., 1961. *The Luwian Population Groups of Lycia and Cilicia Aspera During the Hellenistic Period*. Leiden: Brill.
Howland, R.H., 1958. *The Athenian Agora*, vol. IV: *Greek Lamps and their Survivals*. Princeton (NJ): American School of Classical Studies.
Hrouda, B., 1998. Ergebnisse der Ausgrabung auf dem Sirkeli Höyük, Herbst 1996. *KST* 19/i, 467–82.
Jackson, M., 1999a. A pilgrimage experience at sacred sites in late antique Anatolia, in Baker *et al*. (eds.), 72–85.
Jackson, M., 1999b. The Göksu Valley Project. *Anatolian Archaeology* 5, 26.
Jackson, M.P.C., 2001. Kilise Tepe in Byzantine Isauria. Unpublished PhD thesis, University of Newcastle upon Tyne.
Jackson, M.P.C. & J.N. Postgate, 1999. Kilise Tepe 1997. A summary of the principal results. *KST* 20/i, 541–57.
Jasink, A.M., 2001. Kizzuwatna and Tarhuntašša, their historical evolution and interactions with Hatti, in Jean *et al*. (eds.), 46–56.
Jean, É., 2003. From Bronze to Iron Ages in Cilicia: the pottery in its stratigraphic context, in Fischer *et al*. (eds.), 79–91.
Jean, É., A.M. Dinçol & S. Durugönül, (eds.), 2001. *La Cilicie: espaces et pouvoirs locaux (2e millénaire av. J.-C.–4e siècle ap. J.-C.): Actes de la Table Ronde Internationale d'Istanbul 2–5 novembre 1999*. Paris: de Boccard.
Jerphanion, G. de, 1928. *Une nouvelle province de l'art byzantin: Les Églises Rupestres de Cappadoce*. Paris: Geuthner.
Jones, A.H.M., 1973. *The Later Roman Empire, 284–602: a Social and Economic Survey*. Oxford: Blackwell.
Jones, F.F., 1950. The pottery, in Goldman (ed.), 149–295.
Jones, G., 1984. Interpretation of archaeological plant remains: ethnographic models from Greece, in van Zeist & Casparie (eds.), 43–61.
Jones, G., 1990. The application of present-day cereal processing studies to charred archaeobotanical remains. *Circaea* 6/2, 91–6.
Jones, G., 1998. Distinguishing food from fodder in the archaeobotanical record. *Environmental Archaeology* 1, 95–8.
Jones, R.E., 1986. *Greek and Cypriot Pottery: a Review of Scientific Studies*. (Fitch Laboratory Occasional Paper 1.) Athens: BSA.
Joukowsky, M.S., 1986. *Prehistoric Aphrodisias I. Excavations and Studies*. Louvain-la-Neuve: Institut supérieur d'archéologie et d'histoire de l'art, Collège Érasme.
Kaplan, L., M.B. Smith & L.A. Sneddon, 1992. Cereal grain phytoliths of southwest Asia and Europe, in Rapp & Mulholland (eds.), 149–74.
Karageorghis, V., 1983. *Palaepaphos-Skales: an Iron Age Cemetery in Cyprus*. Konstanz: Universitätsverlag.
Karageorghis, V., E. Vassilika & P. Wilson, 1999. *The Ancient Art of Cyprus in the Fitzwilliam Museum, Cambridge*. Cambridge: The Fitzwilliam Museum & The A.G. Leventis Foundation.
Kardulias, P.N. & R.W. Yerkes, 1996. Microwear and metric analysis of threshing sledge flints from Greece and Cyprus. *JAS* 23, 657–66.
Kataja, L. & R. Whiting, 1995. *Grants, Decrees and Gifts of the Neo-Assyrian Period*. (State Archives of Assyria XII.) Helsinki: Helsinki University Press.
Kazhdan, A. & A. Cutler, 1982. Continuity and discontinuity in Byzantine History. *Byzantion* 52, 429–78.
Keckler, D. 1994. *Surfer for Windows: User's Guide*. Golden: Golden Software Inc.
Keil, J. & A. Wilhelm, 1931. *Denkmäler aus dem Rauhen Kilikien*. (Monumenta Asiae Minoris Antiqua 3.) Manchester: Manchester University Press.
Kennedy, H., 1985. The last century of Byzantine Syria: a reinterpretation. *Byzantinische Forschungen* 10, 141–83.
Kennedy, H., 1992. The impact of Muslim rule on the pattern of rural settlement in Syria, in *La Syrie de Byzance à l'Islam VIIe–VIIIe Siècles*, eds. P. Canivet & J.-P. Rey-Coquais. Damascus: Institut Français de Damas, 291–7.
Kennedy, H. & J.H.W.G. Liebeschuetz, 1988. Antioch and the villages of northern Syria in the fifth and sixth centuries AD: trends and problems. *Nottingham Medieval Studies* 32, 65–90.
Kenyon, K., 1957. Pottery: Hellenistic and later, in *The Objects from Samaria*, eds. J.W. Crowfoot, G.M. Crowfoot & K.M. Kenyon. London: Palestine Exploration Fund. 217–72.
Kilgore, L. & R. Jurmain, 1988. Analysis of the human skeletal remains, in *The Circus and a Byzantine Cemetery at Carthage*, vol I, ed. J.H. Humphrey. Ann Arbor (MI): University of Michigan Press, 257–83.
Kilikoglou, V., A. Hein & Y. Maniatis (eds.), 2002. *Modern Trends in Scientific Studies on Ancient Ceramics*. (BAR International Series 1011.) Oxford: Archaeopress.
Knapp, A.B. & J.F. Cherry, 1994. *Provenience Studies and Bronze Age Cyprus: Production, Exchange and Politico-economic Change*. Madison (WI): Prehistory Press.
Knappett, C., V. Kilikoglou, V. Steele & B. Stern, 2005. The circulation and consumption of Red Lustrous Wheelmade Ware: petrographic, chemical and residue analysis. *An. St.* 55, 25–59.
Kondoleon, C., 2000. *Antioch: the Lost Ancient City*. Princeton (NJ): Princeton University Press in association with the Worcester Art Museum.
Korbel, G., 1987. *Spätbronzezeitliche Keramik. Tarsus (Grabung H. Goldman)*. (Mitt. 5.) Hannover: Institut für Bauen und Planen in Entwicklungsländern.
Korfmann, M., 1983a. Red cross bowl: Angeblicher Leittyp für Troja V, in Boehmer & Hauptmann (eds.), 291–7.

Korfmann, M., 1983b. *Demircihüyük. Die Ergebnisse der Ausgrabungen 1975–1978*, Band I: *Architektur, Stratigraphie und Befunde*. Mainz: von Zabern.
Koşay, H.Z., 1951. *Alaca Höyük kazısı 1937–1939. Les fouilles d'Alaca Höyük*. Ankara: Türk Tarih Kurumu.
Koşay, H.Z. & M. Akok, 1966. *Ausgrabungen von Alaca Höyük: Vorbericht über die Forschungen und Entdeckungen von 1940–1948*. Ankara: Türk Tarih Kurumu.
Koşay, H.Z. & M. Akok, 1973. *Alaca Höyük Excavations, Preliminary Report on Research and Discoveries 1963–1967*. Ankara: Türk Tarih Kurumu .
Kosswig, C., 1969. New contributions to the zoogeography of fresh water fish of Asia Minor, based on collections made between 1964–1967. *Israel Journal of Zoology* 18, 249–54.
Kozal, E., 2003. Analysis of the distribution patterns of Red Lustrous Wheel-made Ware, Mycenaean and Cypriot pottery in Anatolia in the 13th–15th centuries BC, in Fischer *et al.* (eds.), 65–77.
Kramer, C. 1982. *Village Ethnoarchaeology: Rural Iran in Archaeological Perspective*. New York (NY): Academic Press.
Kromer, B., S.W. Manning, P.I. Kuniholm, M.W. Newton, M. Spurk & I. Levin, 2001. Regional $^{14}CO_2$ offsets in the tropospheres: magnitude, mechanisms, and consequences. *Science* 294, 2529–2 [online: 10-1126/science.1066114].
Küçükerman, Ö., 1988. *Turkish House: in Search of Spatial Identity*. Istanbul: Turkish Touring and Automobile Association.
Kulaçoğlu, B., 1992. *Museum of Anatolian Civilizations: Gods and Goddesses*. Ankara: General Directorate of Monuments and Museums.
Kull, B., 1988. *Demircihüyük V. Die Mittelbronzezeitliche Siedlung*. Mainz: von Zabern.
Kuniholm, P.I., B. Kromer, S.W. Manning, M. Newton, C.E. Latini & M.J. Bruce, 1996. Anatolian tree rings and the absolute chronology of the eastern Mediterranean, 2220–718 BC. *Nature* 381 (27 June 1996), 780–83.
Lamb, W., 1936. *Excavations at Thermi in Lesbos*. Cambridge: The University Press.
Lamb, W., 1937. Excavations at Kusura near Afyon Karahisar. *Archaeologia* 86, 1–64.
Lamb, W., 1938. Excavations at Kusura near Afyon Karahisar: II. *Archaeologia* 87, 217–73.
Lapidus, I. M., 1988. *A History of Islamic Societies*. Cambridge: Cambridge University Press.
Laroche, E., 1956. Noms de dignataires. *Revue Hittite et Asianique* 58, 26–32.
Laroche, E., 1960. *Les hiéroglyphes Hittites I*. Paris: CNRS.
Laroche, E., 1966. *Les noms des Hittites*. Paris: Klincksieck.
Last, J., 1996. Surface pottery at Çatalhöyük, in Hodder (ed.), 115–71.
Leake, W.M., 1824. *Journal of a Tour in Asia Minor with Comparative Remarks on the Ancient and Modern Geography of that Country*. London: J. Murray.
Lemaire, A. & H. Lozachmeur, 1987. Les inscriptions araméennes, in Davesne *et al.* (eds.), 365–77.
Lenski, N., 1999. Assimilation and revolt in the territory of Isauria, from the 1st century BC to the 6th century AD. *Journal of the Economic and Social History of the Orient* 42, 413–16.
Leonard, A., Jr, 1994. *An Index to the Late Bronze Age Aegean Pottery from Syria-Palestine*. (SIMA 114.) Jonsered: Paul Åströms Förlag.
Lernau, H., 1986/87. Subfossil remains of Nile perch (*Lates* cf. *niloticus*); first evidence from ancient Israel. *Israel Journal of Zoology* 34, 225–36.
Lernau, O., 1996. Fish remains from Tel Harassim, in *Onat ha-hafirot ha-shishit be-Tel-Harasim (Nahal Barka'i) 1995: din ve-heshbon rishoni 6 [The Sixth Season of Excavation at Tel Harassim (Nahal Barkai) 1995]*, ed. S. Givon. Tel Aviv: Universiat Bar-Ilan, 14–23.
Levi, D., 1976. *Festòs e la Civiltà Minoica*. (Incunabula Graeca LX.) Rome: Institute for Mycenean and Aegeo-Anatolian Studies.
Lilie, R.-J., 1976. *Die byzantinische Reaktion auf die Ausbreitung der Araber, Studien zur Strukturwandlung des byzantinischen Staats im 7. und 8. Jahrhundert*. Munich: Institut für Byzantinistik und Neugriechische Philologie.
Lilie, R.-J., 1993. *Byzantium and the Crusader States, 1096–1204*. Oxford: Clarendon Press.
Lister, A., 1996. The morphological distinction between bones and teeth of fallow deer (*Dama dama*) and red deer (*Cervus elaphus*). *International Journal of Osteoarchaeology* 6, 119–43.
Littauer, M.A. & J.H. Crouwel, 1979. *Wheeled Vehicles and Ridden Animals in the Ancient Near East*. Leiden: Brill.
Lloyd, S., 1972. *Beycesultan*, vol. III/i: *Late Bronze Age Architecture*. London: BIAA.
Lloyd, S. & J. Mellaart, 1962. *Beycesultan*, vol. I: *The Chalcolithic and Early Bronze Age*. London: BIAA.
Lloyd, S. & J. Mellaart, 1965. *Beycesultan*, vol. II: *Middle Bronze Age Architecture and Pottery*. London: BIAA.
Loud, G., 1939. *The Megiddo Ivories*. (Oriental Institute Publications 52.) Chicago (IL): The University of Chicago.
Loud, G., 1948. *Megiddo II: Seasons of 1935–39*. (Oriental Institute Publications 62.) Chicago (IL): The University of Chicago.
Madella, M., 2001. Understanding archaeological structures by means of phytolith analysis: a test from the Iron Age site of Kilise Tepe – Turkey, in Meunier & Colin (eds.), 173–82.
Madella, M., 2003. Investigating agriculture and environment in South Asia: present and future contributions from opal phytoliths, in *Indus Ethnobiology: New Perspectives from the Field*, eds. S.A. Weber & W.R. Belcher. Lanham (MD): Lexington Books, 199–249.
Madella, M., A.H. Powers-Jones & M.K. Jones, 1998. A simple method of extraction of opal phytoliths from sediments using a non-toxic heavy liquid. *JAS* 25, 801–3.
Magness, J., 2003. *The Archaeology of the Early Islamic Settlement in Palestine*. Winona Lake (IN): Eisenbrauns.
Maguire, H., 1990. Garments pleasing to God: the significance of domestic textile designs in the Early Byzantine period. *Dumbarton Oaks Papers* 44, 215–24.
Mango, C., 1966. Isaurian builders, in *Polychronion: Festschrift Franz Dölger zum 75 Geburtstag*, ed. P. Wirth. Heidelberg: C. Winter, 358–65.
Mango, C., 1986. *Byzantine Architecture*. London: Faber/Electa.

References

Mango, C., 1991. Germia, a postscript. *Jahrbuch der Österreichischen Byzantinistik* 41, 297–300.

Manning, S.W. & B. Weninger, 1992. A light in the dark: archaeological wiggle matching and the absolute chronology of the close of the Aegean Late Bronze Age. *Antiquity* 66, 636–63.

Manning, S.W., B. Kromer, P.I. Kuniholm & M.W. Newton, 2001. Anatolian tree rings and a new chronology for the East Mediterranean Bronze–Iron Ages. *Science* 294, 2532–5. [online: 10.1126/science.1066112].

Manning, S.W., B. Kromer, P.I. Kuniholm & M.W. Newton, 2003. Confirmation of near-absolute dating of east Mediterranean bronze-iron dendrochronology. *Antiquity* 77, Proj. Gall. (http://antiquity.ac.uk).

Margueron, J.-C., 1982. Les Coffrets, in *Meskéné–Emar: Dix ans de travaux 1972–1982*, ed. D. Beyer. Paris: ÉRC. 95–7.

Martin, H.P., 1985. Metalwork, in *Graves 1 to 99*, ed. J.N. Postgate. (Abu Salabikh Excavations 2.) London: BSAI.

Matthews, J., 1989. *The Roman Empire of Ammianus*. London: Duckworth.

Matthews, R.J., 1989. Excavations at Jemdat Nasr, 1988. *Iraq* 51, 225–48.

Matthews, R.J., 1996a. Systematic surface collection, in Hodder (ed.), 73–7.

Matthews, R.J., 1996b. Surface scraping and planning, in Hodder (ed.), 79–99.

Matthews, R.J. (ed.), 1998. *Ancient Anatolia. Fifty Years' Work by the British Institute of Archaeology at Ankara*. London: BIAA.

Matthews, R.J., 2003. *The Archaeology of Mesopotamia: Theories and Approaches*. London: Routledge.

Matthews, R.J. & J.N. Postgate, 1987. Excavations at Abu Salabikh, 1985–86. *Iraq* 49, 91–119.

Matthews, R.J. & J.N. Postgate (eds.), 2001. *Contextual Analysis of the Use of Space at two Near Eastern Bronze Age Sites* (http://ads.ahds.ac.uk/catalogue/projArch/TellBrak/).

Matthews, W., 2001. Micromorphological analysis of occupational sequences, in Matthews & Postgate 2001, part 7.

Matthiae, P., F. Pinnock & G. Scandone Matthiae, 1995. *Ebla: Alle Origini della Civiltà Urbana. Trent'anni di Scavi in Siria dell'Università di Roma 'La Sapienza'*. (Exhibition catalogue.) Milan: Electa.

Mays, S., 1998. *The Archaeology of Human Remains*. London: Routledge.

Mee, C.B., 1978. Aegean trade and settlement in Anatolia in the second millennium BC. *An. St.* 28, 121–56.

Mee, C., 1998. Anatolia and the Aegean in the Late Bronze Age, in *The Aegean and the Orient in the Second Millennium*, eds. E.H. Cline, & D. Harris-Cline. (Aegaeum 18.) Liège: Université de Liège, 137–48.

Mellaart, J., 1954. Preliminary report on a survey of Pre-Classical remains in southern Turkey. *An. St.* 4, 175–240.

Mellaart, J., 1955. Iron Age pottery from southern Anatolia. *Belleten* 19, 115–36.

Mellaart, J., 1958a. Second millennium pottery from the Konya Plain and neighbourhood. *Belleten* 22, 311–45.

Mellaart, J., 1958b. The Neolithic obsidian industry of Ilıcapınar and its relations. *Istanbuler Mitteilungen* 8, 82–92.

Mellaart, J., 1961. Early cultures of the South Anatolian Plateau. *An. St.* 11, 159–84.

Mellaart, J., 1963. Early cultures of the South Anatolian Plateau II. *An. St.* 13, 199–236.

Mellaart, J., 1970. *Excavations at Hacilar*. Edinburgh: Edinburgh University Press.

Mellaart, J., 1971. Anatolia c. 4000–2300 BC, in *The Cambridge Ancient History*, vol. I, pt 2, eds. I.E.S. Edwards, C.J. Gadd & N.G.L. Hammond. 3rd edition. Cambridge: Cambridge University Press, 363–410.

Mellaart, J., 1975. *The Neolithic of the Near East*. London: Thames & Hudson.

Mellaart, J. & A. Murray, 1995. *Beycesultan*, vol. III/ii: *The Late Bronze Age Pottery and the Middle and Late Bronze Age Small Objects*. London: BSAI.

Mellink, M.J., 1965. Archaeology in Asia Minor. *AJA* 69, 133–49.

Mellink, M.J., 1966. Excavations at Karataş Semayük in Lycia, 1965. *AJA* 70, 245–55.

Mellink, M.J., 1967. Archaeology in Asia Minor. *AJA* 71, 155–74.

Mellink, M., 1986. The Early Bronze Age in West Anatolia: Aegean and Asiatic correlations, in Cadogan (ed.), 139–52.

Mellink, M., 1989. Anatolian and foreign relations of Tarsus in the Early Bronze Age, in Emre et al. (eds.), 319–31.

Metzger, H., 1972. *Les Céramiques Archaiques et Classiques de l'Acropole Lycienne*. (Fouilles de Xanthos IV.) Paris: Klincksieck.

Meunier, J.D. & F. Colin (eds.), 2001. *Phytoliths: Applications in Earth Sciences and Human History*. Lisse: Balkema.

Meyers, E.M. (ed.), 1997. *The Oxford Encyclopedia of Archaeology in the Near East*, vol. 1. Oxford: Oxford University Press.

Meyza, H. & J. Mlynarczyk, 1995. *Hellenistic and Roman Pottery in the Eastern Mediterranean: Advances in Scientific Studies. Acts of the II. Nieborow Pottery Workshop.* (Research Centre for Mediterranean Archaeology.) Warsaw: Polish Academy of Sciences.

Mietke, G., 1996. Survey der römisch-frühbyzantinische Siedlung bei Akören in Kilikien, 1994. *AST* 13, 35–48.

Mietke, G., 1999. Review of Stephen Hill, The Early Byzantine Churches of Cilicia and Isauria. *Byzantinische Zeitschrift* 92, 120–24.

Miller, D.C., 1998. Palaeobotanical Remains from Kilise Tepe, Southern Turkey. Unpublished M.Sc. dissertation, University of Sheffield.

Miller, P.J. & M.J. Loates, 1997. *Fish of Britain & Europe*. London: Collins Pocket Guides.

Mitchell, S., 1979. Iconium and Ninica. Two double communities in Roman Asia Minor. *Historia* 28, 409–38.

Mitchell, S., 1980. *Aşvan Kale: Keban Rescue Excavations in Eastern Anatolia I. The Hellenistic, Roman and Islamic Site*. (BAR International Series 80.) Oxford: BAR.

Mitchell, S., 1999. Archaeology in Asia Minor 1990–98, in *Archaeological Reports for 1998–99*. London: The Council of the Society for the Promotion of Hellenic Studies

References

and the Managing Committee of the BSA, 125–91.

Mitford, T.B., 1980. Roman rough Cilicia, in *Principat 7.2. Politische Geschichte*, ed. H. Temporini. (Aufstieg und Niedergang der Römischen Welt II.) New York (NY): de Gruyter, 1230–61.

Molleson, T.I., 1994. The eloquent bones of Abu Hureyra. *Scientific American* 217, 59–65.

Moore, J., 1993. *Tille Höyük 1. The Medieval Period*. London: BIAA.

Moorey, P.R.S., 1980. *Cemeteries of the First Millennium BC at Deve Hüyük, near Carchemish, Salvaged by T.E. Lawrence and C.L. Woolley in 1913*. (BAR International Series 87.) Oxford: BAR.

Moorey, P.R.S., 1994. *Ancient Mesopotamian Materials and Industries*. Oxford: Clarendon Press.

Mora, C., 1987. *La Glittica Anatolica del II Millennio A.C.: Classificazione Tipologica. 1, I sigilli a iscrizione geroglifica*. Pavia: Iuculano.

Mora, C., 1990. I sigilli 'post-ittiti' con iscrizione geroglifica, in *Il geroglifico anatolico. Problemi di analisi e prospettive di ricerca*, ed. M. Marazzi. Roma: Dipartimento di Studi Glottoantropologici, Università 'La Sapienza'. 443–57.

Morris, D., 1985. *The Art of Ancient Cyprus*. Oxford: Phaidon Press.

Mountjoy, P.A., 1986. *Mycenaean Decorated Pottery: a Guide to Identification*. (SIMA 73.) Göteborg: Paul Åströms Förlag.

Mountjoy, P.A., 1997. Local Mycenaean pottery at Troia. *Studia Troica* 7, 259–67.

Mountjoy, P.A., 2005. The Mycenaean pottery from the 1934–1939 excavations at Tarsus, in Özyar (ed.), 83–134.

Moutsopoulos-Leon, V., 1991. *Die Basilika am Staatsmarkt in Ephesos. Kleinfunde: 1 Teil: Keramik Hellenistischer und Römischer Zeit*. (Forschungen in Ephesos IX 2/2.) Wien: Schindler.

Müller-Karpe, A., 1988. *Hethitische Töpferei der Oberstadt von Hattuša*. (Marburger Studien zur Vor- und Frühgeschichte 10.) Marburg/Lahn: Hitzeroth Verlag.

Müller-Karpe, A., 1994. *Anatolisches Metallhandwerk*. Neumünster: Wachholtz Verlag.

Mutter, L.G. 1998. An Iron Age Pottery Study from Kilise Tepe, Turkey. Unpublished BA Dissertation, University of Cambridge.

Mylonas, G., 1933. Pre-Persian pottery from Olynthus, in *Excavations at Olynthus*, vol. V: *Mosaics, Vases and Lamps of Olynthus found in 1928 and 1931*, ed. D.M. Robinson. Baltimore (MD): Johns Hopkins University Press, 15–63.

Napoleone-Lemaire, J. & J.-C. Balty, 1969. *L'église à Atrium de la Grande Colonnade*. (Fouilles d'Apamée de Syrie I, 4.) Brussels: Centre Belge de recherches archéologiques à Apamée de Syrie.

Nesbitt, M., 1995. Plants and people in ancient Anatolia. *Biblical Archaeologist* 58(2), 68–81.

Nesbitt, M. & G.D. Summers, 1988. Some recent discoveries of millets (*Panicum miliaceum* and *Setaria italica*) at excavations in Turkey and Iran. *An. St.* 38, 85–97.

Neve, P., 1982. *Büyükkale, Die Bauwerke, Grabungen 1954–1966 (Boğazköy-Hattuša XII)*. Berlin: Gebr. Mann.

Neve, P., 1985. Die Ausgrabungen in Boğazköy-Hattuša 1984. *AA*, 323–52.

Neve, P., 1987. Die Ausgrabungen in Boğazköy-Hattuša 1986. *AA*, 381–412.

Neve, P., 1993. *Hattuša: Stadt der Götter und Tempel. Neue Ausgrabungen in der Haupstadt der Hethiter*. Mainz: von Zabern.

Nicolaou, I. & K. Nicolaou, 1989. *Kazaphani: a Middle/Late Cypriot tomb at Kazaphani – Ayios Andronikos: T. 2A,B*. Nicosia: Department of Antiquities.

Oates, D., J. Oates & H. McDonald, 1997. *Excavations at Tell Brak, vol. 1: The Mitanni and Old Babylonian Periods*. (McDonald Institute Monographs.) Cambridge: McDonald Institute for Archaeological Research/London: BSAI.

Obladen-Kauder, J. 1996. Die Kleinfunde aus Ton, Knochen und Metall, in *Demircihüyük IV, Die Kleinfunde*, eds. A. Baykal-Seeher & J. Obladen-Kauder. Mainz: von Zabern, 209–383.

Orrieux, C., 1985. *Zénon de Caunos, parépidémos, et le destin grec*. (Centre de recherches d'histoire ancienne 64.) Paris: Belles Lettres.

Otten, H., 1988. *Die Bronzetafel aus Boğazköy: ein Staatsvertrag Tuthalijas IV*. (Studien zu den Boğazköy-Texten, Beiheft 1.) Wiesbaden: Harrassowitz.

Otto, A., 2000. *Die Entstehung und Entwicklung der Klassisch-Syrischen Glyptik*. Berlin: de Gruyter.

Ousterhout, R.G., 1998. The cave-dwellers: Cappadocia's mysterious rock-cut architecture. *Archaeology Odyssey* Fall 1(4), 22–7.

Özdoğan, M. & A. Özdoğan, 1998. Buildings of cult and the cult of buildings, in *Light on Top of the Black Hill: Studies Presented to Halet Çambel*, eds. G. Arsebük, M.J. Mellink & W. Schirmer. Istanbul: Ege Yayınları, 581–601.

Özgüç, N., 1968. *Seals and Seal Impressions of Level Ib from Karum Kanish*. Ankara: Türk Tarih Kurumu.

Özgüç, N., 1983. Sealings from Acemhöyük in the Metropolitan Museum of Art, New York, in Boehmer & Hauptmann (eds.), 349–60.

Özgüç, N., 1989. Bullae from Kültepe, in Emre *et al.* (eds.), 377–405.

Özgüç, T., 1948. Excavations at Fraktin near Develi and researches in the Anti-Taurus Region. *Belleten* 12, 260–67.

Özgüç, T., 1978. *Excavations at Maşat Höyük and Investigations in its Vicinity*. Ankara: Türk Tarih Kurumu.

Özgüç, T., 1982. *Maşat Höyük II, A Hittite Centre Northeast of Boğazköy*. Ankara: Türk Tarih Kurumu.

Özgüç, T. 1988. *Inandıktepe: an Important Cult Centre in the Old Hittite Period*. Ankara: Türk Tarih Kurumu.

Özgüç, T. & N. Özgüç, 1953. *Kültepe Kazısı 1949: Ausgrabungen in Kültepe 1949*. Ankara: Türk Tarih Kurumu.

Özgül, N., 1984. Stratigraphy and tectonic evolution of the Central Taurides, in Tekeli & Göncüoğlu (eds.), 77–90.

Özten, A., 1989. A group of Early Bronze Age pottery from the Konya and Niğde region, in Emre *et al.* (eds.), 407–18.

Özyar, A. (ed.), 2005. *Field Seasons 2001–2003 of the Tarsus-Gözlükule Interdisciplinary Research Project*. Istanbul: Ege Yayınları.

References

Panagiotakopulu, E., P.C. Buckland & P.M. Day, 1995. Natural insecticides and insect repellents in antiquity: a review of the evidence. *JAS* 22, 705–10.

Parman, E., 1989. The pottery from St. John's Basilica at Ephesos, in *Recherches sur la Céramique Byzantine*, eds. V. Déroche & J.-M. Spieser. (Bulletin de Correspondance Hellénique, Supplement 18.) Paris: École Française d'Athènes, 277–89.

Parzinger, H. & R. Sanz, 1992. *Die Oberstadt von Hattuša. Hethitische Keramik aus dem zentralen Tempelviertel (Boğazköy-Hattuša XV)*. Berlin: Gebr. Mann.

Payne, S., 1985. Morphological distinctions between the mandibular teeth of young sheep, *Ovis* and goats, *Capra*. *JAS* 12, 139–47.

Payne, S., 1987. Reference codes for wear states in the mandibular cheek teeth of sheep and goats. *JAS* 14, 609–14.

Peacock, D.P.S., 1977. Ceramics in Roman and medieval archaeology, in *Pottery in Early Commerce*, ed. D.P.S. Peacock. London: Academic Press, 21–34.

Peacock, D.P.S., 1984. The amphorae: typology and chronology, in Fulford & Peacock (eds.), 116–30.

Peacock, D.P.S. & D.F. Williams, 1986. *Amphorae and the Roman Economy*. London: Longman.

Pecorella, P.E., 1975. *Malatya III. Rapporto preliminare delle campagne 1963–1968. Il livello eteo imperiale e quelle neoetei.* (Orientis Antiqui Collectio XII.) Rome: Centro per le Antichità e la Storia dell'Arte del Vicino Oriente.

Perlman, I. & F. Asaro, 1969. Pottery analysis by neutron activation. *Archaeometry* 11, 21–52.

Petrie, Sir F., 1927. *Objects of Daily Use*. London: British School of Archaeology in Egypt.

Philip, G., F. Jabour, A. Beck, M. Bshesh, J. Grove, A. Kirk & A. Millard, 2002. Settlement and landscape development in the Homs region, Syria: research questions, preliminary results 1999–2000 and future potential. *Levant* 34, 1–23.

Pınar-Erdem, N. & E. Ilhan, 1977. Outlines of the stratigraphy and tectonics of Turkey, with notes on the geology of Cyprus, in *The Ocean Basins and Margins*, vol. 4A: *The Eastern Mediterranean*, eds. A.E.M. Nairn, W.H. Kanes & F.G. Stehli. London: Plenum Press, 277–318.

Piperno, D., 1988. *Phytolith Analysis: an Archaeological and Geological Perspective*. New York (NY): Academic Press.

Pliny, the Elder, 1982. *Historia Naturalis*, trans. into English by J.I. Whalley. London: Sidgwick & Jackson.

Plog, S., F. Plog & W. Wait, 1978. Decision making in modern surveys, in Schiffer (ed.), 383–421.

Postgate, J.N. (ed.), 1983. *The West Mound Surface Clearance*. (Abu Salabikh Excavations 1.) London: BSAI.

Postgate, J.N., 1994. Review of Finkbeiner *et al.*, Uruk Kampagne 35–37, 1982–1984. *ZA* 84, 291–4.

Postgate, J.N., 1995. The site and its setting, in Baker *et al.*, 139–43.

Postgate, J.N., 1996. Kilise Tepe 1995. A summary of the principal results. *KST* 18/i, 441–56.

Postgate, J.N., 1998a. Kilise Tepe 1996. A summary of the principal results. *KST* 19/i, 209–26.

Postgate, J.N., 1998b. Between the plateau and the sea: Kilise Tepe 1994–97, in Matthews (ed.), 127–41.

Postgate, J.N., forthcoming. *The Chronology of the Iron Age Seen from Kilise Tepe*. Izmir: Ege University.

Postgate, J.N. & R.J. Matthews, 1995. Application to the Leverhulme Trust: detailed statement.

Postgate, J.N. & J.A. Moon, 1982. Excavations at Abu Salabikh, 1981. *Iraq* 44, 103–36.

Procopiou, H. & R. Treuil (eds.), 2002. *Moudre et Broyer: L'interprétation fonctionnelle de l'outillage de moulure et de broyage dans la Préhistoire et l'Antiquité*, vol. 1: *Méthodes*. Paris: Editions CTHS.

Ramsay, W.M., 1890. *The Historical Geography of Asia Minor.* (Royal Geographical Society, Supplementary Papers 4.) London: John Murray.

Rapp, G., Jr & S.C. Mulholland (eds.), 1992. *Phytolith Systematics: Emerging Issues*. New York (NY): Plenum Press.

Rautman, M.L., H. Neff, B. Gomez, S. Vaughan & M.D. Glascock, 1999. Amphoras and roof-tiles from Late Roman Cyprus: a compositional study of calcareous ceramics from Kalavasos-Kopetra. *Journal of Roman Archaeology* 12, 377–91.

Redman, C.L. & P.J. Watson, 1970. Systematic, intensive surface collection. *American Antiquity* 35, 279–91.

Reimer, P.J. *et al.*, 2004. IntCal04: Terrestrial radiocarbon age calibration, 0–26 cal kyr BP. *Radiocarbon* 46/iii, 1029–58.

Reyes, A.T., 2001. *The Stamp-Seals of Ancient Cyprus*. Oxford: Oxford University School of Archaeology.

Rice, D.S., 1952. Studies in medieval Harran. *An. St.* 2, 36–84.

Riis, P.J. & M.-L. Buhl, 1990. *Les Objets de la période dite Syro-Hittite (Âge du Fer)*. (Hama: fouilles et recherches, 1931–1938 2/ii.) Copenhagen: Nationalmuseet.

Riley, J.A., 1979. Coarse pottery, in *Excavations at Sidi Khrebish Benghazi (Berenice)*, vol. II, ed. J.A. Lloyd. Tripoli: Department of Antiquities, 91–467.

Robinson, D.M., 1933. *Excavations at Olynthus V: Mosaics, Vases and Lamps of Olynthus Found in 1928 and 1931*. Baltimore (MD): Johns Hopkins Press.

Robinson, H.S., 1959. *The Athenian Agora*, vol. 5: *Pottery of the Roman Period. Chronology.* Princeton (NJ): Princeton University Press.

Robinson, R.C.W., 1985. Tobacco pipes of Corinth and the Athenian Agora. *Hesperia* 54, 149–203.

Rose, M.J., 1994. With Line and Glittering Bronze Hook: Fishing in the Aegean Bronze Age. Unpublished PhD thesis, Indiana University.

Rosen, A.R., 1986. *Cities of Clay: the Chronology of Tells*. Chicago (IL): University of Chicago Press.

Rosen, A., 1992. Preliminary identification of silica skeletons from Near Eastern archaeological sites: an anatomical approach, in Rapp & Mulholland (eds.), 129–47.

Rotroff, S., 1997. *The Athenian Agora 29. Hellenistic Pottery: Athenian and Imported Wheelmade Table Ware and Related Material*. Princeton (NJ): American School of Classical Studies.

Runge, F., 2001. Evidence for land use history by opal phytolith analysis: examples from the Central African tropics (Eastern Kivu, D. R. of Congo), in Meunier & Colin (eds.), 73–86.

Russell, J.C., 1958. Late ancient and medieval population. *Transactions of the American Philosophical Society* 48(3), 40–45.

Russell, J., 1979. The Necropolis church. *An. St.* 29, 183–5.

Russell, J., 1980. Anemurium: the changing face of a Roman city. *Archaeology* 33, 31–40.

Russell, J., 2001. The Persian invasions of Syria/Palestine and Asia Minor in the reign of Heraclius: archaeological, numismatic and epigraphic evidence, in *In the Dark Centuries of Byzantium (7th–9th C.)*, ed. E. Kountoura-Galake. Athens: National Hellenic Research Foundation Institute for Byzantine Research, 41–71.

Salles, J.-F., 1995. Céramiques hellénistiques de Kition — Bamboula, in Meyza & Mlynarczyk, 397–415.

Salmeri, G. & A.L. D'Agata, 2002. Cilicia Survey 2001. *AST* 20, 207–11.

Sams, G.K., 1994. *The Early Phrygian Pottery.* (The Gordion Excavations, 1950–1973: Final Reports IV.) Philadelphia (PA): The University Museum, University of Pennsylvania.

Sangster, A.G. & M.J. Hodson, 1997. Botanical studies of silicon localization in cereal roots and shoots, including cryotechniques: a survey of work up to 1990, in *Estado Actual de los Estudios de Fitolitos en Suelos y Plantas*, eds. A. Pinilla, J. Juan-Tresserras & M.J. Machado. Madrid: Consejo Superior de Investigaciones Cientificas, 113–21.

Sarre, F., 1925. *Die Ausgrabungen von Samarra II — Die Keramik von Samarra.* Berlin: Dietrich Reimer/Ernst Vohsen Verlag.

Sauer, J.A. & J. Magness, 1997. Ceramics of the Islamic period, in Meyers (ed.), 475–9.

Sayar, M.H., 1992. Strassenbau in Kilikien unter den Flaviern nach einem neugefundenen Meilenstein. *Epigraphica Anatolica* 20, 57–62.

Schaeffer, C.F.A., 1939. *Ugaritica I.* (Mission de Ras Shamra III.) Paris: Geuthner.

Schaeffer, C.F.A., 1949. *Ugaritica II.* (Mission de Ras Shamra V.) Paris: Geuthner.

Schaeffer, C.F.A., 1956. *Ugaritica III.* (Mission de Ras Shamra VIII.) Paris: Geuthner.

Schäfer, J., 1968. *Pergamenische Forschungen II: Hellenistische Keramik aus Pergamon.* Berlin: de Gruyter.

Schiffer, M.B. (ed.), 1978. *Advances in Archaeological Method and Theory*, vol. 1. New York (NY): Academic Press.

Schiffer, M.B., 1987. *Formation Processes of the Archaeological Record.* Albuquerque (NM): University of New Mexico Press.

Schliemann, H., 1880. *Ilios: the City and Country of the Trojans.* London: John Murray.

Schmidt, E.F., 1932. *The Alishar Hüyük, Seasons of 1928 and 1929,* part I. (Oriental Institute Publications 19.) Chicago (IL): The University of Chicago Press.

Schmidt, E.F., 1933. *The Alishar Hüyük, Seasons of 1928 and 1929,* part II. (Oriental Institute Publications 19.) Chicago (IL): The University of Chicago Press.

Schoop, U.-D., 2003. Pottery traditions of the later Hittite Empire: problems of definition, in Fischer *et al.* (eds.), 167–78.

Schreiber, N., 2002. *The Cypro-Phoenician Pottery of the Iron Age.* Leiden: Brill.

Seeher, J., 1987. *Demircihüyük III.1. Die Keramik 1. A. Die neolithische und chalkolithische Keramik, B. Die frühbronzezeitliche Keramik der älteren Phasen.* Mainz: von Zabern.

Seeher, J., 1995. Die Ausgrabungen in Boğazköy-Hattuša 1994. *AA,* 611–21.

Seeher, J., 1998. Die Ausgrabungen in Boğazköy-Hattuša 1997. *AA,* 215–41.

Seeher, J., 2001. Die Zerstörung der Stadt Hattuša, in *Akten des IV. Internationalen Kongresses für Hethitologie,* ed. G. Wilhelm. (Studien zu den Boğazköy Texten 45.).Wiesbaden: Harrassowitz, 623–34.

Seidl, U., 1972. *Gefässmarken von Boğazköy (Boğazköy-Hattuša IX).* Berlin: Gebr. Mann.

Seton Williams, M.V., 1954. Cilician survey. *An. St.* 4, 121–74.

Shanks, M. & C. Tilley, 1992. *Re-constructing Archaeology: Theory and Practice.* London: Routledge.

Shaw, B.D., 1999. War and violence, in *Late Antiquity: a Guide to the Postclassical World,* eds. G.W. Bowersock, P. Brown & O. Grabar. London: Harvard, 130–69.

Sheffer, A., 1981. The use of perforated clay balls on the warp-weighted loom. *Tel Aviv* 8/i, 81–3.

Sheftel, P., 1974. The Ivory, Bone and Shell Objects from Gordion from the Campaigns of 1950 through 1973. Unpublished PhD dissertation, University of Pennsylvania.

Shelmerdine, C.W., 1985. *The Perfume Industry of Pylos.* (SIMA Pocket Book 34.) Göteborg: Paul Åströms Förlag.

Shennan, S., 1997. *Quantifying Archaeology.* Edinburgh: Edinburgh University Press.

Sherratt, E.S. & J.H. Crouwel, 1987. Mycenaean pottery from Cilicia in Oxford. *Oxford Journal of Archaeology* 6, 325–52.

Shipman, P., G. Foster & M. Schoeninger, 1984. Burnt bones and teeth: an experimental study of colour, morphology, crystal structure and shrinkage. *JAS* 4, 307–25.

Silver, I.A., 1969. The ageing of domestic animals, in Brothwell & Higgs (eds.), 283–302.

Simpson, St J., 1999. Modern glass melon beads from Syria and Lebanon. *Bead Study Trust Newsletter* 34 (Winter), 3.

Simpson, St J., et al., forthcoming. *Late Sasanian Remains at Erk-Kala.* (Acta Iranica, Textes et Mémoires = Merv Excavation Reports I.) Louvain: Peeters.

Singer, I., 1984. The AGRIG in the Hittite texts. *An. St.* 34, 97–127.

Skakun, N., 1993. Agricultural implements in the Neolithic and Eneolithic cultures of Bulgaria, in *Traces et Fonction: les Gestes Retrouvés,* eds. P.C. Anderson, S. Beyries, M. Otte & H. Plisson. Liège: Etudes et Recherches Archéologiques de l'Université de Liège, 361–8.

Skelton, P. & G. Teugels, 1992. Neotype description for the African catfish *Clarias gariepinus* (Burchell 1822) (Pisces: Siluroidei: Clariidae). *Ichthyological Bulletin of the J.L.B. Smith Institute of Ichthyology* 56, 1–8.

Snodgrass, A.M., 2002. The rejection of Mycenaean culture and the oriental connection, in *Die nahöstlichen*

References

Kulturen und Griechenland an der Wende vom 2. zum 1. Jahrtausend v. Chr.: Kontinuität und Wandel von Strukturen und Mechanismen kultureller Interaktion, eds. E.A. Braun-Holzinger & H. Matthäus. Möhnesee: Bibliopolis, 1–9.

Sodini, J.-P. & E. Villeneuve, 1992. Le passage de la céramique Byzantine à la céramique Omeyyade en Syrie du Nord, en Palestine et en Transjordanie, in *La Syrie, de Byzance à l'Islam VIIe–VIIIe siècles*, eds. P. Canivet & J.-P. Rey-Coquais. Damascus: Institut Français de Damas, 195–218.

Sodini, J.-P., G. Tate, B. Bavant, J.-L. Biscop & D. Orssaud, 1980. Déhès (Syrie du Nord) Campagnes I–III (1976–1978) Recherches sur l'habitat rural. *Syria* 57, 1–304.

Spaer, M., 1988. Pre-Islamic glass bracelets of Palestine. *Journal of Glass Studies* 30, 51–61.

Spaer, M., 1992. The Islamic glass bracelets of Palestine. *Journal of Glass Studies* 34, 44–62.

Stambolidis, N.Ch. & A. Karetsou, 1998. *Anatoliki Mesogeios: Kupros - Dodekanisa – Kriti*. Irakleio: University of Crete.

Stathakopoulos, D., 2000. The Justinianic plague revisited. *Byzantine and Modern Greek Studies* 24, 256–76.

Steel, L., 1997–98. The social impact of Mycenaean pottery in Cyprus in the 14th and 13th centuries BC. *Bulletin of the Institute for Classical Studies* 42, 203–4.

Stern, E., 1982. *Material Culture of the Bible in the Persian Period 538–332 BC*. Warminster: Aris & Phillips.

Stern, M., 1989. The production of glass vessels in Roman Cilicia. *Kölner Jahrbuch für Vor- und Frühgeschichte* 22, 121–8.

Sterrett, J.R.S., 1884–85. *The Wolfe Expedition to Asia Minor*. Boston (MA): American School of Classical Studies at Athens.

Stone, E.C., 1994. The anatomy of a Mesopotamian city: the Mashkan-shapir project. *Bulletin of the Canadian Society for Mesopotamian Studies* 27, 15–24.

Stone, E.C. & P. Zimansky, 2004. *The Anatomy of a Mesopotamian City: Survey and Soundings at Mashkan-shapir*. Winona Lake (IN): Eisenbrauns.

Süel, A., 1998. Ortaköy-Shapinuwa: Bir Hitit Merkezi. *TÜBA-AR* 1, 37–61.

Summers, G.D., 1993. *Tille Höyük 4: the Late Bronze Age and the Iron Age Transition*. London: BIAA.

Summers, G.D. & M.E.F. Summers, 1998. The Kerkenes Dağ Project, in R. Matthews (ed.), 177–94.

Sykes, Lt-Col. Sir M., 1915. *The Caliph's Last Heritage: a Short History of the Turkish Empire*. London: Macmillan.

Symington, D., 1986. Remarks on the Tarsus Late Bronze Age I pottery in the Adana Museum. *AST* 3, 279–85.

Symington, D., 2001. Hittites at Kilise Tepe, in Jean *et al.* (eds.), 167–84.

Tate, G., 1992. *Les Campagnes de la Syrie du Nord du IIe au VIIe siècle: un exemple d'expansion démographique et économique dans les campagnes à la fin de l'antiquité*. Paris: Geuthner.

Taylor, R.J. & V.J. Robinson, 1996. Neutron activation analysis of Roman African Red Slip Ware kilns. *Archaeometry* 38/ii, 231–43.

Tchalenko, G., 1953-8. *Villages Antiques de la Syrie du Nord: Le massif du Bélus à l'epoque romaine* I–III. Paris: Geuthner.

Tekeli, O. & M.C. Göncüoğlu (eds.), 1984. *Geology of the Taurus Belt (International Symposium 26–29 September 1983, Ankara, Turkey)*. Ankara: MTA (Mineral Research and Exploration Institute).

Tekoğlu, R. & A. Lemaire, 2000. La bilingue royale louvito-phénicienne de Çineköy. *Comptes-Rendus, Académie des inscriptions et belles-lettres*, 961–1006.

Thissen, L., 1993. New insights in Balkan–Anatolian connections in the Late Chalcolithic: old evidence from the Turkish Black Sea littoral. *An. St.* 43, 207–37.

Tobin, J., 2004. *Black Cilicia: a Study of the Plain of Issus During the Roman and Late Roman Periods*. (British Archaeological Reports International Series 1275.) Oxford: BAR.

Todd, I.A., 2001. Early connections of Cyprus with Anatolia, in *The White Slip Ware of Late Bronze Age Cyprus*, ed. V. Karageorghis. (Öster. Akad. der Wissenschaften, Denkschriften der Gesamtakademie XX.) Vienna: Verlag der Öster. Akad. der Wissenschaften, 203–13.

Tomlinson, J.E., 1991. Provenance of Minoan Ceramics by Multivariate Analysis of Neutron Activation Data. Unpublished PhD Thesis, University of Manchester.

Tomlinson, J.E., 1995. Multivariate analysis of neutron activation data on heavy ware stirrup jars from Mycenae, in *The 'Ivory Houses' at Mycenae*, ed. I. Tournavitou. (Supplementary volume 24.) London: BSA, 305–8.

Tomlinson, J.E., 1996. Chemical evidence for a Cretan origin of heavy ware stirrup jars found at Mycenae, in *Proceedings of the Second Symposium of the Hellenic Archaeometrical Society: Archaeometrical and Archaeological Research in Macedonia and Thrace*, eds. I. Stratis, M. Vavelidis, K. Kotsakis, G. Tsokas & E. Tsoukala. Thessaloniki: Hellenic Archaeometrical Society, 371–8.

Tomlinson, J.E., 1997. Statistical evaluation of the Asaro-Perlman neutron activation data on Mycenaean pottery from the Peloponnese. *BSA* 92, 139–64.

Tomlinson, J.E., 1998. Chemical analysis of some Mycenaean pottery from Perati, Attica. *Archaiologiki Ephimeris 1995*, 227–30.

Tomlinson, J.E., 1999. Provenance using neutron activation analysis, in French & Tomlinson, 259–65.

Tomlinson, J.E., 2000. Statistical analysis of neutron activation data on Mycenaean pottery from Gla, Thebes, Eutresis, Kallithea and Tanagra in Boeotia, in *Proceedings of the Third International Congress of Boeotian Studies, Thebes, 4–8 September 1996*, ed. V. Aravantinos. Athens: Society of Boeotian Studies, 253–63.

Tomlinson, J.E., 2004. Statistical evaluation of neutron activation data on Mycenaean pottery found at Lachish, in *The Renewed Archaeological Excavations at Lachish 1973–1994*, ed. D. Ussishkin. Tel Aviv: Institute of Archaeology of Tel Aviv University, 1437–45.

Tomlinson, J.E., forthcoming a. Neutron activation and statistical analysis of Late Helladic Pottery from the Menelaion, the North Hill and Profitis Elias, in *Chemical Analysis of Mycenaean Pottery from the Menelaion and its Vicinity*, eds. R.E. Jones & J.E. Tomlinson.

Tomlinson, J.E., forthcoming b. Statistical analysis of neutron activation data on Mycenaean pottery from the Argolid and Corinthia, in *Well Built Mycenae*. (Fascicule 34: Technical Reports.)

Tomlinson, J.E. & V.J. Robinson, in preparation. Neutron activation analysis of Minoan pottery from Crete: the search for reference groups.

Topçu, Ç., 1984. Seleukeia – Kalykadnos 1984 yılı kazı çalişmaları. *KST* 7, 509–17.

Trombley, F.R., 1998. War, society and popular religion in Byzantine Anatolia (6th–13th centuries), in *Byzantine Asia Minor (6th–12th cent.)*, ed. S. Lampakis. Athens: National Hellenic Research Foundation, Institute for Byzantine Research, 97–139.

Tufnell, O., 1958. *Lachish IV (Tell ed-Duweir). The Wellcome-Marston Archaeological Research Expedition to the Near East. The Bronze Age.* London: Oxford University Press.

Turkey, Geological Map of, 1950–65 (Türkiye Jeolojik Haritası) scale 1:500,000, 18 sheets. Bull. Min. Res. Explor. Inst. Turk.

Tzedakis, Y. & H. Martlew, 1999. *Minoans and Mycenaeans: Flavours of their Time*. Athens: Ministry of Culture and National Archaeological Museum.

Uerpmann, M. & W. Van Neer, 2000. Fischreste aus den neuen Grabungen in Troia (1989–1999). *Studia Troica* 10, 145–79.

Ünlü, E., 2005. Locally produced and painted Late Bronze to Iron Age Transitional Period pottery of Tarsus-Gözlükule, in Özyar (ed.), 145–68.

Ur, J., 2002. Settlement and landscape in northern Mesopotamia: the Tell Hamoukar Survey 2000–2001. *Akkadica* 123 fasc. 1.

Ur, J., 2003. CORONA satellite photography and ancient road networks: a northern Mesopotamian case study. *Antiquity* 77, 102–15.

Van Alfen, P.G., 1996. New light on the 7th-c. Yassı Ada shipwreck: capacities and standard sizes of LRA1 amphoras. *Journal of Roman Archaeology* 9, 189–213.

Van Neer, W. & M. Uerpmann, 1998. Fish remains from the new excavations at Troy, in *Archaeozoology of the Near East III: Proceedings of the Third International Symposium on the Archaeozoology of Southwestern Asia and Adjacent Areas*, eds. H. Buitenhuis, L. Bartosiewicz & A.M. Choyke. (ARC – Publication 18.) Groningen: Center for Archeological Research and Consultancy, Rijksuniversiteit Groningen, 243–54.

Van Neer, W., B. De Cupere & M. Waelkens, 1997. Remains of local and imported fish at the ancient site of Sagalassos (Burdur Prov., Turkey), in *Sagalassos IV: Report on the Survey and Excavation Campaigns of 1994 and 1995*, eds. M. Waelkens & J. Poblome. Leuven: Leuven University Press, 571–86.

Van Neer, W., R.H. Wildekamp, F. Küçük, M. Ünlüsayın, M. Waelkens & E. Paulissen, 2000a. Results of the 1996 survey of fish fauna of the Aksu river and some lakes in southwestern Anatolia and the implications for the fish trade at Sagalassos, in *Sagalassos V: Report on the Survey and Excavation Campaign of 1996 and 1997*, eds. M. Waelkens & L. Loots. Leuven: Leuven University Press, 828–42.

Van Neer, W., R. Wildekamp, M. Waelkens, A. Arndt & A. Volckaert, 2000b. Fish as indicators of trade relationships in Roman times: the example of Sagalassos, Turkey, in *Archaeozoology of the Near East IV: Proceedings of the Fourth International Symposium on the Archaeozoology of Southwestern Asia and Adjacent Areas*, eds. M. Mashkour, A.M. Choyke, H. Buitenhuis & F. Poplin. Groningen: Center for Archeological Research and Consultancy, Rijksuniversiteit, 206–15.

Van Neer, W., O. Lernau, R. Friedman, G. Mumford, J. Poblome & M. Waelkens, 2004. Fish remains from archaeological sites as indicators of former trade connections in the Eastern Mediterranean. *Paléorient* 30(1), 101–48.

Van Neer, W., R.H. Wildekamp, F. Küçük, M. Ünlüsayın, J. Poblome & M. Waelkens, in press. The 1997–1999 surveys of the Anatolian fish fauna and their relevance to the interpretation of trade at Sagalassos, in *Sagalassos VI: Report on the Survey and Excavation Campaigns of 1998, 1999 and 2000*, eds. M. Waelkens & J. Poblome. Leuven: Leuven University Press.

Van Zeist, W. & W.A. Casparie (eds.), 1984. *Plants and Ancient Man*. Rotterdam: Balkema.

Vandier d'Abbadie, J., 1972. *Catalogue des objets de toilette égyptiens*. Paris: Editions des Musées Nationaux.

Varro, M.T., 1978. *Res Rusticae*, trans. into French by J. Heurgon. Paris: Les belles lettres.

Vaughan, S.J., 1987. A Fabric Analysis of Late Cypriot Base Ring Ware: Studies in Ceramic Technology, Petrology, Geochemistry, and Mineralogy. Unpublished PhD thesis, University College, London.

Vaughan, S.J., 1991. Late Cypriot Base Ring Ware: studies in raw materials and technology, in *Recent Developments in Ceramic Petrology*, eds. A. Middleton & I. Freestone. London: British Museum, 337–68.

Vergil, 1988. *Georgics*, ed. R.F. Thomas. Cambridge: Cambridge University Press.

Vidali, M.L., E. Vidali & C.C. Lamberg-Karlovsky, 1976. Prehistoric settlement patterns around Tepe Yahya: a quantitative analysis. *Journal of Near Eastern Studies* 35, 237–50.

Vogelsang-Eastwood, G., 1990. Crescent loomweights? *Oriens Antiquus* 29, 97–113.

von den Driesch, A., 1976. *A Guide to the Measurement of Animal Bones from Archaeological Sites.* Cambridge (MA): Peabody Museum of Archaeology and Ethnology, Harvard University.

von der Osten, H.H., 1937. *Researches in Anatolia VIII: the Alishar Hüyük, Seasons of 1930–32.* (Oriental Institute Publication 29.) Chicago (IL): University of Chicago Press.

von der Osten, H.H. & E.F. Schmidt, 1932. *The Alishar Hüyük, Season of 1927*, part II. (Oriental Institute Publication 7.) Chicago (IL): University of Chicago Press.

von Saldern, A., 1980. *Ancient and Byzantine Glass from Sardis*. Cambridge (MA): Harvard University Press.

Vryonis, S., 1971. *The Decline of Medieval Hellenism in Asia Minor and the Process of Islamization from the Eleventh through the Fifteenth Century*. Berkeley (CA): University of California Press.

Waagé, F.O., 1948. *Antioch-on-the-Orontes. IV.1: Ceramics and Islamic Coins*. Princeton (NJ): Princeton University Press.

Waldbaum, J.C., 1983. *Metalwork from Sardis: the Finds through 1974*. Cambridge (MA): Harvard University Press.

References

Warner, J.L., 1994. *Elmalı Karataş II: the Early Bronze Age Village of Karataş*. Bryn Mawr (PA): Bryn Mawr College Archaeological Monograph.

Webb, P.A.O. & J.M. Suchey, 1985. Epiphyseal union of the anterior iliac crest and medial clavicle in a modern multiracial sample of American males and females. *American Journal of Physical Anthropology* 68, 457–66.

Webster, T.L., J.R. Green & A. Seeberg, 1995. *Monuments Illustrating New Comedy*. 3rd edition. London: Institute of Classical Studies.

Weingarten, J. 1990. The sealing structure of Karahöyük and some administrative links with Phaistos on Crete. *Oriens Antiquus* 29, 63–95.

Whallon, R., Jr, 1980. The systematic collection and analysis of surface materials from a prehistoric site in southeastern Anatolia, in *The Joint Istanbul-Chicago Universities' Prehistoric Research in Southeastern Anatolia I*, eds. H. Çambel & R.J. Braidwood. Istanbul: Edebiyat Fakültesi Basımevi, 207–19.

Whallon, R., Jr & S. Kantman, 1969. Early Bronze Age development in the Keban reservoir, east central Turkey. *Current Anthropology* 10:1, 128–33.

Whitbread, I.K., 1989. A proposal for the systematic description of thin sections towards the study of ancient ceramic technology, in *Archaeometry: Proceedings of the 25th International Symposium*, ed. Y. Maniatis. Amsterdam: Elsevier, 127–38.

Whitbread, I.K., 1995. *Greek Transport Amphorae: a Petrological and Archaeological Study*. Athens: BSA.

Whittow, M., 1996. *The Making of Orthodox Byzantium 600–1025*. Basingstoke: Macmillan Press.

Wickede, A. von, 1990. *Prähistorische Stempelglyptik in Vorderasien*. (Münchener vorderasiatische Studien VI.) Munich: Profil Verlag.

Wilkinson, J., 1971. *Egeria's Travels*. London: SPCK.

Wilkinson, T.J., 2000. Regional approaches to Mesopotamian archaeology: the contribution of archaeological survey. *Journal of Archaeological Research* 8/iv, 219–67.

Williams, C., 1977. A Byzantine well-deposit from Anemurium (Rough Cilicia). *An. St.* 27, 175–90.

Williams, C., 1985. The pottery and glass from Alahan, in Gough (ed.), 35–61.

Williams, C., 1989. *Anemurium: the Roman and Early Byzantine Pottery*. Toronto: Pontifical Institute of Medieval Studies.

Wilson, C.W., 1895. *Handbook for Travellers in Asia Minor, Trancaucasia, Persia etc.* London: John Murray.

Wood, W.R. & D.L. Johnson, 1978. A survey of disturbance processes in archaeological site formation, in Schiffer (ed.), 315–81.

Woolley, C.L., 1921. *Carchemish: Report on the Excavations at Jerablus on Behalf of the British Museum*, part II: *The Town Defences*. London: British Museum.

Woolley, C.L., 1934. *Ur Excavations II. The Royal Cemetery*. London/Philadelphia (PA): British Museum Press and the University Museum of the University of Pennsylvania.

Woolley, C.L., 1955. *Alalakh: an Account of the Excavations at Tell Atchana in Hatay, 1937–1949*. Oxford: Oxford University Press.

Woolley, C.L. & T.E. Lawrence, 1936. *The Wilderness of Zin*. London: Jonathan Cape.

Workshop of European Anthropologists, 1980. Recommendations for age and sex diagnoses of skeletons. *Journal of Human Evolution* 9, 517–49.

Yakar, J., 1985. *The Later Prehistory of Anatolia: the Late Chalcolithic and Early Bronze Age*. (British Archaeological Reports International Series 268.) Oxford: BAR.

Yakar, J., 2000. *Ethnoarchaeology of Anatolia: Rural Socio-economy in the Bronze and Iron Ages*. Tel Aviv: Emery and Claire Yass Publications in Archaeology.

Yalçın, M.N. & N. Görür, 1984. Sedimentological evolution of the Adana Basin, in Tekeli & Göncüoğlu (eds.), 165–72.

Yon, M., V. Karageorghis & N. Hirschfeld, 2000. *Céramiques mycéniennes d'Ougarit*. (Ras Shamra – Ougarit 13.) Paris: ÉRC.

Young, J.H., 1956. Studies in south Attica: country estates at Sounion. *Hesperia* 25, 122–46.

Zerner, C., P. Zerner & J. Winder (eds.), 1993. *Wace and Blegen: Pottery as Evidence for Trade in the Aegean Bronze Age, 1939–1989*. Amsterdam: J.C. Gieben.

Ziegler, L., 1942. Tonkästchen aus Uruk, Babylon und Assur. *ZA* 47 (NF 13), 224–40.

Zohary, D. & M. Hopf, 2000. *Domestication of Plants in the Old World*. Oxford: Oxford University Press.

Zoroğlu, L., 1994. *Kelenderis I: Kaynaklar, kalıntılar, buluntular*. Ankara: Dönmez Ofset.

Zoroğlu, L., H. Adıbelli & M. Doğan, 1999. Tarsus Cumhuriyet alanı 1997. *KST* 20/ii, 463–73.

Artefact Drawings

Architectural fragments — 705–8

Pottery recording sheets — 709

Geological maps — 710

Ceramics — 711
    Early Bronze Age — 711
    Middle Bronze Age — 726
    Late Bronze Age — 731
    Level II — 736
    Geometric — 751
    Mycenaean — 752
    Hellenistic — 754
    Late Roman/Byzantine — 757

Seals — 775

Clay artefacts — 778
    Stoppers — 778
    Figurines — 779
    Counters, discs and clay 'ball' — 781
    Miscellaneous — 782
    Furniture — 783
    Crescents and ovoids — 784

Loomweights — 785

Spindle whorls — 789

Beads and glass vessels — 796

Copper objects — 798

Iron and silver objects — 801

Bone artefacts — 804

Lithics — 805

Stone artefacts — 807

Stele — 813

Artefact Drawings

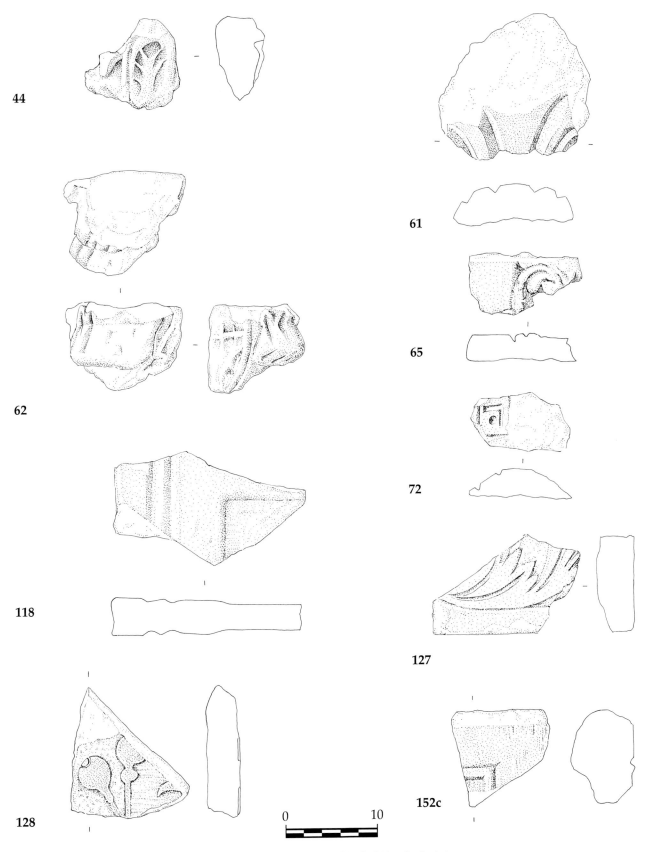

Figure 358. *Architectural fragments: 44, 61–2, 65, 72, 118, 127–8, 152c. Scale 1:4.*

Artefact Drawings

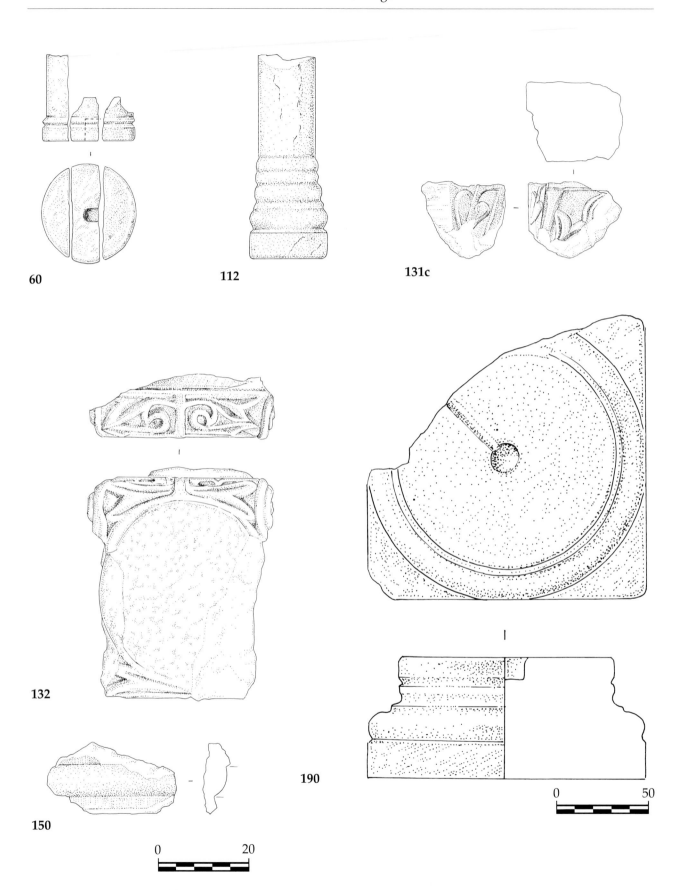

Figure 359. *Architectural fragments: 60, 112, 131–2, 150, 190. Scale 1:8 (112 at 1:2, 190 at 1:10).*

Artefact Drawings

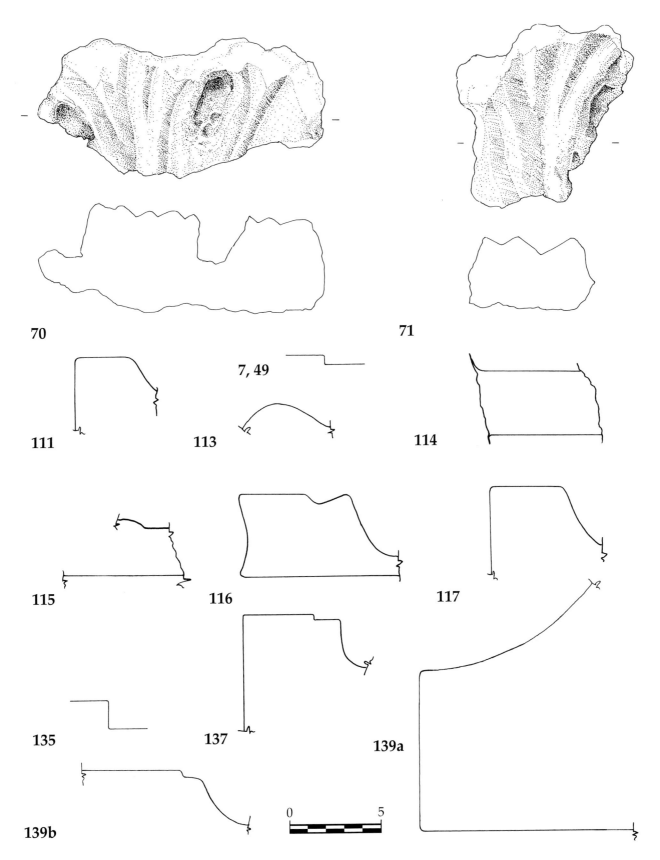

Figure 360. *Architectural fragments: 70–71; mouldings: 7, 49, 111, 113–17, 135, 137, 139a–b. Scale 1:2.*

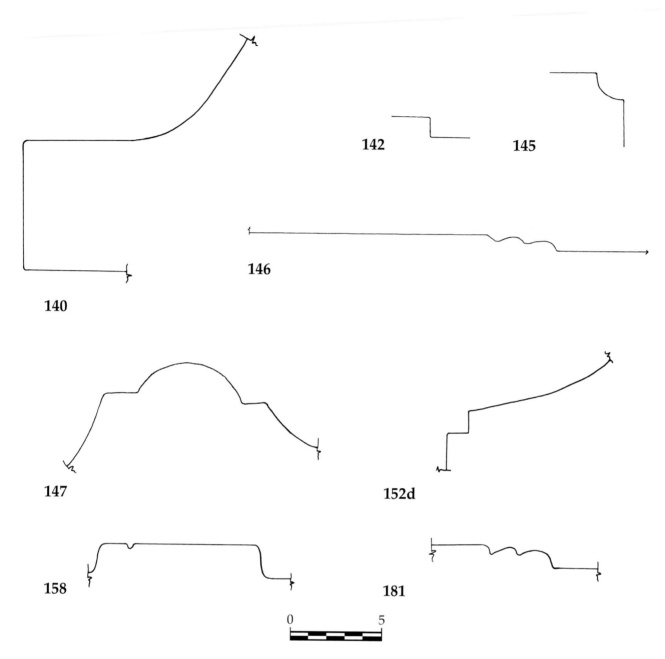

Figure 361. *Architectural mouldings: **140**, **142**, **145–7**, **152d**, **158**, **181**. Scale 1:2.*

Artefact Drawings

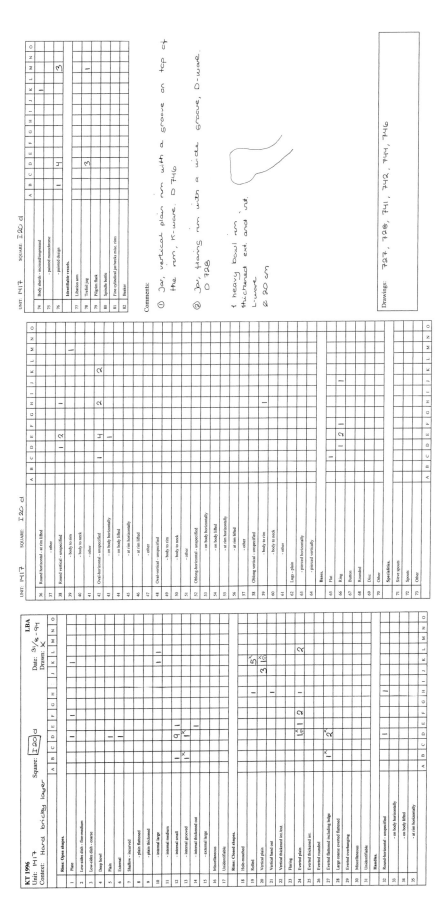

Figure 362. *LBA pottery recording sheet (a).*

Figure 363. *LBA pottery recording sheet (b).*

Figure 364. *LBA pottery recording sheet (c).*

709

Artefact Drawings

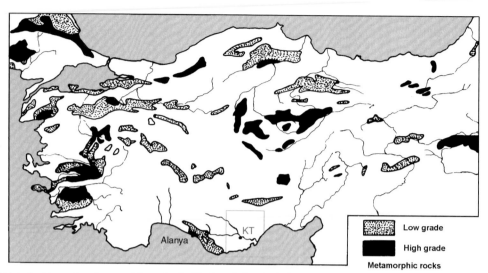

Figure 365. *Distribution of metamorphic rocks in Turkey (after Brinkmann 1976).*

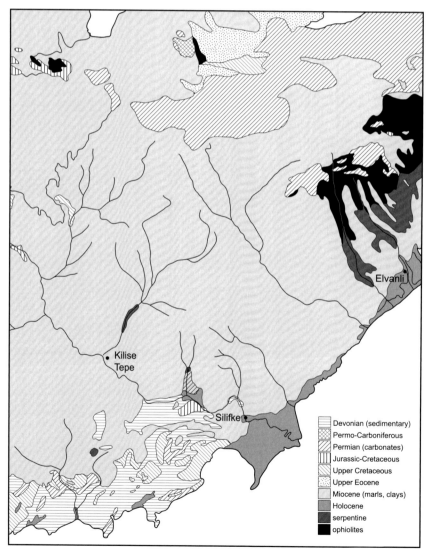

Figure 366. *Geological map of Kilise Tepe area (after Turkey, Geological Map of, 1950–65).*

Artefact Drawings

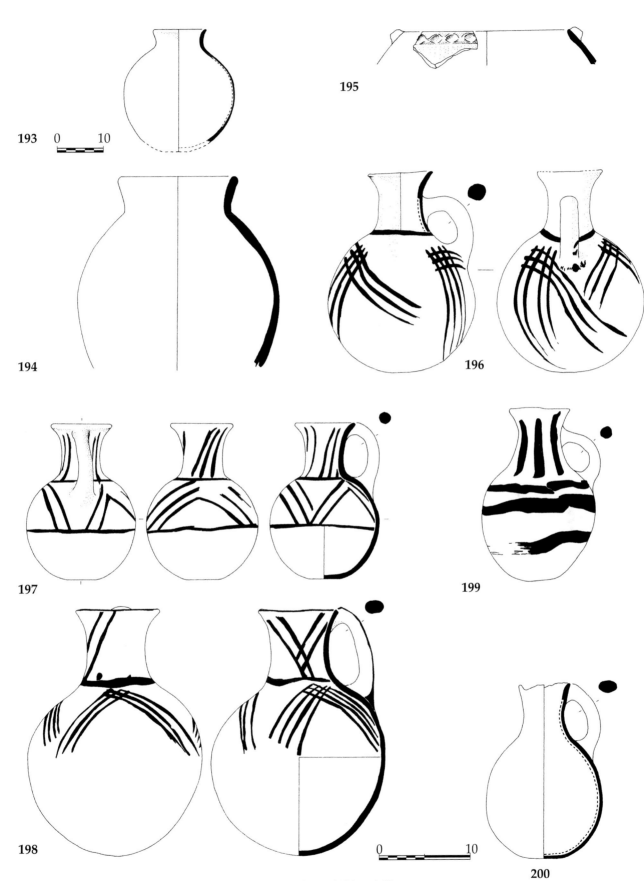

Figure 367. *Early Bronze Age ceramics 193–200. Scale 1:4 (193 at 1:8).*

Artefact Drawings

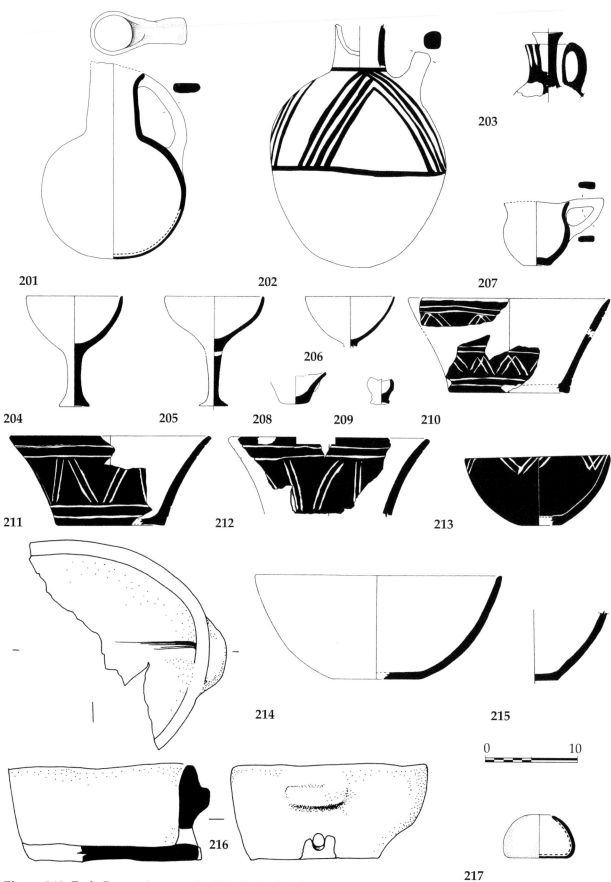

Figure 368. *Early Bronze Age ceramics* **201–17**. *Scale 1:4.*

Artefact Drawings

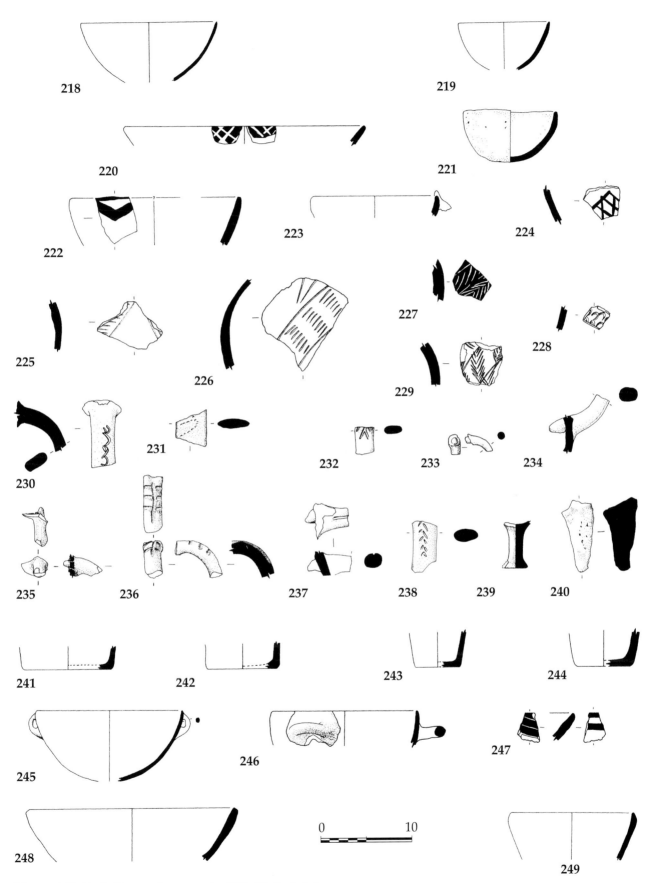

Figure 369. *Early Bronze Age ceramics* **218–49**. *Scale 1:4.*

Artefact Drawings

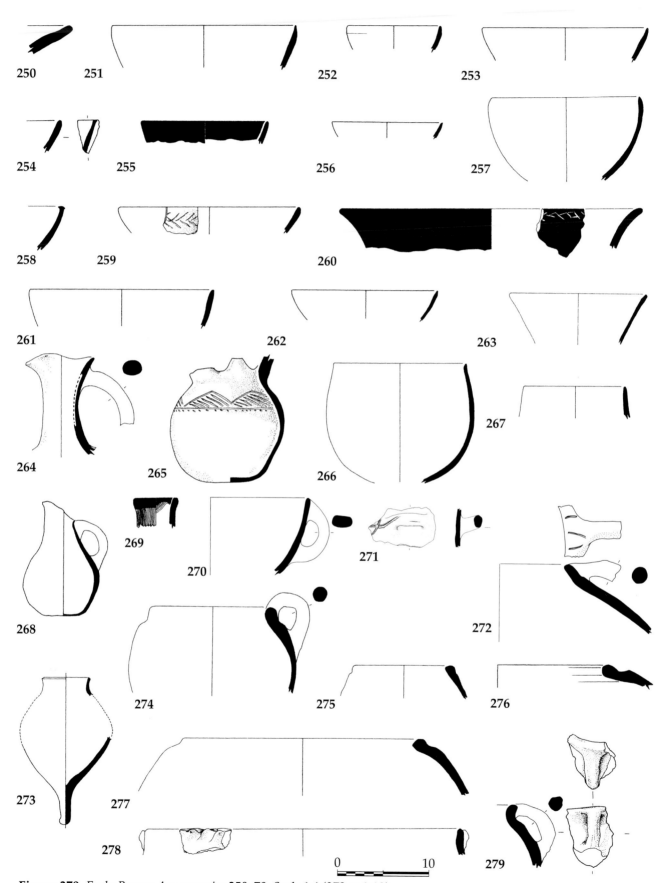

Figure 370. *Early Bronze Age ceramics* **250–79**. *Scale 1:4 (***273** *at 1:10).*

Artefact Drawings

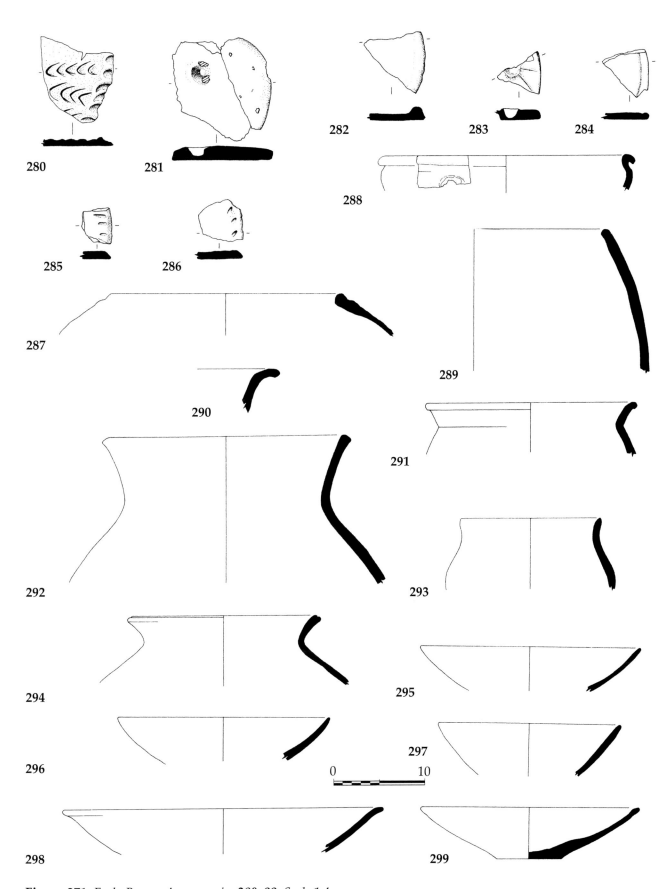

Figure 371. *Early Bronze Age ceramics 280–99. Scale 1:4.*

Artefact Drawings

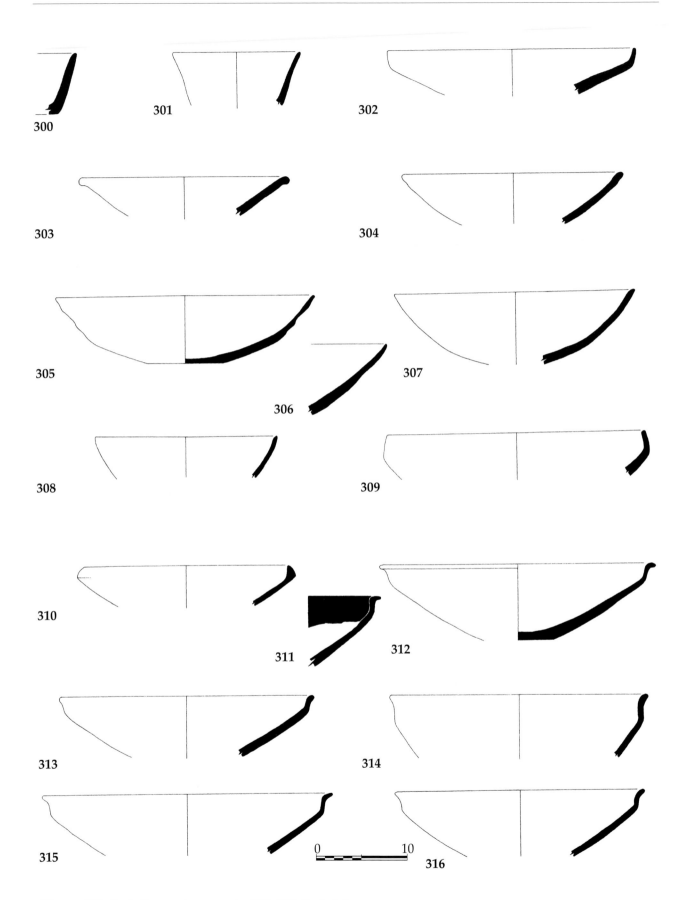

Figure 372. *Early Bronze Age ceramics 300–316. Scale 1:4.*

Artefact Drawings

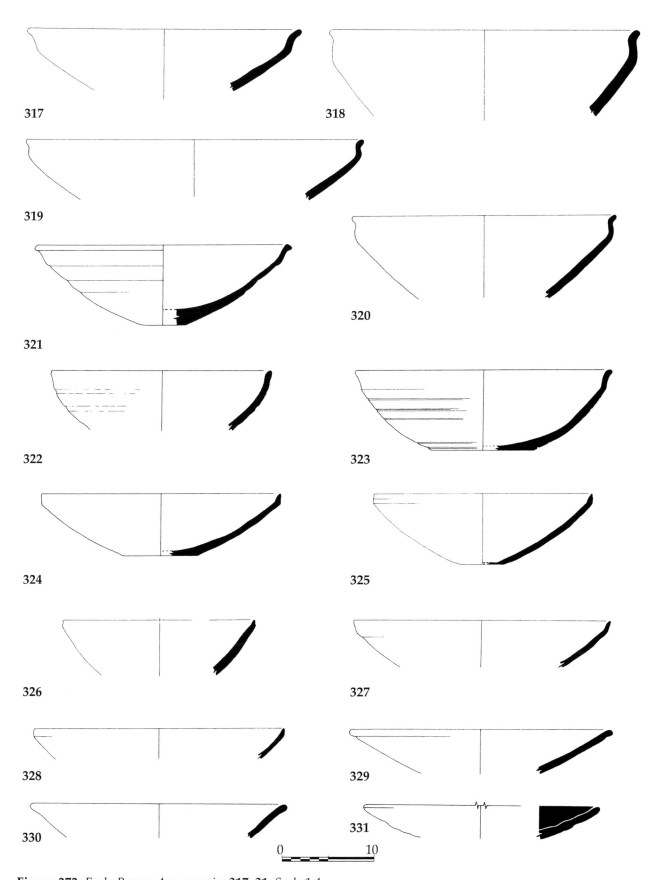

Figure 373. *Early Bronze Age ceramics 317–31. Scale 1:4.*

Artefact Drawings

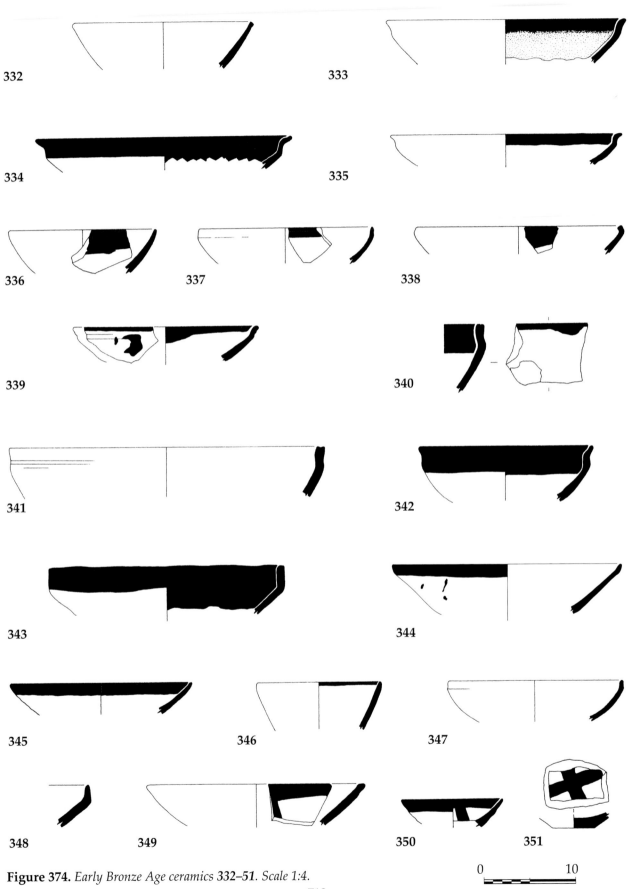

Figure 374. *Early Bronze Age ceramics 332–51. Scale 1:4.*

Artefact Drawings

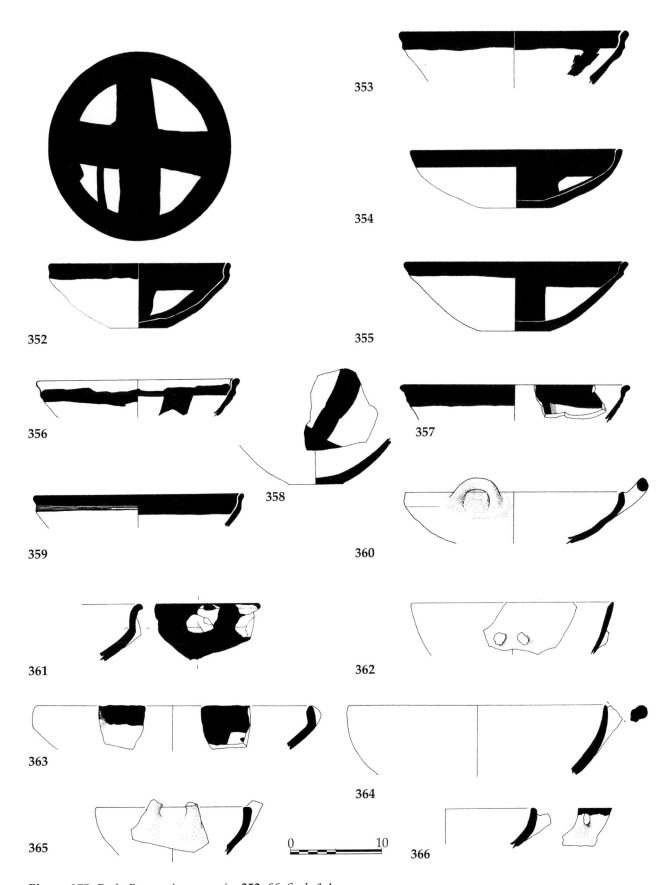

Figure 375. *Early Bronze Age ceramics 352–66. Scale 1:4.*

Artefact Drawings

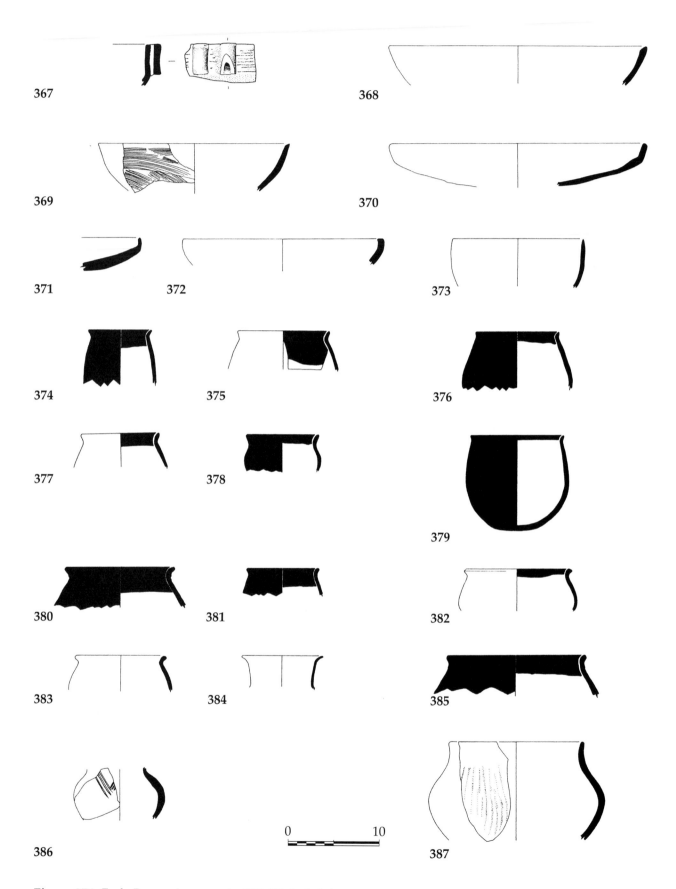

Figure 376. *Early Bronze Age ceramics 367–87. Scale 1:4.*

Artefact Drawings

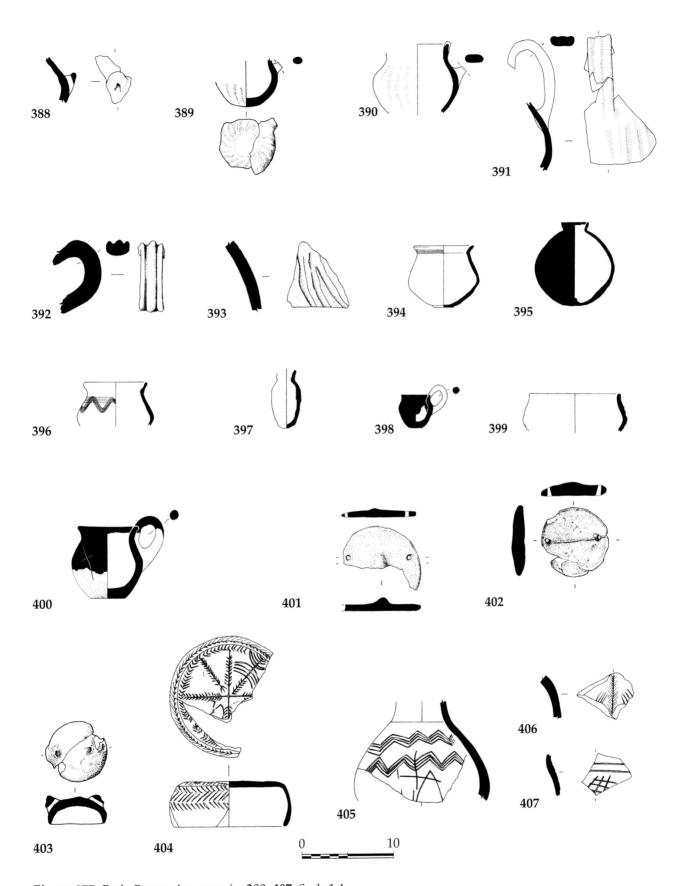

Figure 377. *Early Bronze Age ceramics 388–407. Scale 1:4.*

Artefact Drawings

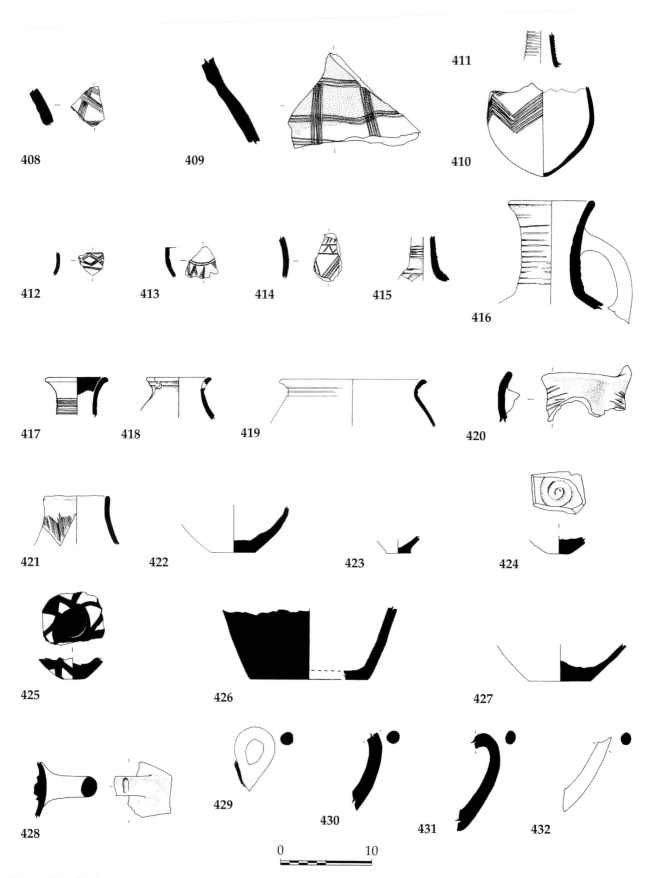

Figure 378. *Early Bronze Age ceramics 408–32. Scale 1:4.*

Artefact Drawings

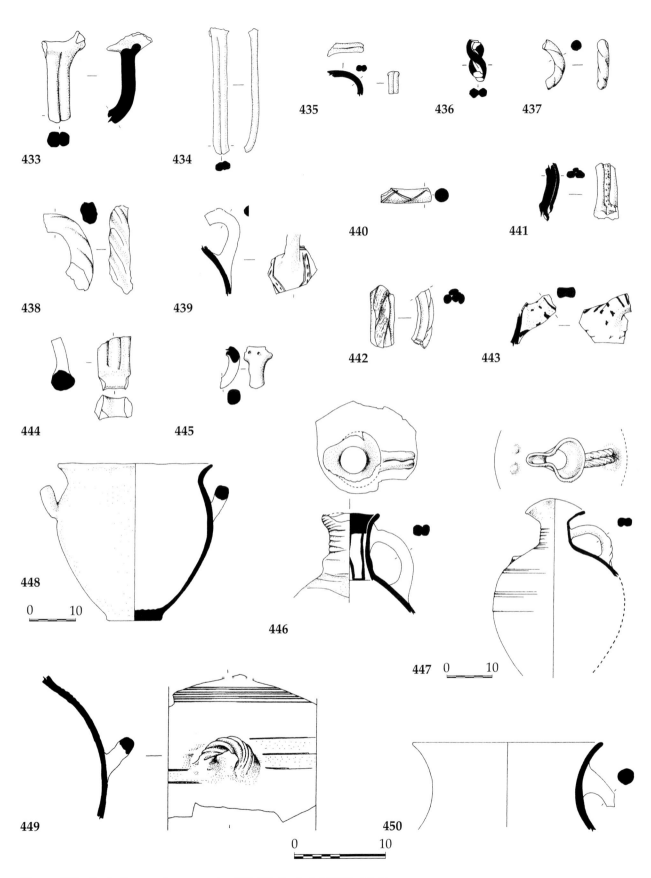

Figure 379. *Early Bronze Age ceramics 433–50. Scale 1:4 (448 at 1:8).*

Artefact Drawings

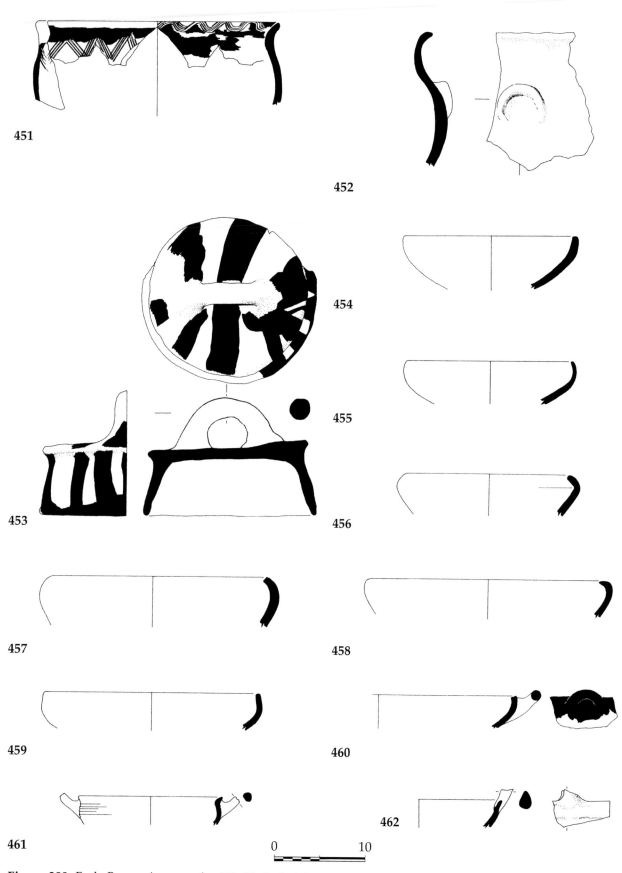

Figure 380. *Early Bronze Age ceramics 451–62. Scale 1:4.*

724

Artefact Drawings

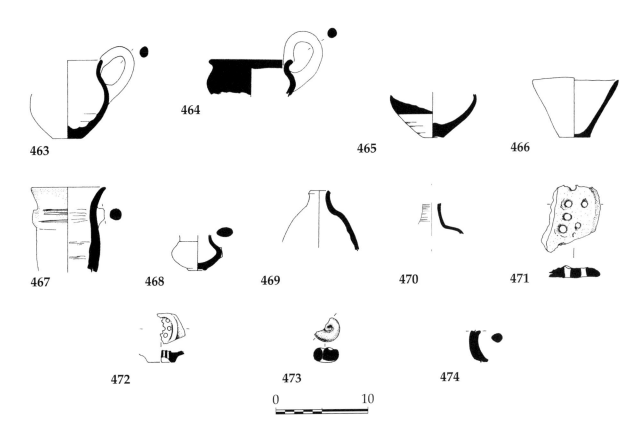

Figure 381. *Early Bronze Age ceramics* **463–74**. *Scale 1:4.*

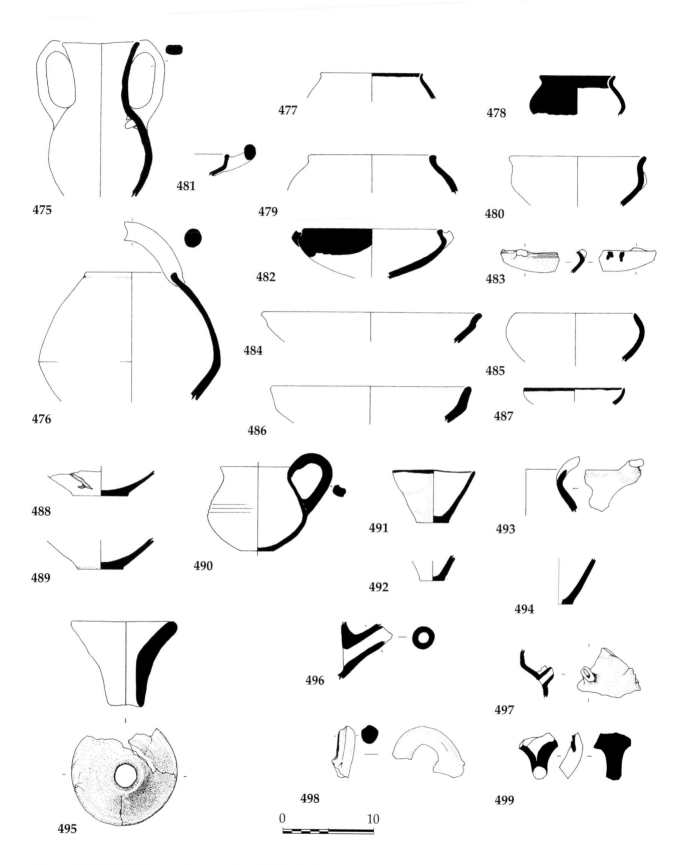

Figure 382. *Middle Bronze Age ceramics 475–99. Scale 1:4.*

Artefact Drawings

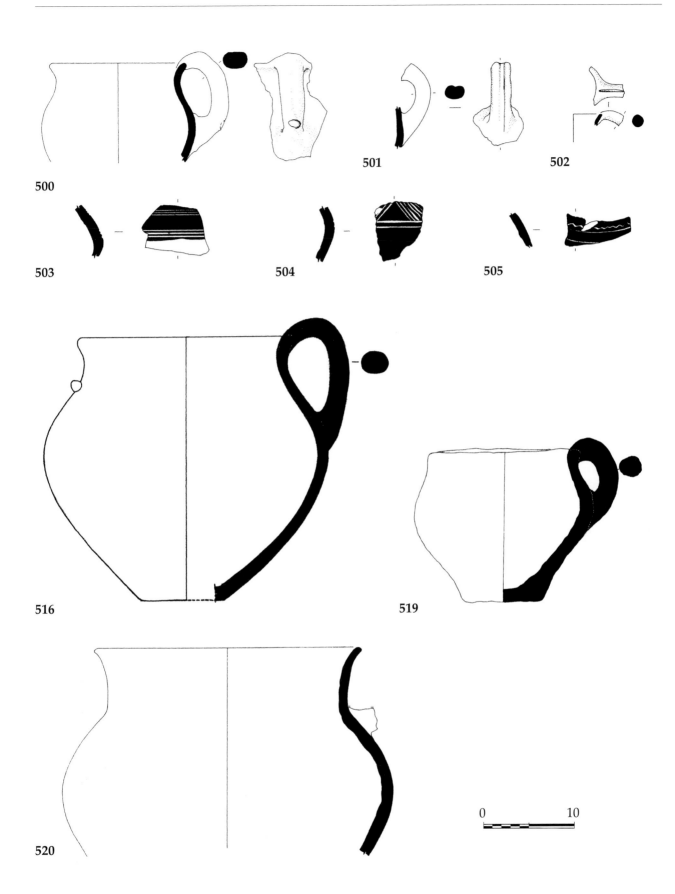

Figure 383. *Middle Bronze Age ceramics 500–520. Scale 1:4.*

Artefact Drawings

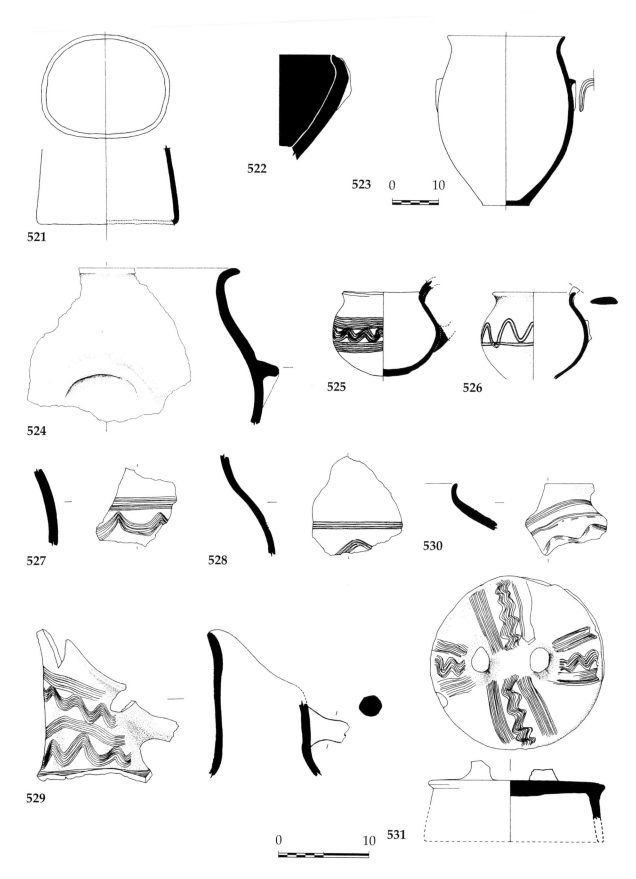

Figure 384. *Middle Bronze Age ceramics* **521–31**. *Scale 1:4 (**523** at 1:8).*

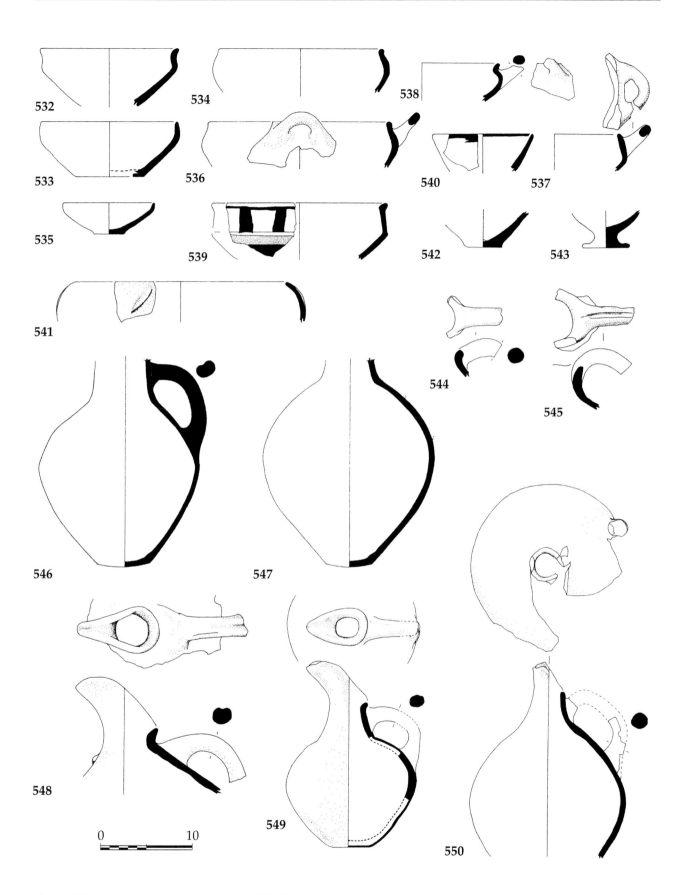

Figure 385. *Middle Bronze Age ceramics* **532–50**. *Scale 1:4.*

Artefact Drawings

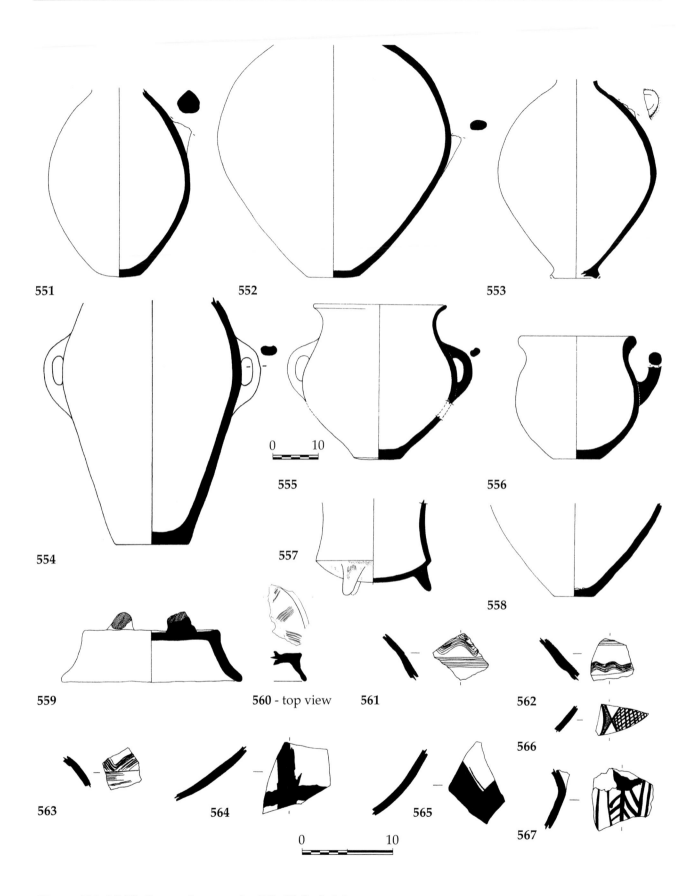

Figure 386. *Middle Bronze Age ceramics 551–67. Scale 1:4.*

Artefact Drawings

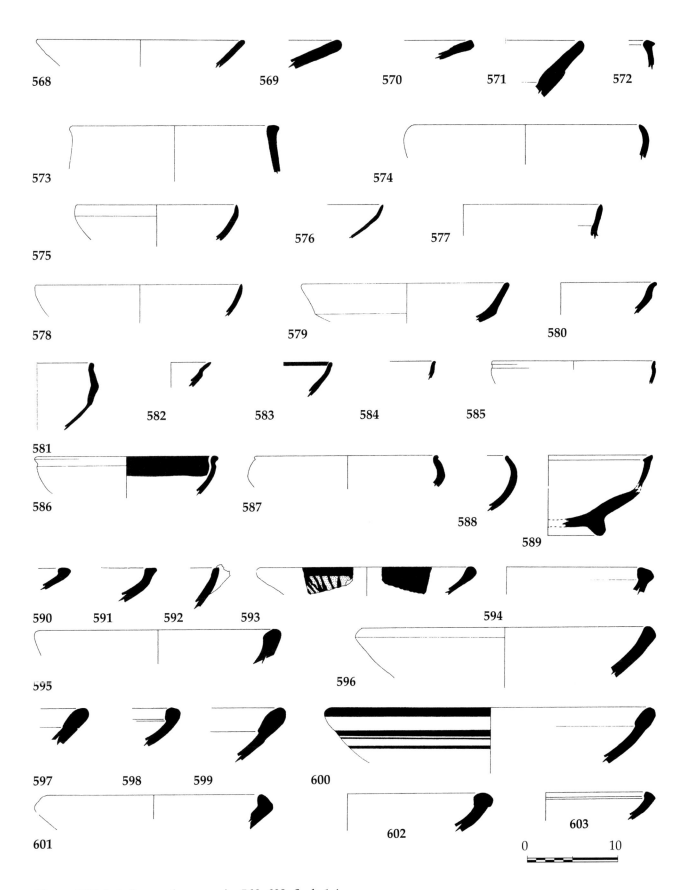

Figure 387. *Late Bronze Age ceramics 568–603. Scale 1:4.*

Artefact Drawings

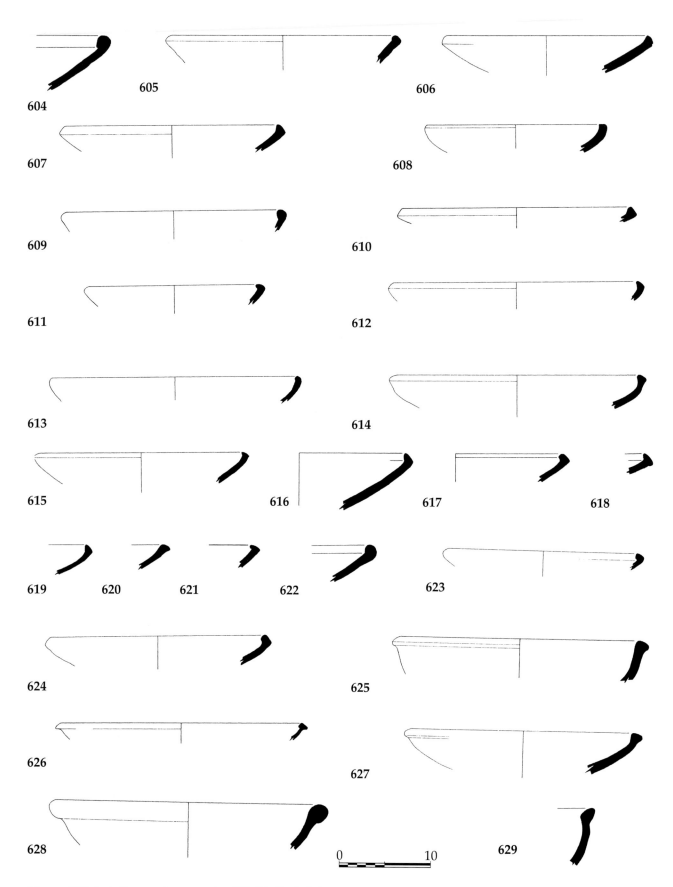

Figure 388. *Late Bronze Age ceramics 604–29. Scale 1:4.*

Artefact Drawings

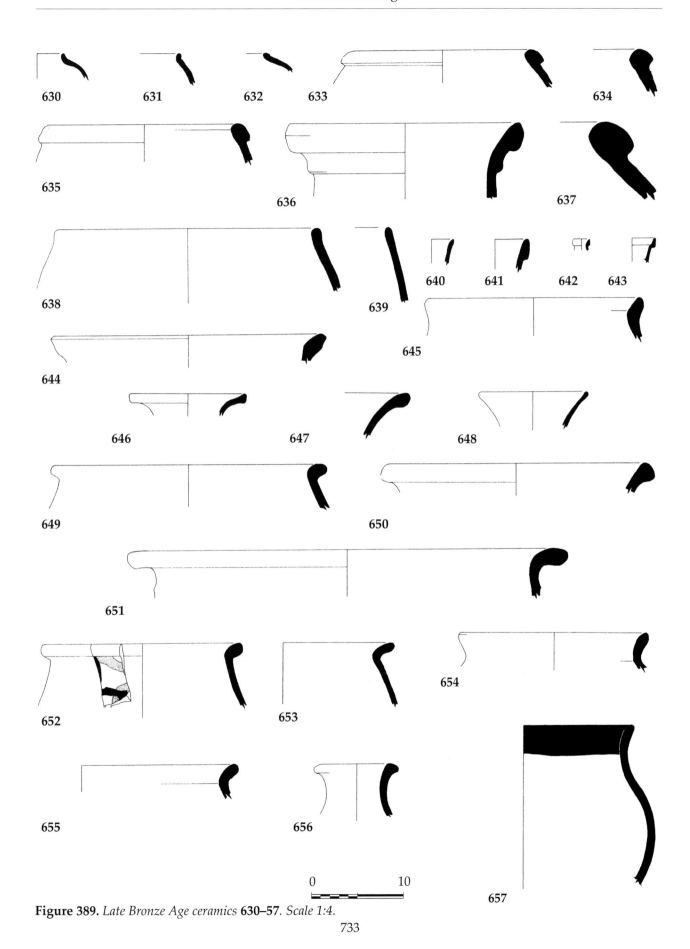

Figure 389. *Late Bronze Age ceramics* **630–57**. *Scale 1:4.*

Artefact Drawings

Figure 390. *Late Bronze Age ceramics 658–77. Scale 1:4.*

Artefact Drawings

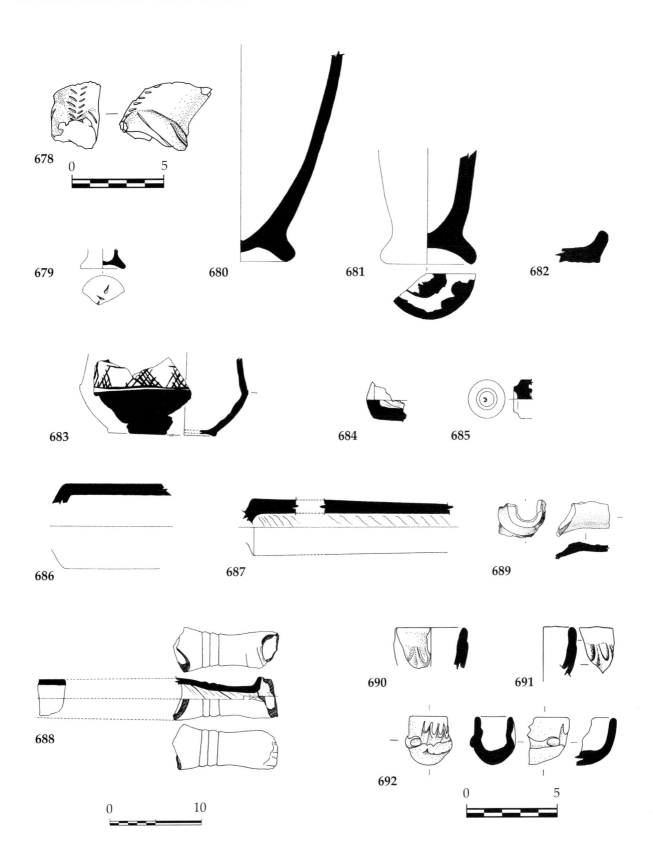

Figure 391. *Late Bronze Age ceramics **678–92**. Scale 1:4 (**690–92** at 1:2).*

735

Artefact Drawings

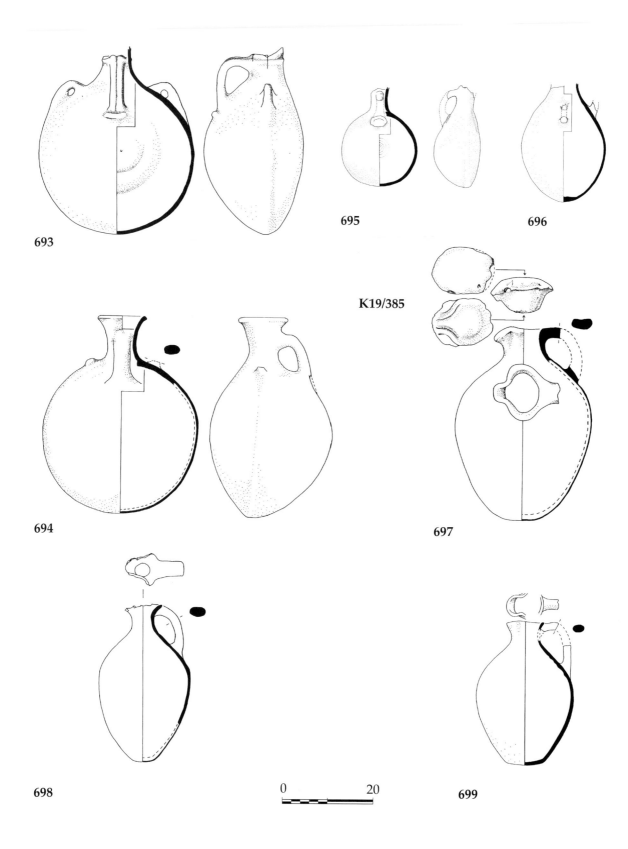

Figure 392. *Level II ceramics 693–9. Scale 1:8.*

Artefact Drawings

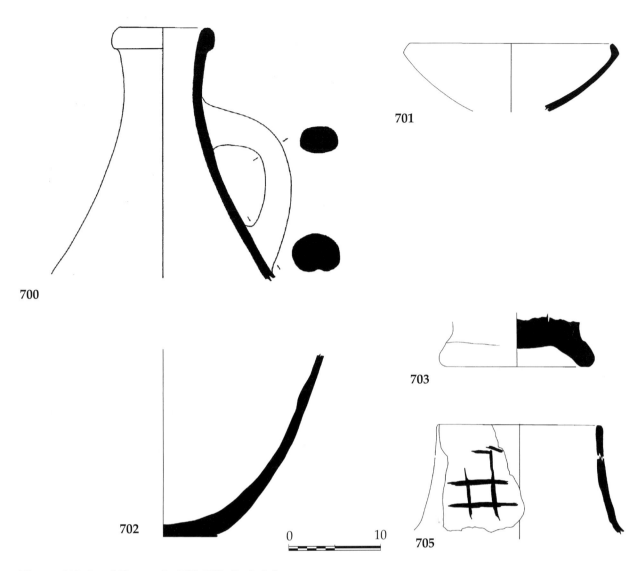

Figure 393. *Level II ceramics* **700–705**. *Scale 1:4.*

Artefact Drawings

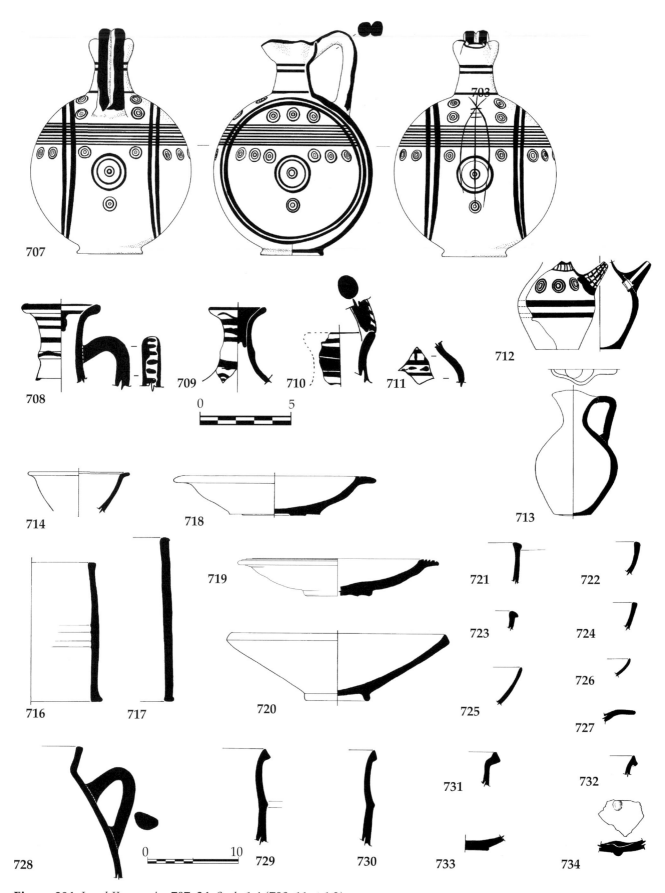

Figure 394. *Level II ceramics* **707–34**. *Scale 1:4* (**708–11** *at 1:2*).

738

Artefact Drawings

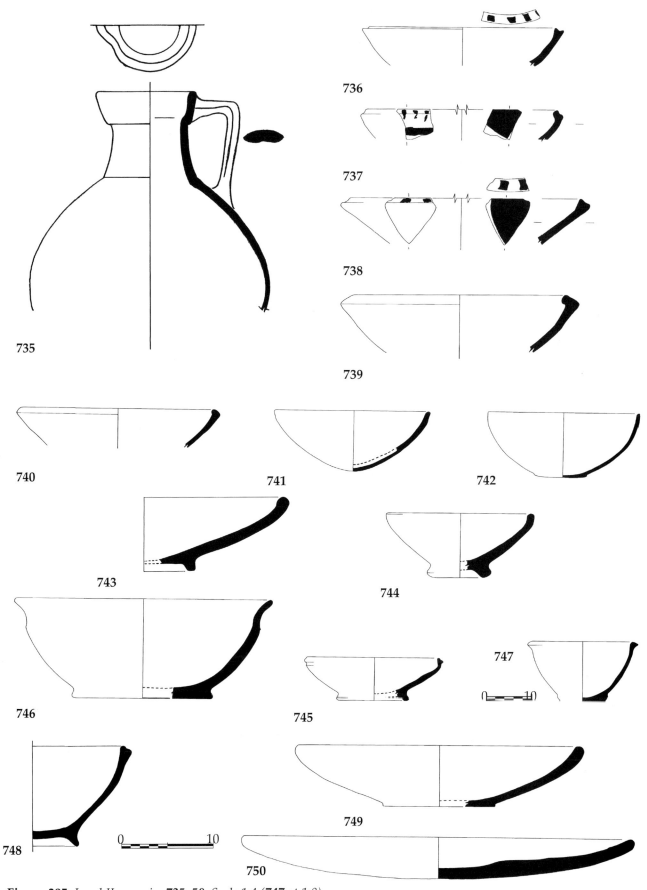

Figure 395. *Level II ceramics* **735–50**. *Scale 1:4* (**747** *at 1:8*).

Artefact Drawings

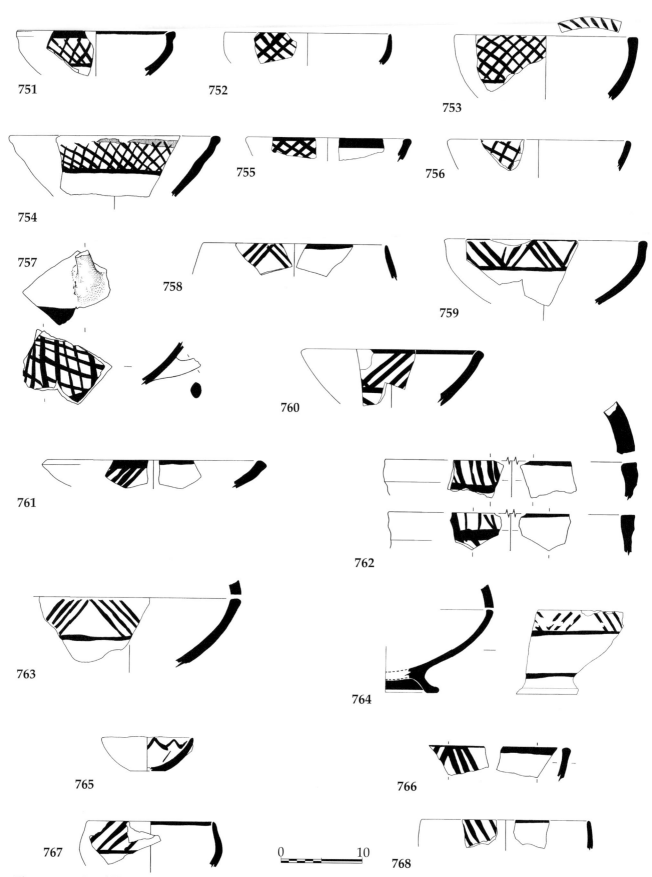

Figure 396. *Level II ceramics 751–68. Scale 1:4.*

Artefact Drawings

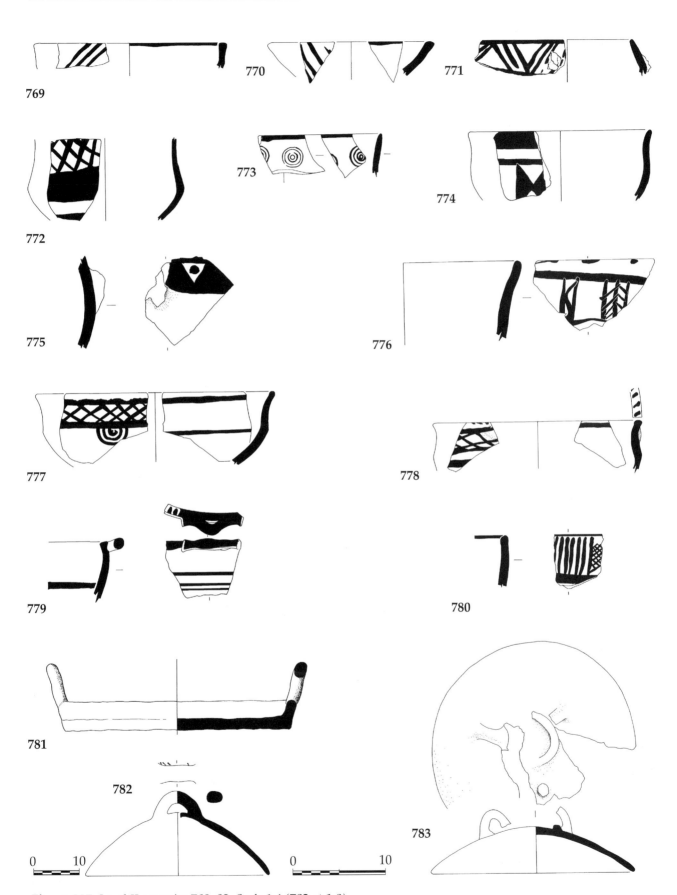

Figure 397. *Level II ceramics 769–83. Scale 1:4 (782 at 1:8).*

Artefact Drawings

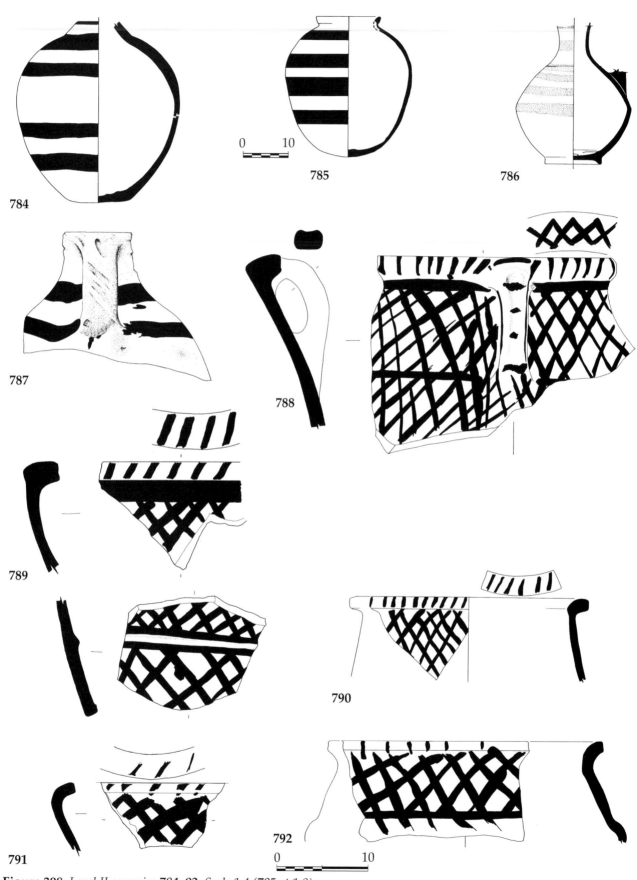

Figure 398. *Level II ceramics 784–92. Scale 1:4 (785 at 1:8).*

742

Artefact Drawings

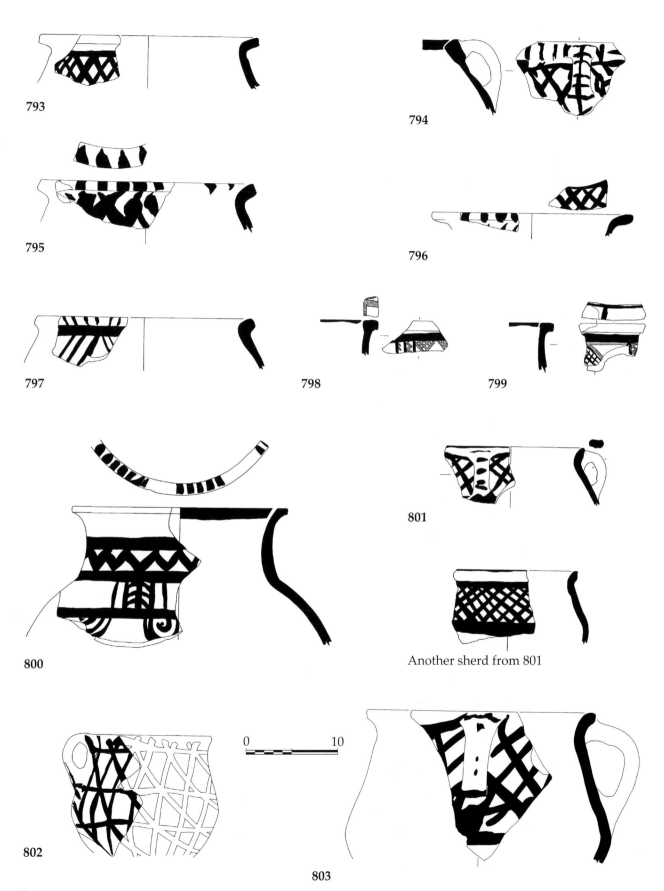

Figure 399. *Level II ceramics **793–803**. Scale 1:4.*

Artefact Drawings

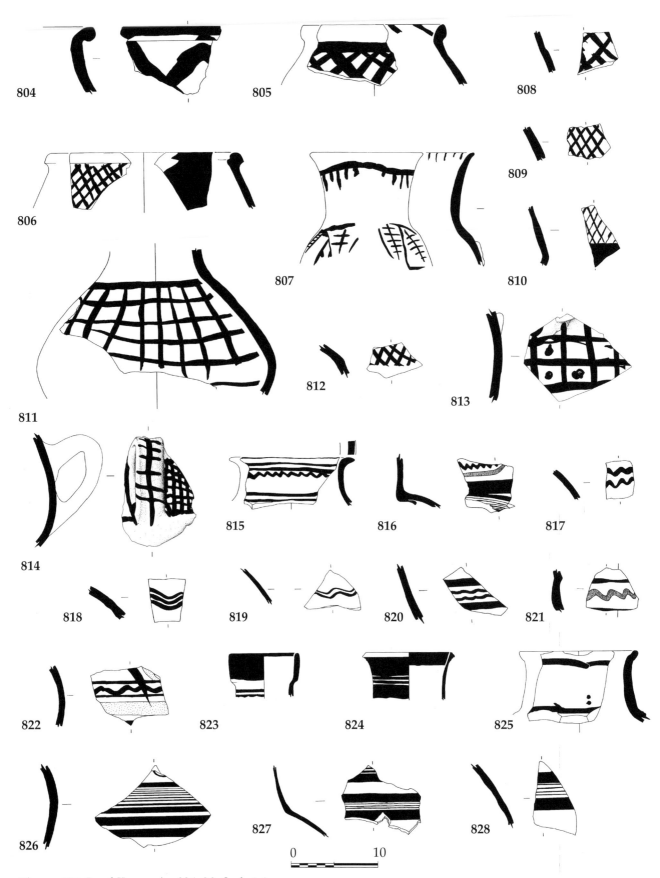

Figure 400. *Level II ceramics 804–28. Scale 1:4.*

744

Artefact Drawings

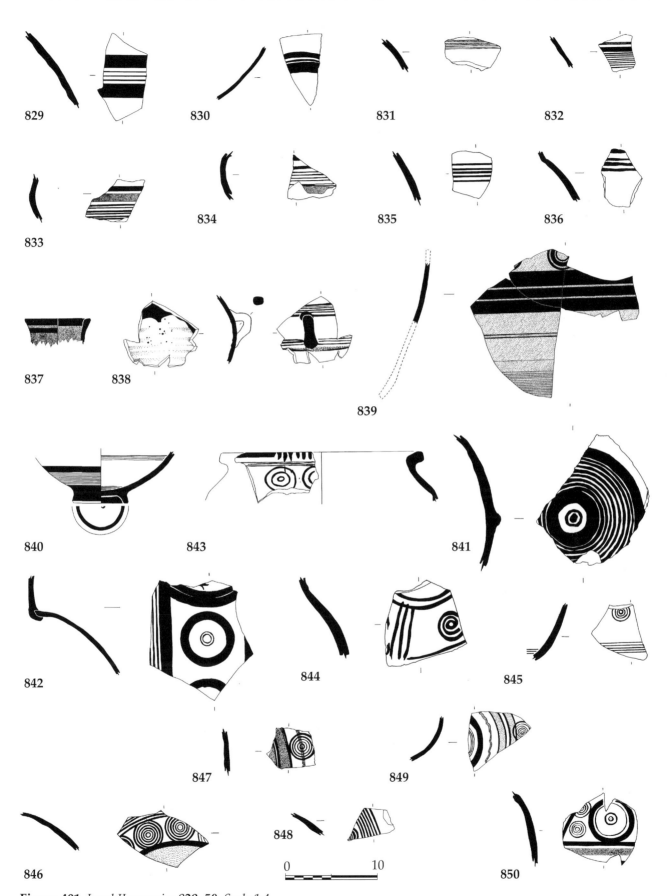

Figure 401. *Level II ceramics 829–50. Scale 1:4.*

Artefact Drawings

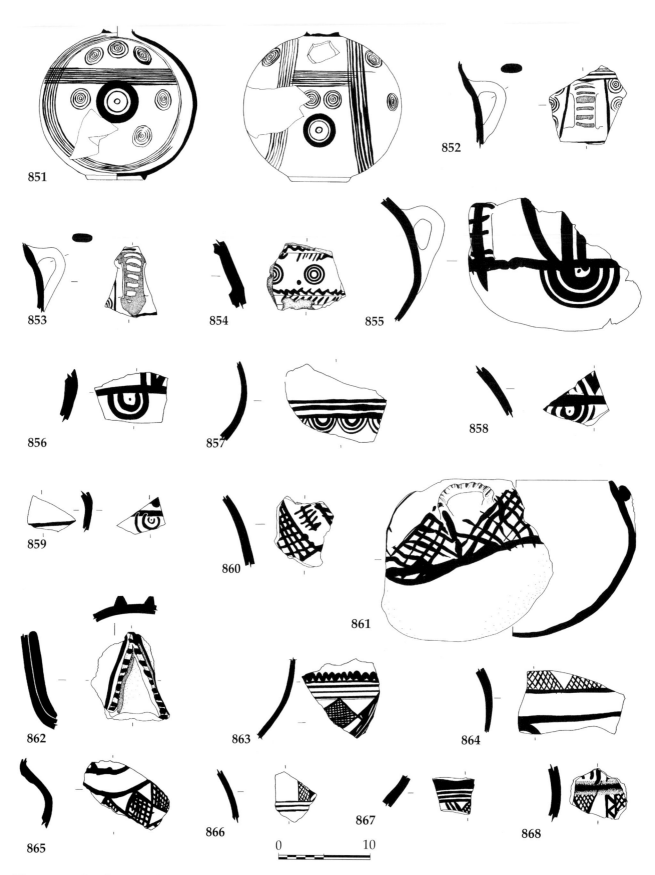

Figure 402. *Level II ceramics 851–68. Scale 1:4.*

Artefact Drawings

Figure 403. *Level II ceramics 869–89. Scale 1:4.*

747

Artefact Drawings

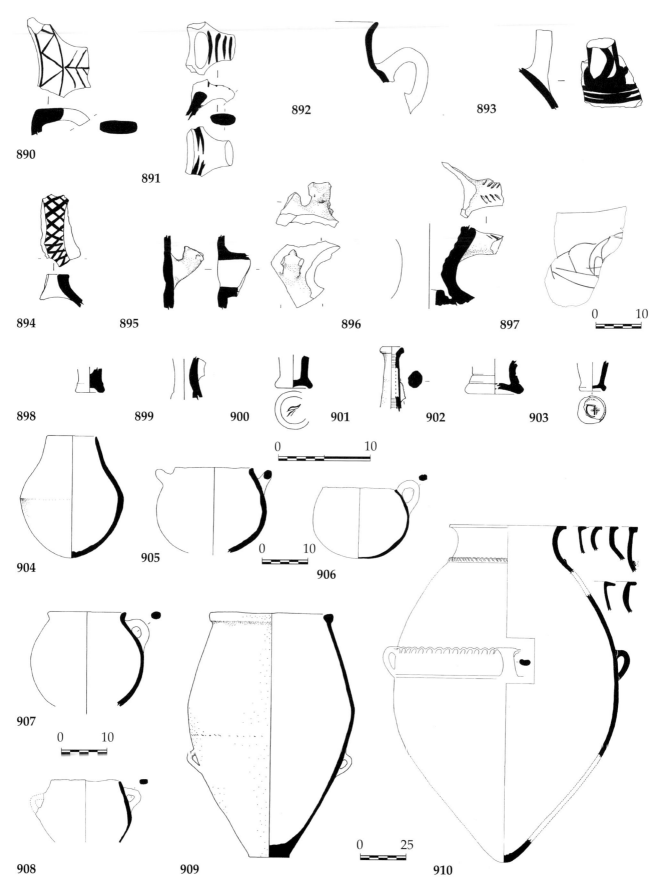

Figure 404. *Level II ceramics 890–910. Scale 1:4 (897, 905–8 at 1:8; 909–10 at 1:20).*

Artefact Drawings

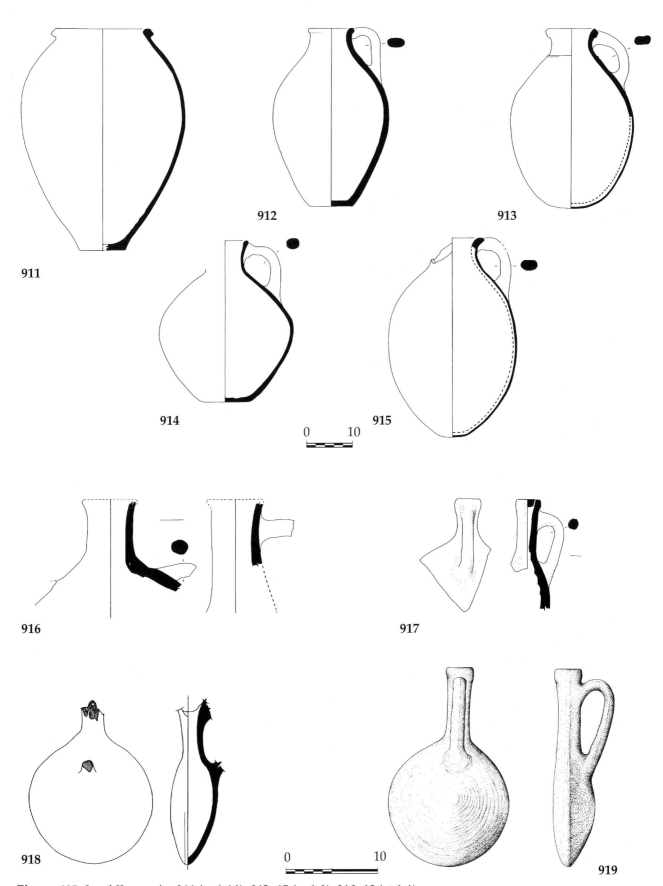

Figure 405. *Level II ceramics **911** (at 1:16), **912–15** (at 1:8), **916–19** (at 1:4).*

749

Artefact Drawings

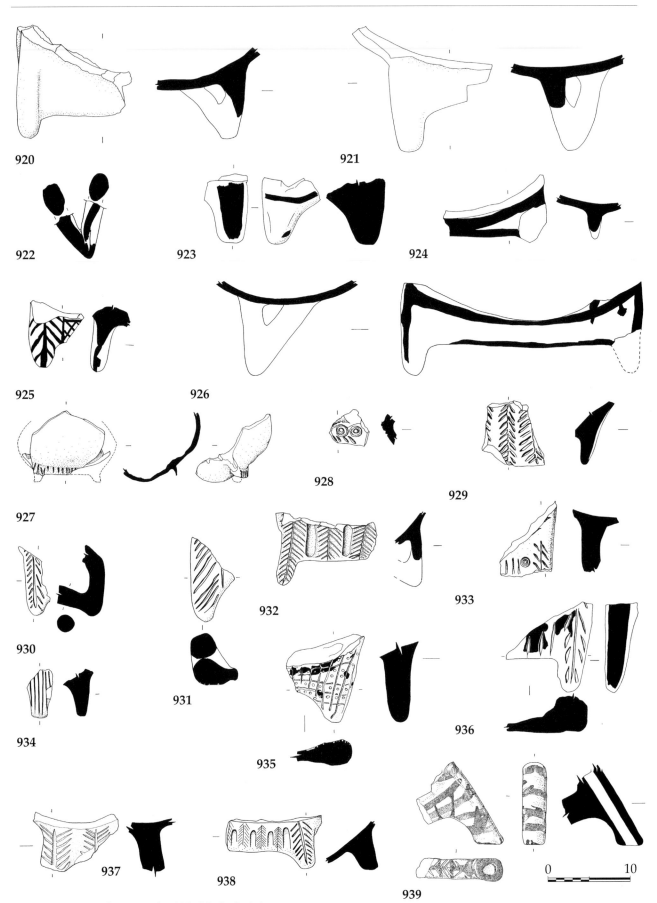

Figure 406. *Level II ceramics* **920–39**. *Scale 1:4.*

Artefact Drawings

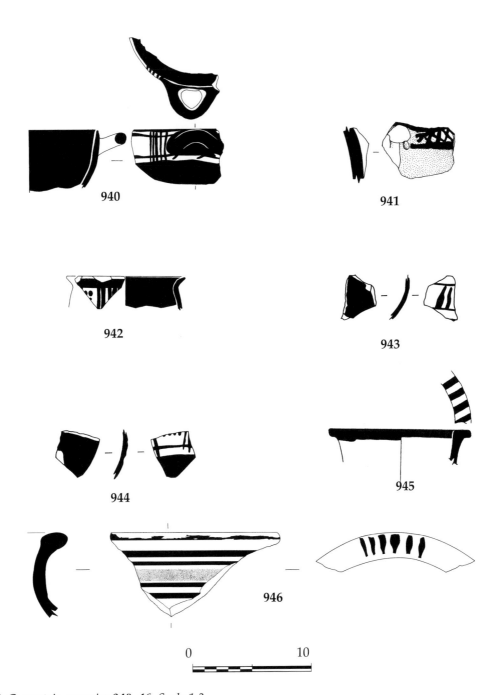

Figure 407. *Geometric ceramics **940–46**. Scale 1:3.*

Artefact Drawings

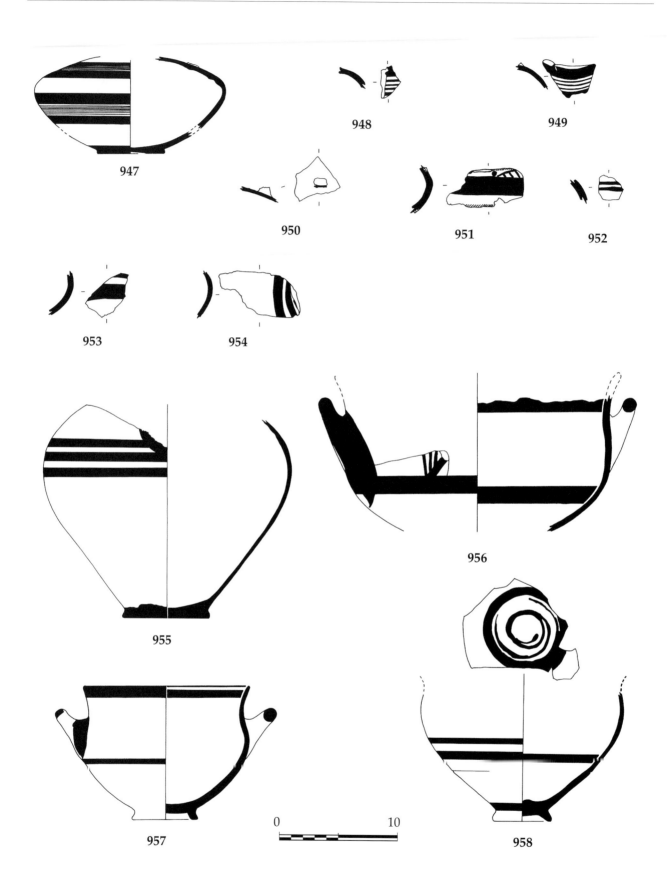

Figure 408. *Mycenaean ceramics 947–58. Scale 1:3.*

752

Artefact Drawings

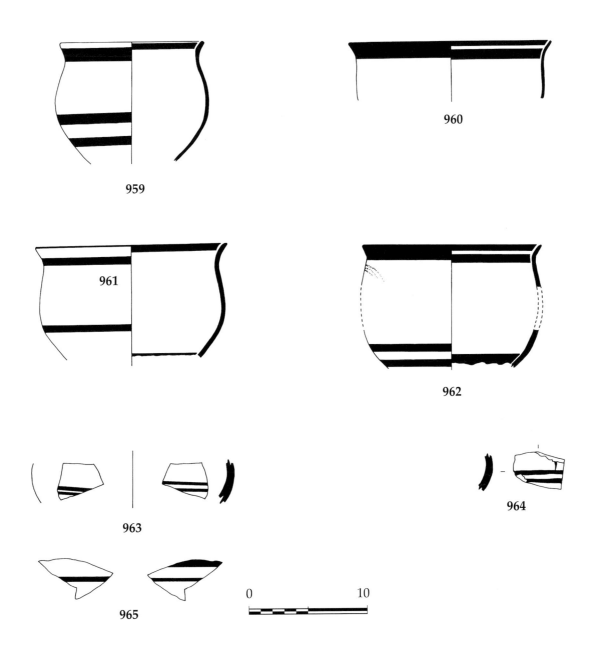

Figure 409. *Mycenaean ceramics **959–65**. Scale 1:3.*

Artefact Drawings

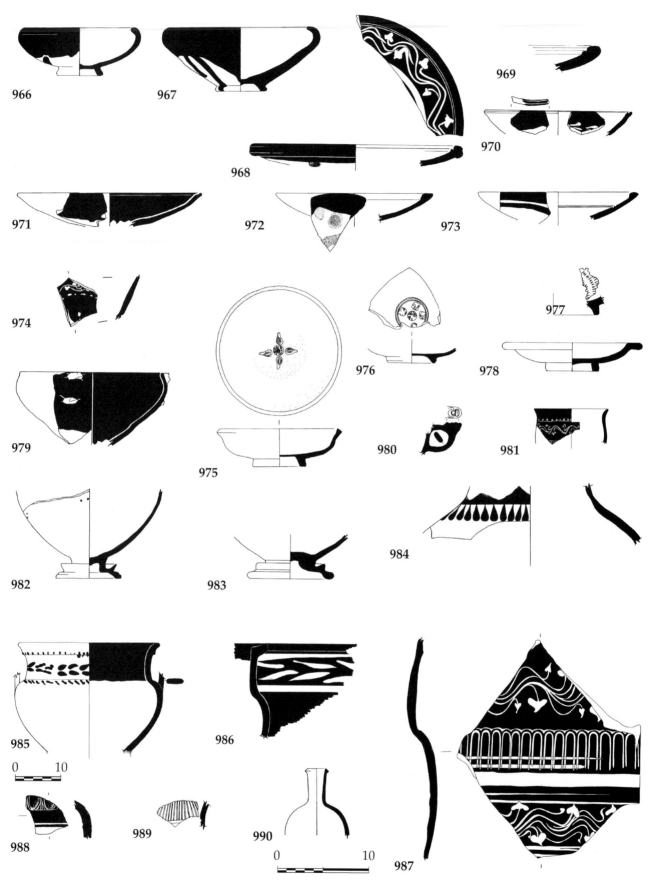

Figure 410. *Hellenistic ceramics* **966–90**. *Scale 1:4* (**985** *at 1:8*).

Artefact Drawings

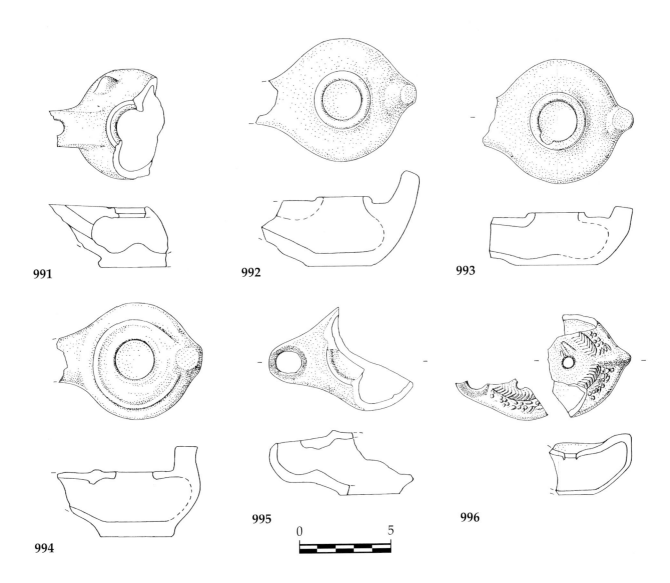

Figure 411. *Hellenistic lamps* **991–5**, *Byzantine lamp* **996**. *Scale 1:2.*

Artefact Drawings

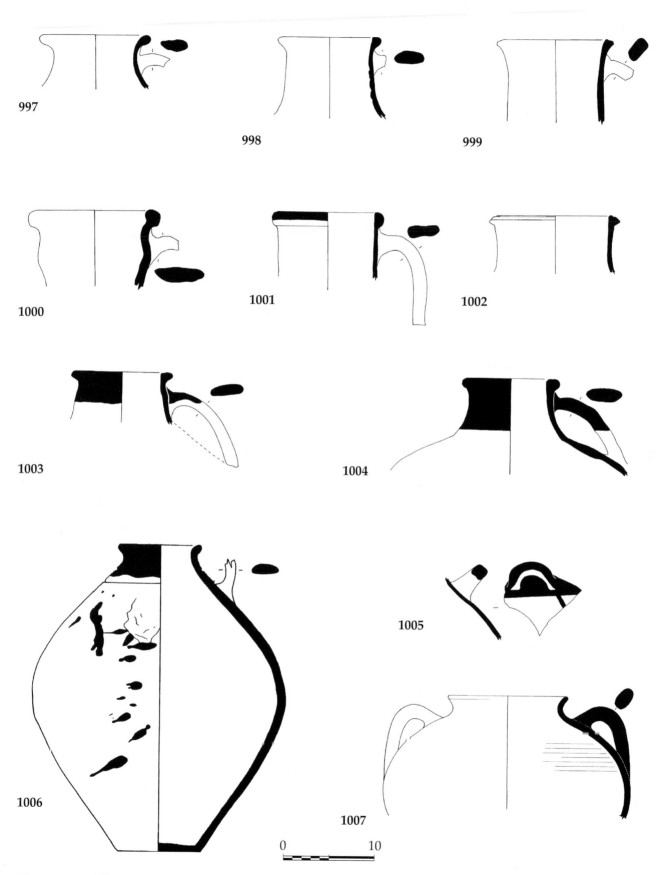

Figure 412. *Hellenistic ceramics **997–1007**. Scale 1:4.*

Artefact Drawings

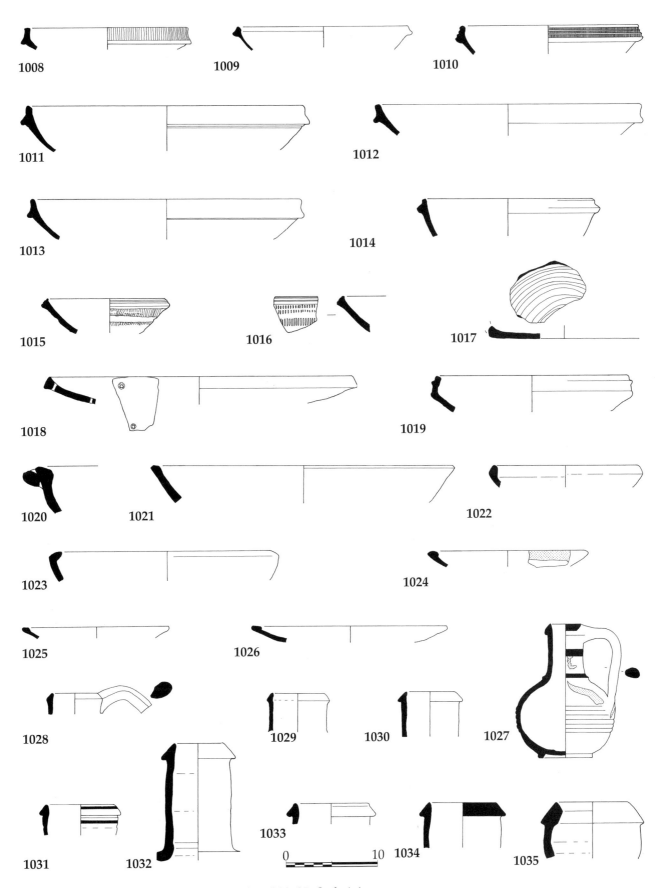

Figure 413. *Late Roman/Byzantine ceramics 1008–35. Scale 1:4.*

Artefact Drawings

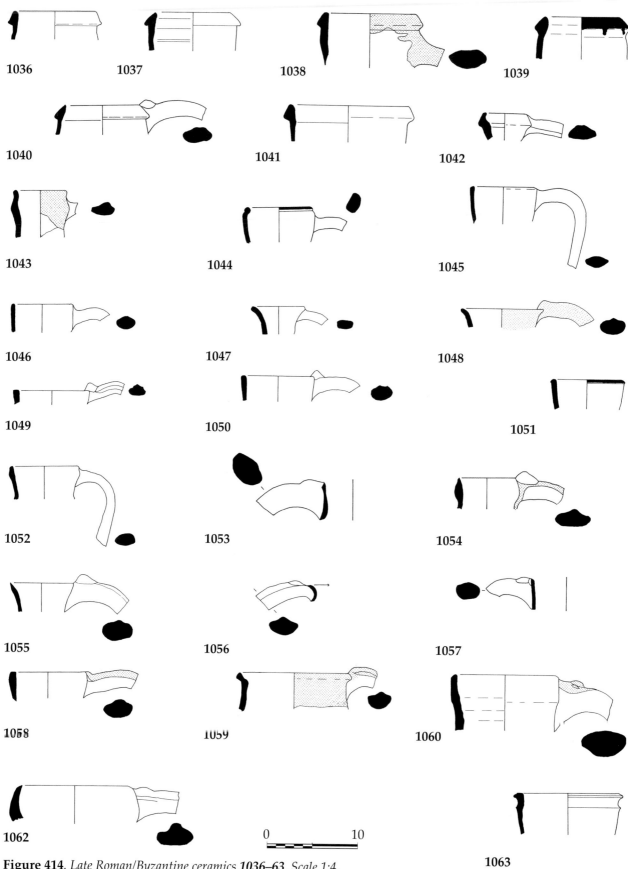

Figure 414. *Late Roman/Byzantine ceramics **1036–63**. Scale 1:4.*

Artefact Drawings

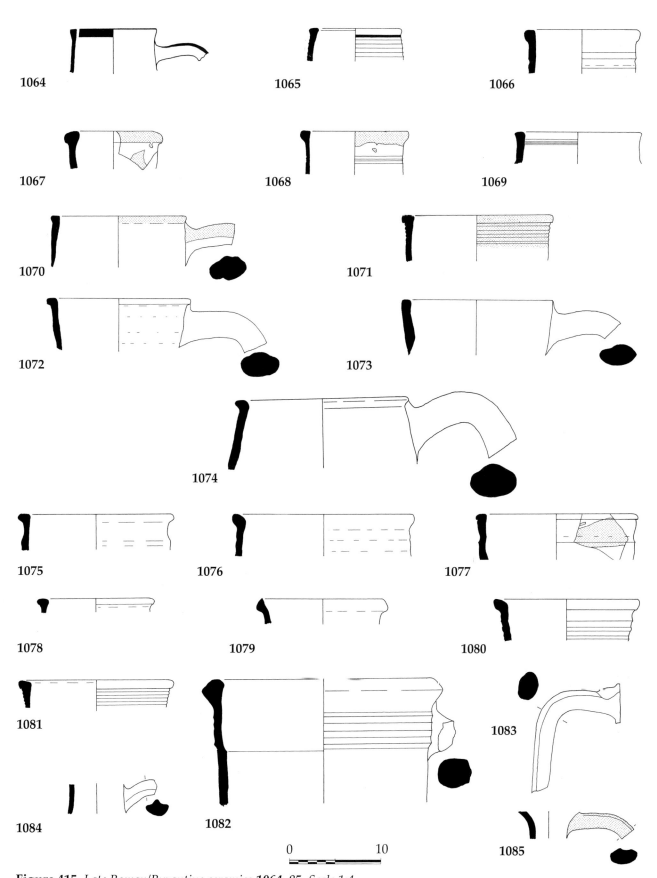

Figure 415. *Late Roman/Byzantine ceramics **1064–85**. Scale 1:4.*

Artefact Drawings

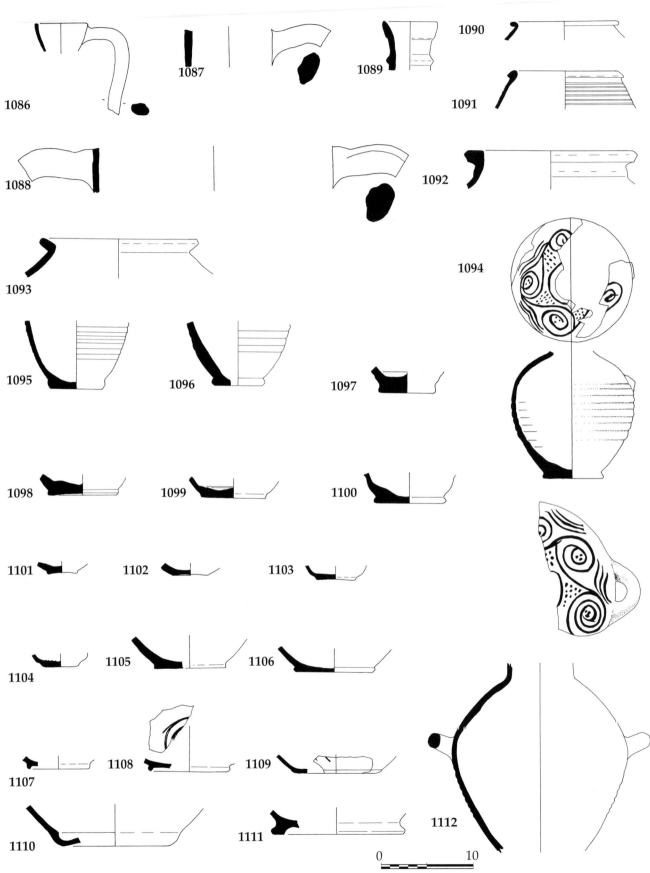

Figure 416. *Late Roman/Byzantine ceramics 1086–112. Scale 1:4.*

Artefact Drawings

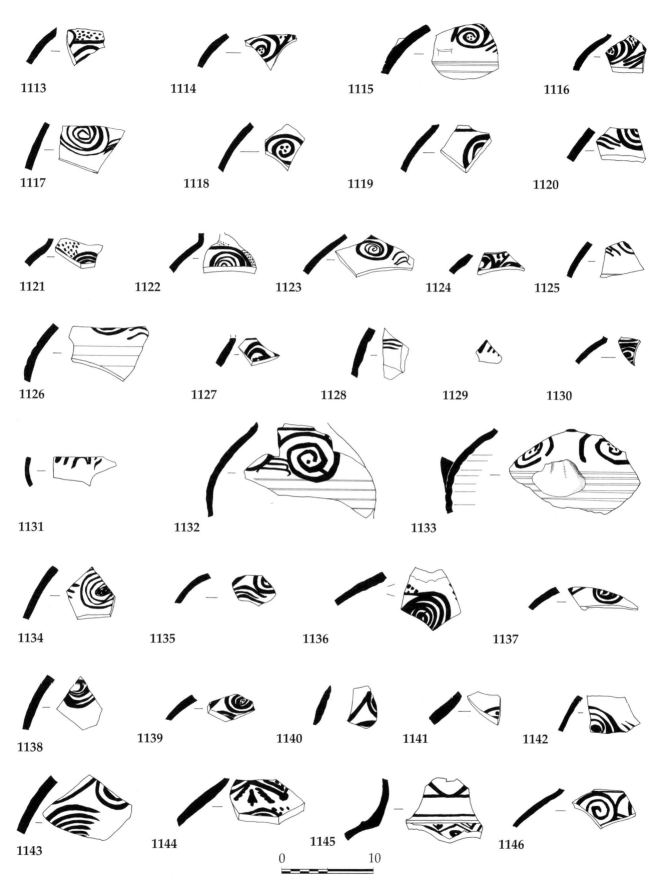

Figure 417. *Late Roman/Byzantine ceramics 1113–146. Scale 1:4.*

Artefact Drawings

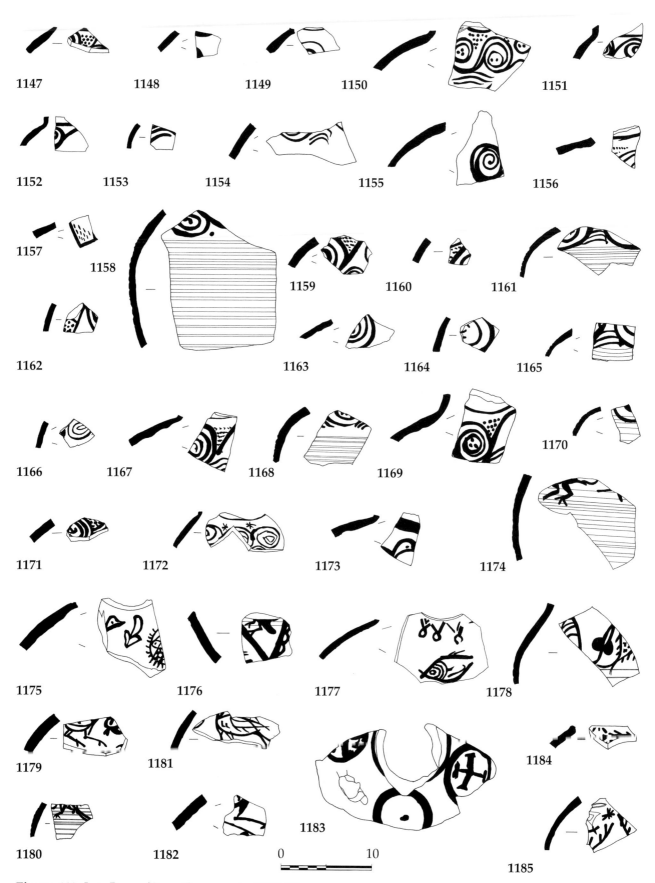

Figure 418. *Late Roman/Byzantine ceramics* **1147–85**.

762

Artefact Drawings

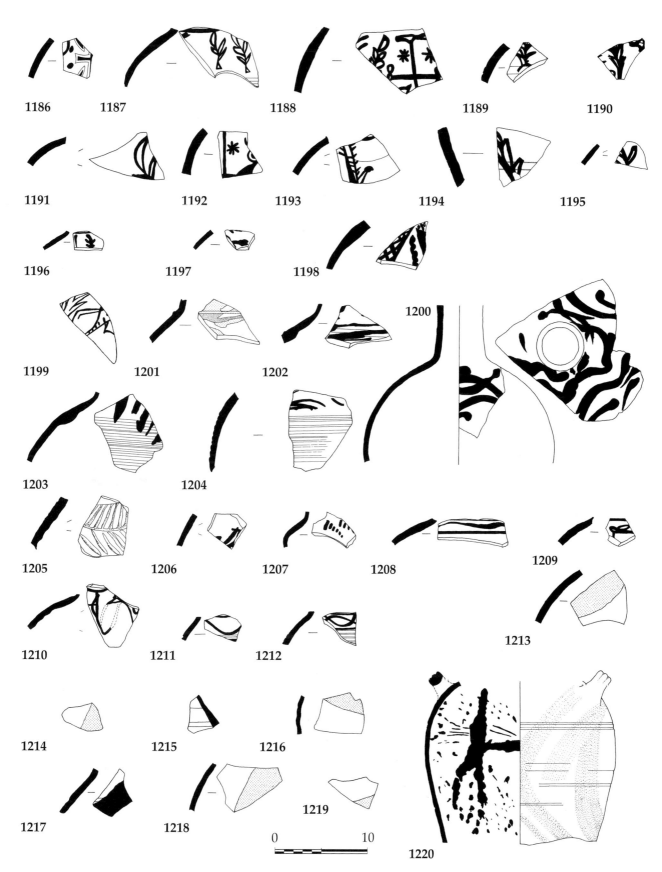

Figure 419. *Late Roman/Byzantine ceramics* **1186–220**. *Scale 1:4.*

Artefact Drawings

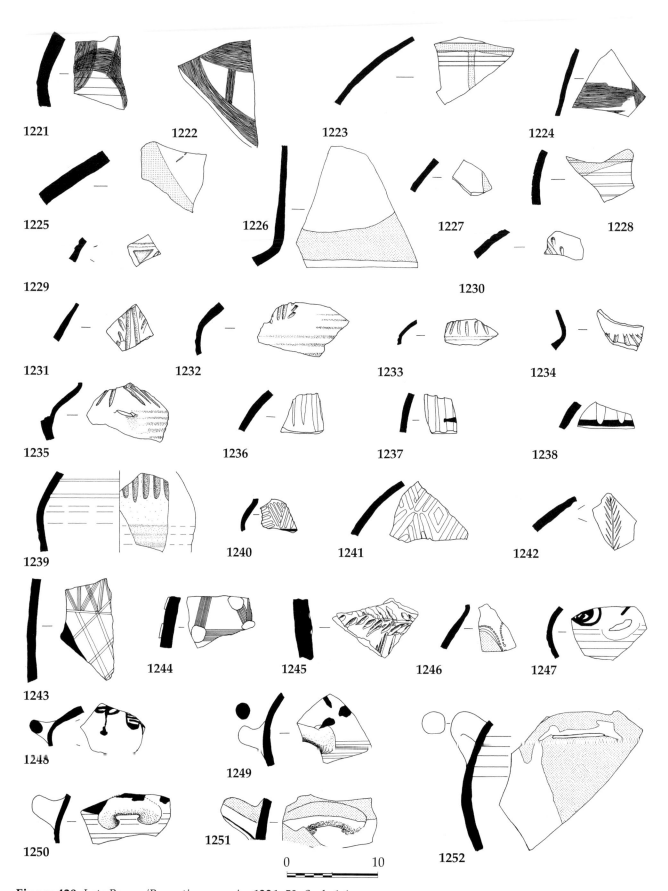

Figure 420. *Late Roman/Byzantine ceramics* **1221–52**. *Scale 1:4.*

Artefact Drawings

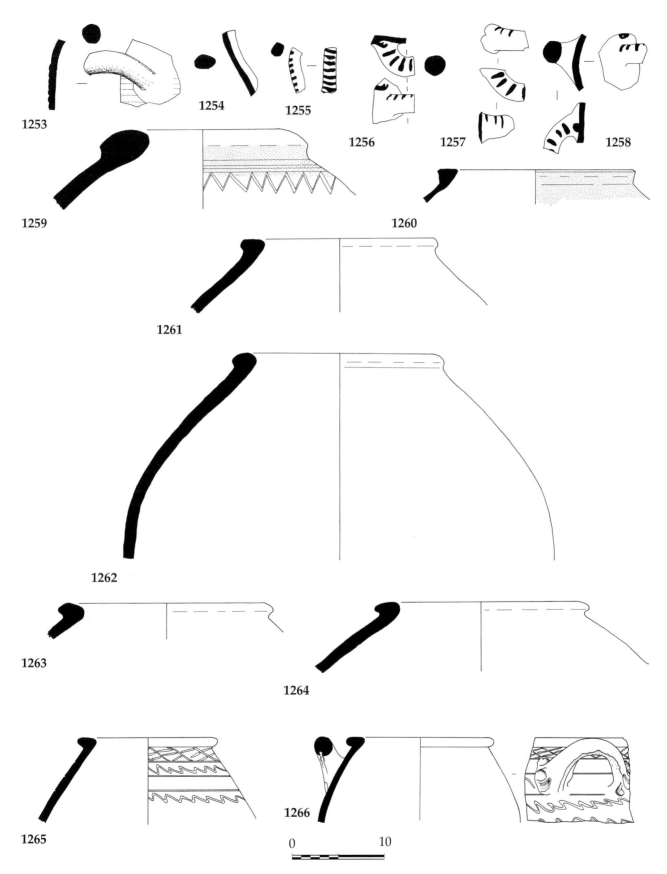

Figure 421. *Late Roman/Byzantine ceramics* **1253–66**. *Scale 1:4.*

765

Artefact Drawings

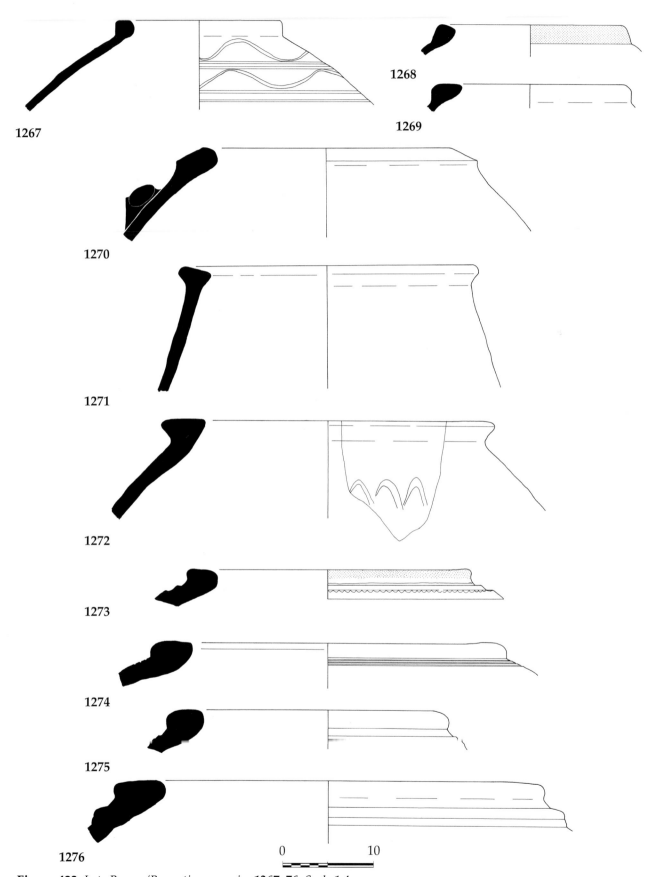

Figure 422. *Late Roman/Byzantine ceramics* **1267–76**. *Scale 1:4.*

766

Artefact Drawings

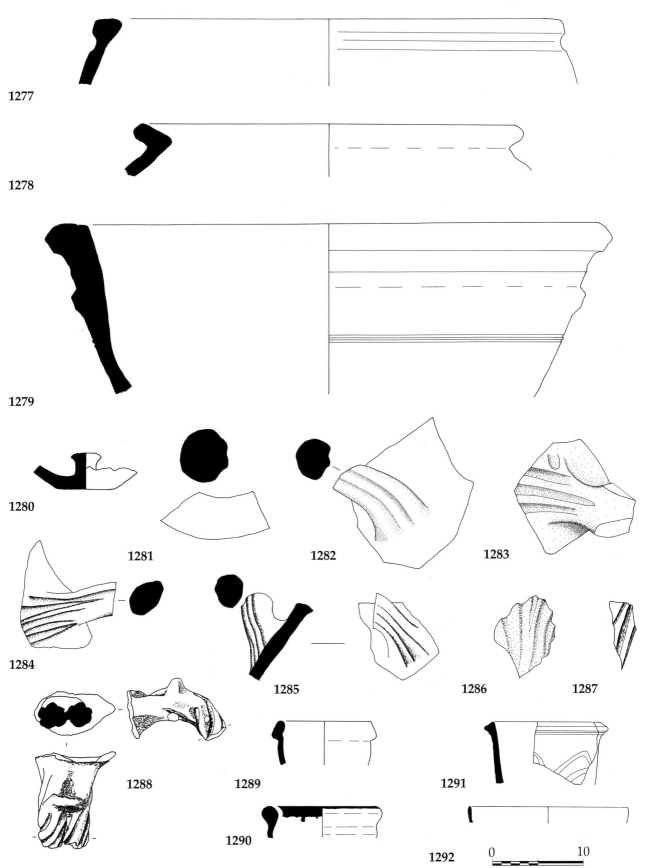

Figure 423. *Late Roman/Byzantine ceramics* **1277–92**. *Scale 1:4.*

Artefact Drawings

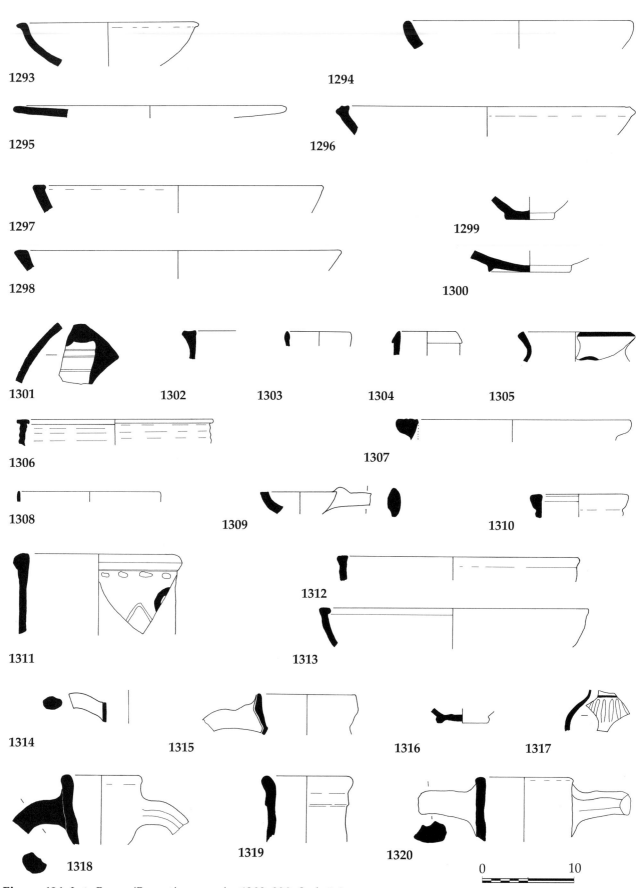

Figure 424. *Late Roman/Byzantine ceramics 1293–320. Scale 1:4.*

Artefact Drawings

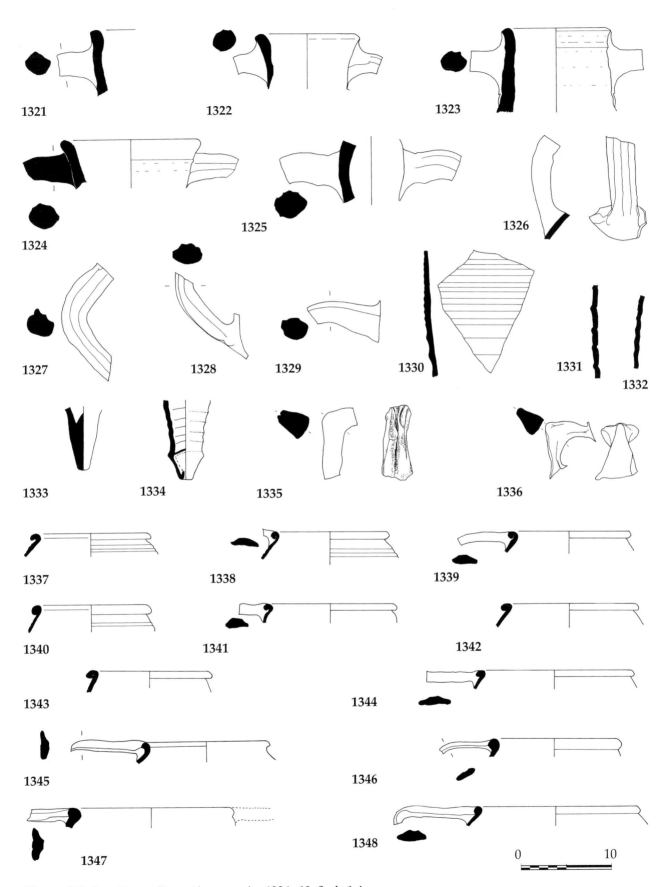

Figure 425. *Late Roman/Byzantine ceramics* **1321–48**. *Scale 1:4.*

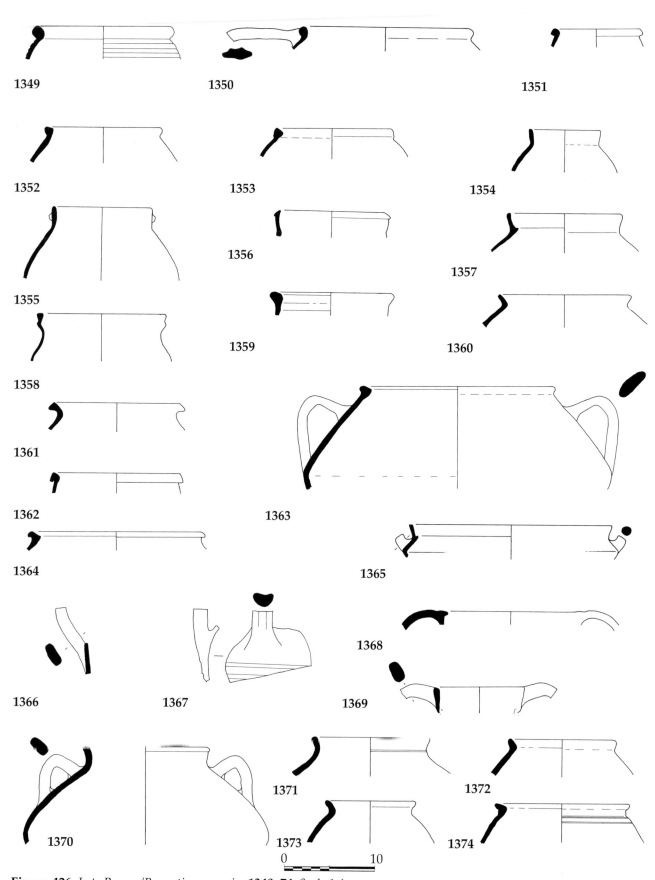

Figure 426. *Late Roman/Byzantine ceramics 1349–74. Scale 1:4.*

Artefact Drawings

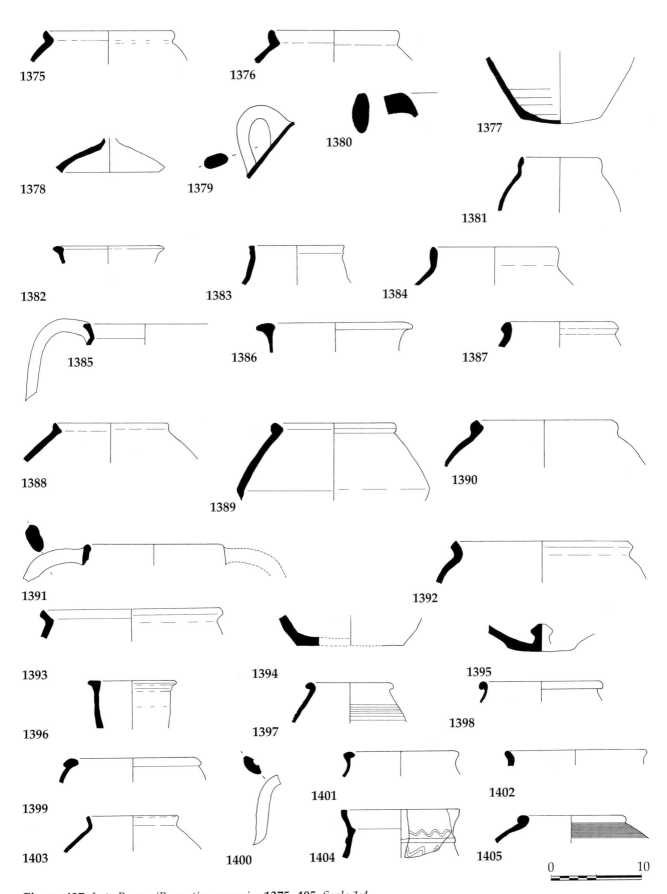

Figure 427. *Late Roman/Byzantine ceramics **1375–405**. Scale 1:4.*

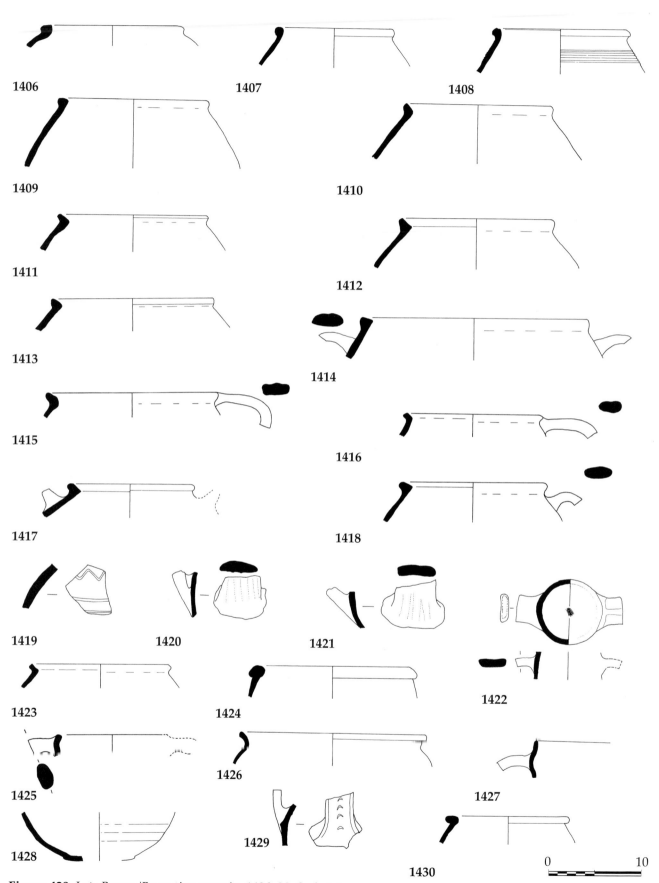

Figure 428. *Late Roman/Byzantine ceramics 1406–30. Scale 1:4.*

Artefact Drawings

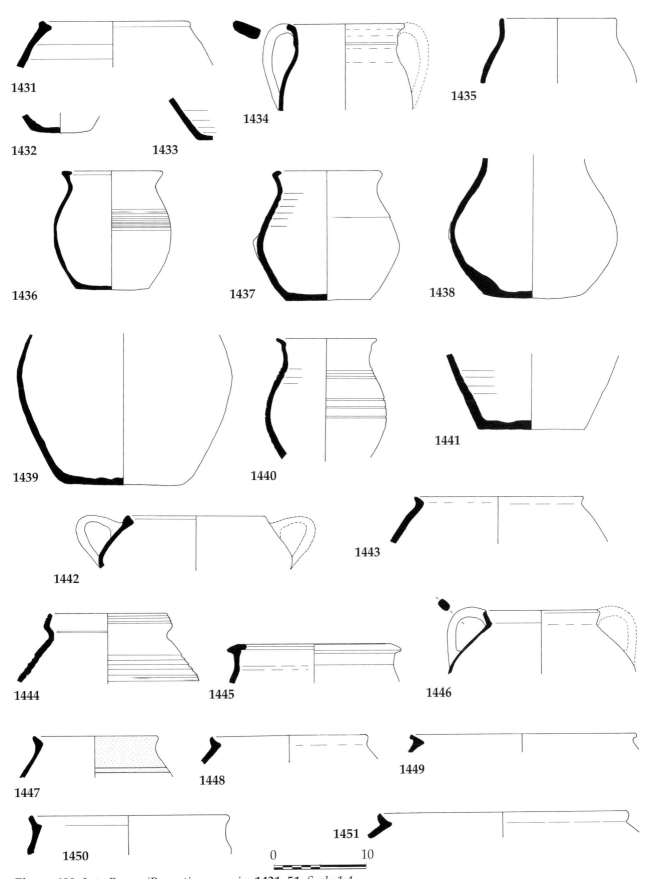

Figure 429. *Late Roman/Byzantine ceramics* **1431–51**. *Scale 1:4.*

Artefact Drawings

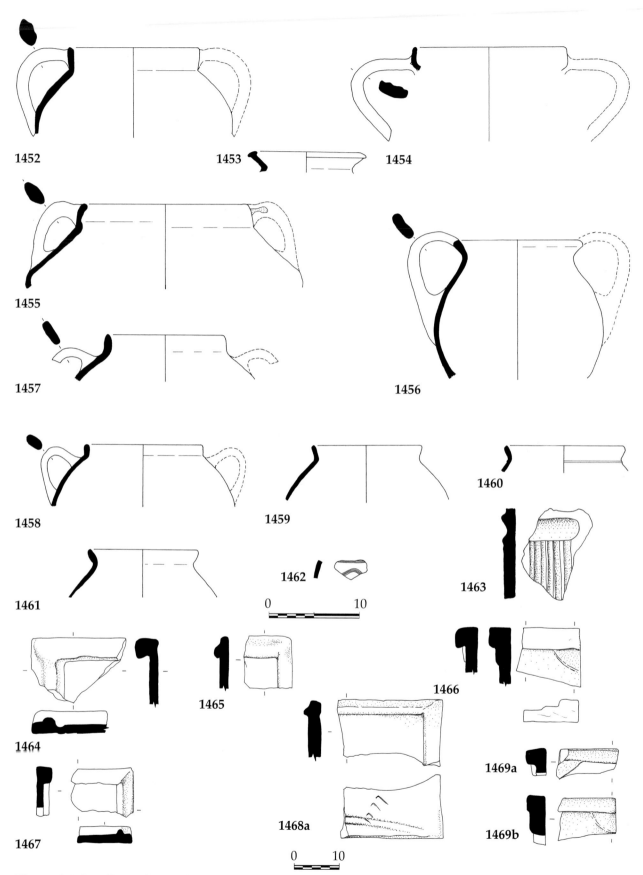

Figure 430. *Late Roman/Byzantine ceramics* **1452–62**; *Byzantine tiles* **1463–9b**. *Scale 1:4 (****1464–9*** *at 1:8).*

Artefact Drawings

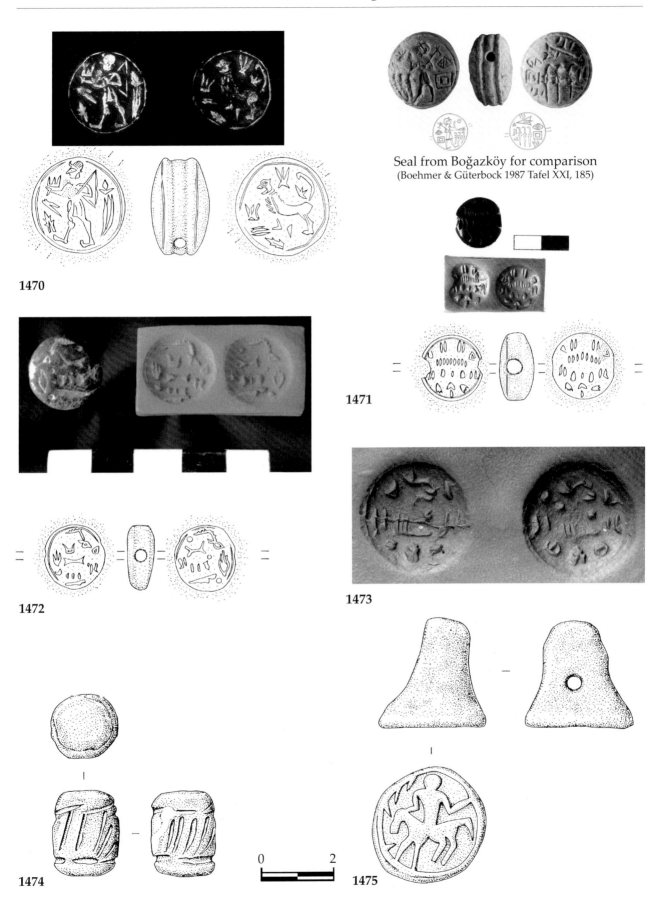

Figure 431. Seals 1470–75. Drawings scale 1:1.

Artefact Drawings

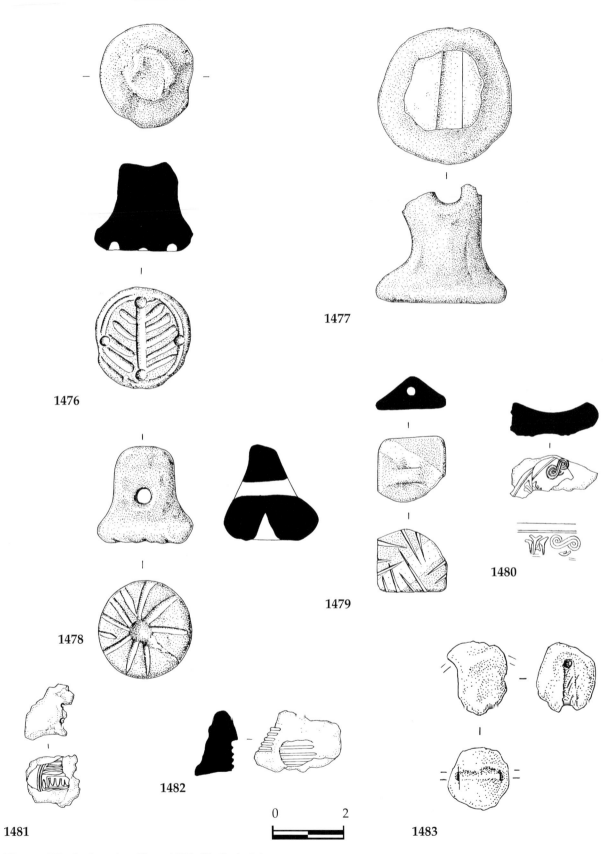

Figure 432. *Seals and sealings* **1476–83**. *Scale 1:1.*

Artefact Drawings

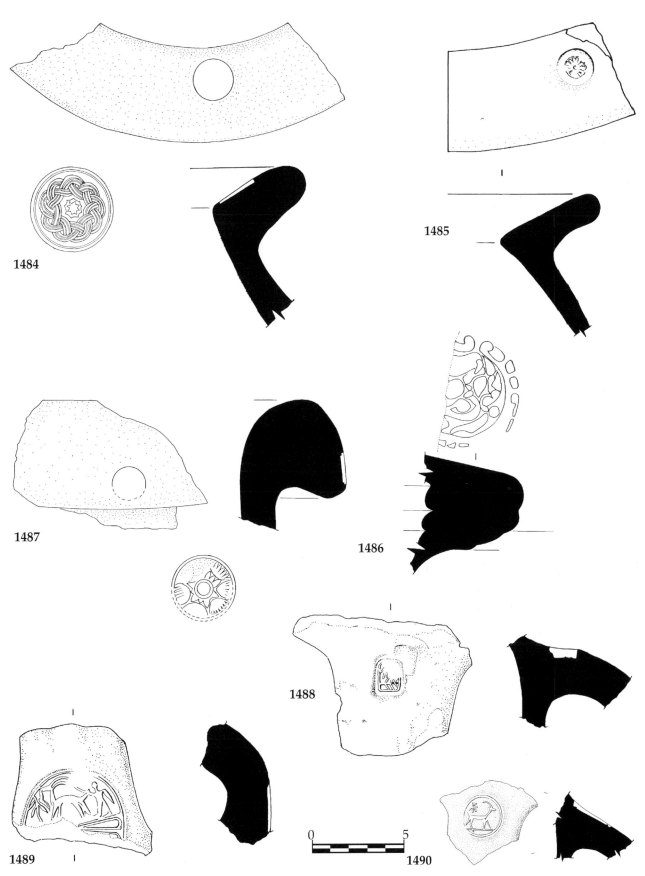

Figure 433. *Sealings on pottery vessels* **1484–90**. *Scale 1:2.*

Artefact Drawings

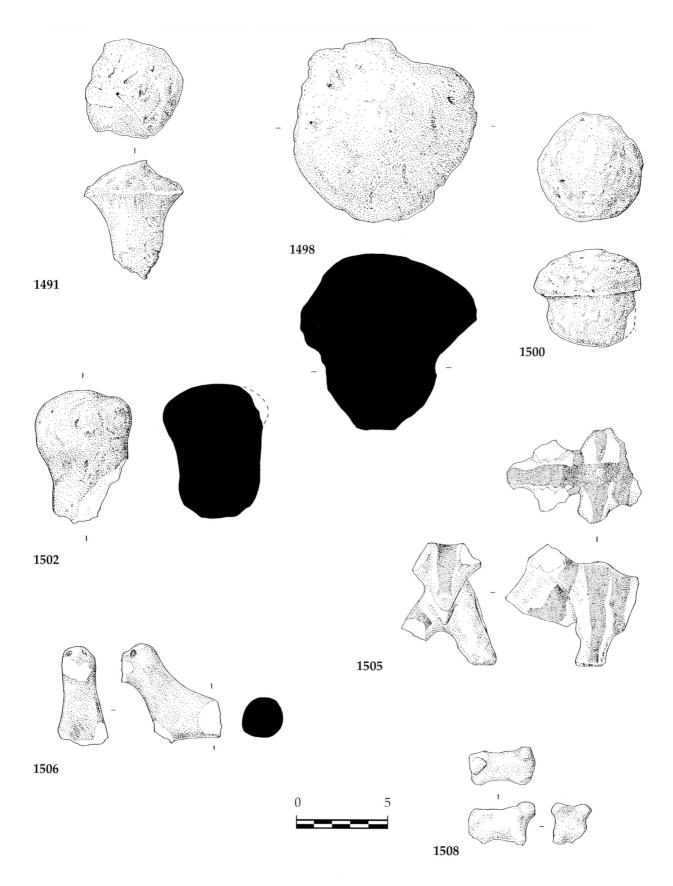

Figure 434. *Clay stoppers (**1491**, **1498**, **1500**, **1502**) and figurines (**1505–6**, **1508**). Scale 1:2.*

Artefact Drawings

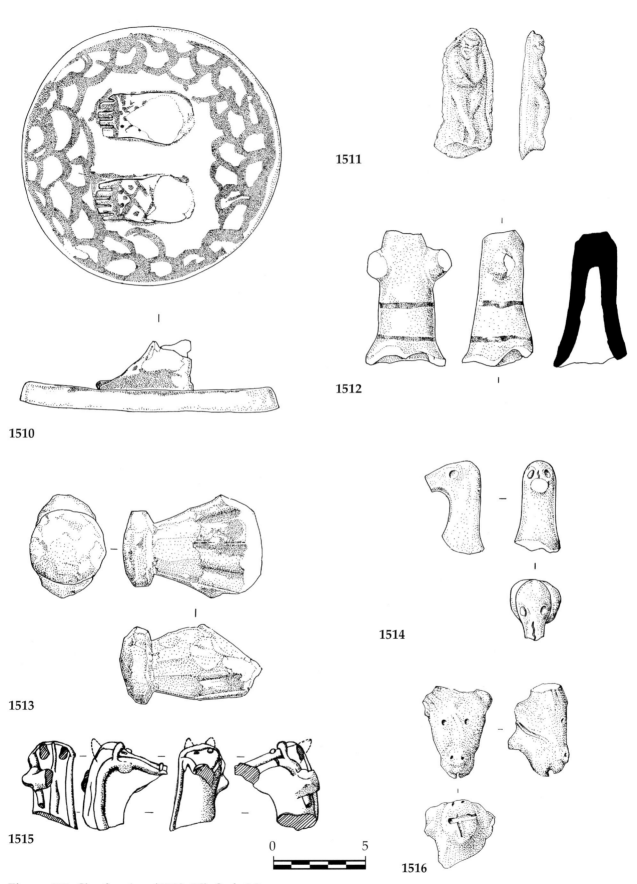

Figure 435. *Clay figurines (**1510–16**). Scale 1:2.*

779

Artefact Drawings

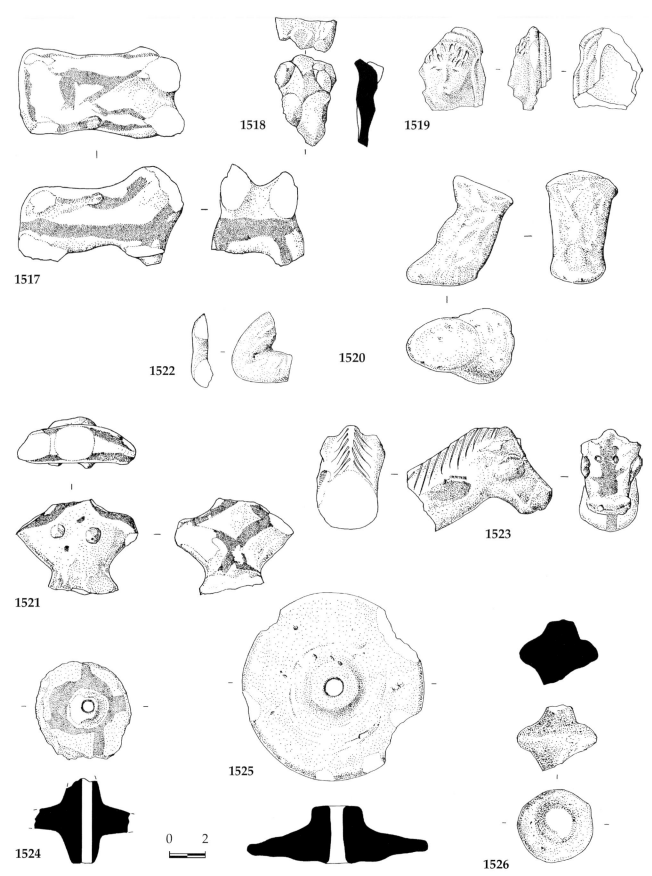

Figure 436. *Clay figurines (**1517–23**) and wheels (**1524–6**). Scale 1:2.*

Artefact Drawings

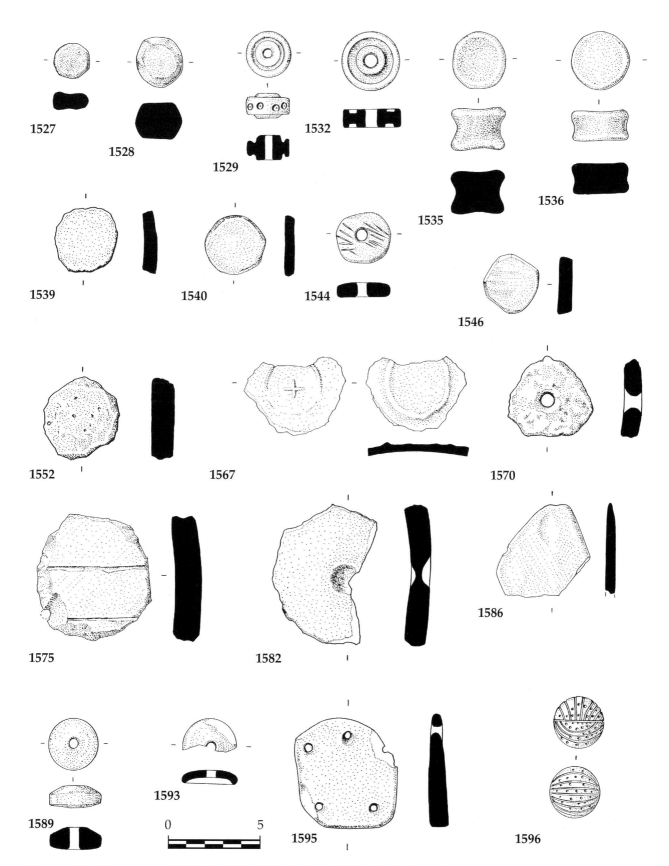

Figure 437. *Clay counters (**1527–9, 1532, 1535–6**), discs (**1539–40, 1544, 1546, 1552, 1567, 1570, 1575, 1582, 1586, 1589, 1593, 1595**) and clay 'ball' (**1596**). Scale 1:2.*

Artefact Drawings

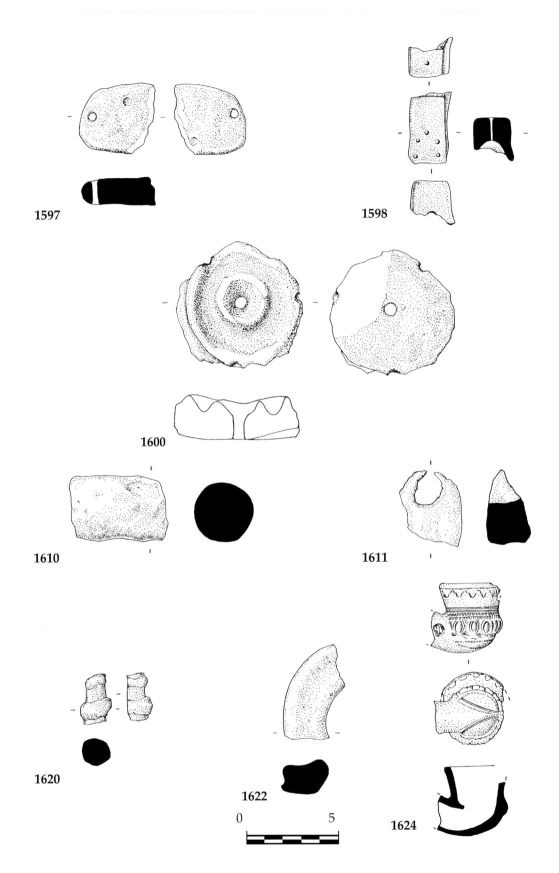

Figure 438. *Miscellaneous clay artefacts (1597–8, 1600, 1610–11, 1620, 1622, 1624). Scale 1:2.*

Artefact Drawings

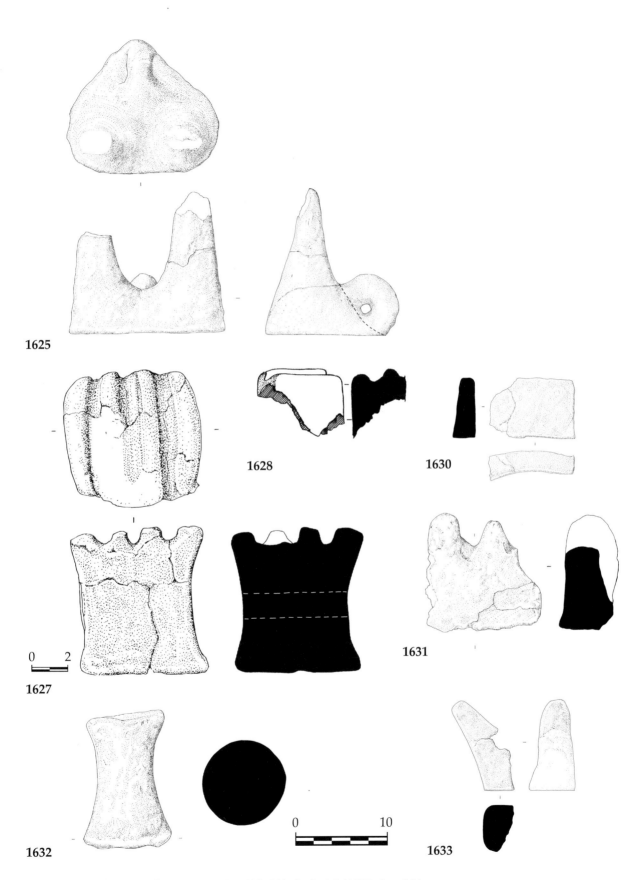

Figure 439. *Clay furniture (**1625**, **1627–8**, **1630–33**). Scale 1:4 (**1627–8** at 1:2).*

Artefact Drawings

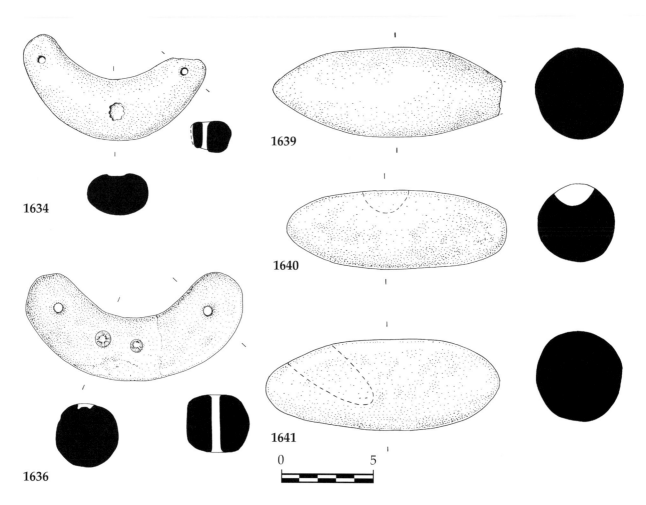

Figure 440. *Clay crescents (**1634**, **1636**) and clay ovoids (**1639–41**). Scale 1:2.*

Artefact Drawings

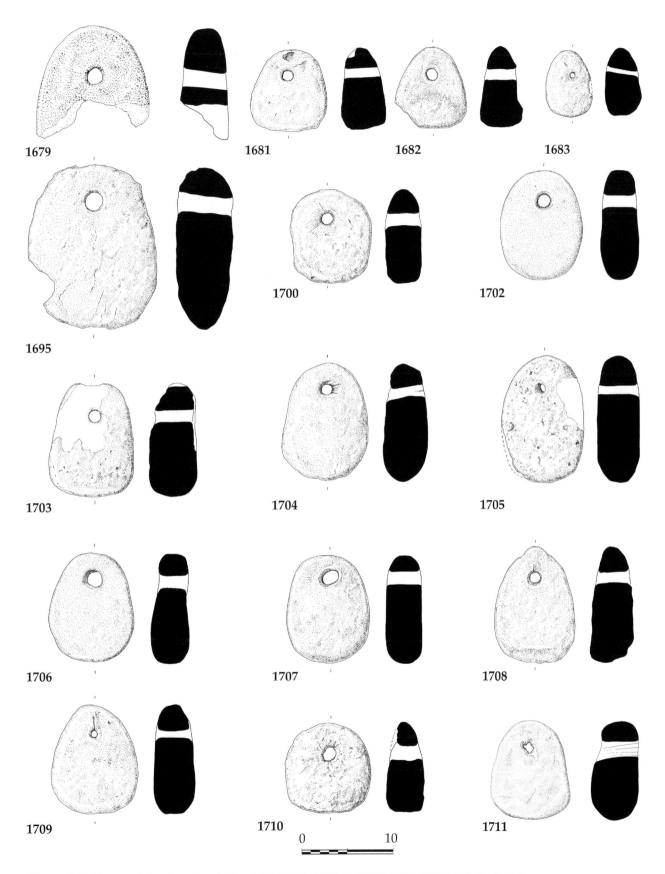

Figure 441. *Loomweights from Level V and IV (**1679**, **1681–3**, **1695**, **1700**, **1702–11**). Scale 1:4.*

Artefact Drawings

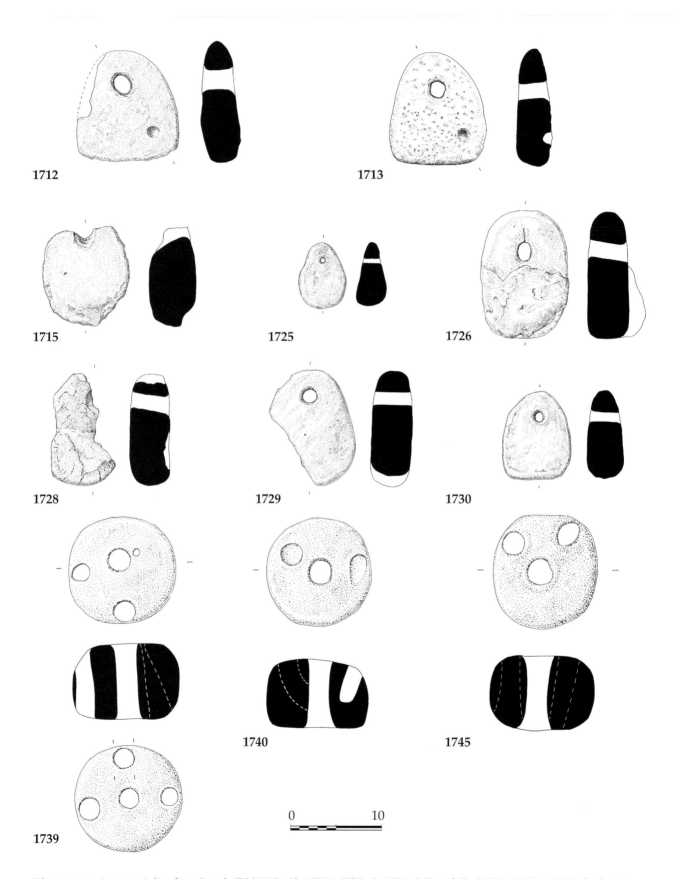

Figure 442. *Loomweights from Levels IV (**1712–13**, **1715**, **1725–6**, **1728–30**) and IIe (**1739**, **1740**, **1745**). Scale 1:4.*

Artefact Drawings

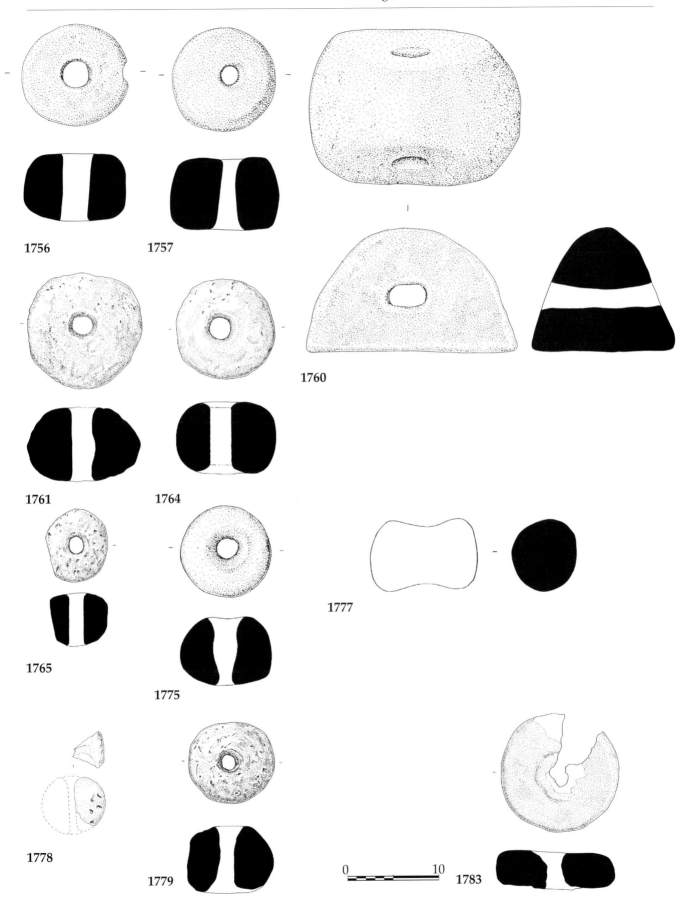

Figure 443. *Loomweights from Levels IIe (**1756–7**, **1760**), and IIf (**1761**, **1764–5**, **1775**, **1777–9**, **1783**). Scale 1:4.*

Artefact Drawings

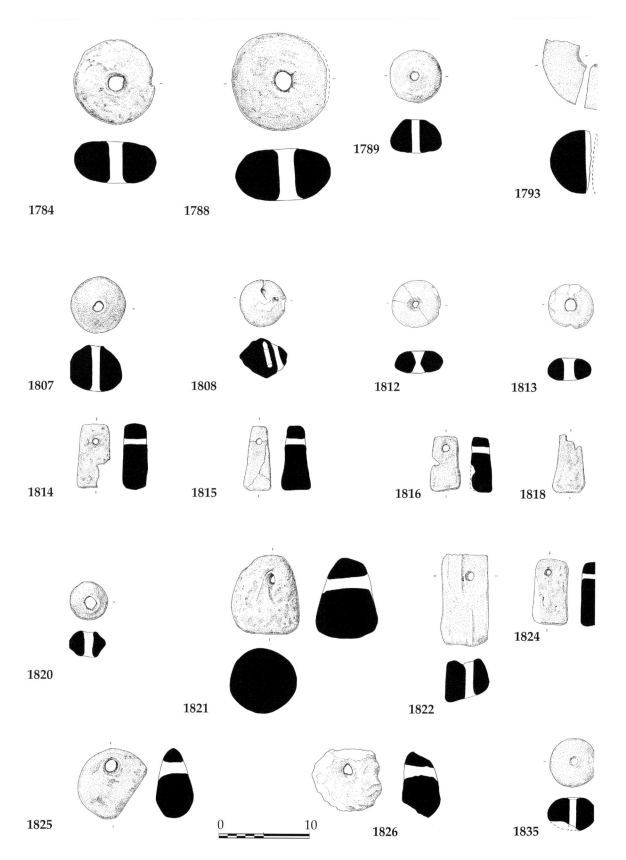

Figure 444. *Loomweights from Level IIf (**1784**, **1788–9**), miscellaneous provenances (**1793**, **1807–8**, **1821–2**, **1824**), Q20 (**1812–16**, **1818**, **1820**), and possible stone weights (**1825–6**, **1835**). Scale 1:4.*

Artefact Drawings

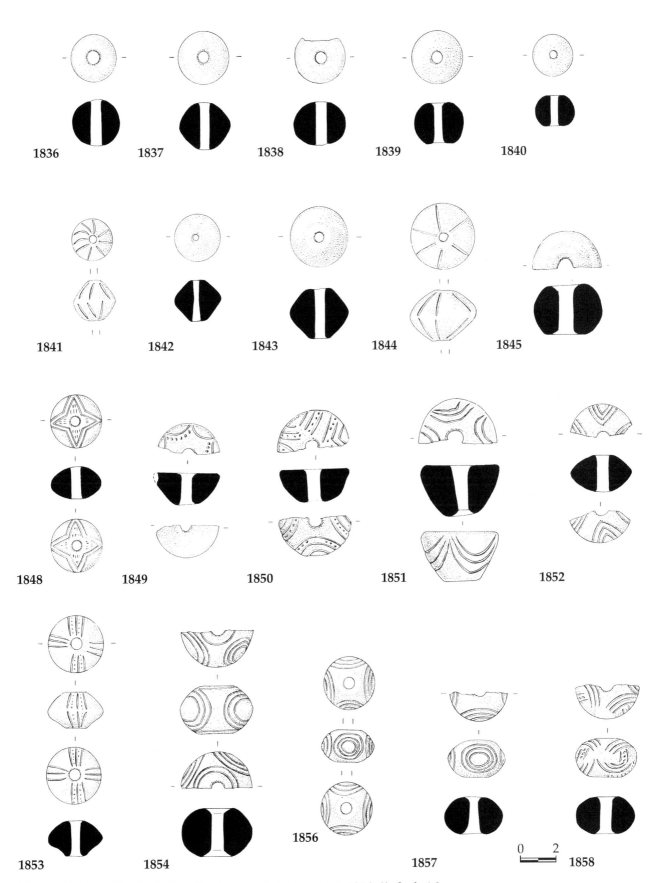

Figure 445. *Spindle whorls from Level V (**1836–45**, **1848–54**, **1856–8**). Scale 1:2.*

Artefact Drawings

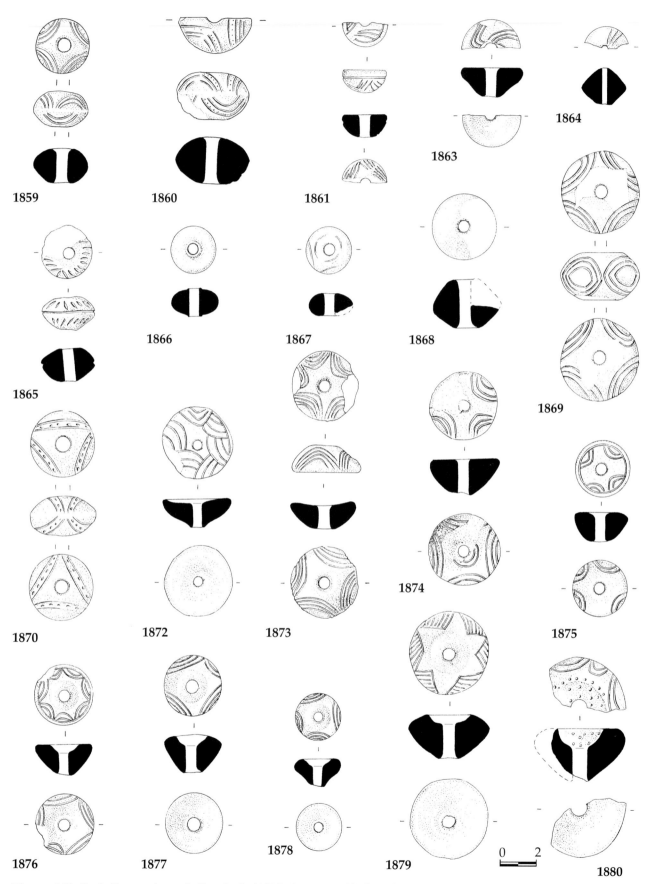

Figure 446. *Early Bronze Age spindle whorls (**1859–61**, unstratified, and **1863–70**, **1872–80** from Level V). Scale 1:2.*

Artefact Drawings

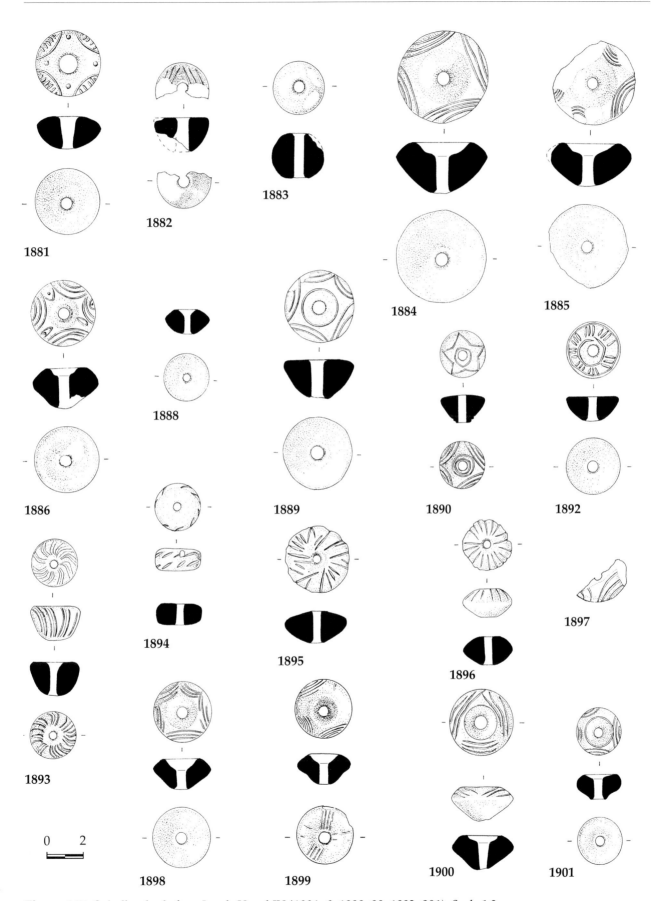

Figure 447. *Spindle whorls from Levels V and IV (**1881–6, 1888–90, 1892–901**). Scale 1:2.*

Artefact Drawings

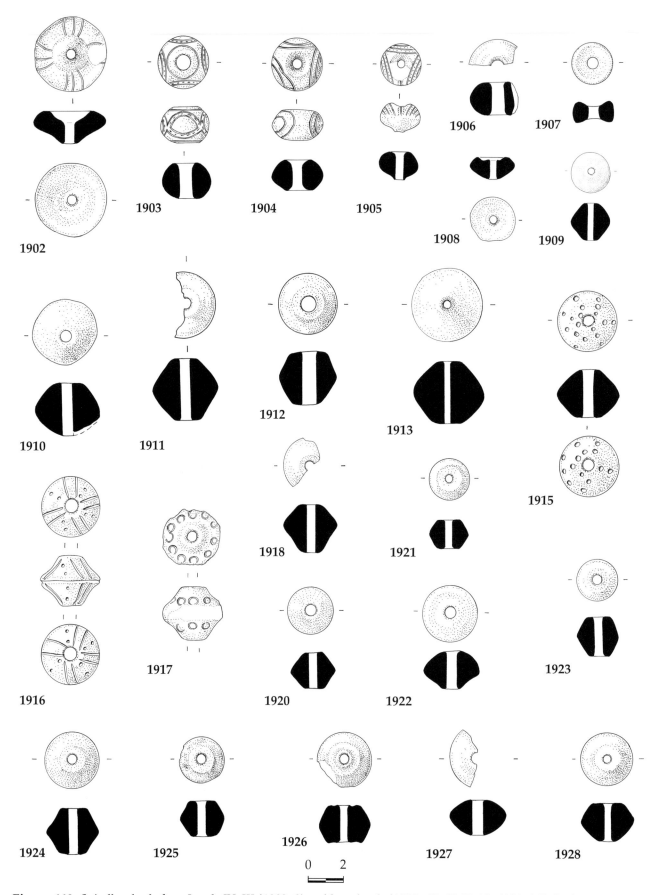

Figure 448. *Spindle whorls from Levels IV–III (**1902–8**) and later levels (**1909–13, 1915–18, 1920–28**). Scale 1:2.*

Artefact Drawings

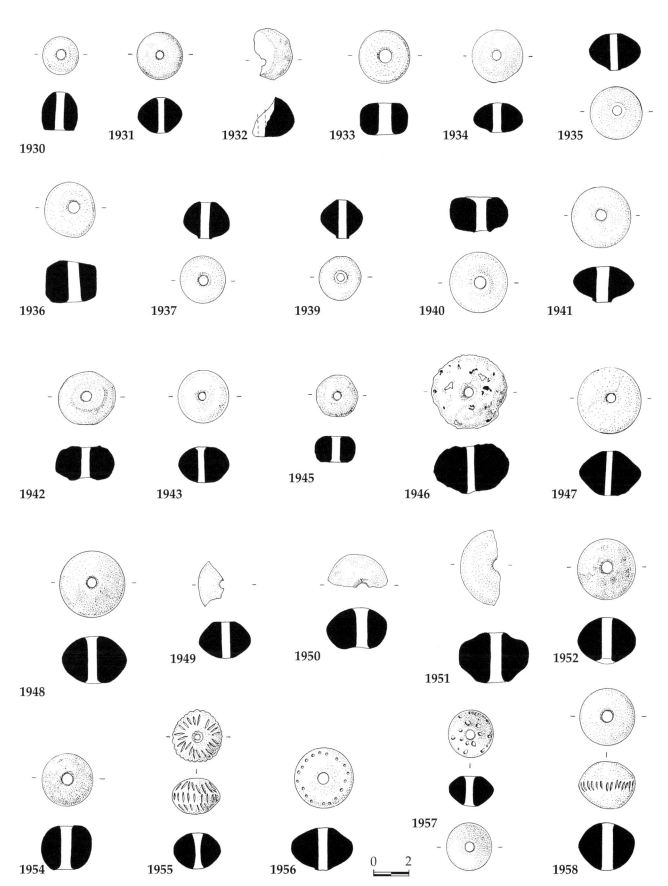

Figure 449. *Spindle whorls from later levels (**1930–37**, **1939–43**, **1945–52**, **1954–8**). Scale 1:2.*

Artefact Drawings

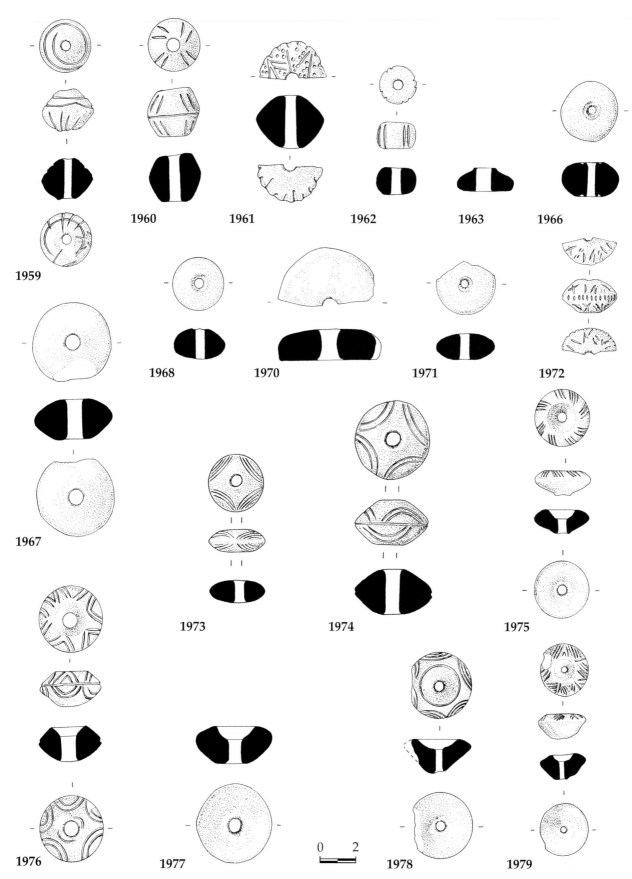

Figure 450. *Spindle whorls from later levels (**1959–63**, **1966–8**, **1970–79**). Scale 1:2.*

Artefact Drawings

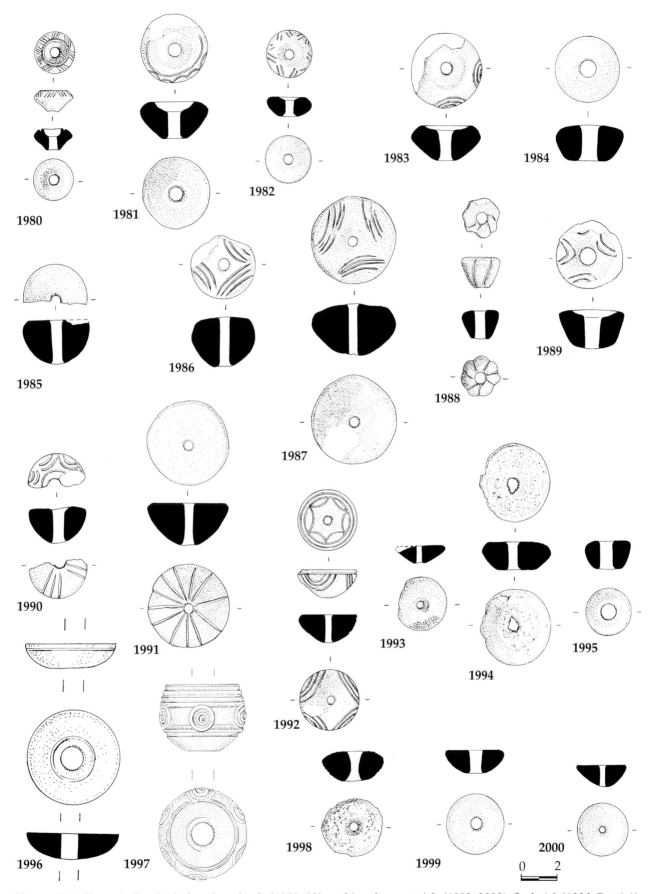

Figure 451. *Clay spindle whorls from later levels (**1980–92**), and in other materials (**1993–2000**). Scale 1:2 (**1996–7** at 1:1).*

Artefact Drawings

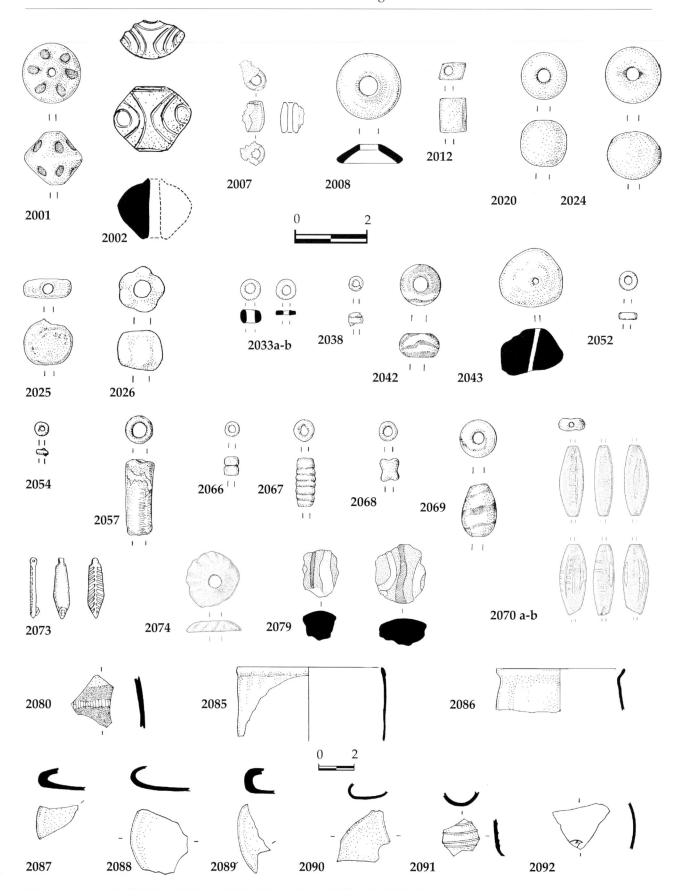

Figure 452. Beads (*2001–2, 2007–8, 2012, 2020, 2024–6, 2033a–b, 2038, 2042–3, 2052, 2054, 2057, 2066–70a–b, 2073–4, 2079; scale 1:1*) *and glass vessels* (*2080, 2085–92; scale 1:2*).

Artefact Drawings

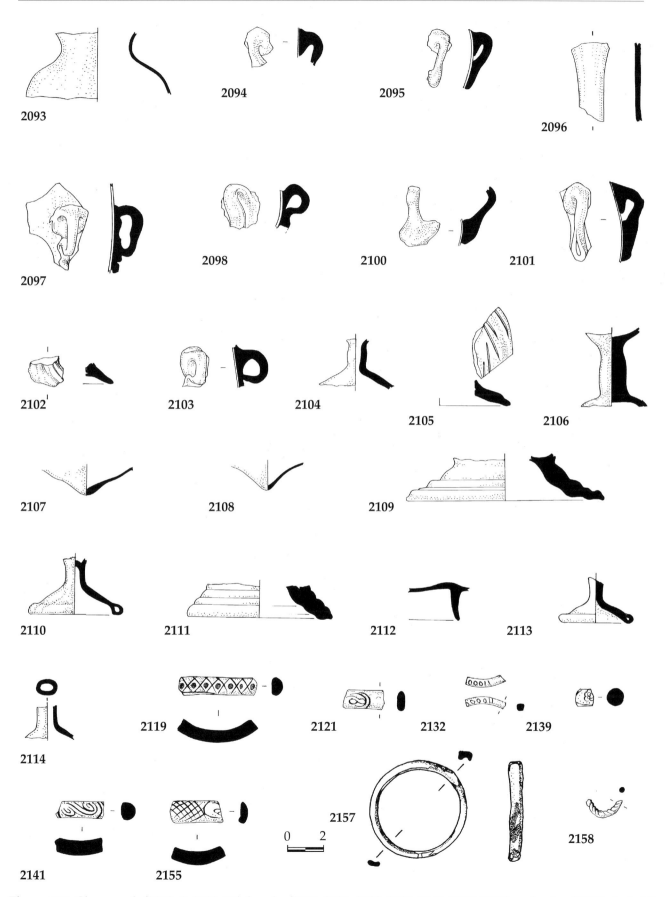

Figure 453. *Glass vessels (2093–8, 2100–14), bangles (2119, 2121, 2132, 2139, 2141, 2155, 2157), and a ring (2158). Scale 1:2.*

Artefact Drawings

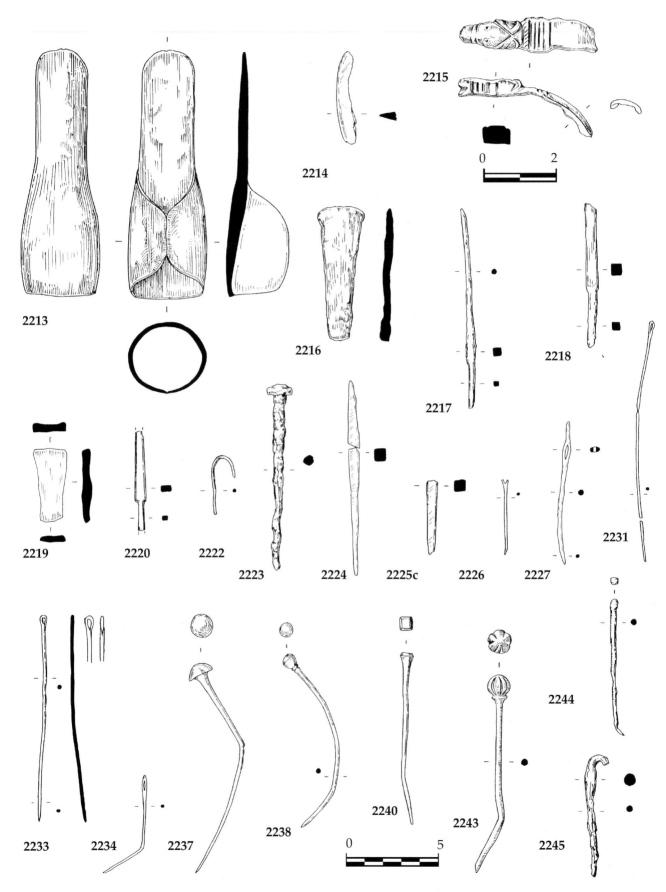

Figure 454. *Copper objects (2213–20, 2222–7, 2231, 2233–4, 2237–8, 2240, 2243, 2245). Scale 1:2 (2215 at 1:1).*

Artefact Drawings

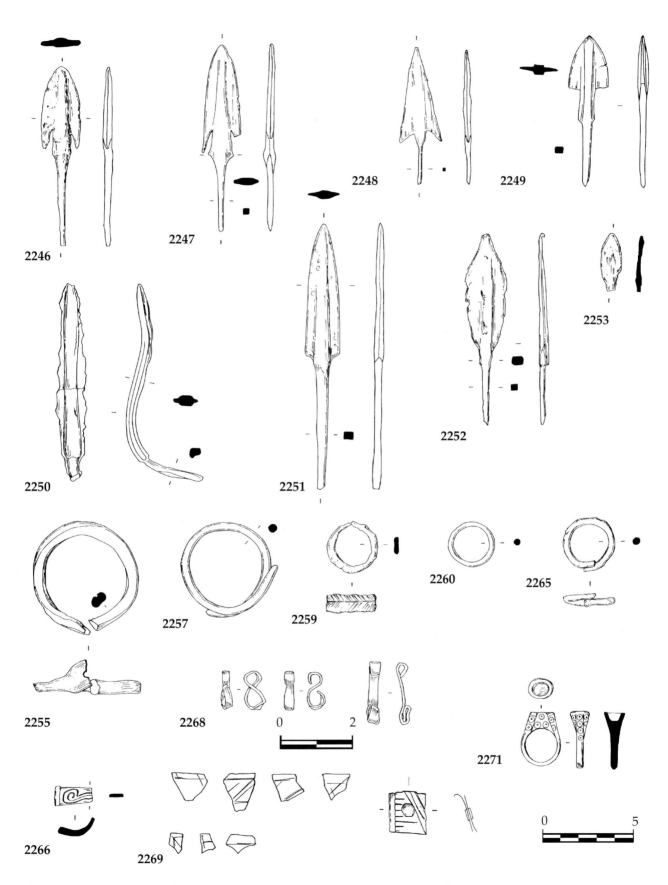

Figure 455. *Copper objects (**2246–53**, **2255**, **2257**, **2259–60**, **2265–6**, **2269**, **2271**). Scale 1:2 (**2268** at 1:1).*

Artefact Drawings

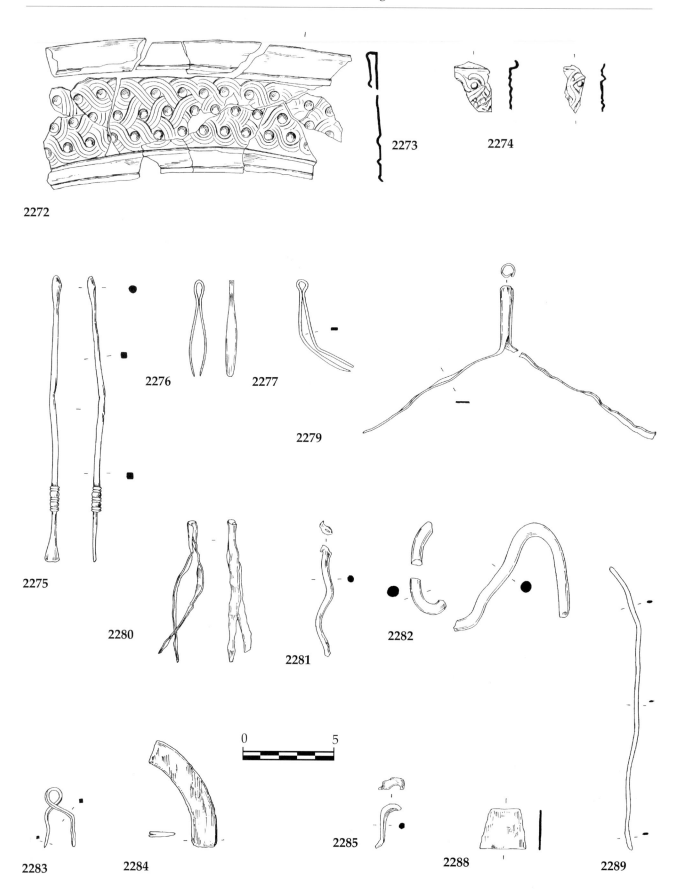

Figure 456. *Copper objects (2272–7, 2279–85, 2288–9). Scale 1:2.*

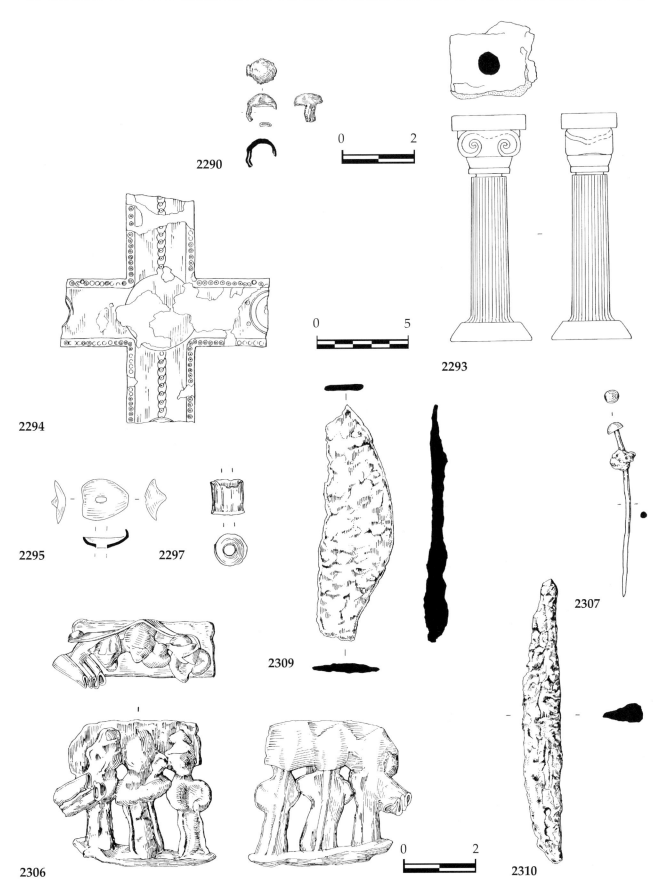

Figure 457. *Objects of copper, silver and iron (**2290**, **2293–5**, **2297**, **2306–7**, **2309–10**). Scale 1:2 (**2290**, **2293** and **2306** at 1:1).*

Artefact Drawings

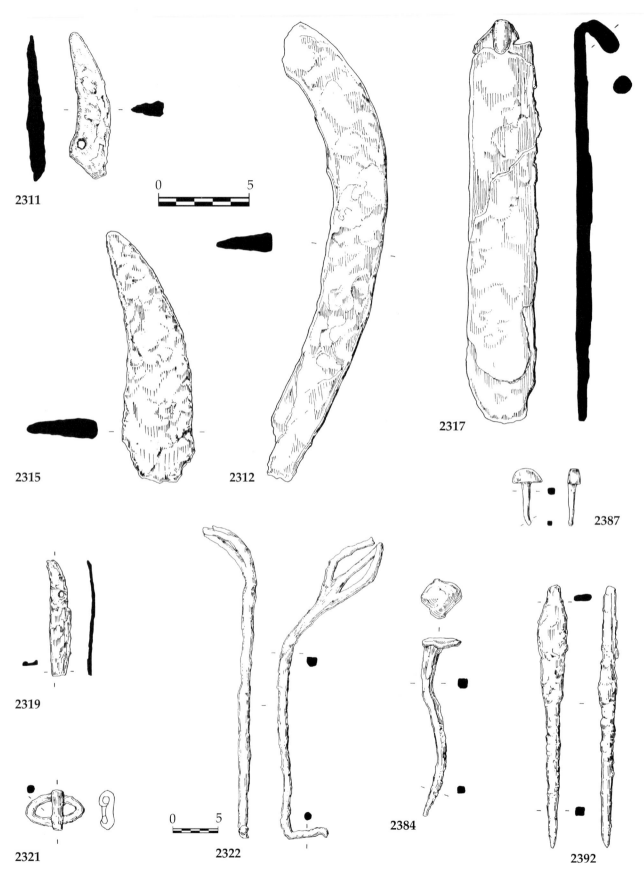

Figure 458. *Objects of iron (**2311–12**, **2315**, **2317**, **2319**, **2321–2**, **2384**, **2387**, **2392**). Scale 1:2 (**2322** at 1:4).*

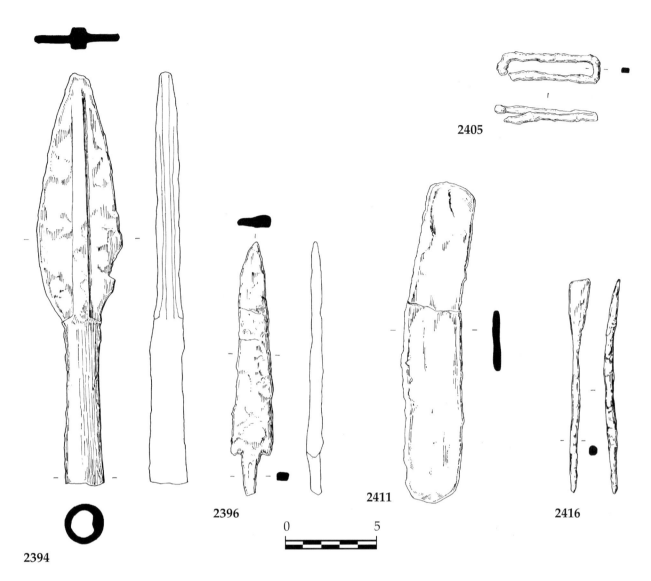

Figure 459. *Objects of iron (**2394**, **2396**, **2405**, **2411**, **2416**). Scale 1:2.*

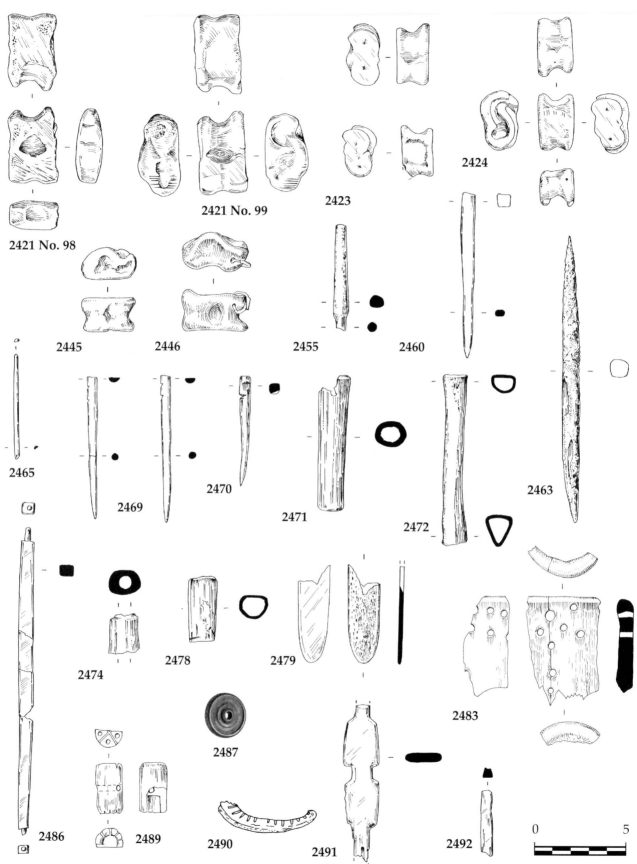

Figure 460. *Bone artefacts (2421, 2423–4, 2445–6, 2455, 2460, 2463, 2465, 2469–72, 2474, 2478–9, 2483, 2486–7, 2489–92). Scale 1:2.*

Artefact Drawings

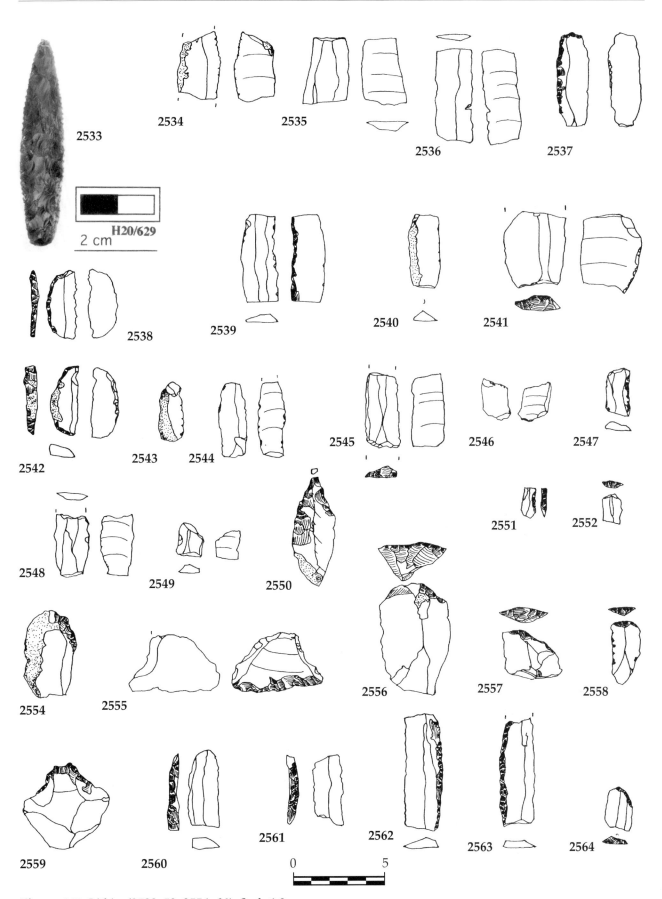

Figure 461. *Lithics (2533–52, 2554–64). Scale 1:2.*

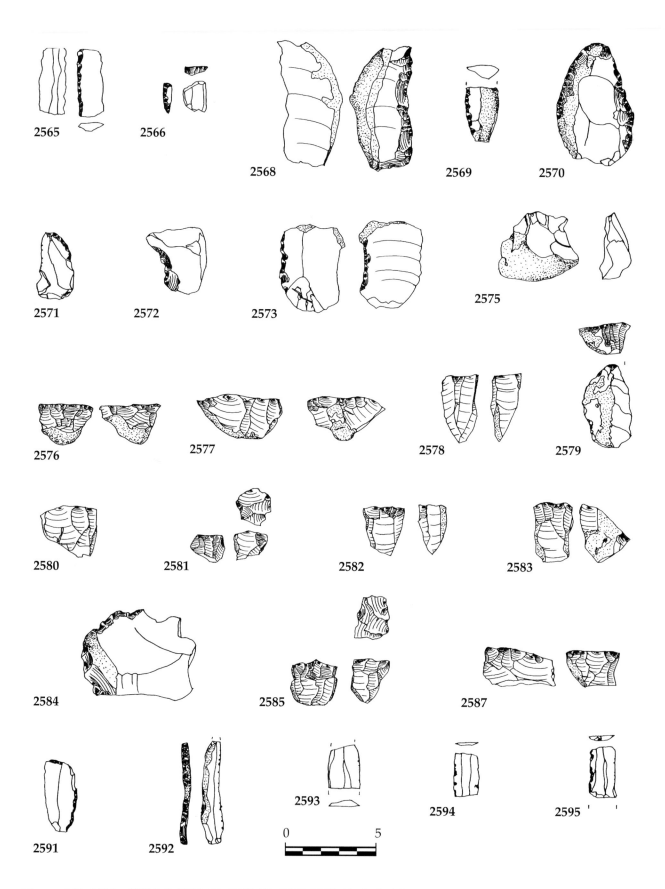

Figure 462. *Lithics (2565–6, 2568–73, 2575–85, 2587, 2591–5). Scale 1:2.*

Artefact Drawings

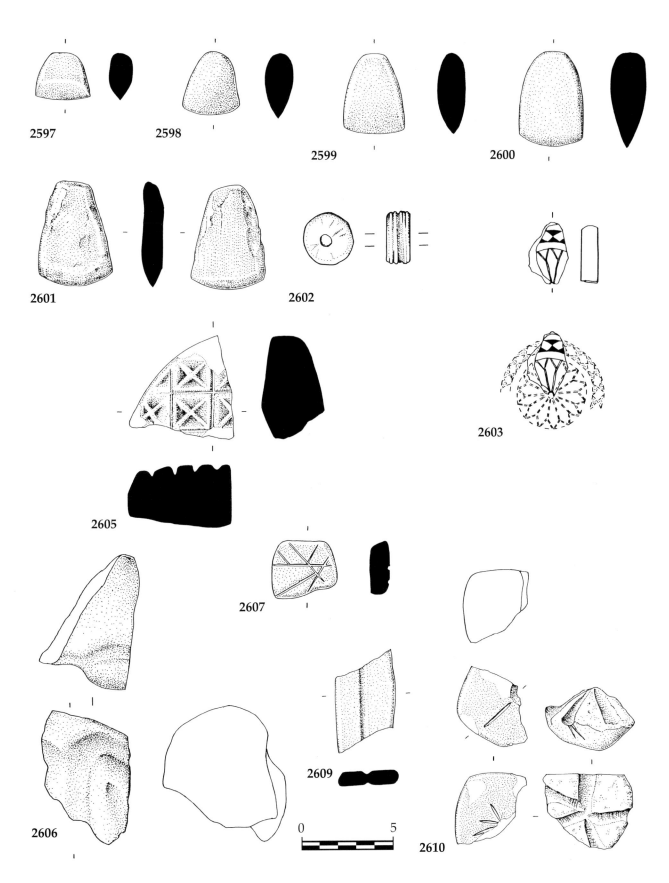

Figure 463. *Smaller stone artefacts (2597–603, 2605–7, 2609–10). Scale 1:2.*

Artefact Drawings

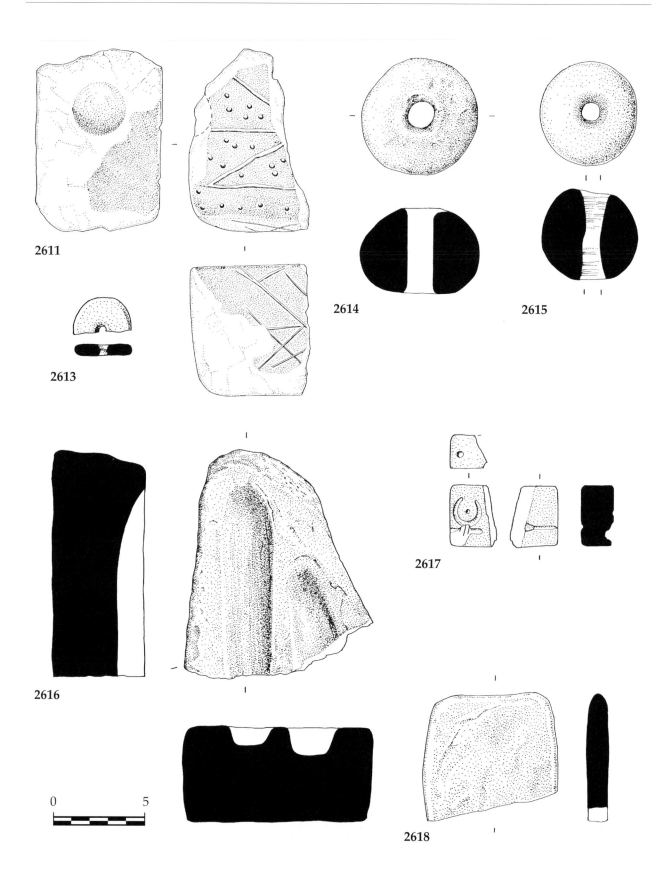

Figure 464. *Smaller stone artefacts (**2611**, **2613–18**). Scale 1:2.*

Artefact Drawings

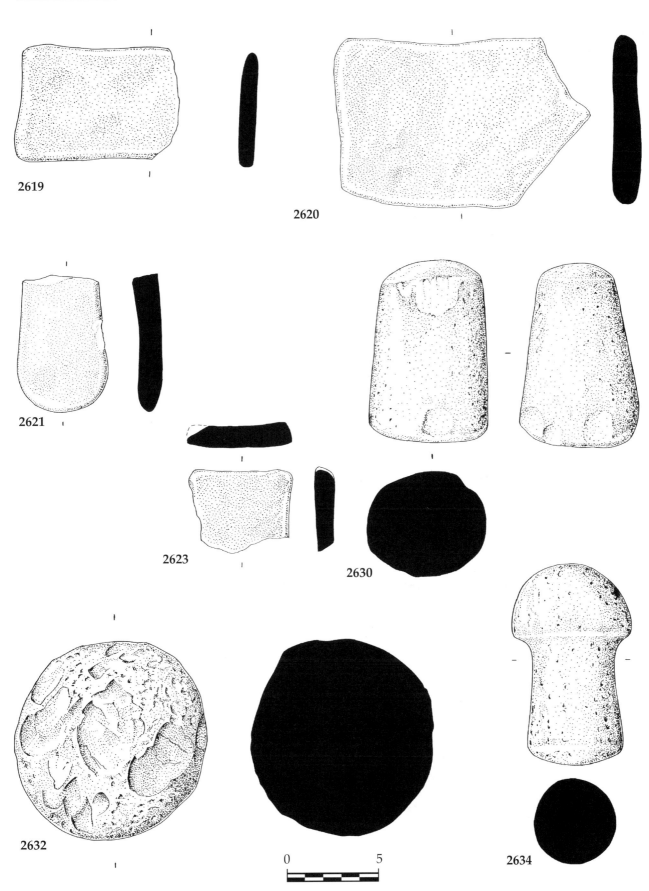

Figure 465. *Smaller stone artefacts (**2619–21**, **2623**, **2630**, **2632**, **2634**). Scale 1:2.*

Artefact Drawings

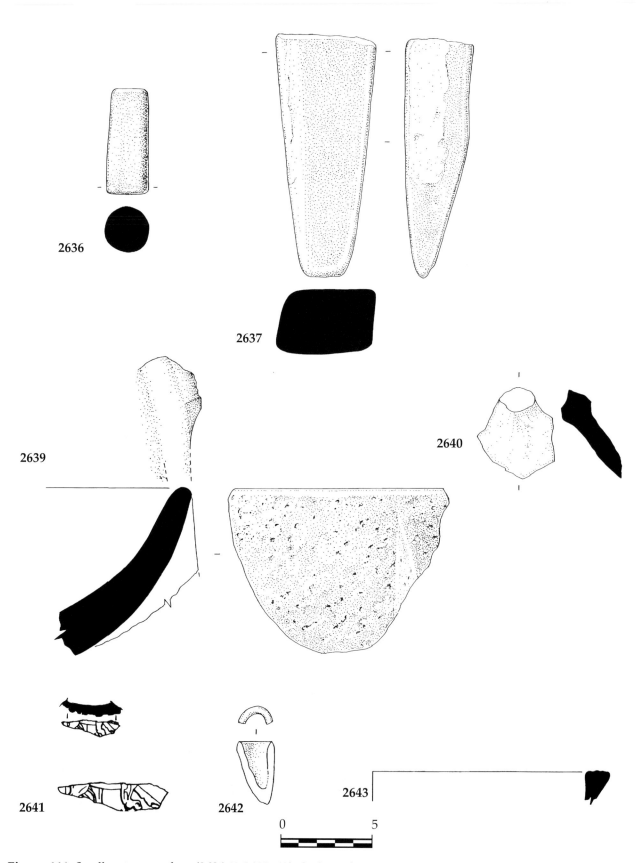

Figure 466. *Smaller stone artefacts (2636–7, 2639–43). Scale 1:2 (2641 at 1:1).*

Artefact Drawings

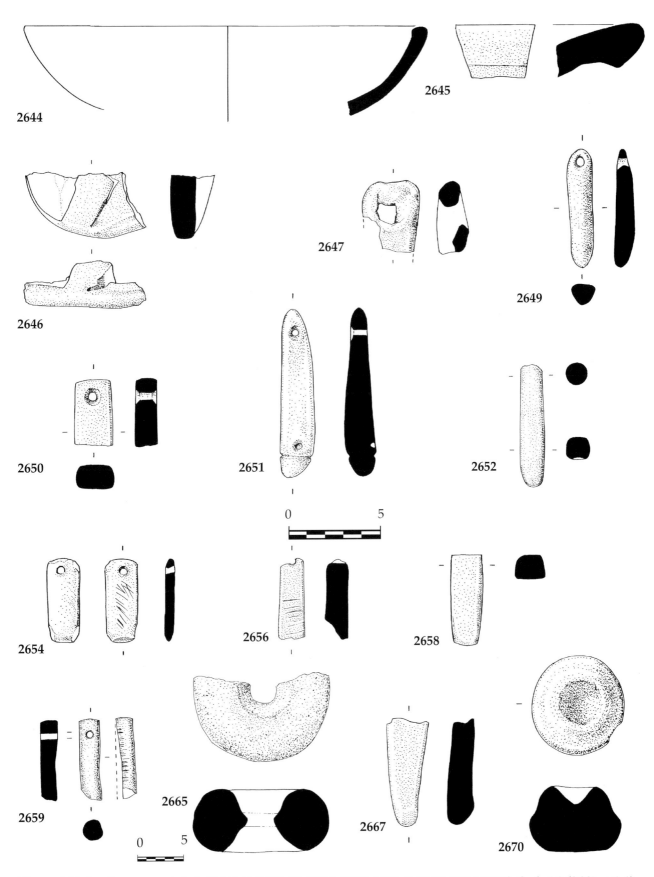

Figure 467. *Smaller stone artefacts (**2644–7**, **2649–52**, **2654**, **2656**, **2658–9**, **2665**, **2667**, **2670**). Scale 1:2 (**2665** at 1:4).*

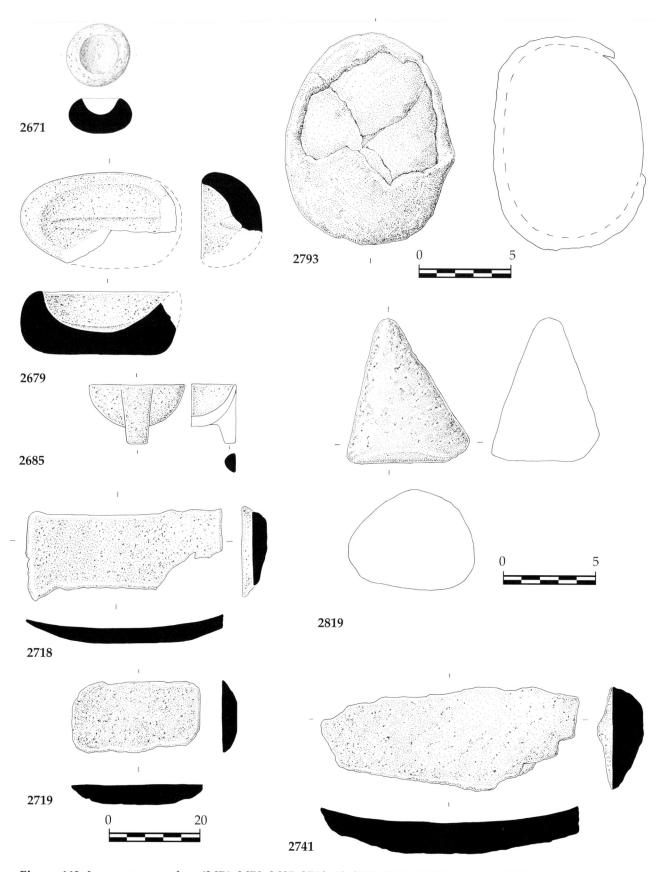

Figure 468. *Larger stone artefacts (**2671**, **2679**, **2685**, **2718–19**, **2741**, **2793**, **2819**). Scale 1:8 (**2679** at 1:10; **2793** & **2819** at 1:2).*

Artefact Drawings

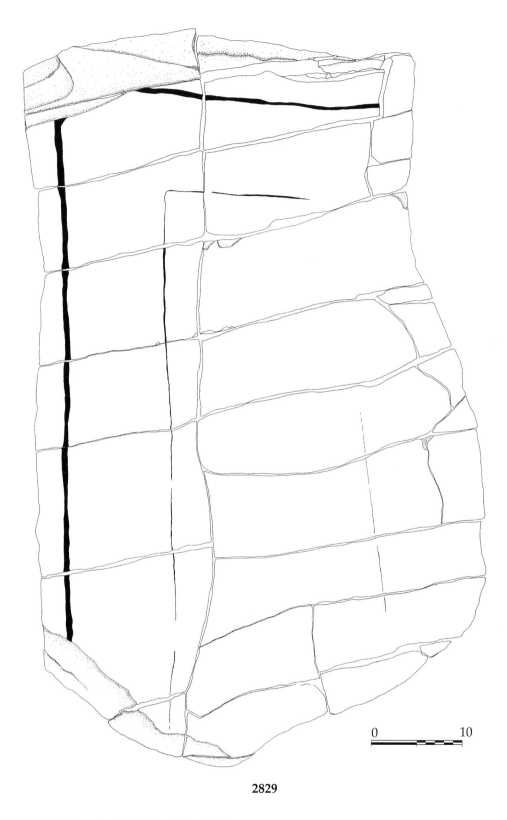

2829

Figure 469. *Stele **2829** from Level IIc, Rm 3. Scale 1:4.*

Maps, Plans and Sections

Maps   817

Stratigraphic and chronological chart   820

Plans   821
- NW corner   821
  - Phases Vl–IVb   828
  - Phases IIIa–e   830
  - Level II   833
- East Slope   841
- Q10   843
- N12   843
- I14   844
- J14   844
- I-M14   845
- Church   846
- NW corner: Level I   847

Sections   849

Maps, Plans and Sections

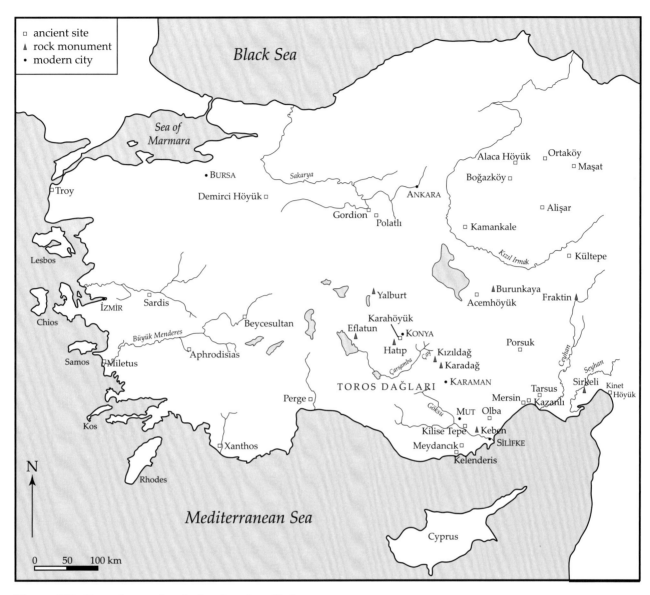

Figure 470. *General map of central and western Turkey.*

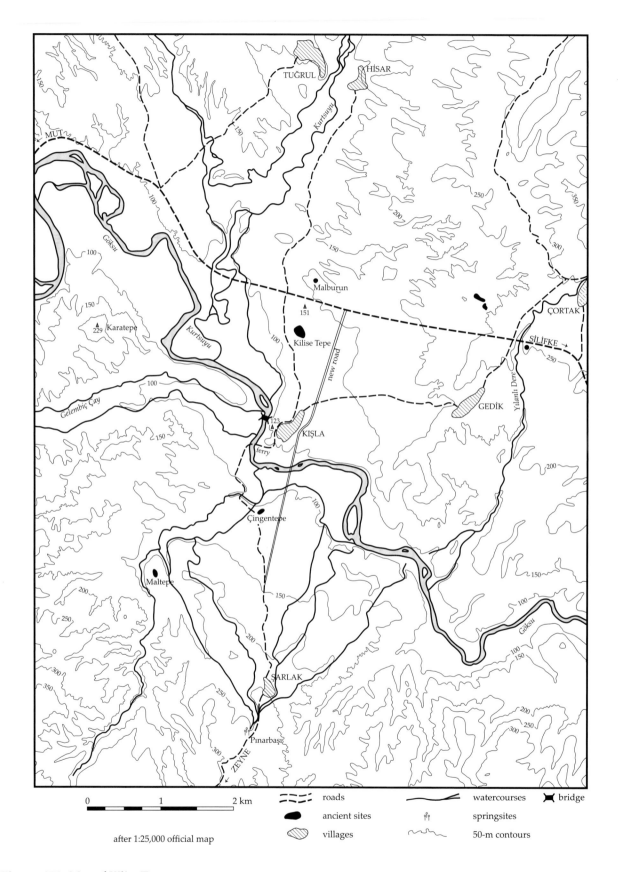

Figure 471. *Map of Kilise Tepe area.*

Maps, Plans and Sections

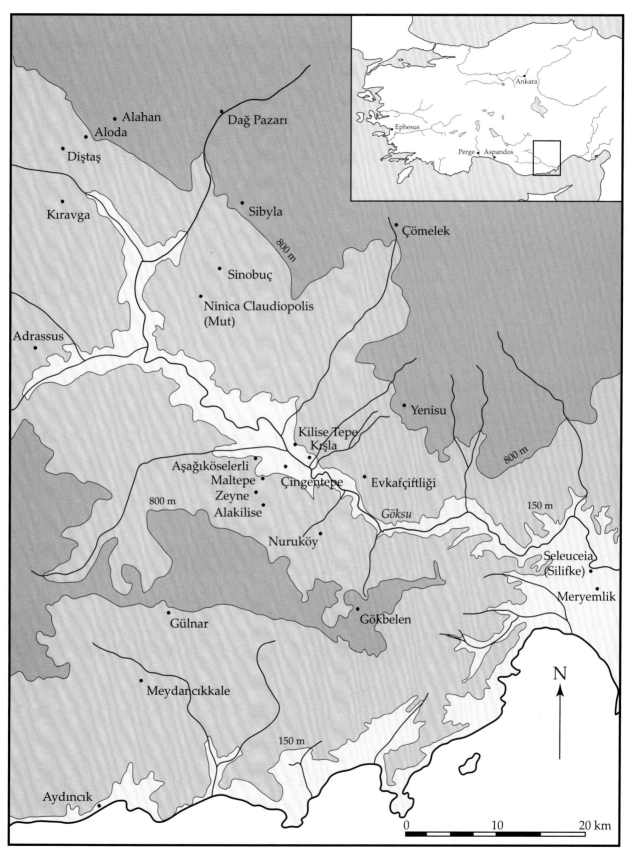

Figure 472. *Map of the Göksu valley.*

Period	Approx. dates	NW corner		Church	I-M14		East slope (Q-S)	N12a	Q10a
					I/J14	K14a			
Byzantine	AD 400–1200	I	e	1	1 Late		E1 (S18)	1	Phase 1
			d						
Late Roman			c						
			b						
Roman	AD 400–300 BC	I	a		1 Early		E2a–c		Phase 2
Hellenistic							E3a–b		
							E4a–c		
Iron Age	1150–650 BC	II	g, h		2k	2 upper	E5a–b		Phases 3–4
			f		2 late	2 middle			
			e				E5c–d		
Late Bronze	1275–1150 BC	II	d		2 early	2 lower			
			c						
			a/b						
	1500–1275 BC	III	e		3				
			d						
			a–c						
Middle Bronze	2000–1500 BC	IV	b						
			a						
Early Bronze III	2400–2000 BC	V	e						
			f						
Early Bronze II	2700–2400	V	g						
			h						
			i						
			j						
			k						
			l						

Figure 473. *Kilise Tepe stratigraphic and chronological chart.*

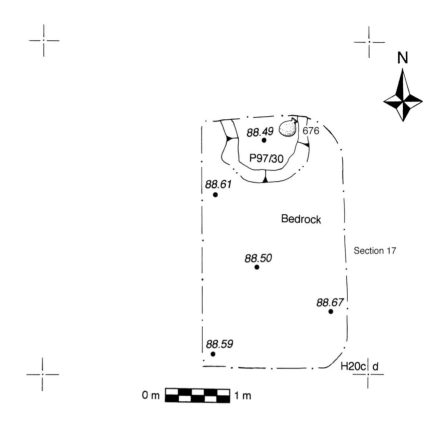

Figure 474. *H20: Phase Vl.*

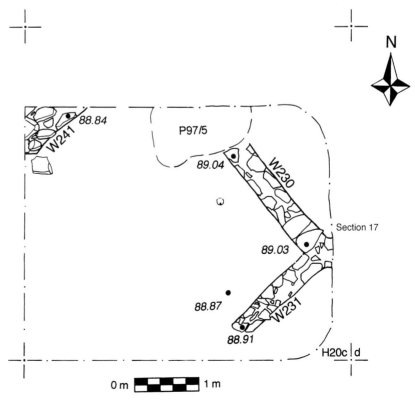

Figure 475. *H20: Phase Vk.*

Maps, Plans and Sections

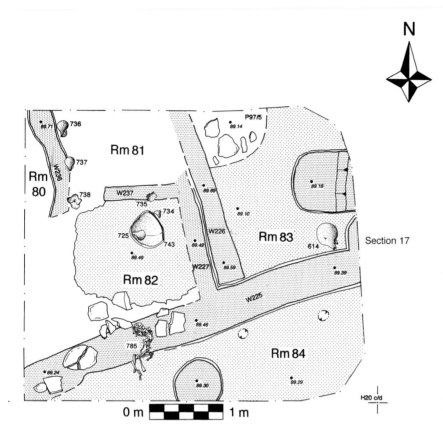

Figure 476. *H20: Phase Vj.*

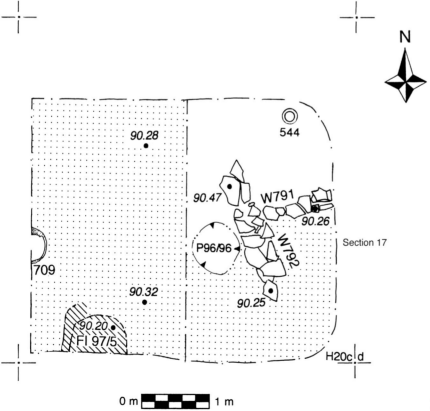

Figure 477. *H20: Phase Vi early.*

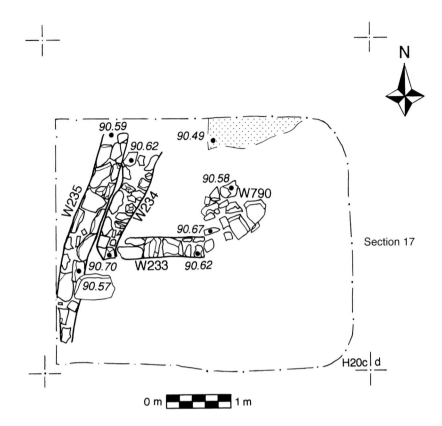

Figure 478. *H20: Phase Vi late.*

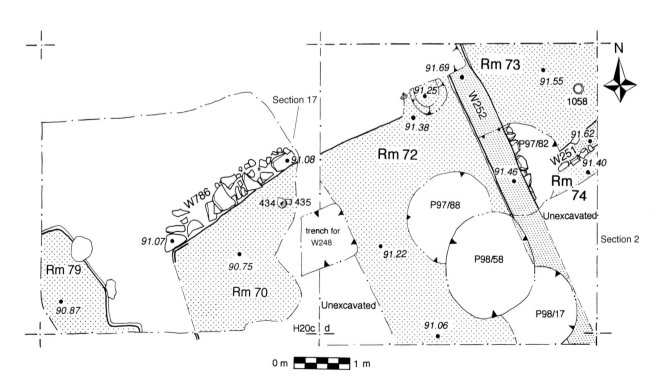

Figure 479. *H20: Phase Vh early.*

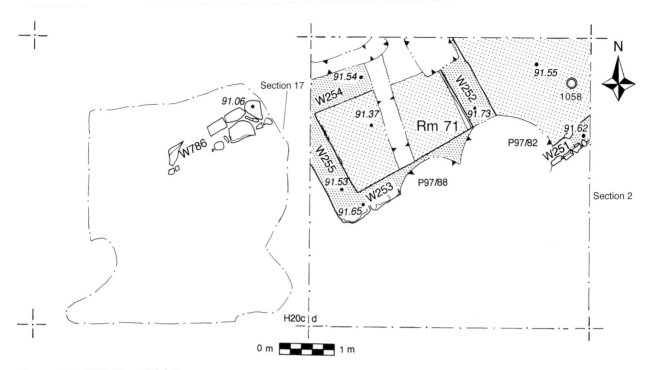

Figure 480. *H20: Phase Vh late.*

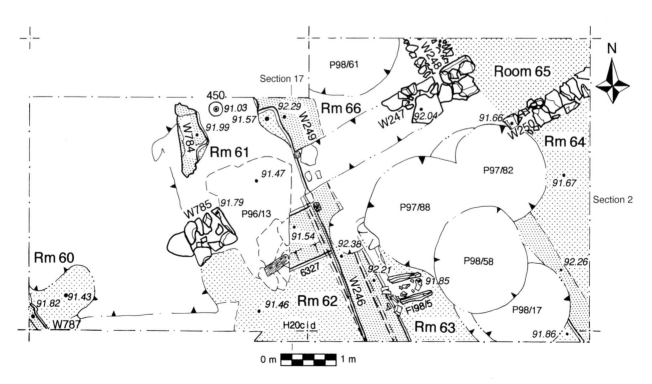

Figure 481. *H20: Phase Vg.*

Maps, Plans and Sections

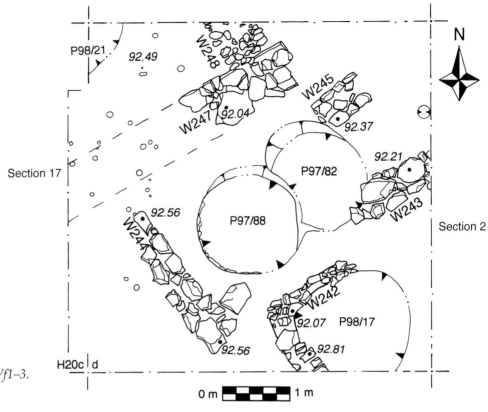

Figure 482. *H20: Phase Vf1–3.*

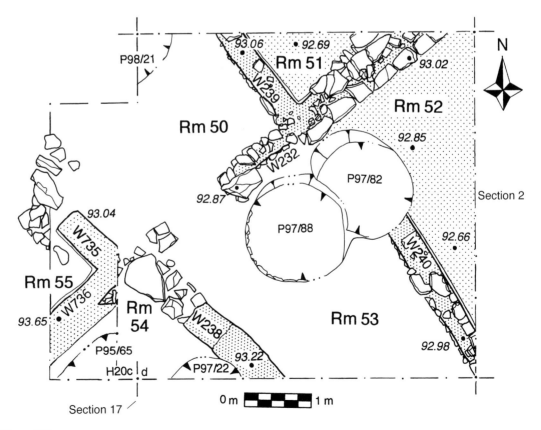

Figure 483. *H20: Phase Vf4.*

825

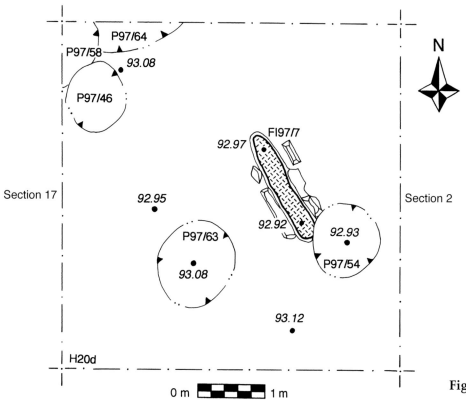

Figure 484. *H20: Phase Ve early.*

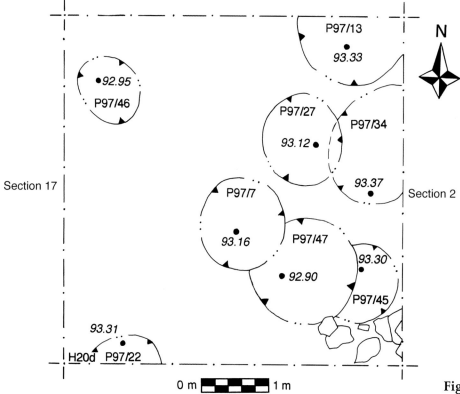

Figure 485. *H20: Phase Ve middle.*

Maps, Plans and Sections

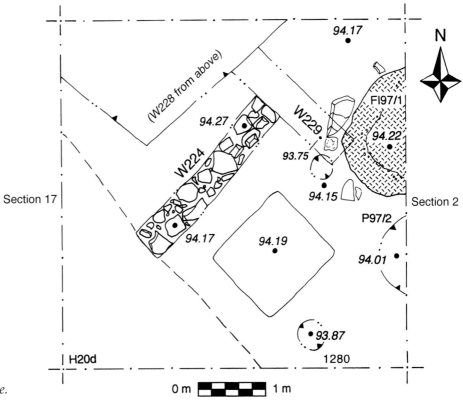

Figure 486. *H20: Phase Ve late.*

827

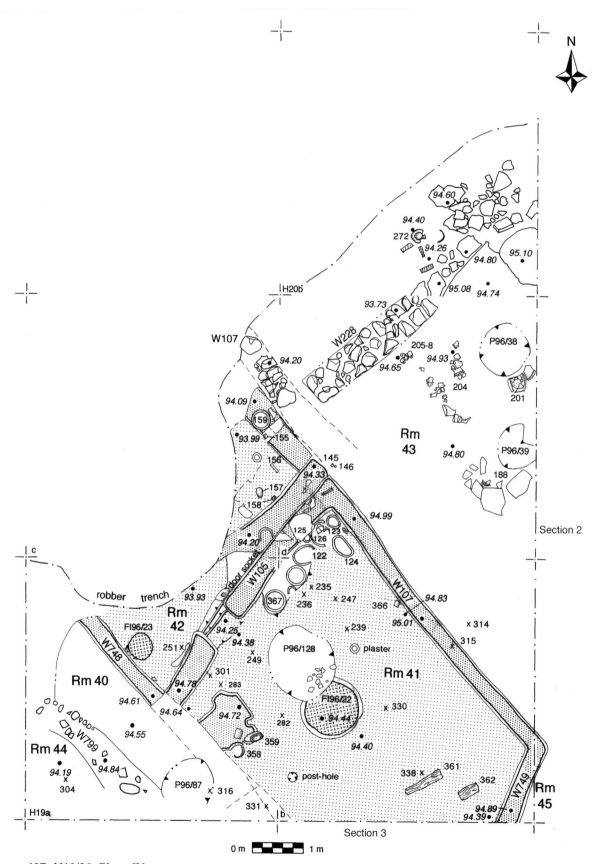

Figure 487. *H19/20: Phase IVa.*

Maps, Plans and Sections

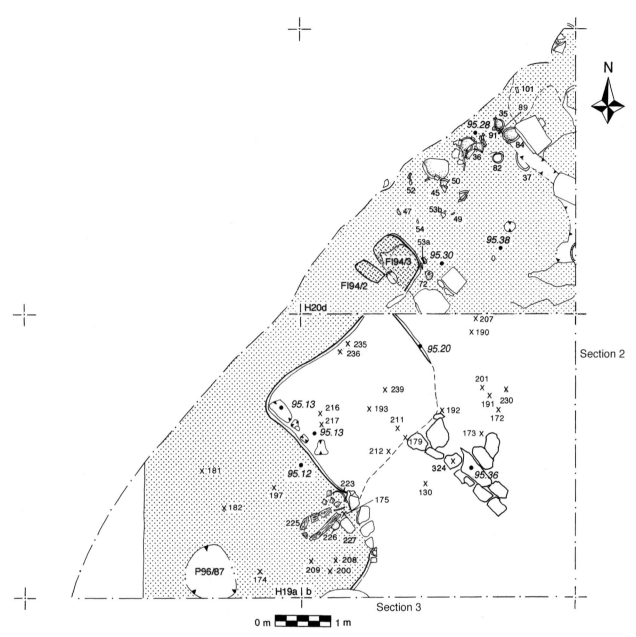

Figure 488. *H19/20: Phase IVb.*

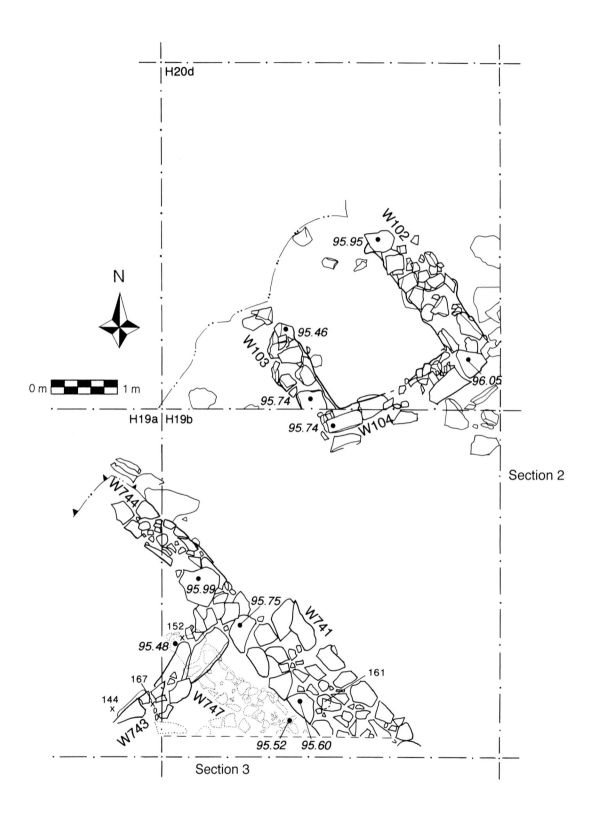

Figure 489. *NW Corner: Phases IIIa–b.*

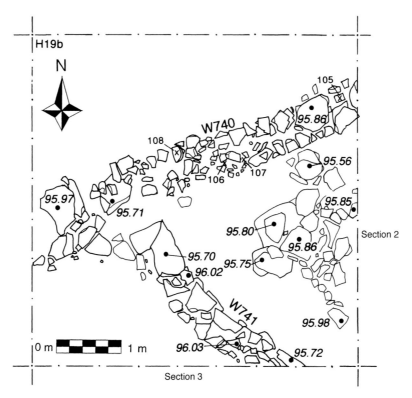

Figure 490. *NW Corner: Phase IIIc.*

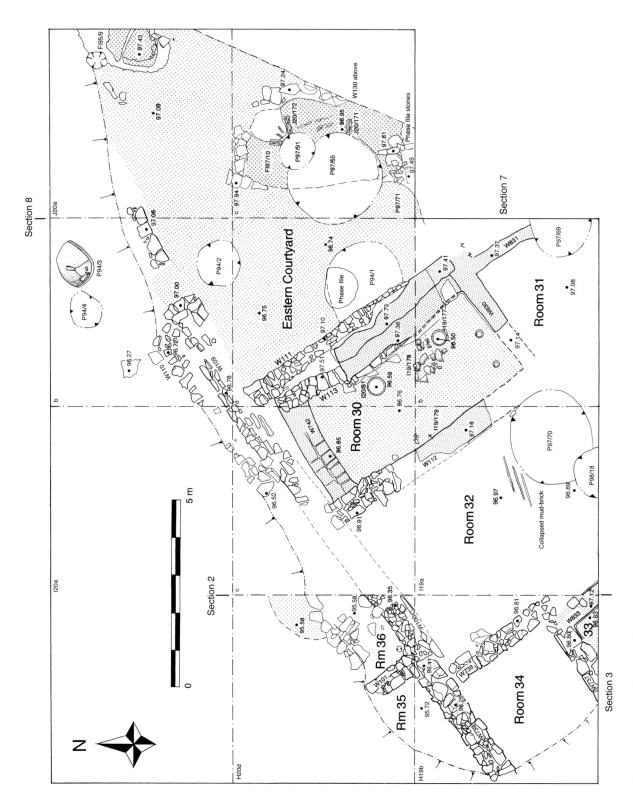

Figure 491. *NW Corner: Phases IIId and IIIe.*

Maps, Plans and Sections

Figure 492. *Level IIc Stele Building and Eastern Building.*

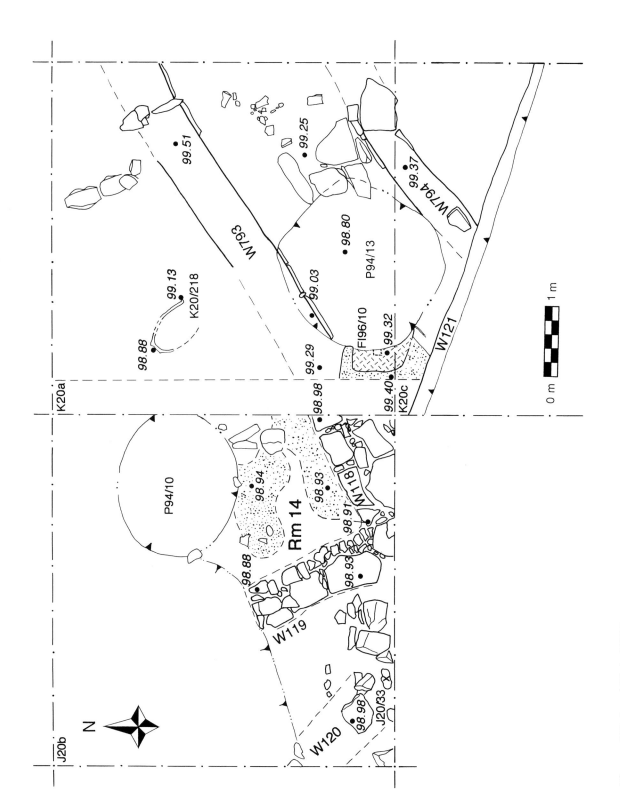

Figure 493. *Level IIb in J/K20.*

Maps, Plans and Sections

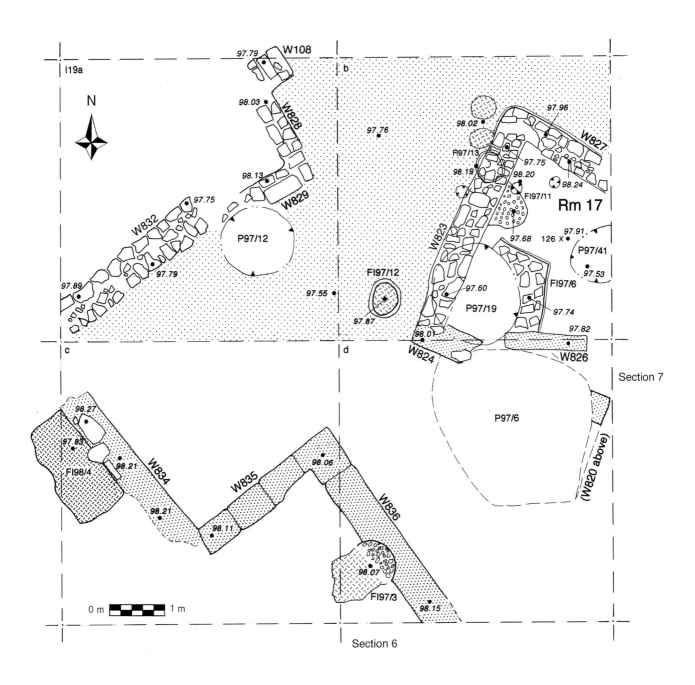

Figure 494. *Level IIa/b Western Courtyard.*

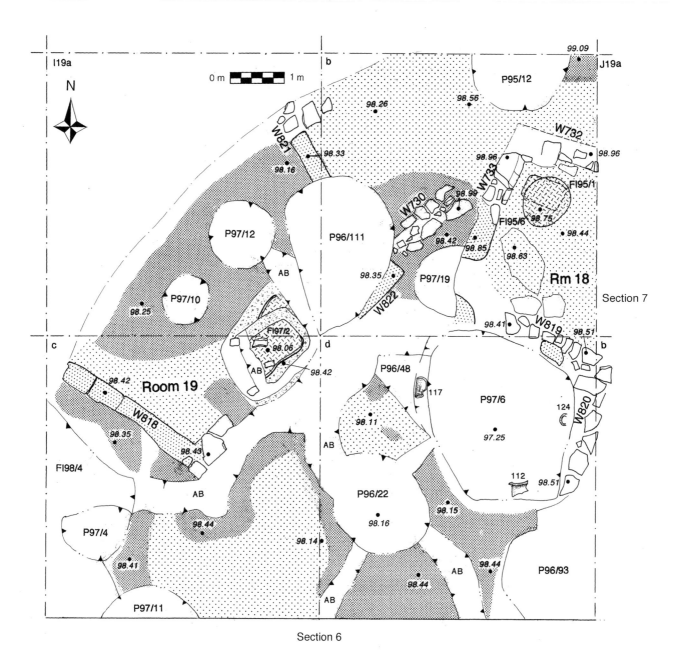

Figure 495. *Level IIc/d Western Courtyard (heavy stippling indicates dark ashy deposit).*

Maps, Plans and Sections

Figure 496. *Level IId Stele Building.*

Maps, Plans and Sections

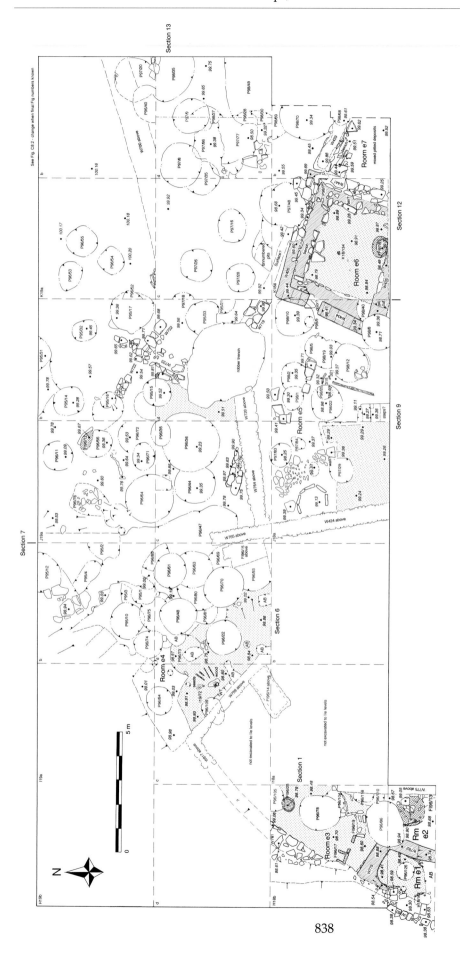

Figure 497. *Level IIe in I19, J18/19, K18.*

Maps, Plans and Sections

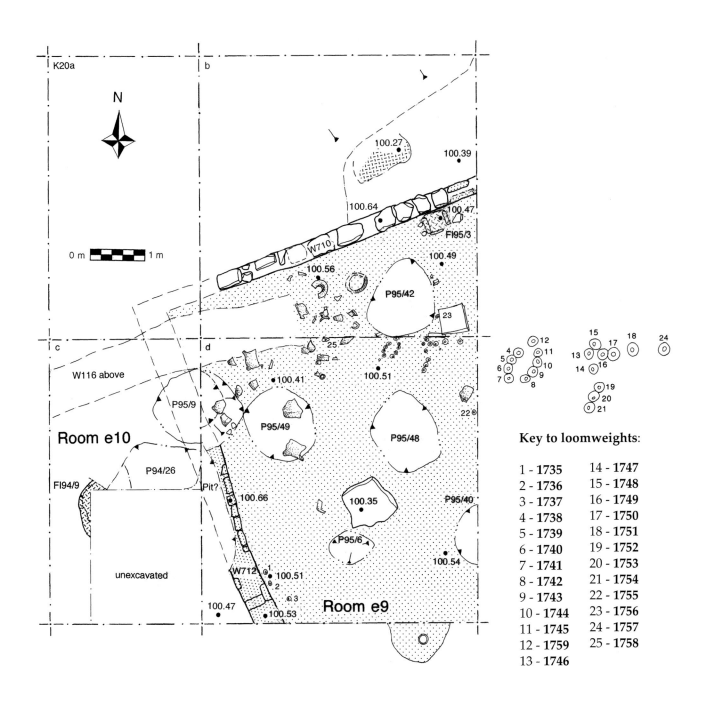

Figure 498. *Level IIe in K20, Rms e9–10.*

Figure 499. *NW Corner: Level IIf.*

Figure 500. *East slope, SE sector (Q19, Q-S18).*

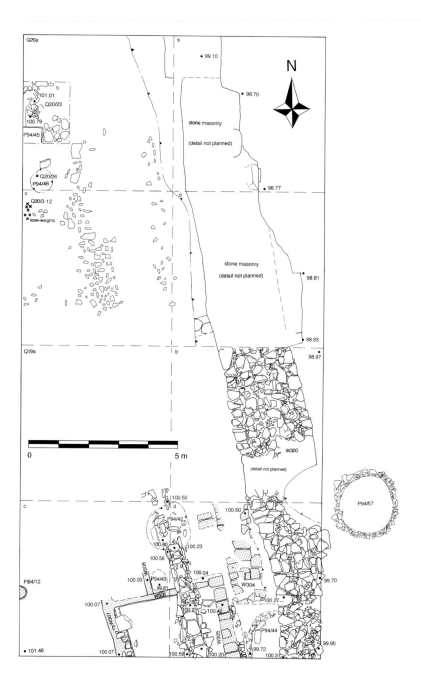

Figure 501. *East slope, NW sector - Q19/20.*

Maps, Plans and Sections

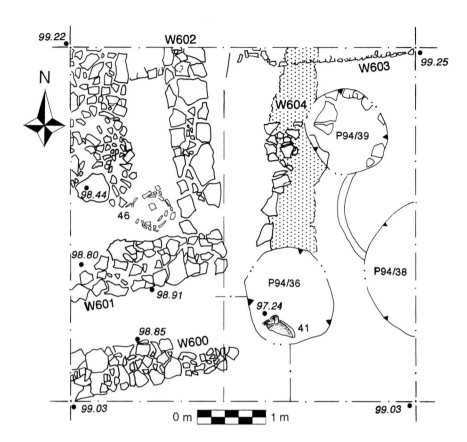

Figure 502. *Q10a.*

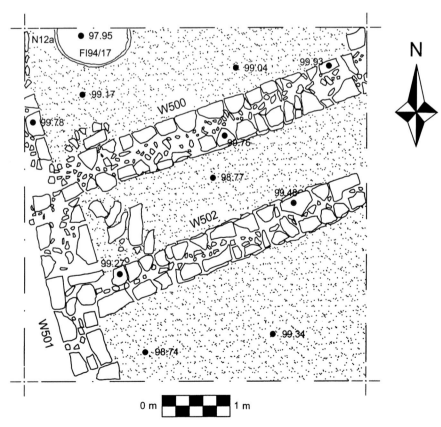

Figure 503. *N12a.*

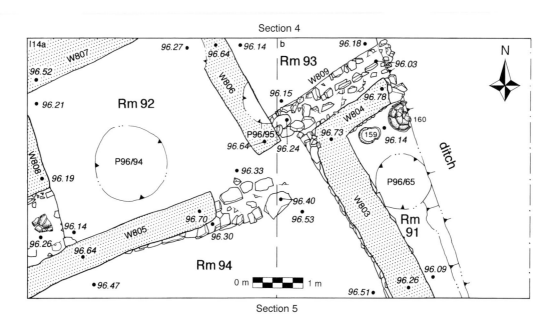

Figure 504. *I14: Level 3, Rms 91–4.*

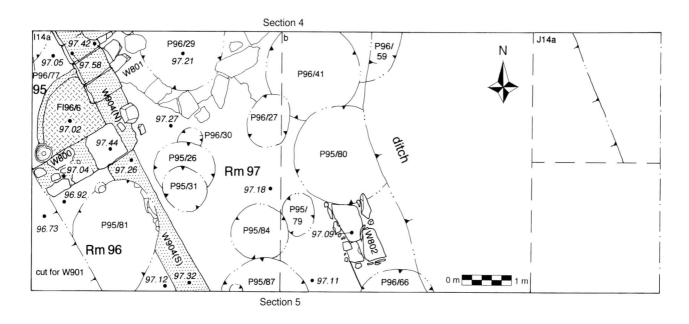

Figure 505. *I14 and J14a: Level 2 early, Rms 95–7.*

Maps, Plans and Sections

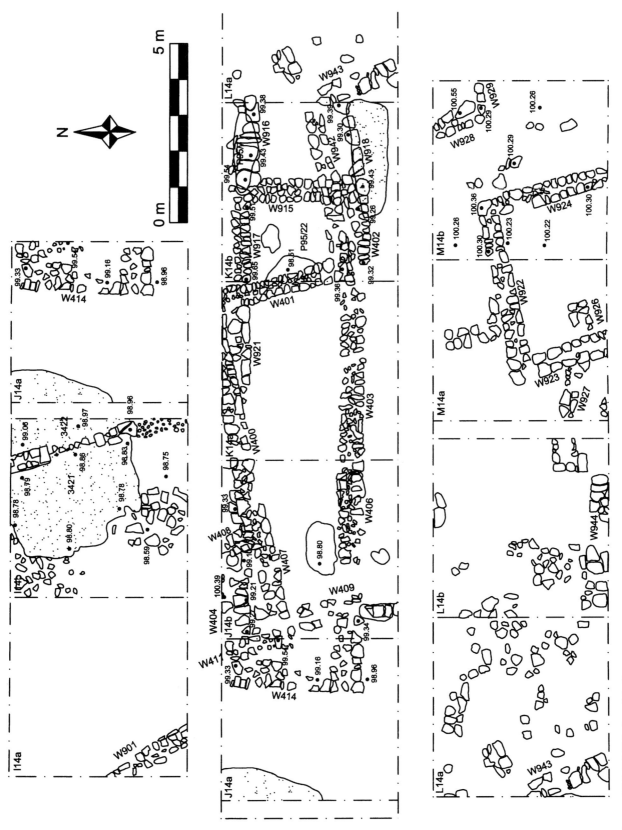

Figure 506. *I–M14: Level 1a/b.*

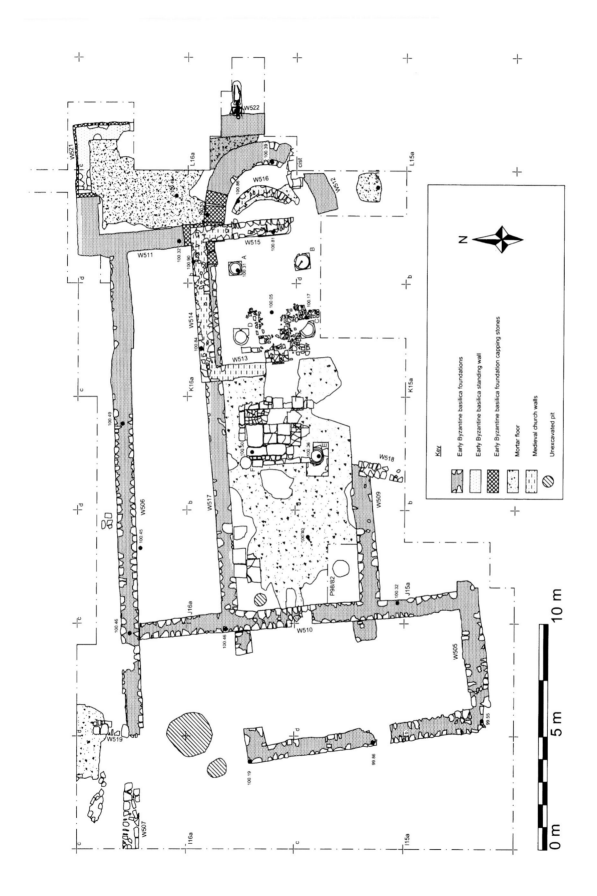

Figure 507. *Church, to show both phases.*

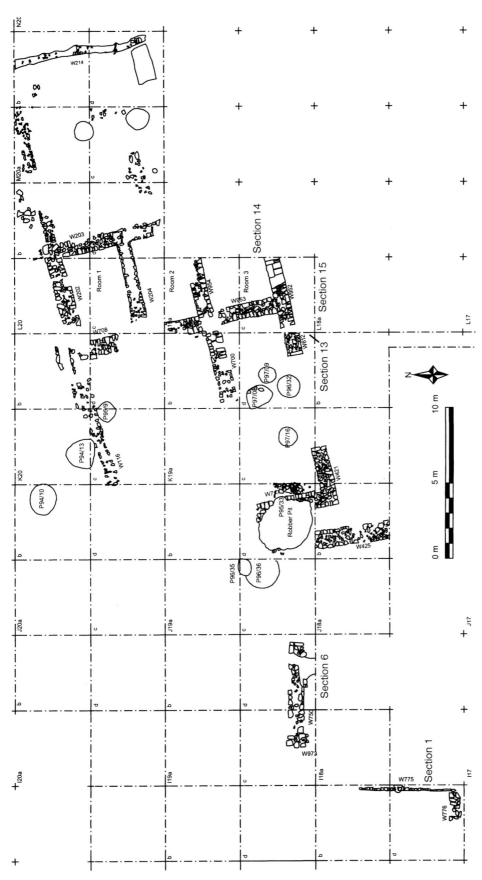

Figure 508. *NW corner Level Ia–b.*

Maps, Plans and Sections

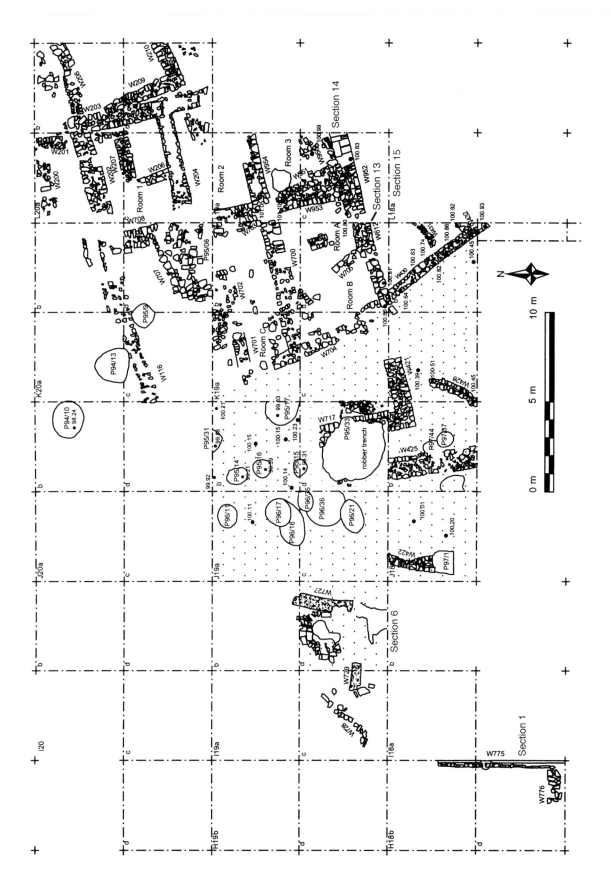

Figure 509. *NW corner Level Ib–d (western part).*

Maps, Plans and Sections

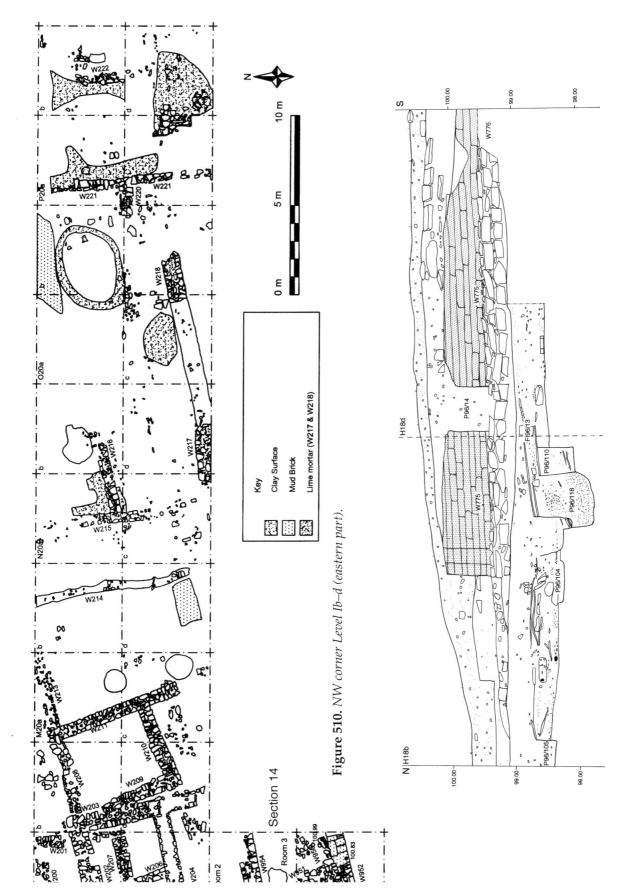

Figure 510. *NW corner Level Ib–d (eastern part).*

Figure 511. *Section 1: H18b/d E section (Levels I & IId/e; see Figs. 497, 499, 508–9).*

Maps, Plans and Sections

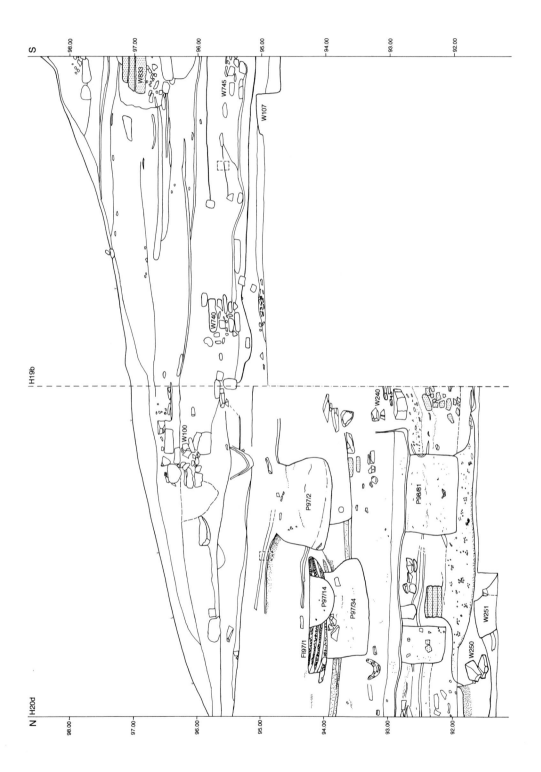

Figure 512. *Section 2: H20d/H19c E section (Level IIIa–c; see Figs. 479–91).*

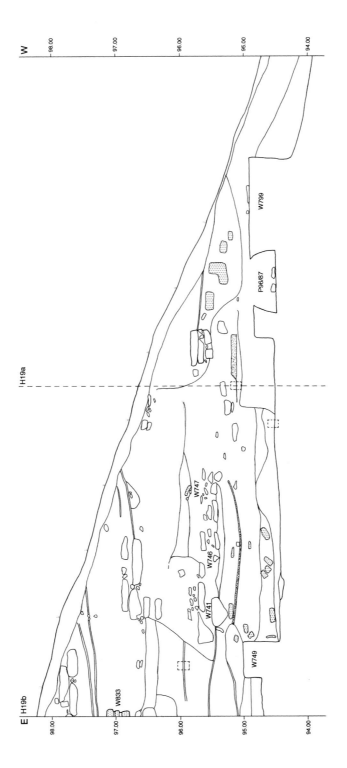

Figure 513. *Section 3: H19a/b S section (Level IIIa–c; see also Figs. 487–91).*

Maps, Plans and Sections

Figure 514. *Section 4: I14a/b N section (Level 2; see Figs. 504–5).*

Figure 515. *Section 5: I14a/b S section (Levels 1–3; see Figs. 504–5).*

852

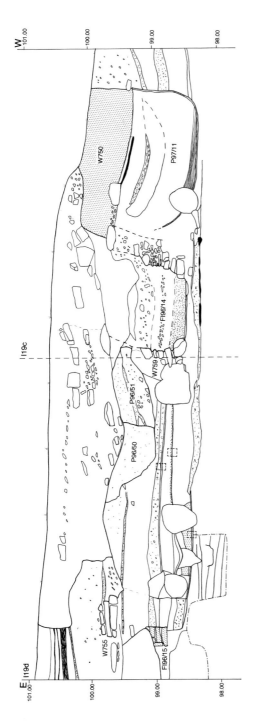

Figure 516. *Section 6: I19c/d S section (Levels I–IIf; see Figs. 494–5, 497, 499, 508–9).*

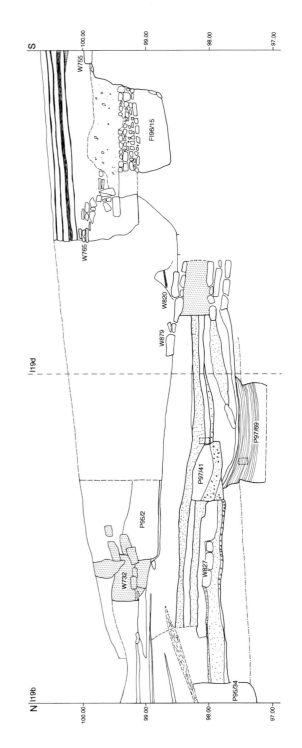

Figure 517. *Section 7: I19b/d E section (Level IIa–f; see Figs. 151, 491, 494–5, 497, 499).*

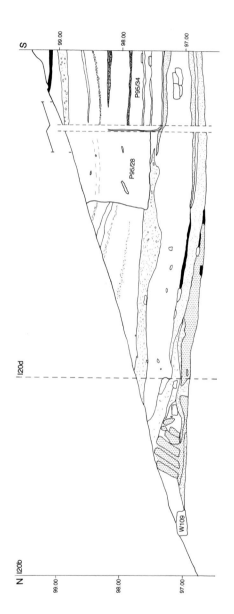

Figure 518. *Section 8: I20b/d E section (Levels IIb–e–IIId–e; see Fig. 491).*

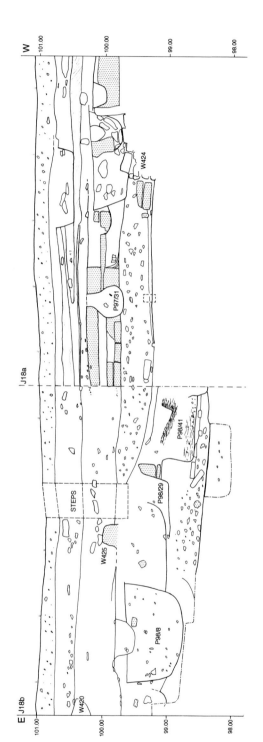

Figure 519. *Section 9: J18a/b S section (Levels I–IIf; see Figs. 492, 496–7, 499).*

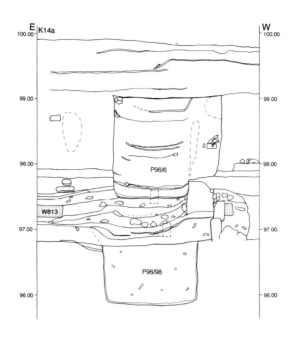

Figure 520. *Section 10: K14a S section (Levels 1–2 lower).*

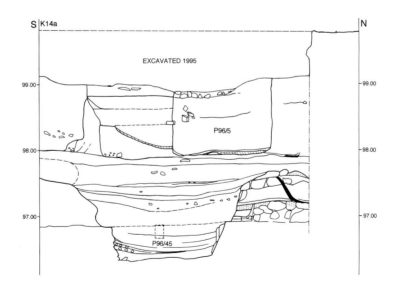

Figure 521. *Section 11: K14a W section (Level 2 middle–upper).*

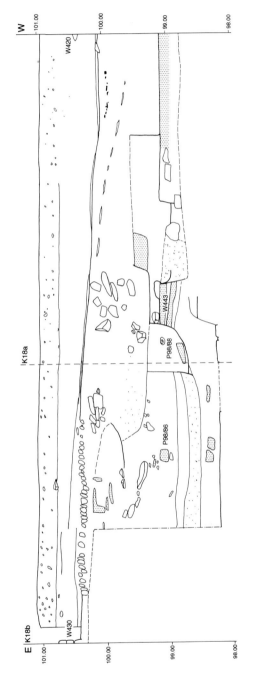

Figure 522. *Section 12: K18a/b S section (Levels I–IIf; see Figs. 492, 496–7, 499).*

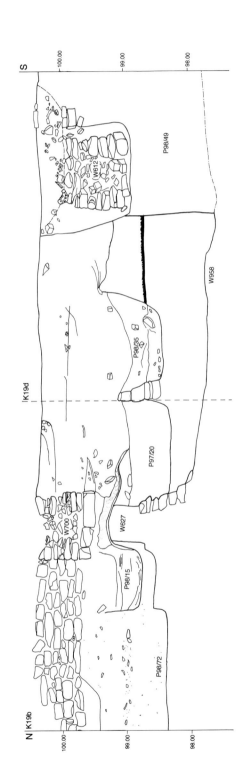

Figure 523. *Section 13: K19b/d E section (Levels I–IIc; see Figs. 492, 496–7, 508–9).*

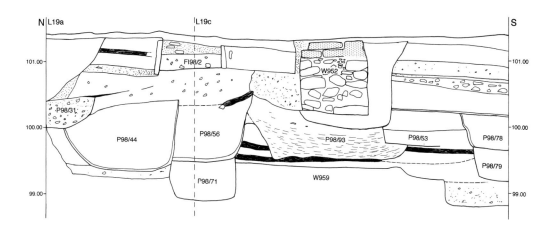

Figure 524. *Section 14: L19a/c E section (Levels I–IIc; see Figs. 492, 508–9).*

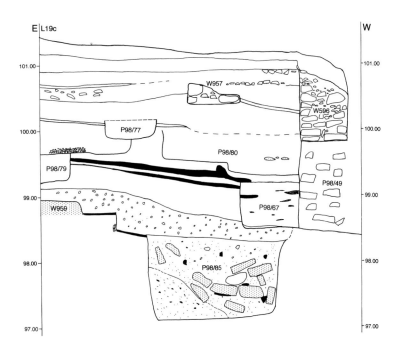

Figure 525. *Section 15: L19c S section (Levels I–IIb; see Figs. 492, 508–9).*

Maps, Plans and Sections

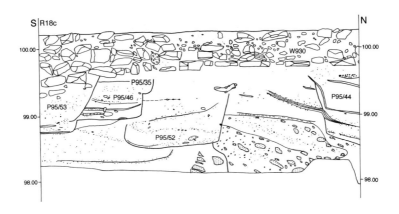

Figure 526. *Section 16: R18c W section (Levels E3a–E5a; see Fig. 500).*

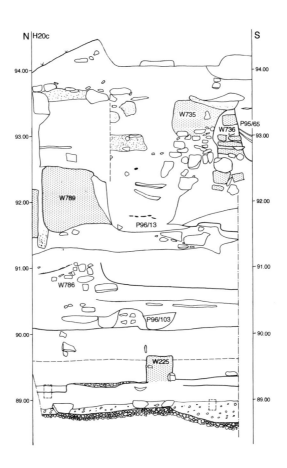

Figure 527. *Section 17: H20c E section (Level Ve/f–VI; see Figs. 474–91).*

858

Colour Figures

Thin sections 861

Ceramics 867

Phytoliths 873

Colour Figures

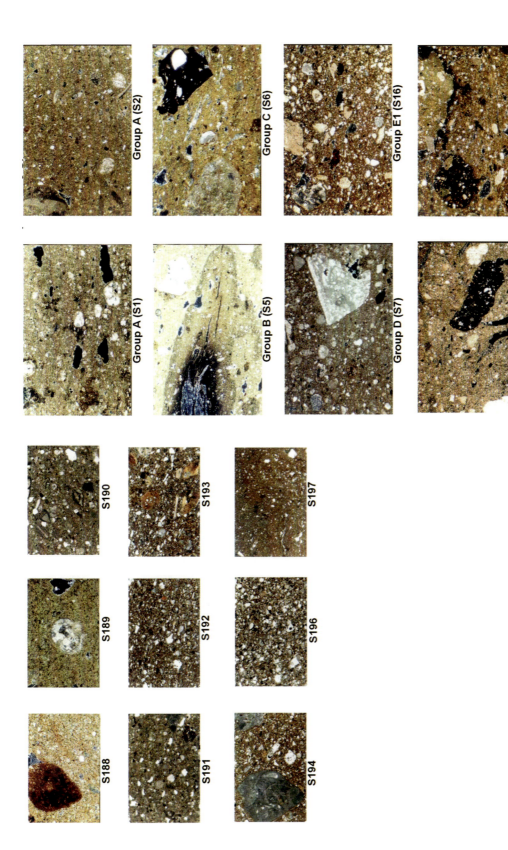

Figure 529. *Thin sections Level Vj–g, Groups A–E1.*

Figure 528. *Thin sections of clay samples: S188–94, 196–7.*

Colour Figures

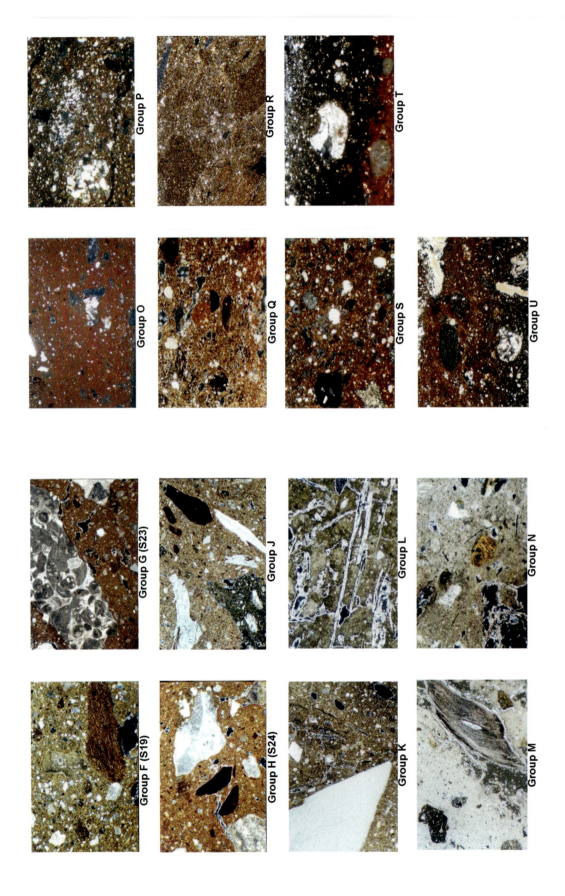

Figure 531. *Thin sections Level Vj–g ctd, Groups O–U.*

Figure 530. *Thin sections Level Vj–g ctd, Groups F–N.*

862

Colour Figures

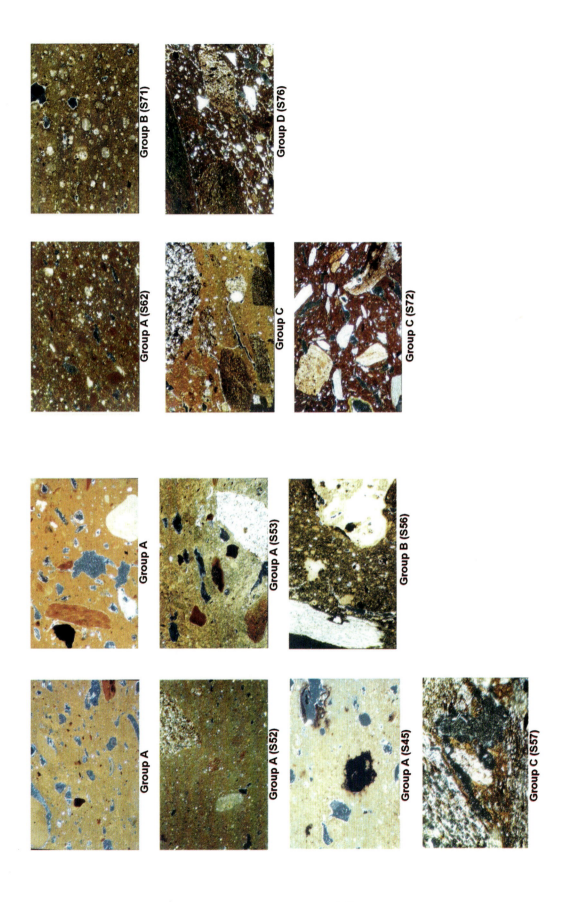

Figure 533. *Thin sections Level IV, Groups A–D.*

Figure 532. *Thin sections Level Vf–e, Groups A–C.*

863

Colour Figures

Figure 535. *Thin sections Level III ctd, Groups D–J.*

Figure 534. *Thin sections Level III, Groups A–C.*

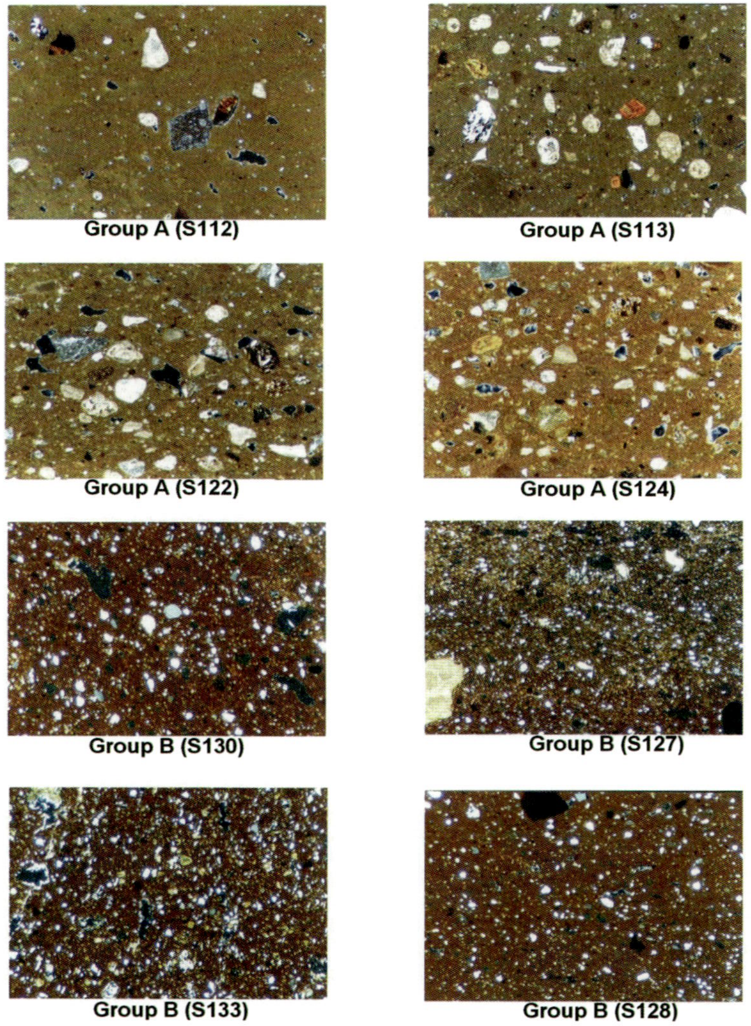

Colour Figures

Figure 536. *Thin sections Level IIa–d, Groups A–B.*

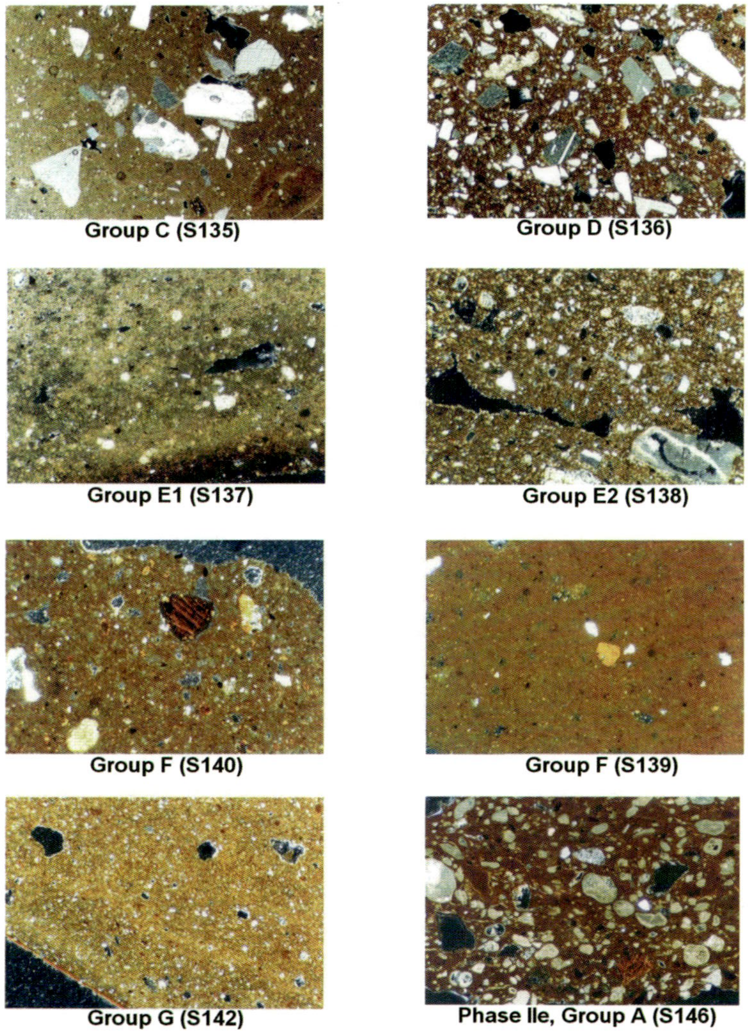

Figure 537. *Thin sections Level IIa–d ctd, Groups C–G and IIe, Group A.*

Colour Figures

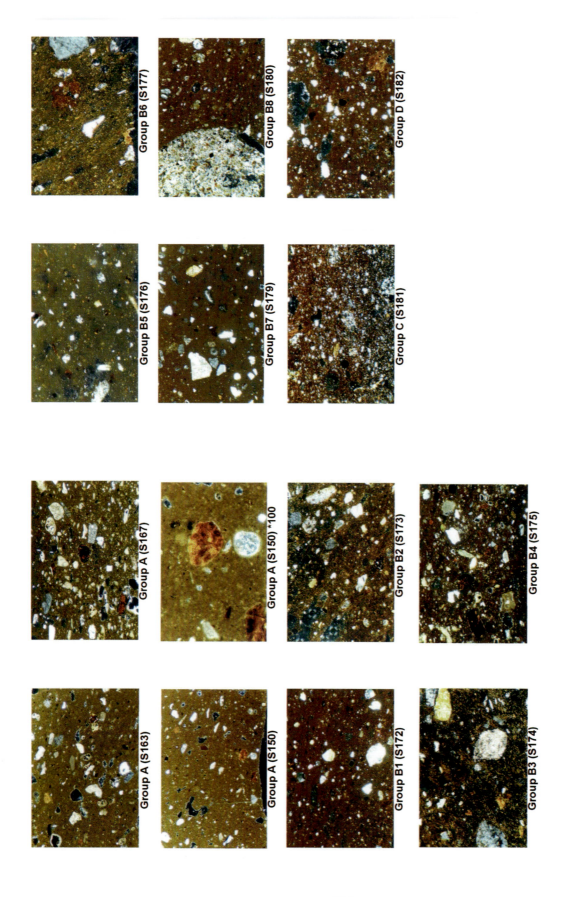

Figure 539. Thin sections Level IIf ctd, Groups B5–D.

Figure 538. Thin sections Level IIf, Groups A–B4.

Colour Figures

Figure 540. *Mycenaean vessel* **955**.

Figure 541. *Assorted Mycenaean sherds. From top left:* **957**, **947** (×2), **960** (×2); **959** (×2), **962**, **958**.

Figure 542. **1001** *(two pieces); waster from unit 2106.*

Figure 543. **1005**, **1003**, **1004**.

Colour Figures

Figure 544. *1011, d533, 1016.*

Figure 545. *1017.*

Figure 546. *1027.*

Figure 547. *1068, 1069, 1031; 1034, 1077, 1071.*

Figure 548. *d5446, 1062, 1053, 1056; 1309 1061, 1054, 1055.*

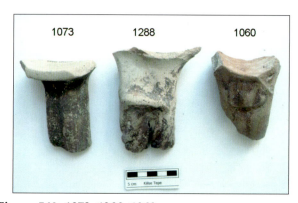

Figure 549. *1073, 1288, 1060.*

Figure 550. *1094.*

Figure 551. *1112.*

Colour Figures

Figure 552. *1146, 1117, 1158; 1136, 1116.*

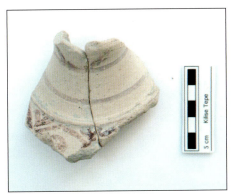

Figure 553. *1145.*

Figure 554. *99/4, 1144, 1167, 1155, 1142, 1143.*

Figure 555. *1185, 1186.*

Figure 556. *1189, 1182; 1178, 1181.*

Figure 557. *1199,* unit *1260; 1187,* unit *194.*

Figure 558. *1177.*

Figure 559. *1188, 1179.*

Colour Figures

Figure 560. *1257, 1255, 1256, 1258.*

Figure 561. *1200.*

Figure 562. *1172.*

Figure 563. *1235, 1241, 1234; 1233, 1231, 1236.*

Figure 564. *1220: a) exterior; b) interior.*

Figure 565. *1266, 1265.*

Figure 566. *1276, 1221, 1284; 1259, 1262, 1281.*

Colour Figures

Figure 567. *1267*, *1268*.

Figure 569. *1335*, *1336*.

Figure 571. *1440*.

Figure 573. *1135*, *1134*, *1118* local painted ware.

Figure 568. *1318*, *1330*, *1328*, *1324*.

Figure 570. *1439*, *1438*, *1437*, *1377*, *1440*, *1441*.

Figure 572. *1436*.

Figure 574. *Glazed wares: unit 5000, d1378 (×2), unit 9600; unit 4801, unit 4800.*

Colour Figures

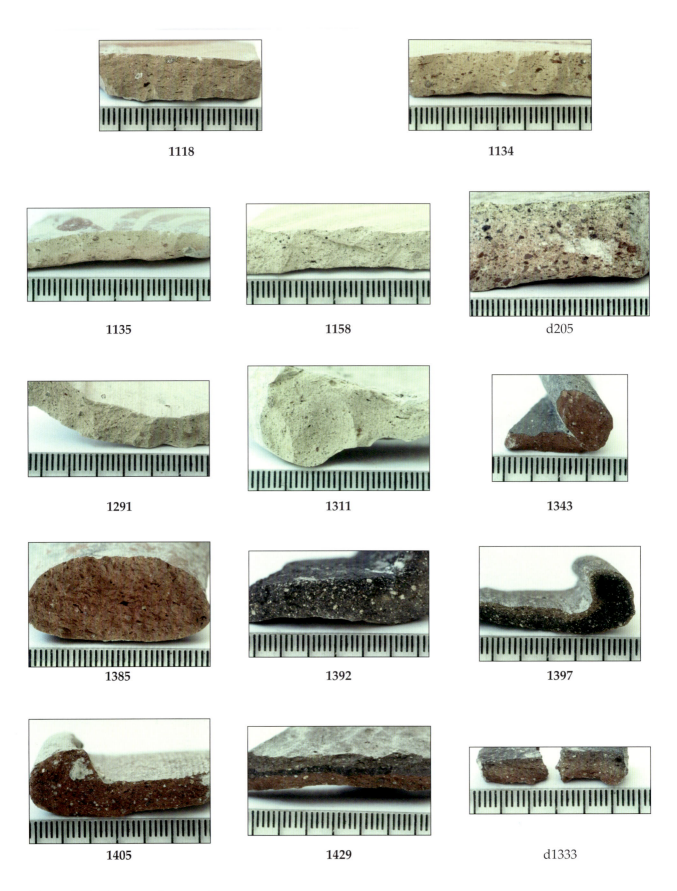

Figure 575. *Close-ups of cross-sections.*

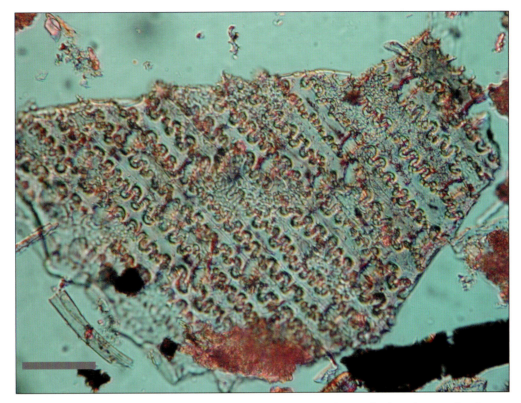

Figure 576. *Silica skeleton of cereal husk, note the dendritic long cells that characterize the epidermal tissues of the grass floral parts. Scale bar equal to 50 microns.*

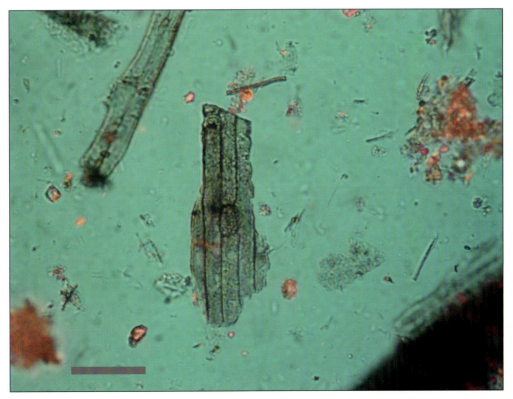

Figure 577. *Silica skeleton of a culm epidermis with typical smooth-sided long cells. Scale bar equal to 50 microns.*

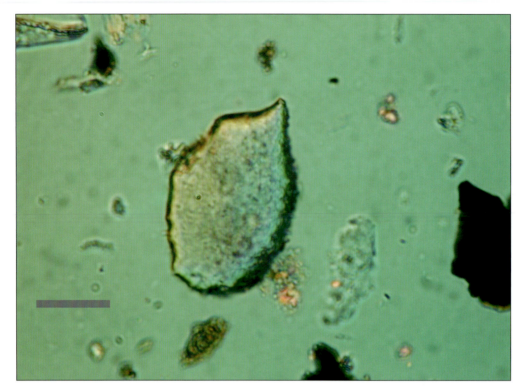

Figure 578. *A bulliform cell from the leaf mesophyll. These types of cells are active in the folding and unfolding of the leaf lamina and they are normally filled with opal silica only at the end of their life, just before the death of the leaf. Scale bar equal to 50 microns.*

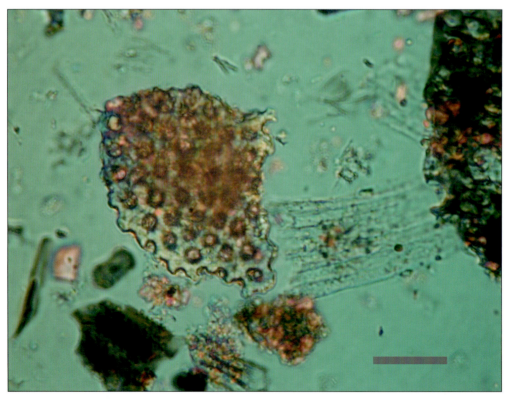

Figure 579. *A phytolith (perforated block) probably from a dicotyledon plant found in the coprolite and the residues from the pots. Scale bar equal to 50 microns.*

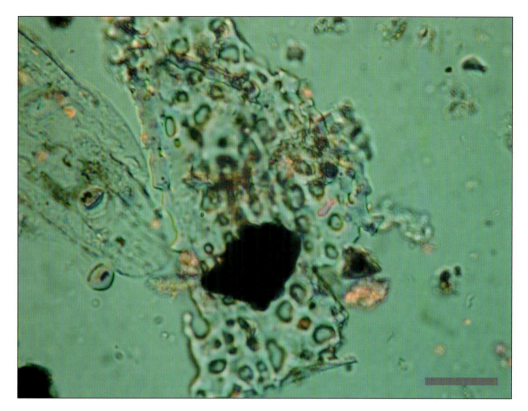

Figure 580. *A phytolith (plate with perforations) from a dicotyledon plant found in the courtyard sediments. Scale bar equal to 50 microns.*

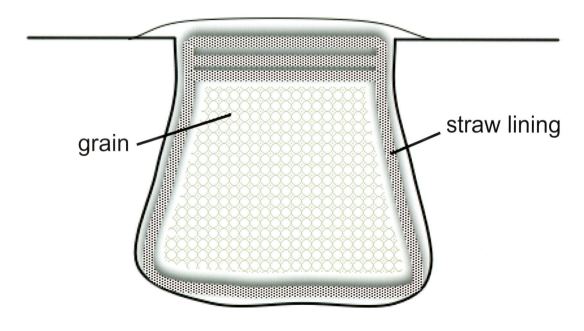

Figure 581. *An idealized reconstruction of Kilise Tepe pits used for the storage of grains.*

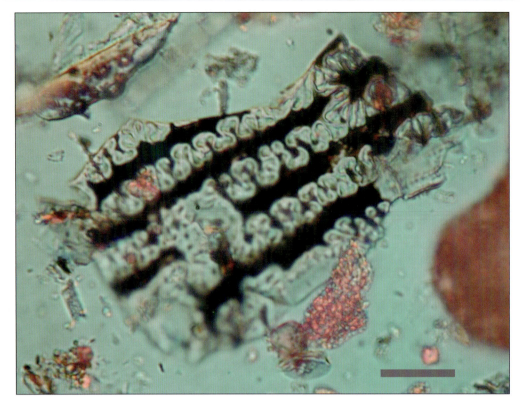

Figure 582. *Typical cereal (wheat/barley) husk silica skeleton. Dendritic long cells are black because some of the organic matter of the original plant tissues has been preserved. Scale bar equal to 50 microns.*

Figure 583. *Silica skeleton from the husk of* Panicum/Setaria *(millets). Note the different pattern of the sides of the long cells in respect to the wheat/barley epidermis (Fig. 582). Scale bar equal to 50 microns.*

Colour Figures

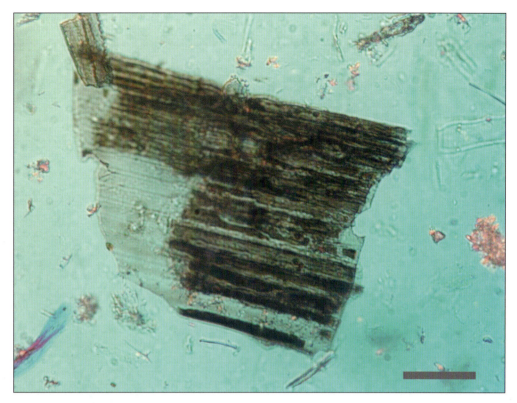

Figure 584. *Silica skeleton from a grass culm with the typical straight cuts produced by the use of the tribulum for separating the grains from the husk. Scale bar equal to 50 microns.*

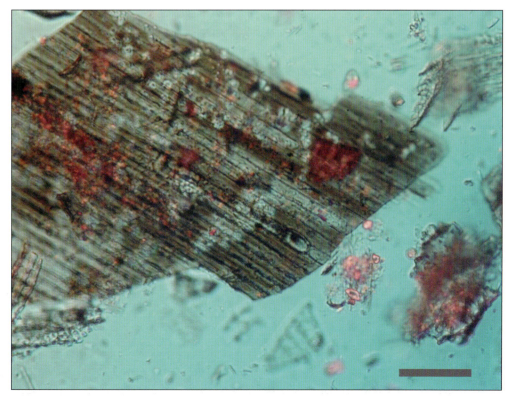

Figure 585. *Silica skeleton from grass culm with stepped cuts produced by the use of the tribulum. Scale bar equal to 50 microns.*